D0119372

BEN FOGLE

LAND ROVER

THE STORY OF THE CAR THAT CONQUERED THE WORLD

WILLIAM
COLLINS

To Willem

William Collins
An imprint of HarperCollins*Publishers*
1 London Bridge Street
London SE1 9GF

WilliamCollinsBooks.com

This omnibus edition first published by William Collins in 2017

22 21 20 19 18 17
10 9 8 7 6 5 4 3 2 1

Land Rover first published in Great Britain by William Collins in 2016
Text © Ben Fogle 2016

Labrador first published in Great Britain by William Collins in 2015
Text © Ben Fogle 2015

Photographs © Individual copyright holders

Excerpt on pages 15–16 of *Labrador* from *The Shipping News* by
Annie Proulx © Dead Line Ltd, 1993; Excerpt on page 121 of *Labrador*
from *Marley & Me* © John Grogan, 2005

A catalogue record for this book is
available from the British Library

All reasonable efforts have been made by the author and publishers to trace
the copyright owners of the material quoted and of any images reproduced
in this book. In the event that the author or publishers are notified of any
mistakes or omissions by copyright owners after publication of this book,
the author and the publishers will endeavour to rectify the position
accordingly for any subsequent printing.

ISBN 978-0-00-796911-1

Printed and bound in Great Britain by
CPI Group (UK) Ltd, Croydon CR0 4YY

MIX
Paper from
responsible sources
FSC
www.fsc.org
FSC™ C007454

This book is produced from independently certified FSC
paper to ensure responsible forest management.

For more information visit www.harpercollins.co.uk/green

CONTENTS

PROLOGUE

LAND ROVER

The Series I, II, IIa, III, 90, 110 and Defender are all members of the iconic 'boxy' Land Rover genre, first produced in 1948, with the current version called Land Rover Defender. To avoid any confusion, in this book I will sometimes refer to them all using Defender as a collective noun. Please don't hate me.

Lode Lane, Solihull is a flurry of activity. The brick walls are still covered in camouflage paint to disguise the factory from German air raids. The waters of the Birmingham canal flow close by, ready to extinguish any fires from falling bombs. Nearby a field has been transformed into a 'jungle track' to test the vehicles. On the factory floor inside, a team of workers are riveting aluminium plates and fixing axles to chassis on cars in various states of deconstruction. This is the famous Solihull Land Rover factory and the workmen are building some of the most iconic cars ever built, the Land Rover Series I, a car that changed the world. But this is not 1948. It is 2016 and I am watching third-generation factory workers making Series I vehicles on the same patch of land that their grandfathers had once done.

Just a few months before, the world had mourned as the very last Defender, the evolution of the Series I, rolled off the factory line. The lights went out on 67 years of iconic history. It had been the end, but now I was back at the very beginning for the rebirth. Where most evolve and advance, here at Lode Lane, workers were using decade-old tools and technology to regress to a simpler time. To make a vehicle born out of post-war rationing to help a country rebuild. This is the reborn project at Land Rover where buyers can spend more money on a 'new' 68-year-old vehicle than a top-of-the-range sports car.

As I bounced, cantilevered and splashed along the very same 'jungle track' once used by the Wilks brothers to demonstrate the capabilities of these workhorse vehicles, I couldn't help but marvel at the ageless charm of these iconic cars. Regressive progression. Nostalgic advancement. The new old. Was this the rebirth? Had the Land Rover ever really died? Or was this really the resurrection we had all dreamed of?

It is an oxymoron but a fitting metaphor for the story of the greatest car ever made.

INTRODUCTION

'Do not go where the path may lead,
go instead where there is no path and leave a trail'
Ralph Waldo Emerson

Sometimes you don't know what you've got until it's gone.

At 9.30am on 29 January 2016, the 2,016,933rd Defender rolled off the production line at Land Rover's factory at Lode Lane, Solihull, on the outskirts of Birmingham. It marked the end of 67 years of continuous production of the world's most famous vehicle. The final Defender.

In all those years, the workhorse Defender had served farmers and foresters, armies and air forces, explorers and scientists, construction and utility companies – in fact, everyone who needed a good, honest vehicle that would do a good, honest job anywhere in the world. And there were a lot more people who bought one just for fun, too – for its sheer brilliant off-road ability and austere utilitarian attitude that made it so different to the rest of today's homogenised, jelly-mould automotive offerings.

'Jerusalem' was sung through the factory line as generations of engineers, mechanics and factory line workers paid tribute to the

Land Rover Defender. This was a funereal send-off for a much-loved car that had conquered the planet. Media, journalists and film crews had descended from around the world to record this death knell. The world held its breath as the last ever Defender was driven silently out of the building.

This was an end that was marked by tears and sorrow, as Land Rover enthusiasts bade farewell to a familiar friend and the historic production line that had produced it fell silent.

The world mourned. This was the day the real Land Rover, the successor to the Wilks brothers' 1948 original, died.

It is said that for more than half the world's population the first car they ever saw was a Land Rover Defender. As quintessentially British as a plate of fish and chips or a British bulldog, the boxy, utilitarian vehicle has become an iconic part of what it is to belong to this sceptred isle. It is a part of the stiff-upper-lipped British psyche; it never complains, and neither do we.

You climb into a Land Rover – literally; in fact some people even need ropes to hoist themselves up into the rigid seats. The doors don't seal properly, and freezing cold rainwater, overflowing from the car's gutter (they really do have a gutter) cascades down your neck as the flimsy aluminium door invariably closes on the seat belt that dangles out of the door. The dashboard consists of a series of chunky black buttons and two analogue dials. Without heated seats, climate control options are freeze or fry. The windows ALWAYS mist, even if you hold your breath. I have to pull up a metal antenna from the bonnet to pick up radio, which I can only receive while driving at 30mph. If I crank her up to her limit of 60mph, the noise from the engine, gearbox, transfer box, differentials, tyres and the wind is deafening, and too loud to have a conversation let alone listen to anything from the speakers. There is no coffee-cup holder or hands-free. The gears grind and the seats cannot be tilted.

So on the face of it there is not much going for the Defender. It is noisy, uncomfortable, slow, uneconomical and, according to the USA, dangerous. So why is it that I, along with millions of other people around the world, am so hopelessly, obsessively in love with this car?

The Land Rover is an integral part of the fabric of our society, a part of the furniture. Nothing lasts forever, but some things come close. The Defender has survived the decades largely unchanged. It transcends fashion while somehow epitomising it. It has an ability to neutralise rational thought or expectation, and it has avoided the homogenisation of our vehicles in modern times.

The Defender is a beacon of safety and security, too. It is favoured by the military, the police, the fire service, NGOs, the UN, the Royal Palace, the Special Forces and explorers alike. These vehicles have discovered new regions, won wars and saved lives. Across the world, the Land Rover symbolises durability and Britishness, with her diversity and rigidity. It is estimated that three-quarters of all Land Rovers ever built are still rattling noisily across country somewhere in the world.

The Defender is a national treasure. We are reassured by its understated presence. It inspires a second glance but never a stare. Unshowy, unpretentious and classless, it is the car in which you can arrive at Buckingham Palace, a rural farm or an inner-city estate.

Over the years I have encountered Land Rovers in the farthest corners of the world. From steamy tropical jungles to remote islands, I have bounced across lonely landscapes in dozens, perhaps hundreds, of Land Rovers, many of them decades old.

Around the world, the Land Rover has become as much a part of the African savannah as acacia trees and elephants. The UK was still a colonial power at the Defender's inception, and the car quickly spread across the Empire; from Tristan da Cunha, where a lone policeman patrols the island's one-mile road in his trusty Defender, one of only a handful of vehicles on the island, to the Falkland Islands, which boast the world's highest per capita Land Rover ownership – one for each of the 2000 residents who live there, earning itself the moniker Land Rover Island.

I have driven through the muddy trails of the Amazon basin and across the deserts of Chile in ancient Land Rovers bound together with baler twine. When my young family first came to visit me while I was working in Africa, there was never any question that we would embark on an expedition across the muddy plains of the Serengeti in anything other than a Defender. It always seems incredible that these international workhorses that have crossed some of the most challenging of landscapes in remote corners of the world originated from a former sewing-machine factory in Solihull, near Birmingham. Such an inauspicious birthplace for arguably one of the world's most iconic vehicles.

When I drive through London in my Land Rover I get stopped not for my autograph or a selfie but for a photograph of my car. I have lost count of the number of notes slipped under the windscreen wiper with offers to buy my beloved car. The children love it. The dogs love it – and so do two million other people in the world.

Everyone from Fidel Castro to the Queen drives a Land Rover Defender. Idris Elba made his entrance at the 2014 Invictus Games' opening ceremony aboard a trusty Defender. Ralph Lauren, Kevin Costner and Sylvester Stallone all drive the rugged vehicles. And now, after 67 years and two million vehicles, the Land Rover Defender has ceased production. It is ironic that the vehicle is more popular in death than it was in life. Interest has reached fever pitch for this icon of Britishness; it is a vehicle that transcended its original remit to knit itself into the fabric of the nation that created it.

A vehicle that can drag a plough, clear a minefield and carry royalty, the Land Rover Defender transcends the rapidly changing world in which we live. As cars become rounder, curvier and shinier, the Land Rover Defender still looks like a child's drawing of a car, with its boxy shape. To climb into a Defender is like stepping back in time into a simpler, classier world.

The Defender was a car that didn't just defy the fickle face of fashion but also changing mechanisation and economics. It was a car that was handbuilt until the end. It took 56 man hours to construct just one vehicle. Two original parts have been fitted to all soft-top Series Land Rovers and Defenders since 1948: the hood cleats and the underbody support strut – but these are just two of the over 7000 individual parts that make up each Defender.

This is a car that is instantly recognisable from its wing mirrors to its wings. Indeed, workers on the Land Rover production line have their own nicknames for parts of the vehicle: for example, the door hinges are known as 'pigs ears' and the dashboard is the 'lamb's chops'.

So what is it about this vehicle that has spawned such an obsessive, loyal following? How did the Land Rover so successfully take over the world? In some ways the Defender mirrors many of our national traits; stiff-upper-lipped and slightly eccentric. In the spirit of the great British explorers Scott, Shackleton, Cook, Livingstone, Fawcett and Fiennes, the Land Rover was a twentieth-century progression of the age of exploration.

The car has spawned an industry that includes dozens of publications, car shows and even model cars tailored to the passion of those who dedicate their lives to the Land Rover. In order to understand why this car is such a national treasure and excites such passion, I decided to embark on a road trip of my own in my trusty Land Rover to meet the people who live for this marque – the enthusiasts, the designers, the military, the police and the explorers who glory in this bastion of quintessential Britishness.

A Land Rover is a living breathing thing. The vehicles become characters. We name them. We learn their unique quirks and foibles. It is a sort of love affair. I know plenty of men who remember more about their old beloved Land Rovers than they do their ex-girlfriends. These cars seduce us with their charm – they are not supermodels, they are dependable, robust and loyal. There is a unique and almost unquantifiable relationship with a Land Rover. It is an emotional attachment like no other. How can a man-made object have such power over us?

Every Land Rover has its own unique story to tell. Here, in these pages, is the story of the world's favourite car and how it conquered the planet and the hearts and souls of those who inhabit it … and me.

CHAPTER ONE

A LOVE STORY

You never forget your first Land Rover. It was a rusty grey pick up that seemed to be held together with baler twine. The doors didn't close properly and baler twine was doing the job of holding them shut. Inside, her seats were ragged and torn, transformed into a fabric reminiscent of Emmental cheese by the farm rats. The front windscreen was cracked and there was a large hole where a stereo had once sat. A thin coat of dust coated the interior and an even thicker layer of mud swamped the footwells. Various gloves and farm tools had been wedged into any spare space. She had a sort of musty, fuely smell that overwhelmed the senses.

On starting, she would rattle and vibrate violently. A thick black cloud of smoke would temporarily envelop the whole car with a toxic cloud of diesel fumes that threatened to choke you as it seeped through the gaping seals where the doors failed to close.

I must have been about 9 or 10 years old; I was on a farm in West Sussex where my parents had rented a tiny cottage, which was next to a working beef and dairy farm that the farmer operated with the help of an ancient Land Rover. I loved that smelly old broken vehicle, built purely for functionality.

So I have a confession to make. My first car was not a Land Rover. My parents didn't drive one, nor did I learn to drive in one. Truth be told, I'm not even that into cars. I suppose to understand how I have come to write a book about the Land Rover, I should begin by exploring my own history with the automobile.

Our first family car was an ambulance. Not any old ambulance, but an animal one. My father, a vet, bought a Honda camper van that he converted into the 'Mobile Animal Clinic', a slogan which was emblazoned down the side in green ink. He wasn't allowed blue flashing lights so the van had a green one instead. She had a little operating table in the middle and oxygen tanks around the sides. Although she was technically a caravan or a mobile home, she was like a little box fitted behind a tiny cab. The seats in the back were configured around the operating table, which meant that not only could we use it to do our homework on the way home from school but we could play endless games of monopoly during long car journeys. She was, without doubt, the most distinctive vehicle on the school run.

Sad was the day when my father retired our little animal ambulance, to be replaced by the Space Cruiser, with its state-of-the-art electric retractable roof. At the time, Toyota was one of the most advanced vehicle manufacturers in the world. Those were the days when Japanese vehicles were really coming into their own, and I think my father had been seduced by the Japanese during many of his lecturing tours. Everything in the Space Cruiser was electric – windows, sunroof – I can still recall my sisters and I standing on the back seat, with our heads protruding through the open roof as we drove through the country lanes of Sussex. Of course, driving regulations and safety requirements were a little more relaxed in the 70s; this was still the era of non-obligatory seat belts and of rear-facing seats in Mercedes-Benz. My abiding memories were of dozens of children crammed into cars and wedged into seats, often sitting on laps, heads lolling out of the open windows. Ah, those were the days!

Alongside the practical vehicles that our family owned, my mother had a lifelong love affair with the Italian Alfa Romeo. Her first was a blue model which she lovingly drove for nearly 20 years until she replaced it with a red Alfa, complete with spoilers and fins. My father could never understand her passion for the Alfa; they were expensive to run and, in his eyes, they weren't even particularly good cars. My mother never agreed. She loved her Alfa.

Apart from my mother's passion for the Alfa, cars were not a Fogle family obsession. They were merely functional; a means of getting from A to B or for transporting wounded animals.

One of my friends had a father who owned a Caterham. I can still remember the joy and exhilaration of being driven down a dual carriageway at more than 100mph with my head sticking out, free in the open air of the convertible. Bugs stung against my cheeks as we sped across Dorset.

When I turned 17, I decided it was time to get my driver's licence. Looking back, I didn't go about it in a particularly clever manner, though. Most people think logically about such important milestones and plan it with their family's help. I was away at boarding school and short of funds so I decided to do one occasional driving lesson at a time, and then do another one once I had saved up enough money. This system worked well at first, but soon having just one lesson a month began to have detrimental effects. I have never been a quick learner and whenever I had a lesson it felt as if I was starting from scratch. This soon became apparent when I failed my first test, and then the second and the third and the fourth ...

It took seven tests before I finally passed. I think this story nicely illustrates several points. First, that I am quite a stubborn individual, and second, that I really wasn't into cars.

For the first year after I passed my test my father kindly lent me the silver-bullet Toyota Space Cruiser whenever I needed transportation. It was without doubt the most uncool car to be seen at the wheel of, but it did the job and I can remember driving piles of friends down to Devon and Cornwall in it. It was, as my father often reminded us, very 'functional'.

The first car that I owned myself was a grey Nissan Micra. It was the archetypal bland, homogeneous car, but it was a very generous eighteenth-birthday gift from my father, who quite rightly pointed out that it was, as ever, economical and functional. My mother had tied a giant red ribbon into a bow on the roof when they presented it to me. I climbed in immediately and drove it to Hyde Park in Central London – and straight into a red Volvo. Within an hour of getting my first car it was a near write-off and was being towed away by a recovery vehicle. Once repaired, though, my little Nissan Micra served me well. I took that little car everywhere – to Scotland, the French Alps, Spain. She was a trustworthy little vehicle that didn't break down once in the seven years I drove her.

Despite my early difficulties in learning to drive, I loved driving. As a family we used to drive a lot. Every weekend we would pack up the Mobile Animal Clinic, and latterly the Space Cruiser, with my two sisters, our two golden retrievers and Humphrey, our African grey parrot.

In the summers, my sisters and I would be packed off to live with my paternal grandparents in Canada, where we experienced another approach to driving. My late grandmother, Aileen, was anything but your ordinary grandparent – agile and strong until the day she died, aged 100, she always stood out from the crowd, so it is probably no surprise that her car of choice was a sports car, a green Camaro with a V8 engine.

The ritual packing of the car would continue on the other side of the Atlantic, as Canadian dogs and cousins were all herded into the tiny sports car for the two-hour journey from the city of Toronto out to my grandparents' little summer cottage on the shores of Lake Chemong.

Land Rovers did not cross my path again in any memorable way until 1999, when I took part in *Castaway* for the BBC. This programme was a year-long social experiment to see whether a group of urbanites could create a fully self-sufficient society from scratch. For this, we were marooned on an uninhabited island in the Outer Hebrides of Scotland, in the Western Isles.

It was a remote, rugged place, and we were left there, isolated from the outside world. We had no internet, telephone nor television. It was just us and the windswept landscape of Taransay. The island had once been inhabited, but all that was left of its one-time occupation was a small farmhouse and an animal steading. Dotted around the island were remnants of its earlier history, in the form of black houses, their crumbling ruins a reminder of the crofters that had long ago worked the land.

The island topography was boggy and mountainous. There were no paths, tracks or roads, and crossing the island would involve a yomp through knee-high bogs and up the steep flanks of the hills that dominated the landscape. The absence of roads made the remains of the island's sole vehicle even more remarkable and curious. Hidden near the animal steading that we had converted into the kitchen and communal area was the rusting body of a Land Rover Series II.

That Land Rover confused me more than almost every other aspect of island life. I couldn't begin to fathom how such a vehicle would have been used, and why it was there. It wasn't just the logistics of getting the vehicle onto the island that baffled me; rather, apart from the small area around which we built our settlement – which was about the size of two football pitches – I couldn't imagine how the Land Rover would get across country. It seemed impossible that any vehicle, even a Land Rover, could make its way through this inhospitable geography.

The car had long since lost its engine, and its skeleton-like remains made a perfect place for the children to play and pretend they were driving somewhere. That island had a strange effect on all of us and even I used to sit in that dilapidated car and imagine I was on a journey, driving across a vast wilderness.

It was then and there that I resolved that I would one day get a Land Rover.

As our only communication with the outside world was via letter, and as the end of the year and the experiment loomed large, I wrote to my father to ask him to help me find a Land Rover for my return. When the end came it was a bittersweet moment. I longed to leave that island but I also worried about adapting to life back in the real world. For a year we had been isolated from the rest of the world, and suddenly, come 1 January 2001, having been stripped of our anonymity, we were about to be thrust back into civilisation – not to mention the public eye. It was a daunting prospect.

We were helicoptered off the island in a carefully choreographed live TV broadcast. I was last to leave. Tears streamed down my cheeks as we crossed that tiny body of turquoise water that separated us from the next main island of Harris.

Several dozen journalists and photographers had braved the Hebridean winter to gather on Horgabost beach ready for our arrival. It was the beginning of a new life in front of the media glare – and it scared me.

We transferred into coaches and began what seemed like a victory drive across the island to the Harris Hotel, where we would begin our decompression. I can't begin to tell you how strange it was to be back in civilisation. A press conference was convened in the hotel's dining room and we were thrust into the hungry grasp of the British press. It was quite a revelation. The questions. The spin. The stories. The money offers. The exclusives. Rival newspapers vied to outbid one another to get the scoop. We castaways became pawns in a game about which we knew very little. We didn't understand the rules and we had very little help to pick our way through the minefield.

We were due to stay in the hotel for a few days to acclimatise and spend time with the show's psychologist, but I found the whole experience overwhelming.

'There's something waiting for you in the car park,' one of the show's executive producers told me.

I escaped the claustrophobia and heat of the hotel and strode out into the wind and rain of the small gravel car park. There, tucked away in the corner, was the unmistakable shape of a blue Land Rover Defender. I pulled the handle of the unlocked door and climbed in. A set of keys had been 'hidden' beneath the sun visor. A smile enveloped my face. It was the Land Rover smile – more of which later.

I relaxed. It was as if all the fears and worries that had been brewing in that small hotel disappeared. I had my first Land Rover. It may seem strange, but I had no idea how it had got there, who had bought it, how much it cost or even if it really was mine. The world had become such a strange place that it never even occurred to me to ask.

While the rest of the castaways had been booked to fly back to civilisation from Stornoway, I had worried about flying back with my Labrador, Inca. She had only known freedom for a year; she hadn't worn a collar nor been on a lead in that time and I couldn't bear the thought of confining her to the hold of a plane in a cage, so driving seemed the natural solution to the problem.

My first night in a proper bed was not the luxury I had been anticipating. I found the central heating stifling and oppressive and the bed was far too soft – even apart from the fact that my mind was spinning and reeling. I was confused and, if I'm honest, I was scared, too.

I'm not sure what came over me or even why it happened, but I woke up in the middle of the night that first night – and left.

In retrospect it was completely out of character. I had planned to spend several more days with the show's execs and the gathered journalists for interviews and photo shoots, but I was over-whelmed by the new situation I found myself in. So, quietly, I packed the Land Rover with my worldly possessions and Inca and placed the key in the ignition. The engine turned several times and then … spluttered to a stop. Several mysterious lights illuminated the dashboard. I tried again, willing the car to start, then finally the engine choked and spluttered to life. The whole car shuddered and vibrated. Inca sat in the passenger seat, her head lolling out of the window as we rolled out of town on the long journey home.

It was midwinter and sunrise was still hours away. I had been in plenty of Land Rovers through the years but this was the first time I had driven my own one. I felt a freedom that I had been deprived of for more than a year – a sense of liberty and sheer happiness at being able to explore, unfettered. That island had been like a prison, we had been confined by its watery limits, but here, now, aboard my mighty Land Rover, I felt invincible.

We drove past small shops selling newspapers that had my face on the front page as I drove up towards the ferry port of Stornoway. That had to be one of the more surreal experiences of my life.

Within hours of leaving the hotel, Inca, my trusty Land Rover and I were sailing away from the Hebrides and into the unknown of Scotland. I didn't have a plan; all I had was my dog, a credit card and my Land Rover. Although I longed to see my friends and family, I wasn't ready to return home just yet.

Aimlessly we drove through the Scottish Highlands. That Land Rover brought with it such a freedom. For more than twelve months I had been restricted to Taransay and now I had a wanderlust that was difficult to shake. Apart from the dizzying euphoria of movement, it was also a fear of stopping that overwhelmed me. If I were to stop I wasn't really sure what would happen or if I would ever get moving again.

We drove until nightfall, when I pulled over to the side of the road and Inca and I curled up in the back of the Land Rover and went to sleep.

And so it was that I disappeared into the Scottish Highlands for a week. It seems strange now, but I don't remember much about that time. I don't recall where I went or even where I stayed. My Defender was like a ghost vehicle, winding its way through the mountains.

That Land Rover was my saviour. It offered so much more than just freedom; it also offered me opportunity and hope. And in many ways, this is the essence of the Land Rover spirit.

I kept that blue Land Rover for the best part of four years, but eventually the loan deal came to an end and I had to buy my own car. I'm not sure what came over me, but I bought a Jeep.

A Jeep? I hear you say. How did someone who had spent their life coveting a Land Rover end up with an American Jeep? It gets worse. It was a special Orvis edition pimped out with black leather seats and tinted windows. I am still genuinely puzzled by my decision to get that car. I wasn't looking for it, it just sort of came into my life at a roundabout near Lord's cricket ground.

You see, I am an experimenter. I like to experiment and test. I don't like repeating myself. Perhaps it was a case of having spent four years bouncing and rattling around Britain in a Land Rover Defender that persuaded me to convert ... to an American car.

To be fair, it was a cool car. Apart from the tinted windows – I hated those. Believe it or not, I didn't notice those until after I had bought it. They didn't stand out in the showroom and it wasn't until I parked it outside my house and my sister commented on my new Gangsta credentials that I became aware of them.

I drove that Jeep for a year before I had a calling. I had been working on BBC's *Countryfile* for several years when I rolled up to a Woad farm one day. 'I thought you'd be more of a Land Rover man,' smiled the farmer. It was like seeing the light. 'But I am a Land Rover man,' I replied, to the farmer's confusion.

The Jeep was sold and I decided to do the unthinkable, what very few true Land Rover aficionados ever do: I bought a NEW one.

What was I thinking? We all know that buying a brand-new car off the factory line is like chucking money down the drain. The car depreciates as soon as the wheels leave the threshold of the showroom. I don't think my parents had ever bought a new car. Not a brand-new one. The Fogles had always been rather sensible with money and we all knew that buying a brand-new car was a waste of money, but for some inexplicable reason I found myself in a Land Rover dealership on the A40 in West London putting in an order.

Buying the Land Rover was a big deal. Sure, I had been lucky enough to have cars of my own before, but this was different. I had worked hard for several years and I had saved up some cash. I have never been an extravagant spender (although my wife will probably disagree with that, but in truth it's more that she is the spendthrift …!). All my life I had dreamed of walking into a showroom and picking out a Land Rover Defender, and here, finally, was my chance to do it. I can remember that day like it was yesterday; the excitement combined with a slight fear of the recklessness and extravagance of buying myself a new car.

The spec was really rather simple. The short wheelbase Defender 90 in silver. I wanted a silver Land Rover. Why silver? I don't know. Car colour is a strange thing. I included some chequer body plating and three seats in the front. Now this is important – the three seats in the front is part of the Land Rover Defender's DNA. If we look back to the early Series I and II they all had three seats in the front. It was part of the Land Rover design, but in the latter-day vehicles came the option to add a glove box in the middle.

I am always surprised by the number of Land Rovers that have gone for this configuration. I love the three seats in the front; it is the height of sociability. I remember peering into a McLaren once; the driver sits in the middle while the two passengers sit either side – the industry joke is that they are the seats for the wife and the mistress. With the Land Rover they are more likely to be for the wife and the calf. Next time you are in your car, have a look around at other vehicles and tell me how many have three passengers in the front. There are very few marques that do this – mostly vans. Have a look. Every van will inevitably have three grown men all sitting shoulder to shoulder. Sometimes there is a dog on one of the seats in place of a person, but you get my point.

There is something rather egalitarian about three seats in the front. It takes away the whole hierarchy thing for a start. What is it about the front seat? When I was a child it was like a throne. The front seat was the holy grail of seats and it was always allocated to a strict and unspoken rule of hierarchy, which was usually dictated by age. When Mum and Dad were both in the car there was never any question that they would sit in the front and we children, dogs and parrot would go in the back, but when it came to the school run and only one parent in the car, it became a war zone. 'Shotgun!' we would cry as we left the house and raced to the front door. Bickering and arguments would invariably ensue, followed by frosty sulking from the 'backees'.

The three-seat configuration in the front gives all three passengers the same experience. It is much more inclusive, but of course there is a catch. Have you ever sat in the middle seat of a Land Rover?

A little like everything else about the Defender, it is not the most comfortable experience, indeed, some might call it uncomfortably intimate. The gear stick has to go somewhere, and in the case of the Defender it is located in front of the middle seat. While vans often have the same scenario, they are blessed with slightly more legroom and width. Not so the humble Land Rover, where the long gear stick is positioned between the middle passenger's legs. Gears three and four are fine, but anything else requires full bodily contact with both gear stick and hand. It helps if you know and feel comfortable with the unfortunate passenger, but where's the fun in that? I have lost count of the number of people I have taxied around in the middle seat of the Land Rover, their bodies contorted in a kind of twirl in order to avoid all physical contact.

Two months later, my Land Rover was ready. I couldn't sleep the night before I collected her. I was surprised by my own emotions at the prospect of collecting a new car. She was a thing of beauty, with that unique factory smell that is impossible to replicate once it is lost. I can honestly say I didn't stop smiling from the moment I stepped foot in that vehicle.

It still amazes me the power of a Land Rover to elicit emotion. Driving suddenly became fun again, and I don't mean in a 'pop to the shops as an excuse to get in your new car' kind of way, but a 'drive to Cornwall and back in a day' kind of way. By this point I was working on a number of UK-based shows and I was covering more than 30,000 miles a year. My Silver Bullet went everywhere; although my growing green feelings erred on the side of train travel, I preferred the freedom and anonymity provided by my trusty steed.

Together we covered most of the British Isles. With my beloved Labrador Inca at my side we would drive the length and breadth of the UK to cover rural affairs for *Countryfile*. A great test of early girlfriends was to see if they could endure a Defender journey to Scotland and back – and I don't just mean to the border, I mean right up to the Highlands and Islands. I'll admit it, they were arduous journeys; the shaking and the noise left one feeling slightly frazzled. I must have done that trip a dozen times in a Defender. With nowhere to put a coffee cup or even a bottle of water and too much noise to listen to the radio, they weren't the easiest journeys, but therein lies the sheer joy of Land Rover travel.

The beauty of the Land Rover lies partly in its characterful imperfections. No matter how noisy or bone-shockingly jarring a journey, I always smiled. She always left me feeling fulfilled. You see, a Land Rover really is so much more than just a vehicle – it becomes an extension of you. You begin to know and understand the nuances and quirks of your car. You can recognise every tiny feature of them. They become something so deeply personal that a criticism of your Land Rover is almost a criticism of you.

It is a well-known fact that the car of choice for the Chelsea mother is a 4×4. Indeed, the characterisation has led to its own term: the Chelsea Tractor. Drive past any school in London's Kensington and Chelsea between 8am and 9am and you will see an ocean of 4×4s.

Now I will admit that living in Kensington and Chelsea and driving a ubiquitous 4×4 sometimes left me feeling a little guilty. 'But I use it mostly in the country,' I would invariably argue when confronted about it by one of my green-conscious friends. Indeed, the Silver Bullet probably saw more of the UK countryside than most Land Rovers, but she still retained an air of urban sophistication that meant she stood out just as much in the countryside. I would often deliberately drive up a couple of verges and through some muddy puddles before arriving at any farms or country fairs. I became conscious of her shiny metallic silver body that jarred against the standard-issue Land Rovers favoured by farmers.

All good things must come to an end, though, and in this case it really was self-inflicted.

Shortly before I rowed the Atlantic in 2005, I had started seeing a beautiful girl, Marina, who would later become my wife. In the early days of our relationship I decided it would be a good idea to drive her down to Devon in the Silver Bullet. It would be the early death knell for the Defender.

Soon after rowing the Atlantic I proposed to Marina. Our lives were amalgamated and Marina gently suggested that the Defender was no longer the most 'suitable' family car.

Now, this is far from unique. It is a time-honoured tradition that when a man gains a wife, he loses a car. Some of us fight for both, but one of them usually goes, and in my case I relented, but we wouldn't lose the marque. We went for a Land Rover Discovery.

Before we took delivery of our black Discovery I had to decide what to do with the Silver Bullet. We didn't need and couldn't afford to keep two cars, so the Defender had to go.

I had let go of cars before, of course, but this was different. She really had become a part of me. Together we had been through so much. We had travelled the country together, she had towed my Atlantic rowing boat, we had been 'papped' together more times than I can recall (although I do remember the time we were papped on the phone together – me and the car, that is).

If I had had the means and wherewithal to keep her safe somewhere for the future, I would have done it in a flash, but she had to go.

I called some Land Rover dealerships to see if they wanted her and eventually settled on one just outside of Oxford. That final journey was like a funeral cortège. There was an overwhelming sadness as I found myself looking mournfully over her bonnet as we drove up the A40.

It may seem strange to mourn a car, and it had certainly never happened to me before, but there was a sense of finality when I handed over her keys. It was like closing a whole chapter of my life. This was the car I had dreamed of owning, and now that dream was over. It was like splitting up from a girl you still really like.

Now, don't for a moment blame my wife. She was quite right. The Defender had served me well as a bachelor, but we needed something more suitable for the two of us. We were a partnership, after all, and it was a case of choosing a vehicle that met both our needs.

Marriage is all about compromise. Much is made about being 'under the thumb' and forced to make decisions you would never normally have made, but in our case it was about twinning our lives. I know of friends who had the same issues with their sports cars, who similarly mourned the loss of their beloved Porsche or Aston Martin on marriage.

Although it was time for the Defender to go, I resolved that one day I would once again drive the noisiest and most uncomfortable car.

The Discovery was a spaceship by compassion. It was like swapping from a Cessna aircraft to a Learjet. She was brimming with shiny lights, buttons and technology that the Defender could only ever dream of. But here's the thing: the perfection obliterated the character and charm of her predecessor. I will admit that longer journeys took on a more comfortable edge, but I'll be honest here, it never felt quite the same as getting into my old Defender. Without the quirks and the imperfections the Discovery became just a tiny bit bland. To use a male dating analogy, it would be like leaving an averagely pretty girl with a great personality for a supermodel. The supermodel is great for a while until you begin to miss character.

It is this that drives the world of the Land Rover aficionado. It is its spirit that we often talk about. The Defender is brimming with character and quirkiness. Each vehicle is different. Each one has its own tale to tell.

HISTORY OF THE LAND ROVER

PART I

The story of the Land Rover begins way back in the dark days of the Second World War. Although the Amsterdam Motor Show of April 1948 is regarded as the birthplace of the marque, it was actually conceived much earlier. The vehicle that started it all had a very long gestation period, brought about by fate – and the war. Look closely at the red-brick walls of the office block at Land Rover's famous factory in Solihull, on the outskirts of Birmingham, and you can still see traces of the camouflage paint applied during the 1939–45 conflict. The idea behind this paint job was to confuse Luftwaffe bombers, and presumably it worked, because while nearby Coventry was flattened the Solihull factory survived intact.

Rover had been building cars in Coventry since 1901, but the war changed its fortunes. In 1940, after the Coventry factory was destroyed by the German Luftwaffe's blanket bombing of that city, Rover continued production of aero engines for the war

effort at a government shadow factory – a few miles away at
Solihull. The company was so successful that after the war the
factory looked for new, civilian projects to keep its staff employed.

Steel was required to rebuild a war-torn world, but it was in
short supply. Like everything else in post-war Britain, this metal
was strictly rationed. What the country desperately needed was
earnings from exports; to get steel, companies had to export 75
per cent of what they manufactured. That was a tall order, even
for a successful car manufacturer like Rover, which had earned a
comfortable living by selling plush saloon cars to the middle
classes on the domestic market in the pre-war years. Now,
although new models were planned, its 1930s designs were
outdated and didn't appeal to British motorists, let alone overseas
buyers. It seemed that Rover had little chance of persuading the
government to allocate the all-important steel it needed. But there
was, on the other hand, mountains of aluminium left over from
the aircraft industry, if only somebody could find a use for it ...

Although quirky four-wheel-drive cars had been in existence
since the early years of the twentieth century, it was in the late
1930s, with the rise of Hitler's Nazi Germany and Japan's imperial
ambitions, and when war looked inevitable, that a go-anywhere
utility vehicle became a necessity. The Americans realised that
they were eventually likely to get involved in the European
conflict, so the US government invited tenders for the 4×4 military vehicle that would eventually become the Jeep (designed by
the American Bantam Car Co and Willys-Overland, but eventually built by both the latter company and, under licence, Ford).

The Jeep played a major part in resolving the war in the Allies'
favour, and when peace was declared in 1945 there was no

shortage of takers for the vehicles that had inevitably been left behind in Europe, now surplus to military requirements. These all-terrain vehicles were particularly popular with farmers – and gentleman-farmer Maurice Wilks was no exception.

In the overgrown graveyard of St Mary's Church at Llanfair-yn-y-Cwmwd, on the Isle of Anglesey, North Wales, is the weathered gravestone of Maurice Wilks, which reads: 'A much-loved, gentle, modest man whose sudden death robbed the Rover company of a chairman and Britain of the brilliant pioneer who was responsible for the world's first gas turbine driven car.'

Like the man himself, the inscription is modest, for it fails to mention the invention for which he is best known – the Land Rover.

Wilks died in 1963, aged just 59. In his all-too-short life he also helped to develop Frank Whittle's original jet engine, but he will forever be remembered for creating the motor car that took the world by storm. Nobody back in the 1940s, 50s and 60s could have predicted how the utilitarian little 4×4 would one day become the car of the stars. When Wilks died, even his family underestimated the importance of the Land Rover. They thought he'd be best remembered for his contribution to Rover's ill-fated gas turbine car, which is why that got mentioned on his gravestone and the Land Rover didn't.

Maurice, engineering director at the Rover car company, owned a rugged 250-acre coastal estate at Newborough, on the island of Anglesey, which was made more accessible thanks to his own ex-US Army Jeep. The truth was, he thoroughly enjoyed the experience of 4×4 off-road driving. Old home movies still in the possession of the Wilks family show him driving it at every opportunity. Whenever he was able to escape the hustle and bustle of the Rover factory for the wilderness of Anglesey, the man and his machine were seldom parted.

One day, his brother Spencer, Rover's managing director, asked him what he would do when the battered warhorse eventually wore out. 'Buy another one, I suppose – there isn't anything else,' was his fateful reply.

Legend has it that the Wilks brothers were relaxing on the beach at the time – at Red Wharf Bay in Anglesey, to be precise – and Maurice began drawing a picture of his ideal 4×4 in the sand. Unsurprisingly, it looked very much like his Jeep. It wasn't long before the rough sketch became reality, though, for the brothers reckoned there was a definite niche for a civilian version of the Jeep, and they decided to build it at Solihull.

Again, circumstances played their part. With steel strictly rationed, Rover decided to create the new vehicle's bodywork from Birmabright aluminium alloy panels. The steel box-section chassis was born of necessity, with strips of steel cast-offs hand-welded together to create a ladder frame. As well as being cheaper to install than a heavy press or expensive sheet steel, it also achieved the level of toughness appropriate for an off-road utility vehicle. Astonishingly, the same basic ladder-frame chassis was used throughout the production of the Series Land Rovers, as well as the Defenders, right up until the manufacture of the last cars in January 2016. The ladder-frame chassis was also the backbone of the first- and second-generation Range Rovers (1970–2002), Discovery 1 and 2 (1989–2003) and the various military specials and forward controls produced at Solihull.

The new 4×4 planned by the Wilks brothers also had great export potential. In 1947, British schoolchildren still toiled in classrooms in which a map of the world took pride of place on the wall, one that showed more than half of the land mass coloured pink – denoting countries that were either British colonies or former colonies (by then part of the British Commonwealth). The sun had not yet set on the British Empire and there were plenty of colonial outposts in the developing world where Rover's projected new all-terrain vehicle would prove an invaluable mode of transport. So although the first Land Rover was designed with the British farmer in mind, its versatility meant that it would be a brilliant workhorse anywhere on the planet where the going was likely to get tough. (And it still is. For example, in the remote Cameron Highlands of Malaysia, extremely battered Land Rover Series Is are even today the main mode of transport in the tea plantations, including some very early 80-inch models, which would be worth a fortune as 'garage finds' in the UK!)

The introduction of the Land Rover marked a fresh start at the company's new Solihull premises, and the enthusiasm of the management for the vehicle was such that it even axed its plans for its projected 'mini' car, the M1 (which had reached prototype stage by 1946), in favour of the newcomer.

The first Land Rover prototype was built in the summer of 1947. Its chassis came from a Willys Jeep, as did the axles, wheels and leaf-spring shackles. It is believed that other components, such as the springs, shock absorbers, bearings, brakes and brake drums, were also of Jeep origin, along with the transfer box and several transmission parts, including propshafts, universal joints and handbrake. The engine was an under-powered 1389cc unit from a Rover saloon. The car differed from the Jeep in that it had a more cramped driving position, because Rover wanted to provide the largest possible payload area in the back and so moved the driver's seat forwards three inches to achieve it. Comfort was extremely rudimentary: just a plain cushion in the middle of the metal seat box, which also covered the fuel tank. With the export market in mind, the vehicle had a tractor-like, centrally-mounted steering wheel to save building separate left- and right-hand-drive models. Thus it became known as the Centre-Steer.

Today, the Centre-Steer prototype is the Holy Grail to many Land Rover enthusiasts. That's because apparently no trace of it exists; although some very respected Land Rover experts are convinced it does. In fact, some believe several Centre-Steers are secreted away somewhere.

The official line is that this very first 1947 Land Rover was abandoned to rot in a shed somewhere in the Rover works at Solihull and was eventually thrown away during a spring-clean. It had certainly disappeared completely a few years later. Some say its remains were shovelled ignominiously into a skip and went for scrap. Others believe an employee with a better sense of history than his bosses succeeded in spiriting away the remains for preservation.

Either way, the Centre-Steer, cobbled together mainly out of Jeep parts, is actually a bit of a red herring when it comes to the genesis of the Land Rover that would eventually go into production. Rover's engineers quickly realised that the Centre-Steer wasn't a viable proposition and opted instead for the conventional wisdom of separate right- and left-hand-drive vehicles. Although the development engineers borrowed some ideas from the Jeep – notably the 80-inch wheelbase – the parts for the new vehicle were all designed and built by Rover. Work continued through 1947 and in February 1948 they began to build the first pilot prototypes. It had been decided that the new vehicle – by now christened the Land-Rover (note the hyphen between 'Land' and 'Rover', which wasn't lost until a decade later) – would be launched at the Geneva Motor Show in early March, but it soon became clear that the prototypes wouldn't be completed in time, so it was decided that it would launch at the Amsterdam Motor Show instead.

Thus it was, in the Dutch capital, on 30 April 1948, that the Land Rover legend was born. Two prototypes – left- and right-hand-drive variants – were on public display. One was a standard model, the other equipped by PTO (power take-off)-driven welding equipment, to demonstrate the versatility of the strange-looking little vehicle.

The initial 80-inch wheelbase Land Rovers that were sold to the general public remained very agricultural in every respect. Heaters were non-existent, as were passenger seats, door tops and roofs, but that hardly mattered because cabs and hard tops were yet to be introduced and Solihull's new arrival was intended to be very much open plan, with the driver exposed to the elements. Nothing unusual there; contemporary tractors, combine harvesters and other farm machinery of that era didn't have modern comfortable cabs either.

Nobody minded the Spartan comforts anyway once they had encountered the new vehicle's amazing capabilities. They didn't even bat an eyelid when the original purchase price of £450 was jacked up to £540 in October 1948. The first year's production was 3048, but this more than doubled to 8000 the following year, doubling again to 16,000 in 1950. What had been seen as a stop-gap exercise, cobbled together from Rover car components and other bits copied from the original Jeep, was now a very important vehicle in its own right, and one that would eventually outsell – and indeed outlive – Rover cars. The company clearly had a success story on its hands.

Land Rover plodded on. There were developments aplenty in the following years, but they were evolutionary rather than revolutionary. Today, more than 60 years on, you can stand one of the last Defenders alongside the earliest Series I and there's no mistaking the family resemblance.

The first prototypes were powered by a 1398cc engine, which developed a mere 48bhp. This, however, was deemed inadequate, so the production vehicles were equipped with the 1595cc side-valve unit that had been designed for the Rover P3 60 saloon car. Various drivetrain and axle changes along the way were also dictated by contemporary saloon variants until, in August 1951, the vehicle received the very welcome 1997cc overhead valve engine, which delivered a 26 per cent increase in torque at low engine speeds.

In 1953, the wheelbase was extended to 86 inches, and a long wheelbase version at 107 inches was also introduced. In 1956, these were further extended to 88 and 109 inches to accommodate the bigger 2052cc diesel engine, which became available for the first time a year later.

The very earliest Land Rovers were available in light green only. Legend has it that the company managed to secure a bulk purchase of war surplus paint used to decorate the interiors of RAF bombers, and it was only when that ran out that Land Rovers were sold in the familiar dark green (known as Bronze Green) now synonymous with the marque. It was some years before further colour options – blue and grey – became available.

Although the choice of paintwork was limited, the sky was the limit as far as other options went. The simple, bolt-together construction of the vehicle and its generous provision of power take-off points meant that it could be readily adapted for industrial as well as agricultural use. In fact, a fire-engine variant had been included among the original prototypes, proving that the company was on the ball from the start. Mobile compressors and welders were among the special vehicles available direct from Solihull, but like the 1948 coach-built Tickford Station Wagon, they were not a financial success. Also, many modified variations on the Land Rover theme were – and still are – produced by independent specialists. Today, these are mainly luxury, bespoke variants created by companies like Nene Overland (who produced my own distinctive set of wheels).

The Tickford Station Wagon, Land Rover's first foray into comfortable transport, failed because of the eye-watering levels of purchase tax imposed by the government on luxury goods in the immediate post-war years. However, the company returned to the abandoned Station Wagon theme late in 1954 with a seven-seater on the short wheelbase 86-inch chassis, and accommodation (albeit rather cramped) for ten in the long wheelbase 107-inch version. Alloy-framed bodies replaced the expensive wooden frames of the earlier Tickford version and, although the long wheelbase model in particular looked for all the world as though it had been assembled from a Meccano set, both were an immediate and enduring success.

Enthusiasts love the rugged simplicity of the Series I. Its lack of creature comforts and austere lines give it an aesthetic purity unrivalled by any other motor vehicle, before or since. But it is also a brilliantly practical vehicle for travel in the most remote parts of the world, and, like many early Land Rovers, much revered and much sought-after.

CHAPTER TWO

THE RANGE OF ROVER

HOW LAND ROVER BECAME THE MODERN EXPLORERS

Britain has a long heritage of exploration and adventure; Captain Cook, Captain Scott, Ernest Shackleton, Livingstone, Raleigh, Drake ... the list is endless. In many ways, the Land Rover became the mechanical evolution of the great heroic era of exploration. It provided access to places that had once been inaccessible. It allowed modern-day explorers to push geographic boundaries and penetrate deep into some of the Earth's greatest and hitherto unexplored wildernesses.

British, strong, lantern-jawed, rugged, reliable and determined, the qualities of the Land Rover were not lost on professional explorers. Where once the adventurer had relied on packhorses and mules to carry their loads, this vehicle stepped in as their new mechanical workhorse. A Land Rover could go anywhere that a horse had gone, without fear of fatigue. It could carry heavier loads, too.

One of the first explorers to use the Land Rover was Colonel Leblanc, who drove from Britain to Ethiopia in 1949. The Rover company were impressed at his audacity, and soon he became a travelling salesman for the company. In this role Leblanc helped to sell new models of Land Rovers and Rover cars by leading them in small convoys into faraway remote regions, demonstrating their endurance abilities to the watching world.

However it was Laurens Van der Post who helped to establish the Land Rover as the perfect expedition vehicle. Van der Post was commissioned by the BBC to make a six-part documentary in search of the Bushmen in the Kalahari. *The Lost World of the Kalahari* was a huge hit and Land Rover suddenly realised the power of the brand in helping and endorsing overland expeditions around the world. The vehicles acted like mobile advertising billboards.

One of the most celebrated Land Rover adventurers was an adventuress named Barbara Toy. In 1955, the Australian adventuress drove an 80-inch Land Rover called Pollyanna around the globe. Her book, *Pollyanna*, documenting the journey became a bestseller, further cementing the Land Rover as the explorer's car.

But it is the 1955–6 Far East expedition undertaken by Oxford and Cambridge Universities that caused Land Rover to become the iconic symbol of discovery and adventure. The expedition was on an unprecedented scale and had numerous sponsors, including the Royal Geographic Society. It involved an overland journey across Europe and Asia from London to Singapore. It was the first time such an expedition had been attempted. Two

86-inch Series I station wagons had been loaned to a team of students from Oxford and Cambridge Universities. The Land Rovers were painted in the light and dark blues of the respective universities.

It was a gruelling journey that included the daunting prospect of the dense impenetrable jungles of Southeast Asia. The former commissioner of the BBC, a then unknown David Attenborough, commissioned a film about the expedition.

The film included the crossing of the virgin desert between Damascus and Baghdad and the traverse of the Ledo Road between India and Burma that was later closed. The vehicles forded rivers and streams and often had to build their own bridges to cross the deeper bodies of water. They drove the narrow, dizzying roads of Nepal and risked both bandits and headhunters in their quest to drive to Singapore. The team were forced to hack new paths through northern Thailand's virgin forest.

The vehicles provided Land Rover with invaluable data on their tolerance and resilience in tough conditions, but above all, the iconic images and the later film provided advertising that money couldn't buy of the Land Rover as the go-anywhere vehicle.

The Oxford and Cambridge Expedition arrived in Singapore on 6 March 1956, six months after leaving Hyde Park the previous year. It was a huge success. The vehicles had negotiated 18,000 miles of roads, tracks and jungle. One of the Land Rovers is still on display at the Heritage Centre in Gaydon today.

The success of the expedition was soon followed by a second Oxford and Cambridge overland journey across South America in search of the geographical centre of Brazil.

Not to be outdone by the educated elite, working-class Londoner Eric Edis set out in 1957 to circumnavigate the entire world in a Land Rover. Without sponsorship, he led a team of sixteen in three Land Rovers on a two-year journey. Only one of the Land Rovers survived the gruelling expedition, but once again the Land Rover had proved its credentials while also acting as a mobile billboard, reaching people and places other brands could only dream of achieving.

One of my favourite expeditions, visually, was the Joint Services Expedition in which four Forward Control 101s crossed northern Africa and the Sahara Desert – travelling 7500 miles from the Atlantic Ocean to the Red Sea. They completed the gruelling journey in 100 days, and it was the superb performance of the vehicles on this expedition that led to the Land Rover being taken up by the British military.

These were the days of the great explorers – adventurers who pushed not just geographical boundaries, but took on what to others may have seemed eccentric and even impossible. When I was 14 I met one such man, a character who arguably changed the course of my life.

I was at boarding school in Dorset and one Saturday morning we were entertained by an explorer who looked like a throwback to the Victorian era. He was clad in safari jacket, pith helmet and jungle boots, and he completed his look with a python draped around his neck.

Colonel Blashford Snell, better known as Blashers, had come to our school to talk about his various expeditions around the world. He was notorious for having crossed the Gobi Desert, been shot at in Libya, carried a grand piano into the Amazon, and taken part in searches for the elusive yeti and the fabled two-snouted dog of Bolivia. He was a man of eccentricity and I was immediately drawn to him by his charm and charisma.

It would be a further 20 years until I finally got to meet my hero again, at a reception with Her Majesty at Buckingham Palace – but that sounds like bragging, so I shall move on. Of all the expeditions around the world, Blashers is arguably most famous for taking a Land Rover where this vehicle had never been before. For a car that had transformed the world with its 'go everywhere and anywhere' accessibility, this was really saying something. Of course, this book would not be complete without the story of Blashers' legendary expedition, so I just had to go and visit him and hear the story in his own words.

I have always loved Dorset. It is probably because it holds so many childhood memories. This was the county of my formative years and it still has a soothing, calming effect on me. Once again I found myself rumbling through the tall hedgerows that tower over the narrow snaking country lanes.

This is Land Rover country. I must have passed twenty Defenders as I made my way up the A31 from Poole to Blandford Forum. I was on my way to the Colonel's house but along the way I was making a detour to visit Rosie, a Land Rover enthusiast I had come across on social media. We had arranged to meet at her house deep in the Dorset countryside to talk all things Land Rover, and particularly the part that this marque plays in her life.

Rosie and her partner Jon are obsessed with coffee. They were fed up with the rise of the high-street coffee chains and they wanted to return to the art of artisanal coffee making – to put the love back into coffee without the capitalist approach. They couldn't afford a shop and, besides, they liked the idea of providing coffee to consumers who cared about their produce, so they planned to serve it at farmers' markets and food festivals. What they needed, though, was a mobile coffee wagon.

Jon suggested a Land Rover, so they began their search for a suitable vehicle to transform into a mobile barista. They soon found a Series III on Gumtree for £2000. They put in an offer and a few days later the owner arrived with his entire family and the Land Rover on a trailer.

'They were all crying their eyes out,' marvels Rosie. 'It was like a bereavement for them to say goodbye to the car. It had been lovingly fitted with bench seats and you could tell this had been a much-loved family car. We didn't have the heart to tell them what we planned to do with it,' she added, sounding embarrassed.

Rosie and Jon had named their coffee company Grounded – a combination of ground coffee and the fact that a Land Rover is rooted to the ground as a 4×4.

I stood at the little counter under the weak spring sunshine while Rosie worked the Italian machine. They had converted the Land Rover themselves and you could see the passion and love that had gone into this project. As I sipped on my cappuccino, Rosie proudly showed me the scrapbook full of photographs from the beginning of the restoration project.

'Jon will be gutted not to be here,' she admitted. He still had to work shifts in the pub, but according to Rosie it was he who was the Land Rover fanatic.

At markets and shows, the car, named Arthur, is always swamped with people wanting to take a photo of it. 'It makes people smile,' she laughs.

I asked Rosie what it's like to drive her.

'Well, she leaks, she's slow and she's really really cold,' she admits. 'But I love her.'

Rosie knew nothing about Land Rovers before they bought Arthur (although Jon was a self-confessed enthusiast), and by her own admission her family think she and Jon are crazy, but with this vehicle they have managed to combine their two passions: coffee and Land Rovers. And you can't argue with that.

With my Land Rover-made coffee injecting a much-needed caffeine boost around my body, I said goodbye to Rosie and Arthur the Land Rover and continued on my way to find Blashers.

If you were to imagine what a Victorian explorer's house looked like, the Colonel's house was probably it, brimming with treasures, guns, art, textiles, bows and arrows and other stuff from his various global expeditions. In the hall was a huge Vickers machine gun that he had bought from a 'local choir boy who is also an arms dealer'. The man himself chuckled, 'everyone marvels at the gun but no one ever asks if it's legal.'

The room was filled with photographs and paintings from around the world. There were muskets and guns mounted on the walls and all sorts of indigenous and tribal objects hanging from every nook and cranny.

'It's a museum of exploration,' he explained.

We moved on to his expedition stores. The entrance contained a carefully indexed library of thousands of travel, adventure and exploration books, all catalogued by country. Next was the film room, bursting at the seams with VHS tapes, DVDs and hundreds of cylinders of old cinematic film which Blashers was in the process of transferring into digital format. One wall was dedicated to a series of little doors labelled: HOT ARID DRY, HOT TROPICAL WET, COLD DRY, COLD DAMP, and so on. I pulled one door open to find a cupboard brimming with khaki shirts and jackets. There were dozens of hats and pith helmets. It was like a props cupboard, except this had all been worn in anger.

Another wall was piled high with boxes full of rations, tents, canteens, plates, cutlery, lamps, stoves and torches. This was the room of a travelling hoarder. My eyes were overwhelmed. Bows and arrows and spears were propped up in every corner. Each one of them had a story. 'This one nearly killed me,' Blasher told me, holding up a knife. It was a living museum of Blashers' extraordinary life.

We headed outside to an outbuilding – 'expedition base,' he explained. When I visited him he had only recently returned from a recce to Colombia and was soon to lead an expedition across Mongolia. Pretty impressive for an almost 80-year-old.

'So how important have Land Rovers been in your life?' I asked him.

'Vital,' Blashers answered. 'I have driven them in Ethiopia and used them to clear mines in Libya, I have been shot at in Omagh in Northern Ireland and in Cyprus and used them to support expeditions to explore the Blue Nile.'

Land Rovers really have loomed large in Blashers' life and they have saved his life on more than one occasion, too. As a sapper in the army, the Land Rover was a vital piece of kit. The cars provided access to the inaccessible. They were packhorses that never tired. 'I remember the Land Rovers we used to drive had a big sign on the inside of the windscreen which read, "This vehicle cost £1400, please look after it.'"

He told me the story of one Land Rover that overheated as they drove through the desert. The open-topped Rover had become red hot, igniting a polyester sleeping bag stowed in a cage at the back. 'We had to jettison all the spare fuel to save the vehicle from igniting,' he smiled at the memory.

Blashers is also credited with setting up Operation Raleigh in 1984, which today still enables volunteers to travel to remote places around the world and help local communities. When Prince Charles was given a 110 by Land Rover, he kindly handed it on to Blashers as a donation to Operation Raleigh, for which he was patron.

The walls of Blashers' home are papered with mosaics of expedition images, and among the hundreds of heroic shots are the unmistakable shapes of Land Rover Series vehicles. 'The Queen particularly liked the photograph from the Darien Gap,' he smiled proudly. 'We were invited to Buckingham Palace after we made it through the Gap; the Queen told me she particularly admired the photograph of the Series II Land Rover flying the Union flag.' He showed me a photograph of the vehicle afloat on a river. It's a great image that sums up the derring-do of the go-anywhere do-anything Land Rover.

Which leads us on to perhaps Bashers' most famous expedition: the Darien Gap.

The Pan American highway had transformed trade and travel between North, Central and South America. The highway ran seamlessly until it reached Panama, where it came to an abrupt halt at a notorious jungle crossing known as the Darien Gap. This hostile, steamy jungle had defeated engineers, who were unable to find a way through the impenetrable swamp between Panama and Colombia.

In the late 1950s, several expeditions were mounted by international teams in an attempt to cross the gap, and in 1971 Blashers seized the opportunity. He asked his engineering chief if he thought it was a good idea for him to go. For the army, these were the twilight years between conflicts, and the military were looking for opportunities for adventurous training. The Darien Gap project would be a perfect combination of technical problem-solving, engineering, mechanics and jungle training.

Blashers sent an Irishman on a recce of the jungle, during which he nearly died, but he reported back to the Colonel that, with enough time, men and resources, the crossing would be possible. So the Royal Engineers were enlisted, along with a small army of scientists, zoologists, botanists, geologists and anthropologists. Now all they needed was a vehicle.

By now Land Rover had built their luxury car, the Range Rover, which they were preparing to launch onto the market. They saw the Darien Gap project as the perfect platform for doing just that, and to prove its off-roading credentials at the same time. It was a brave marketing move – and certainly a gamble.

Two brand-new Range Rovers were supplied by Land Rover, and were carefully driven from Alaska to Panama, where the jungle expedition would begin. The team had 100 days to cover 250 miles of virgin jungle.

'The problem was the Range Rovers had very powerful engines,' explained Blashers, 'but the ground was unseasonably wet, turning it into a muddy quagmire, so the torque of the engines ground the wheels into the mud where they stuck.' After that, the differentials on the Range Rovers exploded – 12 of them – before Land Rover began to panic and sent out their own engineers.

Meanwhile, it became apparent to Blashers that what they needed was a Land Rover; not a poncy Range Rover, but a light-weight Series Land Rover to help clear the way ahead of the two heavier vehicles. A runner was dispatched back to Panama City where they purchased on old Series II for $100, which was duly delivered by helicopter to the middle of the Darien Gap to join the expedition. It was named the Pathfinder – and without the electrics of the Range Rovers and with its lightweight body, it performed effortlessly.

However, Blashers needed more men. 'I hired 100 murderers and rapists from the local prison in El Real,' he explained matter-of-factly. 'I swapped them for a case of Scotch whisky and the promise that I would release them in Colombia.'

The press had found the idea of the expedition intoxicating – it was a tale that combined old-school exploration with modern motor vehicles. The *Daily Telegraph* had dispatched their own reporter to cover the expedition, and he confided in Blashers that he wasn't sure if he was covering an expedition or a disaster.

Eventually the team made it through – but not without losses. Dozens of men died during the expedition, but the biggest casualty came when a group of soldiers was ambushed while attempting to join them from the Colombian side. A dozen were shot and killed by warring locals. This was a hostile country at a hostile time.

The surviving explorers were much feted at a celebratory march in Medellín, in Colombia, where they laid a wreath at the statue of the city's liberator, Simón Bolívar. The expedition was deemed a success and Land Rover had saved face. The Range Rovers returned to the UK where Blashers was asked to drive them around the country as a form of marketing for Land Rover – the Series II Pathfinder, however, was sold in Colombia.

'They offered to sell the Range Rovers to me at a discount,' recalls Blashers. 'But I couldn't afford the fuel, so I got a Volvo instead.'

The Land Rover had cemented itself as the car that could go anywhere. It had become an indispensable necessity for modern-day explorers, and the images of these cars ploughing their way through these gruelling expeditions captured the nation's imagination. The vehicle's ability to traverse the world's most inhospitable landscapes also helped secure it one of the most incredible statistics: it has been said that for more than half the world's population, the Land Rover was the very first vehicle they ever saw.

However, with the hallowed days of the great explorations now becoming history, and with explorations becoming fewer and fewer, Land Rover sought other forums in which to test the versatility and endurance abilities of their cars. The Land Rover was about to make its metamorphosis from simple workhorse to high-tech rally car. The world of competitive endurance rally racing was really taking off, and it was only a matter of time before the Land Rover came of age.

In 1970, Derbyshireman Drew Bowler decided he wanted to have a go at rally driving. He didn't have any money to buy a car so he looked around the farm and found an old Series I Land

Rover. He fitted it with roll bars and a new engine and thus was born the Land Rover Bowler.

As rallying really started to take off in the UK throughout the 1970s and 80s, Drew became more and more shrewd when it came to his interpretation of the rules. While most drivers were competing in 'off the line' vehicles, Bowler was busy adapting and transforming existing vehicles into something unique. Thus he was arguably one of the pioneers in the Land Rover modification cottage industry that had cropped up around the country. Most significant in his designs was the fact that Drew realised he didn't have to use the Land Rover chassis; by changing it he could alter a farm vehicle into something capable of taking on the Paris Dakar Rally.

The Tom Cat was the first Bowler production Land Rover, but it was soon followed by the Wild Cat. Both vehicles bear a striking similarity to the Land Rover Defender and Series, but radical plastic surgery had been done to her body, as well as an overhaul of her internal organs.

The world of Rally Racing exploded. The Paris Dakar was seen as the pinnacle of this circuit, the race making plenty of headlines around the world with its tales of derring-do as modern-day adventurers took to Mad Max vehicles to race across the deserts of West Africa.

Current price tags for an individual to take part in a fully supported race car run upwards of a million dollars, and while there are still plenty of wealthy hedge fund managers willing to part with that kind of cash, Drew realised there was a market for those enthusiasts who sat somewhere in between. At the lowest end, in particular, were the maverick home engineers who built cars in their spare time in their garages, and Drew saw this as an untapped market of people keen to enter the world of endurance rally racing.

The Rally Raid, a series of 600-mile-plus endurance races across Europe, was the perfect fit for his Land Rover and these wannabe racers. Cars needed to be equipped to travel distances of up to 375 miles unassisted, which entailed carrying massive 88-gallon fuel tanks weighing upwards of half a ton. This necessitated stronger suspension, which in turn required a stronger chassis.

The Wild Cat was essentially a Land Rover on steroids – 40 per cent Defender, the rest handmade. Drew created the greatest rally car on the market.

While other marques had official rally car divisions racing under their brand, Land Rover never had such a dedicated department. Instead, under an informal agreement, Bowler become the official Land Rover rally car and the development of the Bowler came about with full design assistance of Land Rover.

Drew Bowler had tapped into a market where enthusiasts would be prepared to spend £100,000 on a race-ready rally car, and he soon had upwards of a dozen competing in the famous Dakar Rally. However, Bowler's market was restricted to the UK. 'Elsewhere in Europe and beyond, the Land Rover was seen as a premium vehicle not an off-road vehicle,' admits Drew.

The early 1990s were not Land Rover's finest years, and were memorable only for the production of the much-derided Freelander 1. Added to this was Land Rover's aggressive pursuit of the luxury market with their Range Rover. Beyond British borders, it seemed, the Land Rover had lost its way, but Bowler had given them a platform to remind people of their cars' serious off-road capabilities, even if it meant a car that had been assembled from only half a Defender.

The relationship with Land Rover remains strong, as Drew pointed out to me when I visited him at his workshops in Derbyshire.

'We were one of the first businesses to be recognised, supported and endorsed by Land Rover,' Drew admits proudly. As if to reiterate this, he took me to a 'secret room' where a team of designers worked at banks of computers with high-speed CAD (Computer Aided Design) links to Land Rover's headquarters.

Rally cars required a number of modifications from a standard off-road vehicle. As we walked around the factory floor Drew showed me bumpers that had holes cut out to save weight, but also for ease of cleaning after a race. 'A rally car picks up 40–60 pounds of mud during a race,' he explained. 'They need to be easily hosed down, and the holes help.'

Perhaps most astonishing to see were the massive support trucks that accompany the rally vehicles around the world. Standing some 20 feet tall and weighing in at a staggering 27 tons, I was dwarfed by one six-wheeler truck. Essentially mobile workshops, they also need to be able to navigate across the course. 'There was a point when they were faster than some of the cars,' Drew laughed. They too are fitted with full roll cages and rally seats. Nothing has been omitted in the detailed design of these cars, with upwards of one a week being made by a team of 27 staff. Not to be outdone, though, next to the Goliath was a similar-sized Czech vehicle that had once been used as a mobile nuclear missile launcher.

As the popularity of rally driving continued to grow, Drew spotted another hole in the market: those who wanted a road-legal Defender in which they could weekend rally. Thus the Defender Challenge Land Rover was born – a short wheelbase Defender modified into a highly able rally vehicle. The interior was stripped out and roll bars and rally seats were fitted, along with all the other safety requirements. The result was a car that was original Defender on the outside, but something far more sporty inside.

As far as cost goes, a mere £50,000 buys you the car, a further £20,000 will ensure its entry into the six-part Defender Challenge series, and Bowler will even maintain and manage the cars for you. Like stabling of the finest racehorses, the company will deliver the Bowler Defenders to the rally course then take them away at the end and clean and make any necessary adjustments afterwards. The owners just need to turn up, race and go home.

I asked Drew what made Derbyshire such a good place for his manufacturing.

'Rural communities have the ability to fix things,' he explained. 'We have some of the greatest engineers and manufacturers. Locally we have Rolls-Royce, Bombardier and Toyota.' If you want something made, come to Derbyshire.

Intrigued to know why he had continued with Land Rovers, I asked him why he still worked with this marque.

'They're like a fungus that you can't get rid of,' he replied. 'I learnt to drive in a Series I and it was the same car I started rallying in. Today people want the nostalgia of the cars from their past or their childhood; we revert back to what we know, there is reassurance in something we remember. We have every customer from billionaires to builders; they are all drawn to the classless car.'

In the corner of the workshop stood another Series I that looked unlike anything I had ever seen before.

'This one has been totally rebuilt for a customer in the Middle East. It has power steering, air conditioning, V8 engine, proper brakes,' Drew explained.

It was a stunning-looking vehicle, and I wondered if perhaps this was the next period of evolution in the cottage industry of Land Rovers.

'There was near panic and hysteria last year,' admitted Drew. 'People heard that production of the Defender was about to stop and there was a mad scramble to get a car.

'There are two types of Land Rover enthusiasts,' he continued, 'those who wanted to get one as an investment and those who had always wanted a Land Rover and thought they'd get one before it was too late.'

Bowler has a loyal customer base.

'Our customers often have a top-of-the-range Range Rover, and a Defender, and they complete the set with a Bowler rally car,' Drew revealed.

I wondered whether wives ever have much input. Drew rolled his eyes and smiled.

'"It's an investment, darling," is the most common excuse for buying a Bowler Land Rover. We always have to handle the wives,' he admitted. 'The second most common reply from a prospective customer about to sign for a car is, "I'll just check with my wife."'

The worst, though, Drew revealed, is the customer who arrives with his 'enthusiastic mate' who is invariably a hobby mechanic.

The 'friend' will moan and complain about the engineering and mechanics and quite literally talk his friend out of the business.

'The Land Rover is an assuring vehicle,' Drew said. 'We see them used by search and rescue, the police, the coastguard, ambulance service and the military, and we think, if it's good enough for them, it's good enough for me.'

Rally cars aside, Land Rovers had so far proved to be the ultimate vehicles for the adventurous for more than two decades. Yet the most adventurous event of all was about to hit the scene. The 'Olympics of 4×4', as it was dubbed, began in 1980 with the Camel Trophy. These new adventure races started with a course that took drivers along the Trans-Amazonian highway in Series II Land Rovers. The events were all about adventure and expedition, and in the early years they took place in Sumatra, Papua New Guinea, Zaire, Brazil, Borneo, Australia, Madagascar (the first north–south crossing) and Sulawesi, before returning to the Amazon.

These gruelling tests of human endurance brought together teams from around the world who hoped to triumph in some of the most treacherous off-road conditions imaginable. Teamwork and camaraderie were crucial. The competitive element came in a series of 'Special Tasks' – such as winching and timed driving routes – in which the national teams competed against each other.

Between 1981 and 1998, Land Rover was the primary sponsor of the Camel Trophy adventure competition. In each of those seventeen years the company provided a fleet of vehicles for the international teams to use; however, the only event that featured Series IIIs as team vehicles was the one that took place in 1983.

That year the Camel Trophy was held in Zaire and featured crew from several countries. The 1000-mile journey crossed terrain ranging from knee-deep mud to desert sand, but the biggest obstacle was the heat – 45 degrees centigrade in the shade, with humidity at 95 per cent.

In the 1990s, the Camel Trophy headed to Siberia and the USSR, followed by Tanzania, Burundi, Guyana, Argentina, Paraguay, Chile (the 'Road to Hell' event), Belize, Mexico, Guatemala, El Salvador, Honduras (controversially serving 500 out-of-season lobsters at a dinner), Kalimantan (1000 miles and 18 rollovers to celebrate the first crossing of the island 100 years previously) and Mongolia.

The Camel Trophy, however, did not simply change venue; over the years the event evolved from a mud-plugging expedition to include elements of adventure sport, such as kayaking, mountain biking and winter sports. Teams were selected by each competing nation in competitions held nationally, designed to test the athletic, engineering and driving prowess of potential candidates.

Changing environmental sentiments and respect for the Earth began to impact the race as people questioned the damage that the cars caused to the natural landscapes they traversed. So by 1993 the race included green tasks such as building an environmental monitoring station in the jungle so that biologists could accurately study the flora and fauna of an area that had barely been explored previously. In all the events, the convoy's progress reopened roads and tracks that had fallen into disuse and frequently rebuilt bridges and repaired sections of damaged tracks.

In 1998 the Camel Trophy returned to Argentina and Chile for the penultimate Tierra del Fuego event. It was here that the Land Rover Freelander made its debut, when it was used to speed the competitors 6000 miles across the remote and snowy terrain. Outdoor pursuits dominated that event, and shortly afterwards Land Rover, still a major sponsor, felt that the Camel Trophy was moving away from adventure and exploration and issued a press release that indicated they would not sponsor future events. This ultimately led to the cancellation of the 1999 event, which was planned for Peru.

What we have left now are memories of the competition's glory years of the 1980s and 90s, when the Camel Trophy's distinctive yellow-orange Land Rovers travelled to diverse places across the globe.

That was not quite the end, though, as Land Rover's role as the mainstay of tough off-road adventure was briefly reprised in 2003 with the Land Rover G4 Challenge. This hugely expensive event was staged by Land Rover itself, and although slicing through jungles was out of the question, special off-road stages were held to test the capability of the vehicles as well as the skills of the drivers, using Defenders, Discoverys, Freelanders and Range Rovers.

The obligatory gruelling aspect of this event came from physical challenges such as kayaking, orienteering, mountain biking and abseiling. The first competition was won by Belgian fighter pilot Rudi Theoken, who turned down the first prize of a brand-new Range Rover and requested two Defenders instead!

Following the first G4 Challenge, in 2003, G4-Edition Defenders became available for the general public to buy. As well as the distinctive Tangiers Orange livery of the competition vehicles, yellow and black versions were also produced. Defender 90 and 110 versions were available, with front A-bar, roll cage, side steps and front spotlights as standard, as well as G4 badging.

Another G4 Challenge followed in 2006 and a third was scheduled for 2009, but the costly event was scrapped in 2008 by new owners Tata, who decided the return wasn't worth the outlay, and instead diverted funds into creating new models and the frenetic launch activity for them that we have witnessed in recent years.

These days the world is a smaller place and there aren't so many unexplored corners left to encourage budding explorers to jump into a Land Rover and get out there. But there are still plenty of adventures to be found for the thoughtful Land Rover owner. In the UK, there are Land Rover clubs up and down the land which meet most weekends and together drive the nation's green lanes – byways that have vehicular rights and can be legally driven. For the more adventurous, though, there are companies that lead expeditions to all corners of Europe and North Africa, which you can join in your Land Rover. Morocco and the Sahara Desert are particularly popular destinations, following an overland drive through France and Spain, before catching a ferry across the Strait of Gibraltar.

Although the days of the big set-piece events are over for Land Rover, their role as expedition vehicles continues in occasional challenges. Most recently, Land Rover sponsored the Pole of Cold, a 7500-mile journey from the UK to Oymyakon in the Sakha Republic of Russia which chased winter across Europe and Siberia in a red, specially modified Land Rover Defender. The expedition enabled geographic researchers to reach the coldest place in the Northern Hemisphere, Oymyakon, in northeastern Russia, which has recorded temperatures as low as minus 67 degrees centigrade.

For this journey the Defender was equipped with a Webasto engine heater and extra insulation around the engine bay and suspension. An additional layer of glass was fitted to the windows to create an insulating double-glazed effect and enabled the team to see through side windows whatever the conditions. In three months the Defender covered 18,750 miles. Over the next four months the team drove the length of Norway and Finland, crossing the Arctic Circle twice, before driving the breadth of Eurasia, returning via Altai, Tuva, Sweden and Denmark – all in the depths of winter. In all, the team drove some 22,500 miles and experienced temperatures as low as minus 58.9 degrees centigrade. During the expedition the team spent time with a variety of people recording wide-ranging perspectives on winter, from fishermen in Norway to aurora scientists in Finland, Shaman in Tuva and reindeer nomads in Yakutia.

HISTORY OF THE LAND ROVER

PART II

The huge success of the original Land Rovers of the 1950s and 60s encouraged the company to launch other models, which would in turn greatly influence the design of future Defenders. In fact, the development of all future Land Rover models would become hopelessly intertwined, sharing engines, gearboxes, suspension set-ups ... the list is endless. For example, the 200Tdi, 300Tdi and Td5 turbodiesel engines developed for the Discovery transformed the performance of Defenders throughout the 1990s and 2000s. But all the other models, of course, were inspired by the original Land Rover.

Through the 1970s, Land Rover's position as the world's best 4×4 utility had been eroded in many of the world's markets by cheaper alternatives from other manufacturers – particularly Toyota.

Toyota's story begins in 1941, when the Japanese Imperial Army invaded the Philippines and found a Bantam MkII Jeep abandoned by the Americans. It was shipped back to Japan and handed over to Toyota, who were inspired by it. The resulting AK prototype was used until the end of the war in 1945, and then largely forgotten until 1951, when Toyota re-entered the 4×4 market with the BJ prototype. Again, it was very much based on the American Jeep and the Series I Land Rover (which in itself was based on the Jeep). But the Toyota was bigger and more powerful than both, with a six-cylinder, 3.4-litre petrol engine producing 84bhp.

By 1954, Toyota coined the name Land Cruiser in a bid to attract the same sort of audience as the Land Rover and to boost overseas sales. By 1968, Toyota had sold 100,000 Land Cruisers – and increased the vehicle's attraction greatly by introducing a powerful Mercedes diesel engine to it.

The Toyota was also cheaper than the Land Rover in most markets, and in places like the Australian Outback it achieved a justified reputation for reliability. Meanwhile, those Land Rovers that were produced through the strike-prone 1970s and early 1980s under British Leyland rule were often of dubious quality and had a reputation for breaking down – often.

Toyotas were cheaper, more powerful and more reliable. It was a no-brainer. And by the time Land Rover did anything about this changing state of the market, the Japanese had made huge inroads into the company's traditional strongholds in Australia, Southeast Asia and Africa.

In fairness, it was lack of cash from the struggling BL parent company that held back development at Land Rover. While money was ploughed into absurd products like the Austin Princess, Triumph Toledo, Austin Metro and Morris Ital, the

Series III of the early 1980s was in most ways little changed from the Series II launched back in 1958.

The arrival of the Range Rover, however, was the tipping point for the company's fortunes. The car was given a starring role in Blashers' daring Darien Gap expedition, but it was officially launched on 17 June 1970 – the very last day of Labour Prime Minister Harold Wilson's first term of office. The following day Wilson was deposed by Ted Heath and the Tories. It was ironic, really, as Wilson had pledged back in 1964 to embrace 'the white heat of technology', and the new offering from Solihull was that and more.

By the summer of 1970 the Swinging Sixties were over. The Beatles were tearing themselves apart, while England, who had won football's World Cup back in 1966, were about to lose their champion status in the heat of the 1970 tournament in Mexico.

Most of the optimism of that landmark decade had evaporated as Britain plunged into a new era of industrial strife, decline and inflation. Things were no better at Land Rover. The runaway success of the ultimate go-anywhere utility, launched back in 1948, had begun to slow in recent years, to the extent that sales of the company's only model – the Series IIA – had become a disappointment. A new model was needed.

These were some of the darkest days of the once-proud British motor industry. In 1968, Rover had been lumped together with much of the remaining, ailing, domestic automotive manufacturers to become part of the British Leyland conglomerate – a name that would become synonymous with poor design, shoddy build quality and disastrous labour relations throughout the 1970s. And it was against this backdrop that British Leyland boss Lord

Stokes gave the go-ahead for a new and rather different Land Rover. He was under government orders to launch two new models a year and Range Rover was the first 1970s debutant (the Triumph Stag sports car being the other).

The news wasn't exactly welcomed by all who worked behind the gates at Land Rover's plant in Solihull. Many reckoned an off-roader with a touch of class was against the company's no-frills principles, while others said there'd be no market for it. Yet, against all odds, a small team of engineers and designers who did believe in the new model worked tirelessly around the clock to produce the vehicle that was to become – and remains – a world leader.

What a shock it was, back in 1970, when a fire-breathing V8 4×4 with coil springs and disc brakes all round was released onto the market. This, remember, was a pre-decimalisation time when we carried pounds, shillings and pence in our pockets. Morris Minors and original Volkswagen Beetles were still being manufactured. The last steam trains on British Rail had only been taken out of service two years earlier. The arrival of the Range Rover on our roads was as startling a sight as a Martian knocking on your front door.

At Land Rover, nobody was really sure who the original Range Rover should be aimed at. So in the best tradition of Land Rover's famed versatility, they steered it towards farmers and provided an easy-clean interior that included rubber mats and vinyl seats. Rover had been working on a larger version of the Land Rover for several years. Back in the early 1950s, Rover engineer Gordon Bashford headed up a project to develop a so-called 'Road Rover', but despite reaching prototype stage it was axed in 1958. It wasn't until 1966 that Bashford and fellow Rover engineer Spen King began work on a new model.

Charles Spencer King – better known by his nickname, Spen – was the nephew of the Wilks brothers. Born in 1925, he left school in 1942 and initially joined Rolls-Royce as an engineering apprentice. But in 1945 he joined Rover and, in 1959, became chief engineer of new vehicle projects. He helped develop the P6 and 2000 Rover saloon cars before his greatest achievement of all: the Range Rover. He died in 2010, aged 85, in a cycling accident near his Warwickshire home.

Spen King is acknowledged to be the godfather of the Range Rover. In the late 1960s Spen was senior project engineer and led the team that devised, designed and produced the vehicle that redefined 4×4 vehicles and which became the benchmark for the legions of SUVs to follow. Within a year they had created a prototype, and by 1969 the design was complete. Work began on a batch of 26 engineering development prototypes, which were badged 'Velar' as a decoy for when they were spotted during road tests.

They were certainly eye-catching. The new Range Rover was unlike anything that had gone before, and, after its launch in 1970, the Louvre museum in Paris exhibited one as an 'exemplary work of industrial design'.

It is often said that the Range Rover was the company's answer to the customers who had requested a bit of luxury. But don't for one moment think that this new model was upmarket. There were no carpets and the seats were covered in vinyl – all the better for hosing out the mud. The dashboards were plastic, there was no air con, nor power steering. Only a two-door version was available. All the luxury stuff was to come much later, but at the time it was the ultimate countryside vehicle, with unparalleled on- and off-road performance, thanks to long-travel coil springs, disc brakes all round and the legendary Rover 3.5-litre V8 (actually a 1950s American design, developed by the US manufacturer Buick, but bought by Rover).

However, demand was so great for this car that there was soon a lengthy waiting list of prospective buyers, and for several months after its launch secondhand models were appreciating in value and, when sold, often fetched more than new ones!

Improvements to this model were gradual, due to a lack of funding from the parent company (British Leyland) rather than lack of ambition by the frustrated Rover bosses. In 1975 the whole strike-prone shooting match was effectively nationalised and once-proud marques began to sink without a trace. Land Rover could have so easily disappeared, too, had not fate stepped in. As part of the restructuring of BL in 1978, Land Rover was granted autonomy. Four years later, with the demise of Morris cars, Rover car production was moved to Cowley, Oxford, and the Solihull site was devoted exclusively to 4×4s.

From the very start, the Range Rover had proved that its off-road credentials were a match for its illustrious Land Rover stablemates. The original Range Rover remained in production until 1996, although for the last two years of its life it was re-badged as the Range Rover Classic, to avoid confusion with the second-generation Range Rover that had been launched in 1994. It was as though Land Rover, having enjoyed such huge success with the original Range Rover, was reluctant to let it go, but at the same time it didn't want the presence of the old model to harm the sales of the new one, so only a restricted range of Classic variants was made available. Bizarrely, the cheapest variants of the second-generation Range Rover were actually cheaper than the top-end Classics.

At the time, Land Rover said that production of the Range Rover Classic would continue as long as there was a demand, but that demand fairly quickly diminished. The final production run, in the autumn of 1995, was a batch of 25 right-hand-drive 25th-anniversary models finished in Oxford Blue metallic, with retro chrome bumpers and beige leather upholstery, Freestyle Choice wheels with Goodyear Wrangler tyres, a CD player and special badges. The Range Rover had been in production for over 25 years and over 300,000 had been built in that time.

The Range Rover transformed the fortunes of Land Rover, and its success became key to the evolution of the Defender itself.

CHAPTER THREE

RIOT ROVER

I was once in a riot.

I told this story to a *GQ* journalist. The *Daily Mail* decided it was too good to be true and printed a claim that I had lied. Their lawyers insisted I provide proof that it happened, which I did. They printed the story questioning my account anyway. So, for the record, I shall tell it again. And I can assure you it is true.

We were holed up in a Northern Irish village. It was a slightly depressing-looking place with a small shop, a church, a pub and row upon row of terraced two-up two-down homes. A few battered Ford Cortinas and Escorts cruised the largely deserted streets, and on the outskirts of town was an army barracks.

We were drinking in a pub when a Snatch Land Rover arrived. Heavily armed soldiers stormed the pub and suddenly grabbed my mate, and before we knew what had happened, he had been spirited away in their armoured vehicle. Things escalated pretty quickly after that and suddenly I was in the midst of a full riot.

Petrol bombs were being thrown as the sleep-deprived soldiers approached us, riot shields and batons at the ready.

We threw objects, hollered and heckled. It's amazing what adrenaline can do to courage, and before I could stop myself I was at the front of the crowd, kicking and grabbing at their riot shields. Somehow I managed to leverage a shield from one of the soldiers. I didn't think about the baton in his other hand which was soon falling forcefully onto the bridge of my nose.

And that, ladies and gentlemen, was how I first broke my nose. In a riot.

Of course, it wasn't quite what it seemed. We were in fact in Longmoor Military Camp in Hampshire in a mock Northern Irish village as 'actors' testing new recruits to the army. We were there as fictional residents of the village and the scenario had slowly escalated to a full 'controlled', or in my case 'partly controlled', riot.

To be fair to the soldiers, we had given them hell by keeping them awake all night by running metal rods up and down the corrugated wall around their barracks, and we had been warned we would get as good as we gave.

I found myself in an ambulance. (An interesting aside; I met a beautiful blonde 'rioter' called Lindsey that night and we ended up dating for several years. Every cloud has a silver lining ...)

Long before the 'riot', I was a child of the Troubles, despite living many miles from the epicentre of the violence consuming Northern Ireland. I grew up in the middle of London's West End during the 1970s, when the capital was regularly bombed by the

Irish Republican Army. I can still recall the sound of bombs going off in the city. We were once sealed inside our house while bomb-disposal officers defused a bomb in a car parked outside. I can remember the excitement of hiding under a table after it was deemed too dangerous to leave our house. We lived opposite a police station and we would often hear the collective siren of dozens of police cars heading off to deal with another detonation.

Perhaps my most vivid memory was the time my father walked to Marble Arch to get to McDonald's. His life was narrowly saved by a vigilant black cab driver who had seen armed IRA men firing from a nearby hotel.

Of course, throughout the Troubles I was merely a spectator on the sidelines of a conflict that drove a stake into the heart of Northern Ireland. That conflict on home territory killed thousands.

An escalation in the threat of terrorism and violence in Northern Ireland provided a new challenge for the Northern Irish Police Force known as the Royal Ulster Constabulary (RUC). Facing increasing danger, they needed a vehicle that could provide them with armoured protection. A Series I 109-inch wheelbase Land Rover was first adapted in 1957. It was basic by today's standards, designed to protect both the vehicle and the officers from bricks and bottles thrown during public disorder. The windows and headlights were protected with metal grilles to protect them from being smashed and the pick up on the rear of the vehicle was encased with a metal cage and lined with hardboard as a prevention to sharp objects used to pierce the cage.

Violence soon became more organised and officers now needed protection from bullets as firearms became more common. The early riot Land Rover was extremely vulnerable to weapons and ballistic plates of steel were fitted for extra protection. The adaptations helped against small arms and low velocity weapons but the vehicles were heavy and parts of the Land Rover were still vulnerable.

A new approach was needed and the RUC developed the Hotspur, named after the brand of armour plate made in Wales. The Hotspur was made from armoured steel that was bolted onto the chassis of a civilian 109 station wagon. The thin aluminium roof was also replaced by armoured steel to protect against IEDs and petrol bombs. The doors were fitted with bulletproof glass and sliding pistol ports were added to give officers the chance to fire from the vehicle if it was ambushed. Plates of ballistic steel were attached on both sides of the Land Rover. The vehicle essentially became an armoured box that could protect the crew from armed terrorists or a riotous crowd. The front windscreen was also replaced with bulletproof glass and a retractable metal grille was bolted to the bonnet that could be pulled up over the windscreen and side windows to protect against flying missiles and paint bombs.

The Hotspur was a success. Over the years there were a number of modifications and adaptations to make the vehicle safer. To reduce the damage and dents from riots and civil disorder the vehicle's relatively weak lower panels were replaced with polycarbonate. The first-generation Hotspur had been vulnerable to base attacks. Beer kegs were rolled under the vehicles to try and immobilise them. To prevent these attacks a metal grille was fitted around the bottom of the vehicle to give further protection against missiles and IEDs. As petrol bombs became more ubiquitous during escalating violence, later modifications included a fire-extinguishing system that could be activated from the driver's seat. One button would turn off the vehicle's fans and a series of pipes would discharge and extinguish into the engine and over the windscreen and bonnet.

Soon the Hotspur was superseded by the Simba, a purpose-built vehicle with an armoured steel body. Where the Hotspur had merely been an adapted civilian vehicle, the Simba was built for business. The armoured steel provided 360-degree protection from high velocity weapons, IEDs and petrol bombs as well as common bricks and bottles. The Simba was a far superior vehicle but the suppliers simply couldn't keep up with demand. The Hotspurs were coming to the end of their lifespan and the RUC needed a solution. The Troubles were headline news and the government wanted to see swift action against the civil disorder. The Land Rover Tangi was born.

The retiring Hotspurs were cannibalised for their armour kits and they were fitted to the new Defender 110. The civilian vehicles were available in the quantities required and the adaptations were quicker than the Simba. As the donor kits ran out, the RUC began to weld them in their own workshops. Thanks to trial and error the transparent polycarbonate used on the headlights for protection was soon replaced by the older metal grilles from the Hotspur. Civil disorder was becoming more sophisticated. The rioters learned the vehicle's weak spots. The Tangi was fitted with remote-controlled spotlights and flashing blue lights, all fitted with metal cages to prevent them from being smashed. Both the fire extinguisher system and the side skirt cage were kept as a preventative to objects being thrown under the Land Rover. The increasing use of petrol bombs provided a nightmare scenario to officers inside the vehicles. They faced the impossible decision to stay in the burning vehicle or to face the baying crowd. A strip of fabric was used around the bonnet edge and the hinge between the bonnet and the front bulkhead to protect the engine bay from petrol. With a further 3mm metal grille to protect the engine radiator, the first Tangi was deployed in 1986. It was a game changer for the embattled RUC and was more effective and loved than its predecessor. The heavy weight from the body armour meant that the air conditioning, power steering and disc brakes improved both the performance and working environment for the vulnerable RUC.

Soon the RUC faced another new threat. The roofs of the vehicles were still a vulnerability. During a riot in Belfast's Dawson Street police were only saved from an 'aerial' drogue bomb by their riot shields, which by chance had been packed into the roof cavity. This led to another new addition, the 'Dawson's roof'. These new roofs provided another second skin of armour to protect against roof top attacks. Of course the rioters were quick to adapt their own weapons and soon developed IEDs that were fitted with tiny drogues at the rear that could be thrown horizontally at the side of the Tangi like a rugby ball, penetrating the lesser protected side of the Land Rover. The RUC responded with another modification, this time a second skin of ballistic steel separated from the hull by several inches, creating an air gap that could buffer a detonation. This meant bombs would detonate before they struck the main vehicle, reducing their impact and damage. These heavily armoured, Robocop-type Land Rovers have stood the test of time and they still patrol the streets of Northern Ireland today.

Painted in dark grey, the Tangi was used for patrolling Northern Ireland. They were designed to transport two passengers in the front and up to five in the back, a squash with riot shields, helmets and body armour. They must have been as intimidating to be in as they were to be confronted with. A number of people were killed after being hit by these vehicles over the years. Today the vehicles are used for 'crowd control'. The Good Friday Agreement and the resulting peace process meant that nearly half the 450 armoured Land Rovers were decommissioned. Indeed Chris Patten advised in his 1999 report that all vehicles should be retired to aid the peace process. The Tangi has become an enduring symbol of the Troubles. Long gone is the battleship 'grey' of the Troubles, however. The remaining Land Rovers have been repainted in a less confrontational white, yellow and blue and are used by police forces across the UK.

I got to experience Land Rovers doing what they do best in Northern Ireland, albeit in peace-time patrols. I was invited to visit the Police Service of Northern Ireland (PSNI) – formerly known as the Royal Ulster Constabulary (RUC) – who took me out in an armoured Pangolin Land Rover around the conflict zone between the Unionist and Republican communities of West Belfast.

My chest is squeezed by the heavy padding of my bulletproof vest as I bounce around in the back of the Land Rover. The rest of the crew are also dressed in Kevlar flak jackets and black fire-resistant suits, and are all heavily armed. I peer through the

tiny 'sniper' windows as we edge our way out of the heavily fortified compound.

It is hard to believe that I am not in the midst of some war zone
but out to patrol one of the UK's biggest cities, Belfast, in a police
car. But then this, of course, is no ordinary patrol and this is no
ordinary Land Rover.

The Pangolin, formerly the Tangi and before that the Simba,
has played a pretty crucial role during the Troubles, and perhaps
some of the most iconic images from the 1970s and 80s were of
these grey armoured Land Rovers driving through a sea of civil
unrest. What is perhaps more astonishing is that despite the
peace process, the PSNI still relies on upwards of 400 armoured
Land Rovers to police Northern Ireland.

From the largely Protestant East Belfast we drive through the
centre of the city, which is a hive of business activity. The
armoured Land Rover takes a hard right as we leave the main
road and drive down a tiny cul-de-sac – and it is as if I have
arrived on a different planet.

Two neat rows of detached houses are festooned with red,
white and blue. There is Union bunting above the streets and the
houses are covered in Union Jacks of every size and shape. Even
in the greatest shows of nationalistic pride in England I have
never seen such a display of patriotism. Behind the houses,
though, looms a towering twenty-foot wall to prevent missiles
being hurled by the Loyalist and Republican neighbours at one
another.

We leave the red, white and blue for the Republican green, and
soon we are cruising down two of Belfast's most notorious roads:
Shankill and Falls. The largely loyalist Shankill Road runs parallel

to the largely nationalist Falls Road, and the area has seen numerous flash points over the years.

'Has anyone on board been caught up in a riot here?' I ask the crew. There is laughter. 'Too many times to recall,' the driver answers.

The Land Rover Pangolin is a car that has been adapted exclusively for the streets of Belfast, which needed an agile, tough vehicle with easy manoeuvrability that could be heavily armoured against ballistics and petrol bombs. Working in teams of five vehicles, the Tangi and Pangolin Land Rovers helped control the Troubles when they were at their peak with their ability to get into the midst of riots and civil unrest and allow police officers to control the situation from within.

While the level of terrorism in Northern Ireland may have fallen, 'recreational rioting' is still very much a unique phenomenon in Belfast, particularly in the summer months, during the 'marching season'.

Chief Inspector of the Tactical Support Group, Garrath McCreery, explains, 'Our Land Rovers have come under live fire and attack from improvised explosive devices, petrol bombs, paint bombs and an array of missiles. They have on occasions been attacked with sledgehammers and crowbars, and last year a home-made rocket-propelled grenade was fired at one of our vehicles. The crew was fortunate because the device didn't detonate on impact. An automatic rifle was also used to attack one of our Land Rovers.'

The Pangolin is brimming with kit. There are riot shields, weapons, truncheons, fire extinguishers. The exterior is fitted with CCTV cameras so that the driver can see behind the armoured back door. Fortunately for the crew, a quirk of the weight of the armour means the Land Rovers are almost impossible to be pushed over by rioters.

The image of the car is certainly at odds with the 'peace' of Northern Ireland. As we wind our way through the peaceful-looking streets of Belfast, the Pangolin is a reminder that for many this is still a place of conflict. The crew are very aware of their environment. They are ready for anything. Eyes scan the streets. There is an uneasy feeling. I wonder if it is real or imagined.

We are on an active anti-terror patrol. What is sobering is that the would-be terrorists are not fanatical Islamic State thugs but home-grown activists intent on disrupting the peace process. The conflict lies between the two opposing communities: the Loyalists and the Republicans.

A large wall was erected between the two communities which is now nearly twenty feet tall and is referred to as the 'peace wall'. Several gates within it are controlled remotely, allowing the police to close off the two roads, which they do every evening at around 9pm.

'Kids often come along and block them with obstructions, then when we turn up to clear the debris, we sometimes come under attack,' one of the officers tells me.

The walls are covered in murals from each side; the largely Catholic nationalists, or Republicans, have large murals of Gerry Adams and more intriguingly have now compared themselves to the PLO and Gaza, while around the corner are the Union flag-festooned murals of the largely Protestant Unionists, or Loyalists, intent on remaining within the British Union.

Unusually, the Unionists have taken sides with Israel, and there are plenty of Israeli flags alongside Union flags in the city.

The current 'flash point' is at Ardoyne in North Belfast. Loyalists set up a peace camp three years ago when Unionist Orange marchers were not allowed to walk along a section of the Crumlin Road. They have held a nightly protest ever since. Policing the protest has sometimes involved dozens of Land Rovers.

We pull up in our four-ton Land Rover next to the camp covered in Unionist posters: 'Respect Our Culture', 'Maintain the Union', 'Liverpool supports Ulster'. Another large sign warns that 'no alcohol is to be consumed in the camp', there are Union flags on every lamppost and large oil drums all along the street. The area is deserted. There are no cars. No people. No sign of anyone. It has the feel of an abandoned settlement.

'Sometimes a major policing operation in Belfast may require up to 40 units,' explains the Chief Inspector. 'That's 40 units, each one with five Pangolin Land Rovers.'

I try to imagine so many armoured Land Rovers parked along narrow streets and roundabouts, including here in the Ardoyne area. It must look like a war zone. The image is as startling as it is troubling.

The last time major trouble erupted in the city was late 2012 and early 2013 during the so-called 'Flag Protest'. At that time, thousands took to the streets to protest against Belfast City Council's vote to limit the days on which the Union flag flies from Belfast City Hall. The flag that had flown every day since 1906 had been limited to just 18 days of the year, and the Ulster loyalists responded with protests that resulted in some of the city's worst riots in recent times. Scores of Pangolin Land Rovers were deployed alongside Tactical Support Group officers as parts of the city descended into rioting. The police responded with baton rounds and water cannon. The Ulster Volunteer Force (UVF) and the Ulster Defence Association (UDA) were implicit in the rioting that cost millions of pounds to police.

The Pangolins came under concerted attack by rioters throwing petrol bombs, heavy masonry, scaffolding and an array of other missiles. Seeing the photographs from the rioting, it is obvious why the police in Northern Ireland respect their Land Rovers so much; these are fortified vehicles.

'I'm not sure you should get out,' warns McCreery. 'You're high-profile, you might be recognised.'

I want to tell him it is part of the job description, but his voice conveys something different. This is a place where the scars of the Troubles run deep.

Three officers in full gear hop out with me as I walk around the deserted road. Buildings and pubs look like they have been abandoned. Their windows are covered in metal shutters. I am assured this is merely for safety.

Our Land Rover suddenly looks more aggressive, with her riot shield over the windscreen and her 'skirt' of metal that almost touches the road to prevent IEDs being slipped underneath. Her lights have all been caged to prevent them being smashed. The only thing to soften her appearance is that she is no longer a militaristic grey, allowing her to blend in with the urban cityscape. She is white with the PSNI livery and a Crimestopper logo along the side.

I have been to Belfast many times over the years but this is the first time I have felt slightly vulnerable. Turning up with heavily armed officers in a riot Pangolin obviously doesn't help, but it is a raw, visceral reminder that the Troubles may have left the headlines but they are far from over.

As we walk back to the car a handful of men appear seemingly from nowhere. Another officer has joined them on the other side of the road. 'Who's that?' they ask, pointing to me. I can tell the officers feel uncomfortable and they beckon me back to the Land Rover.

'A message has gone out that we are here,' explains one of the officers. Before I have time to offer my autograph, we have left.

The Land Rover Pangolins rarely work alone. The benefits of the Land Rover in Belfast lie in their size and ability to work together. Orchestrated like a ballet, the vehicle's success was and is as much about the ability of the driver as it is about the vehicle itself.

McCreery reminds me of the aptitude of the drivers themselves. 'They need to be able to manoeuvre the armoured Land Rovers in narrow streets often surrounded by active rioters. Ultimately the drivers are accountable to the law, irrelevant of the circumstances.'

He means that if they hit or injure a rioter with the Land Rover, the police driver can be prosecuted. Rioters have, on occasion, run into the road in front of moving Land Rovers in a bid to hamper the deployment of the Tactical Support Group. This is where the driver's experience to react to a situation becomes crucial.

At night the Land Rovers become most vulnerable as street lights have sometimes been disabled and the rioters deliberately attack the vehicles' lights. The metal grilles are little protection against a crow bar. The biggest hazards are paint or petrol bombs exploding on the windscreen. The fire extinguishers in the vehicle are testament to this threat, but a paint bomb can be equally disabling. Often the whole windscreen is obscured. The wing mirrors have been removed, giving the driver very limited capabilities, so that sometimes the back door needs to be opened so that he can drive backwards, away from a situation. Sometimes he must rely on the following vehicle to direct him by radio communications.

'They sometimes place planks of wood with nails in the middle of the road to puncture the tyres,' explains one of the policemen.

'Have any of you driven with flat tyres?' I ask, and they all nod.

Soon we pass back through the gate at the peace wall and past more murals. Here on the streets of Belfast, the humble Land Rover has taken on another persona. It has become a lingering symbol of the Troubles, and their continued patrol of Northern Ireland undoubtedly causes anguish and resentment. Indeed, Chris Patten, in his report on policing in Northern Ireland, suggested ridding the police of their fleet of riot Land Rovers.

'It's simply too dangerous,' argues the Chief Inspector. 'There are parts of Belfast and Londonderry that would be impossible to police without armoured protection.'

Soon we leave North Belfast and head back through the centre of town and into another world. It is like Belfast has two faces – the one we read about in the press, that of a progressive city with a healthy housing market, vibrant culture and a booming economy; and then there is the other side where resentment lingers in communities who bear the scars of the Troubles and who still live under a dark cloud.

As we pull back into the heavily fortified police station I watch a new batch of female recruits go through their training. They are simulating forcing rioters to retreat using arm pads. I watch, mesmerised, as they beat back their would-be attackers, sweat dripping from their brows.

'How important have these Land Rovers been in Northern Ireland?' I ask the Chief Inspector.

'It's fair to say that as well as protecting thousands of officers, they have prevented many civilian casualties over the years in their ability to control escalating conflict,' he replies.

And yet, important as they are, the continued use of the Land Rover remains a troubling reminder that peace is only skin-deep.

HISTORY OF THE LAND ROVER

PART III

It was 1983 before the world finally saw a radical replacement for the ageing Series III, and by then Solihull's frustrated bosses were definitely in the mood for change. What should logically have been the Land Rover Series IV was never granted a series suffix. Thus the Land Rover One Ten was launched in March 1983 with a flat front, which echoed the distinctive Stage One V8 that had been launched in 1979. The name of the newcomer was derived from its wheelbase. A year later, its stablemate, the Land Rover Ninety, arrived (actually with a wheelbase of almost 93 inches).

The Ninety and One Ten were, of course, destined to become the Defender 90 and 110 – the most accomplished off-road vehicles known to mankind. By now, the Wilks brothers' original concept for an agricultural workhorse had become a do-everything vehicle embraced by all and sundry to get out there in the rough and plough through anything that stood in its way. It was the dawn of the leisure off-road movement.

Thus 1986 saw the lowest annual production figure for more than 30 years, with fewer than 20,000 utility Land Rovers emerging from the Solihull factory. Luckily the Range Rover was increasing in popularity – and profitability – at the same time, and its success possibly saved the marque from extinction.

From the 1980s onwards, Land Rover began to appreciate the Defender's increasing popularity as a recreational vehicle. The utilitarian pick up and hard top (van) versions were seen very much as workhorses, but the station wagons, particularly the County-spec 90s and 110s, were given improved interior trim and more comfortable seats. Levels of luxury were stepped up every year, in line with other manufacturers of the era. But the striped body decals, radio-cassette players and lifestyle accessories (including surfboard carriers!) were really just the window dressing. The main reason for the new model's success compared to the old Series models was the much-enhanced ride comfort from the coil-spring suspension that had replaced the old leaf springs.

Meanwhile, Maggie Thatcher's reforming Conservative government was eager to privatise the thorn in its side known as BL. Attempts to hive off the strike-prone company to the American General Motors in 1986 failed in the face of public and parliamentary protests, but two years later, under the management of Graham Day, the company was finally sold to British Aerospace. With the burden of state-owned bureaucracy finally pared away, Land Rover was at last free to indulge in what it knew best – namely innovation and individuality.

The Solihull plant became a hive of imaginative industry as the unshackled staff looked at the changing world around them and followed their instincts as to where 4×4 vehicles would fit in.

Land Rover had had an eye on the main prize for some time and had quickly spotted the ever-growing gap between the basic Land Rover and the upwardly-mobile Range Rover. That gulf was bridged in 1989 with the mid-priced Discovery. At the time, some insiders worried whether the advent of the Disco would have a detrimental effect upon the more utilitarian Ninety and One Ten models, but in fact the newcomer was to give its work-horse stablemates a very beneficial boost, as the 200Tdi diesel engine developed for the Discovery was also deployed in the Ninety and One Ten.

In September 1989, the Soviet Union was still a communist state. The Berlin Wall still separated East and West Germany. But two months later that Wall would fall along with the old Soviet Bloc. However, at the same time there was another momentous event taking place in Germany: at the Frankfurt Motor Show, a new vehicle was being unveiled that would have an enormous impact on Land Rover fans everywhere. That vehicle was the Land Rover Discovery.

At the time of its launch, the future of Land Rover hung by a thread. These were difficult times for the Solihull-based company. In its 40-year history it still had just two products – the Land Rover and the Range Rover – and although sales of both vehicles had been sufficient to keep the company profitable through the boom years of the 1980s, a recession was starting to bite.

Back in 1989, Land Rover didn't go around launching new models at the drop of a hat like it does today; it took ten years for Solihull to replace its original Series I with the Series II. The

Series III came 13 years after that. And Range Rover had been around for 19 years when Discovery burst upon the scene. But times were changing and the motoring public expected a raft of exciting new models.

These were the dying days of the British car industry – that ailing dinosaur was slowly being killed off by the intense competition from foreign manufacturers. Land Rover itself was under attack by a new wave of 4×4s from Japanese companies that could produce more reliable and affordable vehicles.

Land Rover had the utilities known as the Land Rover Ninety and the Land Rover One Ten (although on the bonnet they were badged Land Rover 90 and Land Rover 110) and the more upmarket Range Rover, which was by now almost 20 years old. That meagre range of options was under attack from manufacturers who could offer a choice of capable vehicles that fell between the two extremes. It was clear that Land Rover itself needed to do the same if it was to survive.

Happily, the Discovery ticked all the boxes. The new model created a similar impact to that enjoyed by the Range Rover back in 1970 and it was an instant hit with everybody who saw it. Even more importantly, its sales surpassed the company's own expectations. It was a vehicle that captured the mood of the times, and the income it generated was enough to see Land Rover through the hard times that were about to deal fatal blows to other British car manufacturers.

But why was this so? What was so special about the Discovery? It certainly wasn't a ground-breaking new vehicle by any means. The original Discovery shared the same 100-inch wheelbase ladder-frame chassis as the Range Rover, upon which was placed a welded new body. In fact, because of the relatively low produc-tion volumes of the One Ten and Ninety and Defenders, Land Rover alone could never have justified the huge investment in developing these new engines, but the company was aiming for mass-market appeal with the Discovery and was prepared to gamble (a gamble that was to pay off very quickly, as Discovery soon became Europe's bestselling 4×4).

This was no scaled-down Range Rover – it carved out an iden-tity all of its own, with its stepped roof and raised floor that provided the so-called 'stadium seating' that allowed the back-seat passengers to enjoy a great view. The cabin itself was espe-cially light and airy, thanks to styling by design guru Sir Terence Conran, who specified a light blue finish on all early models. The big windows also let in plenty of light, aided by the alpine windows and twin sun roofs.

With the benefit of hindsight, it is easy to mock the early Discovery's heavy use of body graphics and decals on the outside, and the pock-marked 'golf-ball' finish to the acres of blue plastic within. But nearly 20 years ago it very much captured the spirit of the time. In other words, most cars from that era looked just as garish. Contemporary owners were probably thrilled with the huge stick-on decals, which included an illustration of a compass that the powers-that-be obviously thought was appropriate on a vehicle named 'Discovery'.

The Discovery could seat five adults in comfort, as well as two more in some degree of discomfort on the folding, inward-facing seats in the boot (known as 'dicky seats'). With the rear seats folded forwards, it also provided a hugely capacious, van-like interior. In fact, the Discovery was probably the most versatile vehicle that Land Rover ever produced. On-road comfort was matched by the typical, uncompromising off-road ability expected by any model bearing the green oval badge. Its bulk and power also made it the best tow car on the road – as confirmed by the hundreds of awards bestowed upon this vehicle over the years since its conception.

The first Discoverys were available only with three doors – a deliberate ploy by Land Rover management, afraid that offering a five-door variant might hit sales of the Range Rover. They needn't have worried. In fact, the whopping success of the Discovery meant the Range Rover was free to abandon the middle ground and move ever more upmarket. As the Disco became established as a bestseller, so too did the model range. The V8 gained electronic fuel injection in 1990, and the much more sensible five-door option appeared the same year. Alloy wheels, an automatic gearbox and a 3.9-litre version of the V8 started to expand the options list.

The same year saw Land Rover's new owners, BMW, take the helm. To some purists it might have seemed sacrilege for a vehicle so British to have passed into foreign ownership, but realists recognised that the financial investment and strict quality-control standards upheld by the Germans could only enhance Land Rover's future. That certainly proved to be the case. And as the Range Rover became even more exclusive and expensive, the Discovery began to move more upmarket, featuring leather trim, airbags and electric seats.

The North American market didn't receive the Defender until 1993. Although the Range Rover had been sold in the USA and Canada since 1987, this was the first time a utility Land

Rover had been sold there for almost 20 years. To suit the new market, the North American Specification (NAS) Defenders were fitted with 3.9-litre V8 petrol engines because, with cheap petrol available, the Americans had no need for diesel engines. These cars had full external roll cages, larger side indicators and tail-lights and air conditioning. The first batch – all but one painted white – comprised 525 Defender 110 County Station Wagons. The exception was one painted black, for fashion guru Ralph Lauren.

In 1994, an NAS Defender 90 became available – originally only as a soft top, but later with an optional fibreglass roof or regular Station Wagon layout. The spec gradually improved until, towards the end of US production, the engine was increased to 4 litres and mated to an automatic transmission, but in 1998 strict new US regulations required the fitting of airbags for both front-seat passengers in all vehicles, as well as side-door impact requirements. The Defender could not be fitted with these without major modifications, so the brilliant NAS Defenders were withdrawn from North America at the end of 1997.

In the UK in 1992 the first special edition Land Rover Defender was produced. It was the 90SV (SV because it was finished off by Land Rover's Special Vehicle department). It was painted turquoise-blue and fitted with a black canvas soft top and alloy wheels as well as disc brakes all round (standard models still had drum brakes at the rear). The engine was the standard 200Tdi turbodiesel engine. Only 90 were made.

By 1994, Land Rover had achieved a justifiable reputation for getting it right. From the hugely successful original Series I to the Range Rover and then the bestselling Discovery, everything it touched seemed to turn to gold. Then along came the second-generation Range Rover (known as the P38).

The original Range Rover was always going to be a hard act to follow. It had been around since 1970 and was loved by the general public and Land Rover bosses alike. In fact, the latter were so fond of it, they refused to let it go. So they let it live on for a couple of years as the Range Rover Classic; always in the background as the new kid on the block tried to make an impact. As it turned out, the newcomer did make an impact, but for all the wrong reasons. Soon after its launch came reports of things going wrong – particularly those things that were controlled by electronic wizardry that the traditional cold-steel approach of Land Rover spannerism couldn't put right.

The truth was, Land Rover had tried too hard. They wanted the new vehicle to surpass its predecessor in levels of luxury and sophistication, and in order to achieve that they stuffed it with technical innovation, using the latest advances in computer technology. But much of the new stuff was unproven and, with so much of it, the law of averages dictated that things were likely to go wrong.

One of Land Rover's biggest balancing acts was attempting to please existing Range Rover fans while attempting to make the new model attractive to new customers. The company had commissioned market research which revealed that there wasn't much wrong with the existing model, so it was decided that the new Range Rover had to be very much like its predecessor – only better. The top brass reckoned that new features and more luxury would allow it to compete on equal terms with marques such as BMW and Mercedes-Benz.

The new model was incredibly sophisticated, with a state-of-the-art electronic engine and systems management system that was largely unproven. Just recall the sort of home computers people were using in those days: generally slow, underpowered and dogged by irritating software bugs that had to be fixed. Why should Range Rover's computerised systems be any different?

Land Rover's paymasters at the time were British Aerospace, who, like British Leyland before them, were strapped for cash. Maybe if BMW had taken over a couple of years earlier, the second-generation Range Rover would have turned out to be a very different vehicle. Either way, although the new model sold well initially, the bad press it got alarmed the top brass at Land Rover – and their BMW bosses – to the extent that its replacement became a matter of priority.

The third-generation Range Rover duly arrived early in 2002, to massive critical acclaim and sighs of relief all round. The Range Rover 2 – the P38A, the codename used by Land Rover when the model was still in development – was one of the most unloved products ever to emerge from Solihull. It has a reputation for unreliable electrics and suspension and was prohibitively expensive to run. It was very much overshadowed by its replacement, the new Range Rover – which was quickly recognised as the world's best luxury 4×4.

By 1997, Land Rover production of its range of vehicles had reached more than 100,000 a year. Its bestselling model at the time was the Discovery, but that wasn't going to last: a very different Land Rover was about to make its debut which would steal the top spot. In fact, it would soon become Europe's bestselling 4×4. It was the Freelander.

Once billed as the 'baby' Land Rover, the Freelander was resented by many Land Rover enthusiasts who were afraid that it would somehow dilute the brand. It was, after all, very different to the norm, with its monocoque body and relative lack of ground clearance. It didn't have a low box or diff lock either, although it did have traction control as well as option Hill Descent Control – aka HDC, the first of the acronyms that would prove so popular on the new models that would follow. HDC allowed you to safely negotiate steep descents while off-roading – with the traction control automatically applying braking in rapid bursts, similar to but even faster than the so-called cadence braking employed by experienced racing drivers to prevent their wheels locking under heavy braking.

Eventually the Freelander did shake off its unkind label as a hairdresser's car and was welcomed into the Land Rover family by most enthusiasts. Even the doubts about its toughness were largely dispelled when the Freelander was employed in the 1998 Camel Trophy, which, although rather tame compared to the legendary Camel Trophy events of previous years, was certainly gruelling enough to show that this was a vehicle that had earned its green oval badge. Freelanders were also among the Land Rover models used in the 2003 G4 Challenge.

The Freelander has introduced a lot of people to the delights of the Land Rover marque. Although the driving position in a Freelander is not as commanding as you get in a Defender, Discovery or Range Rover – it isn't quite so elevated because the Freelander isn't as tall as its stablemates – it is still very different to the experience of driving an ordinary saloon car. Many Land Rover fans started out in Freelanders before moving on to more capable members of the Land Rover family – most notably Defenders.

When Freelander burst onto the scene in 1997 it was very different to any Land Rover that had gone before. Its lack of a transfer box offering lower gears meant that it would always be limited when it came to slow, precision off-road driving. Despite Land Rover's protestations at the time that the Freelander was best in its class off-road, this was a car that was better suited to tarmac. It was also the first Land Rover to be designed by a man bearing an uncanny resemblance to the Queen guitarist, Brian May. That man was Gerry McGovern, who in those days wore a mane of long curls. These days Gerry wears his hair a lot shorter, and as the undisputed design guru of Land Rover he has helped create a crop of new models, such as the Range Rover Evoque, which have followed in the original Freelander's tyre tracks by being aimed at the on-road driver.

Freelander also set a milestone in Land Rover history, because it had abandoned the trademark box-section chassis in favour of a semi-monocoque affair and boasted ABS/traction control and automated hill descent as extra-cost options. The question back in 1998 was, would such new technology appear in other new models in the future? As enthusiasts got ready to celebrate the big event of 1998 – Land Rover's fiftieth anniversary – few could have foretold what the next two decades would bring.

CHAPTER FOUR

FIGHTING ROVER

DOGS OF WAR, ROVER FIGHT
AND THE WOLF

The year 1982 saw one of the strangest conflicts in recent history, when Britain found itself forced to come to the rescue of 1800 British subjects on a small South Atlantic archipelago that had been invaded by a major South American nation.

The ownership of the Falkland Islands has been disputed between Argentina and Britain since the eighteenth century. The archipelago held strategic importance for Britain; indeed, the islands were vital as a Royal Naval base during both the first and second World Wars, so Britain wasn't going to give it up easily.

The recession of the 1980s put huge stress on the newly elected Conservative government under the leadership of Margaret Thatcher. Budget cuts, strikes and riots were blighting the UK. In a perfect storm, on the other side of the Atlantic, nearly 8000 miles from Britain, Argentina was also going through financial turmoil. Inflation was running at over 100 per cent.

President Galtieri, as head of the military government, saw an invasion of the Falklands as a way of distracting attention from the debilitating inflation that was strangling Argentina, while at the same time being seen to flex Argentina's muscle against the imperialistic squatters. A speedy victory in the Falklands, or Las Malvinas as it was known to the Argentines, would appeal to a battered nationalistic sentiment.

Relations between the two nations deteriorated, and, following an invasion of the uninhabited South Georgia, conflict looked inevitable. The British government called the island's governor, Rex Hunt, to warn him of a possible invasion, and on 1 April 1982 the Argentine Special Forces landed at Mullet Creek and proceeded to attack the capital, Stanley. The British were quick to respond and a task force was deployed to liberate the islands. Amongst this, 43 merchant ships were requisitioned to join the armada of Royal Naval warships on the 8000-mile journey, and among their cargoes were hundreds of Land Rovers.

The British government knew that the Land Rover would be invaluable to success in the Southern Ocean, and more than 600 emergency Series III Land Rovers had been ordered by the government. They were commissioned to a reduced spec called CL, meaning Commercial. They were loaded aboard one of the merchant ships, *Atlantic Conveyor*, which got hit by an Argentine Exocet missile. All 600 Series IIIs ended up on the bottom of the Atlantic Ocean. The impact of their loss cannot be overstated;

indeed, it introduced 'yomping' into the English language, necessitating soldiers to take to foot where once they would have travelled by wheel.

The Land Rover was already the vehicle of choice for most Falkland Islanders, so the invading army confiscated any such vehicles they could find and converted them into Argentine fighting vehicles. The Land Rover was the only vehicle capable of tackling the Falklands' boggy terrain, so the task force began to requisition any remaining Land Rovers for their own use on the battlefield.

There are many stories of extreme heroism and bravery from islanders who helped the British during the war. I first visited the Falkland Islands in 2001 and it was there that I met Terry Peck, a no-nonsense gruff islander who had single-handedly helped to win the war. Over dinner in the Upland Goose pub in Stanley, Terry told me how he had once been the island's Police Chief. Once the war broke out, he dressed himself as a builder and stole motorbikes and Land Rovers and drove around the island taking photographs of key installations using a camera hidden inside a drainpipe. His photographs of anti-aircraft missile sites were smuggled out and later appeared in the hands of the army and navy intelligence officers back in London.

Terry spent weeks in Camp, as the countryside is known, sleeping under the stars and evading capture by persuading young Argentine conscripts that he was a builder or a plumber on his way to repair damaged buildings. After the war, Terry was awarded an MBE for his bravery during the conflict, although in a bizarre twist he was later charged with stealing one of the motorbikes on which he had carried out his daring mission.

'They had to, the Police Chief couldn't be seen to be getting away with stealing,' he laughed and shrugged.

Another astonishing story was that of local Trudi McPhee, who single-handedly helped escort a convoy of Land Rovers, tractors and military trucks across the notoriously boggy landscape of the island. The tough sheep farmer advanced on the enemy ahead of the vehicles, using a white glove to indicate silently which direction to take to avoid 'bogging' in the peat bogs. In the darkness of Camp and with headlights off for the hazardous journey, the movements of those white gloves were the only signals for the lead vehicle behind her. McPhee and the convoy advanced under fire from Argentine positions, as she led the convoy from her farmer's Land Rover to their destination near Mount Longdon for what was to be the bloodiest battle of the war.

Trudi had been just one of the heroic islanders to volunteer in the war effort. She even wrote a 'final' letter to her parents before she headed out into the front line in her trusty Land Rover. She and the team of local farmers provided invaluable knowledge of the terrain, as well as winter driving skills and Land Rovers that proved to be a crucial factor in the gruelling cross-country push to reclaim the islands.

Miss McPhee's actions earned her a commendation for bravery after the war from Admiral Sir John Fieldhouse, the commander-in-chief. But her response was typical of the defiance, courage and, when possible, resistance to occupation that was displayed by her fellow islanders during the war.

For the ill-equipped and under-prepared Argentine occupiers, the local Land Rovers were also an essential piece of kit, and plenty were requisitioned by the invading force, which led to the unusual scenario of British-made Land Rovers fighting against one another on British sovereign soil.

It would take 74 days to liberate the islands from Argentina. The costs were high: 255 UK servicemen and three Falkland civilians died in the conflict, as well as a further 650 Argentine troops, many of them young, inexperienced conscripts.

I am still haunted by a handwritten note from one of the Argentine conscripts that had been handed to a Falkland Islander: 'We're sorry, but we're hungry ... please if you can, buy us these things. 2 toothbrush, 3 wafer Cadbury's, 4 Mars, 3 regal Cadbury, 1 orange Cadbury, 8 whole nut Cadbury's, a piece of ham, and if you can buy other things for eating. Thank you.'

The war was wretched for all involved. I have often wondered whether the conflict would have been resolved sooner had those 600 Land Rovers made it across the Atlantic.

Land Rovers have a rich pedigree in the islands. As I've said, the Falkland Islands is sometimes called Land Rover Island, and although I had heard this before I first visited in 2001, nothing could have prepared me for the Land Rover fest that greeted me in Stanley.

Given that the Falklands is an overseas territory for which Britain was willing to go to war, it is perhaps unsurprising that the car of choice was the Land Rover. Series I, II and III in various states of repair were parked alongside 90s and 110s. I had never seen such an array of Land Rovers, but here of all places in the world these cars were truly in their own environment. In the countryside beyond the city limits – the Camp – the Land Rover was king. I was often left speechless at the ability of this vehicle to get through the boggy, mountainous terrain. If there were ever a natural home for the Land Rover it would be the Falkland Islands.

Of course, the Land Rover has a rich history of involvement in post-World War II conflict in other parts of the world. They were used in Korea, Vietnam and the Balkans, not forgetting countless coups and military uprisings. Shortly after the Second Gulf War and the capture of Saddam Hussein, his Centaur Land Rover came onto the market via eBay. The bullet-riddled vehicle had been Saddam's personal vehicle.

The story of the military Land Rover pre-dates the marque itself. Its origins are in the development of the US military Jeep, from which two Land-Rover prototypes were designed and built between late 1947 and early 1948, during the hangover from World War II, and with their military provenance it is perhaps unsurprising that two of the prototypes were sent to the Ministry of Supply.

The American Jeep had impressed the British military in its role during World War II and the army was keen to create a British version of the all-round utility vehicle. A contract had been awarded to Austin to build the Austin Champ, but the order had been delayed and the War Office decided to buy some Land Rovers as insurance.

They were a huge success. The British Army received 2000 Series Is during 1949, while the RAF and Navy received their first vehicles in 1950. The military Series Is had a slightly longer 81-inch wheelbase and a larger 2.8-litre Rolls-Royce petrol engine. With double the power output, the Rolls-Royce engine could travel at 80mph. In their first conflict, the 1950–52 Korean War, they were a huge success.

Meanwhile, the delayed Austin Champ finally entered service in 1952, but by now the Land Rover had become so popular with soldiers that by 1958, when Series I production ceased, around 15,000 Land Rovers were in service with the British military around the world. The Champ had met its end.

The success of the military Land Rovers hadn't gone unnoticed, of course, and soon orders were flooding in from militia around the world. In 1951, Belgian company Minerva reached an agreement with Land Rover to build military Series Is under licence, followed a year later by the West German company, Tempo. The hugely successful Spanish Santana followed in 1955. Australia (Perentie) and Turkey (Otokar) also built military Land Rovers under licence from the 1960s.

Of course, the armed forces of dozens of nations also bought large numbers of military-spec Land Rovers. The new Series II, in 1958, continued to impress and saw new 88-inch and 109-inch models produced for the military. These models had double bumpers, NATO-style tow hitch, split-rim wheels and military convoy lighting. Some had strengthened axles and twin fuel tanks.

Land Rover launched their forward control model to the civilian market in 1962. With its huge payload, it was developed as a heavy delivery vehicle, but once again the military saw its potential. The problem was that it was underpowered, but the evolution of the 101 Forward control changed all that.

Specifically designed for military use and powered by the popular Rover V8 3.5-litre petrol engine, the 101 Forward was developed to fill the gap between the standard military Land Rovers and the 4-ton Bedford trucks, and it was also capable of towing a trailer-mounted Howitzer gun. In 1975, 2300 101s entered service with the British Army, with more following right up until production ceased in 1978. The 101FC, also known as the One-Ton, served many roles for the military, from gun tractor to field ambulance.

The military remained an important customer for Land Rover, and throughout the 1960s engineers worked on a number of experimental military designs. The military needed a lightweight vehicle that could fit inside a transport plane that should weigh no more than 2500 pounds, so that they could be carried under a Wessex helicopter.

It was a huge task to shed half the Land Rover's weight, and, what's more, the vehicles had to be of a size to fit two abreast inside the Argosy transport plane. An 88-inch Series IIA was used as the prototype; the Land Rover was stripped down to its skeleton and then rebuilt using only the materials necessary to make it mobile. The car was picked clean of its doors and windscreen, and some body panels, roof and rear seats were left out, too. Angles were cut off from the traditional boxy shape and the resulting near-naked vehicle had a simple angular body with a narrow bulkhead and axles to fit in the Argosy. The vehicle needed to be transported unladen. The spare wheel, body sides, hood, bumper and other parts were designed for quick removal in the field, so that they could be flown separately once the vehicle had been airlifted to the battlefield, keeping the weight down.

Meanwhile, the development of more powerful helicopters meant that by the time the Lightweight came into service, they didn't need to be so light after all! Despite that, nearly 3000 Series

IIA Lightweights entered service until production of this model ceased in 1971. A year later, Series III Lightweight production began. This time orders also came from overseas buyers, including Belgium, Brunei, Guyana, Holland, Hong Kong, Indonesia, Jamaica, Libya, Saudi Arabia and the Sudan. In military speak they were officially referred to as the 'Land Rover Series IIA Truck, Utility, ½ ton, 4×4', which possibly slips off the tongue.

Production of the Lightweights stopped in 1983, by which time nearly 18,000 had been built. Many remained in service into the new millennium, handed down to the Territorial Army as they were replaced by 110s and 90s and Defender XDs.

The 110s and 90s entered service in 1985, but it wasn't until 1994 that Land Rover created a dedicated, unique, high-spec vehicle: the Defender XD (XD stands for 'xtra duty') which was powered by turbodiesel 300Tdi engines. The Wolf, as it became known, had a much stronger chassis, with fibre webbing around the welded joints and other stress points to increase load capacity. Used for supply, communication and patrol duties, the XD was available both as a Defender 90 and 110.

Land Rover continued to equip its military Defenders with the 300Tdi engine even after 1998, when it was replaced by the Td5 in the civilian versions. Although the Td5 engine had proven reliable in trials, it was decided that servicing and repairing its electronic control systems would be too complicated in battlefield conditions, because they were reliant on diagnostic computers. There were also concerns that the Td5's electronics could be rendered useless by the electromagnetic pulse generated by a nuclear weapon, although you can't help thinking that would be the last of your worries in the event of a nuclear holocaust ...

However, following successful trials of the Td5 Land Rover by the Australian Defence Force, the British MoD purchased a small fleet of Td5 Defender 110s which were deployed in the Falkland Islands as troop carriers and communications vehicles for use by the Royal Marines and UK Special Forces. A small number were also ordered for the Royal Navy. These were painted navy blue and also went to the Falklands. The extra power from the Td5 engine was considered better able to traverse the rugged terrain of the islands.

Modern warfare has moved on since then, and these days light 4×4s do not have such an important role to play on the battlefield. The British Army's fleet of Defender XDs faced criticism following the recent operations in Iraq and Afghanistan. The majority of military Land Rovers carried no armour plating and were vulnerable to roadside bomb attacks. The Wolf or Defender XD is still in service, however, and the current fleet will stay in service until 2030, so despite the end of the Defender, the military Land Rovers will continue to appear in the theatre of war for many years to come.

There have been plenty of other developments over the years for specialised vehicles that could be used for specific tasks. The Normandy landings by the Allied troops that hastened the end of World War II convinced the War Office of the strategic necessity of amphibious vehicles, so Land Rover developed several prototypes between the 1950s and 1960s.

In early prototypes the Land Rover was kept afloat thanks to various buoyancy aids, including air bags inflated by the vehicles' exhaust gases. Propulsion on water was made possible via a propeller fixed to the rear power output. None of these prototypes was very successful and all were quietly forgotten by the end of the 1960s.

There were further concept developments throughout the same period to convert Land Rovers into tank busters, armed with big recoilless rifles or missiles. Some entered service with the British Army, and in 1977 Marshalls of Cambridge completed an order of 100 Series III Lightweights equipped with 106mm M40 recoilless rifles for the Saudi Arabian National Guard.

One of the strangest military Land Rovers was the Centaur half-track, developed from 1977 by Laird (Anglesey) Ltd, who replaced the rear axle of a Series III Stage One V8 with a three-quarter track, creating a vehicle that looked like a Land Rover–tank hybrid. It had impressive cross-country capability but only two were ever sold – to Oman, in 1978. The project was abandoned in 1985. One of these vehicles ended up in the hands of Colonel Gaddafi.

Perhaps the most famous military Land Rover of all, though, is the Pinky or the SAS Pink Panther. The SAS – or 22 Special Air Service – Regiment's primary role is to operate behind enemy lines. In the 1950s the Regiment had adapted 88-inch Land Rovers for these purposes, and during the 1960s its own work-shops modified some 109s, which offered more space and proved much more effective for the task.

By the middle of the 1960s the Regiment was operating in Oman, supporting the Sultan's forces against guerrillas in the country's southern district of Dhofar. Here, they swiftly recog-nised the need for specially developed vehicles capable of carry-ing a three-man crew, weaponry for attack and self-defence, communications equipment and enough crew equipment and supplies of fuel, ammunition and water to remain self-sufficient for several days at a time.

It was Marshalls of Cambridge who produced the famous Pink Panthers. In 1968 Marshalls delivered 72 long-range desert-patrol vehicles to the SAS, built on the Series IIA 109-inch chassis and transformed specially for the Regiment. They were delivered in standard green, but many were repainted in pink, which was then believed to be the best camouflage paint for the desert.

Brimming with guns and equipment, during the First Gulf War they proved invaluable as they even outperformed the Americans' Hummers. The 2.2-litre petrol engine was tweaked from the standard 69bhp to 77bhp for extra power, and fuel was carried in four tanks with a total capacity of 100 gallons for long-range assaults.

Pink Panthers had no doors, windscreen or canopy – all were considered unnecessary for desert driving, but thanks to all the extra equipment and fuel they weighed in at nearly half a ton heavier than standard Land Rovers.

The Defender is for many a symbol of safety and security, and it has long been used in varying degrees to provide protection against a number of different threats beyond the natural environment. To this end, Land Rover engineered an armoured version of the Defender. Protected to B6 (equivalent to VR7) levels, the Armoured Defender provided a defence against ballistic threats, while its Kevlar floor could survive grenade attacks. To counterbalance the heavy and cumbersome armour protection, Land Rover incorporated better suspension and improved the brakes, which meant they remained a strong agility and performance vehicle.

These armoured Defenders were used by government and non-government organisations around the world. One of the biggest markets was journalists working in dangerous hostile environments. The BBC, ITN, NBC, CBS and multitudes of other news-gathering agencies saw the value of a vehicle that could protect them in increasingly volatile war zones.

Back on home soil, the British police have used Land Rovers for many years. Due to the ongoing terrorist threat and prolifer-ation of public order disturbances, the Police Service of Northern Ireland has employed armoured and hardened versions for well over 40 years.

One of the most impressive of these tailored vehicles was the Shorland armoured car, introduced by the Royal Ulster Constabulary in 1965. Built by the Belfast companies Short Brothers and Harland Ltd, it was armour-plated and carried a 7.62mm machine gun. The current PSNI armoured public order vehicle is based upon a heavy-duty Defender 110 chassis fitted with upgraded suspension, brakes and drive train. The bonnet, wings and roof are produced from armoured composite materials while the body is manufactured from a range of armoured steel and composite materials.

Today there is a booming market in ex-military Land Rovers. They have become hugely popular with enthusiasts and usually fetch a higher price than civilian models. Fans know that, although many of these vehicles were abused by squaddies and led punishing lives, they were also scrupulously maintained by engineers who invariably replaced worn and damaged compo-nents with new ones. Nothing but the best for military vehicles. Most were also built tougher in the first place, too – particularly the 300Tdi Defender Wolfs with their extra-strong reinforced chassis. Although most of these military Defenders will stay in service until 2030, some have been retired to the civilian market, giving enthusiasts the unique opportunity to own a piece of Land Rover military history.

CHAPTER FIVE

KAHN AND THE ART OF LAND ROVER MAINTENANCE

The Land Rover is often described as classless. It is everyman (and everywoman's) car. By driving a Land Rover you effectively join a club of like-minded people who quietly admire the vehicle.

One of my favourite aspects of driving a Defender is the acknowledgement that you give and receive whenever you pass a fellow Land Rover driver. Sometimes it is a subtle finger lift or an almost imperceptible nod of the head. Other times I have seen and been known to give anything from a regal wave to a thumbs up. However, when I find myself in another marque I sometimes forget that and unconsciously start waving wildly at a passing Defender, only to find myself ignored.

Range Rover, Discovery and Freelander drivers don't do this. It is the exclusive preserve of the Series and Defender driver. A subtle acknowledgement of a subtle car. We don't like to gawp or make a scene. In my mind Defender drivers are a modest lot. We care about our car but we don't want to be ostentatious. A little like the trend for pre-washed clothes and even ripped jeans, we want our vehicle to look like it has been used and loved for years, which of course is often the case.

Unlike other vehicles and marques, Land Rover have always been rather narrow-minded when it comes to modifications and spec. Indeed, there are several components that have been used in the Land Rover unchanged since the Series I was born. Leaking, rusting and misting is part of the package. You don't like it? You can get another car. This is part of the reason why the cottage industry around the Land Rover has boomed in recent years, as customers clamber to fix faults and personalise their vehicles to their own specification.

I had done just this with my Defender. I had wanted a soft-top short wheelbase, which Land Rover simply wouldn't produce, so I found a company called Nene Overland to do the works for me.

Former farmer Andrew Harrison-Smith spotted a market for modifying factory spec Land Rovers in 1988, and so he started Nene Overland. The spectrum of adaptations they have undertaken over the years is as varied as it is diverse; but there is one company that has taken things to a whole new level, quite literally turning the humble Defender onto its head.

Bradford is an unlikely place for a luxury car dealership. I wound my way out of Leeds towards Bradford, along streets lined with sari shops and curry restaurants. This West Yorkshire city, situated in the foothills of the Pennines, was once an international centre for textiles. Historically, wool had been king here, and it was that industry that helped Bradford cement – or should I say knit – itself as the wool capital of the world. The area's proximity to coal and iron ore facilitated this growth, and the city is still filled with impressive Victorian architecture, including the grand Italianate City Hall.

The textile sector collapsed in the mid-twentieth century. Today, Bradford is perhaps best known for its football club and in recent years as a location for Bollywood films. But of course I wasn't here for the architecture, or the film locations, but to visit a firm responsible for transforming the humble Land Rover into something extraordinary.

Afzal Kahn creates some of the most bling Land Rover Defenders on the market under the marque Project Kahn, now known as The Chelsea Truck Company. A strong character, his reputation goes before him and I had heard plenty of stories about him during my journey through the world of Land Rover enthusiasts.

Whilst a Land Rover is in essence the symbol of understated utilitarian modesty, a Kahn vehicle is anything but. These are the Robocops of the Land Rover world. Bolted with body armour, they look like futuristic military vehicles. They are aggressive, some might even say scary.

I had wanted to meet Kahn for some time. His success seemed to conflict with the very essence of the Land Rover. The appeal of the Defender had always been its ability to blend in. I have lost track of the number of times people have defined the Land Rover as 'classless', a vehicle in which you could arrive at Moss Side in Manchester or Buckingham Palace in London and not look out of place.

The attraction for me has been the ability to morph according to my environment. Let me explain. If you pull up at a set of traffic lights in a Lamborghini or a Ferrari you are more likely to get the finger from other waiting cars. Flashy cars have a way of antagonising people: 'hey, look at me with my big car' – or, as my wife calls it, 'the small willy complex'.

Cars, like so many aspects of our lives, say a great deal about us. We use a car as an extended metaphor of our own personality. In many cases, it is used to mask inadequacies. The humble Landy, however, transcends this. Like a chameleon, it has the ability to be everyone's car, as comfy rumbling across a field as it is in a city street.

Kahn's reputation precedes him. In 2014 he hit the headlines when he announced he was putting his numberplate F1 on the market for £10 million. This just six years after he bought it for £440,000. According to newspaper reports, he turned down an offer of £8.5 million from a buyer in the Middle East. The plate, registered to his million-pound Bugatti, was offered for sale alongside 4HRH – on the market for a snip at £275,000.

Yorkshire-born Kahn started working for the family ice-cream business while he was still at school. 'We had a Datsun,' he explained, 'and I became obsessed with cars.' The ice-cream business taught him to 'hustle' from an early age. 'I was a wheeler dealer,' he confessed.

Meanwhile, his family set up an amusement arcade in the middle of Bradford, but Kahn, still obsessed with cars, had other ideas. He spotted an early niche for carbon-fibre bumpers for Ford Escorts and Granadas. The problem was that he didn't know enough about how to work with carbon fibre as a material, so he did the logical thing and went to work for a coffin maker.

'It was the time of the Falklands War and there was a huge demand for floating coffins for Argentine soldiers killed in action.'

'Floating coffins?' I repeated, perplexed.

'Made of carbon fibre,' he explained, 'they were made to float down the rivers. Like a funeral cortège.'

He would make coffins in the morning, and in return his boss gave him the use of the workshop in the afternoons to perfect his carbon-fibre bumpers. He made his first one, put an advert in *Autotrader* and sold it. Soon business was booming and he could barely keep up with demand.

Kahn had tapped into an early trend for the personalisation and modification of cars. He quickly diversified into selling alloy wheels, and Kahn Designs was born.

Kahn worked on a BMW conversion with Oakwood and sealed his ability to convert luxury cars. In 1999 he bought the Bradford showroom and in 2004 he spotted a gap in the market for adaptations of the Range Rover. The Project Kahn Range Rover had Kahn wheels, leather interior and the Kahn badge across the bonnet.

By 2007 he was buying 100 Range Rovers a year from Land Rover, but it was a racist attack in 2005 that really changed everything. He was beaten senseless by baseball-bat-wielding thugs in Bradford.

'I suffered racism all my life,' he explained matter-of-factly; 'my family, my friends, we all experienced it, but this attack changed my life.'

Battered and bruised, both physically and mentally, he decided to escape Bradford to visit a friend in London's Knightsbridge. It was a revelation. 'I loved it,' he smiled, 'it was so liberating, and for the first time I didn't feel defined by my race.'

So he bought a house in London and in 2012 he established the Chelsea Truck Company. And this is where the humble Defender came into his life.

Up until this point Kahn had experienced plenty of periods of boom and bust. He had owned plenty of expensive sports cars, 'but life changes,' he explained, for he had always seen Defenders as agricultural vehicles, until now. He rang Land Rover to see if they wanted to do a collaboration. They didn't, so he bought a car himself and kitted it out complete with Harris Tweed interior.

However, of all the makeovers Kahn has completed, he is perhaps most famous for the Flying Huntsman, a six-wheeler behemoth which also counts as the most expensive Kahn Land Rover, on sale at £250,000. Until 2012 Kahn Project vehicles had been almost exclusively Range Rovers, but suddenly everyone wanted a Defender. He couldn't keep up with demand.

Today Kahn Project arguably dominates the Land Rover luxury overhaul department. The forecourt of Kahn Design was bursting with 'macho' Defenders when I visited.

Thick layers of 'body armour' have been bolted on with large rivets. Matt black paint and huge alloy wheels complete the look. Future militaristic, verging on Mad Max. While the exterior is certainly bold, the interior is a world away from the factory line spec of a Defender – orange and black leather seats and steering wheels is just one of the looks.

Perhaps most strikingly, though, the gear shift has been removed from all Kahn vehicles and replaced by a simple automatic system, the roof trip has been fitted with tiny LED lights and the engines have been completely overhauled.

In the case of the self-named Huntsman Longnose, the bonnet has been lengthened by several inches to make way for the bigger engine – looking just like a large nose or a trunk. To be honest, it looks nothing like a Defender, which is probably one of the reasons why it no longer even has the Land Rover badge – Kahn has taken the car so far from the original design that he isn't even legally able to call it a Land Rover. And here lies the future: 'I want to become a coach builder. Kahn is the only company in the UK that designs, engineers and manufactures,' he says proudly. 'My dream is to became a coach builder and make the cars themselves.'

So who buys a Kahn? While plenty of their adaptations involve simply converting them from diesel to petrol for the Middle East market, he assures me that most of the cars – 95 per cent – go to 'white Englishmen'.

'We have sent cars to Barbados, Kuwait, Saudi Arabia, Greece ... but most stay here,' he reveals.

This perplexes me. Throughout this journey of discovery, every person I had met had concluded that the popularity of the Defender lies in its classlessness, its ability to blend into the environment like a chameleon. It is the everyman car that makes it impossible to judge the driver. Whereas a Kahn car, I'd argue, is making a massive statement. It's shouting from the roof tops, 'look at me'. Kahn's works are made to turn heads. These are statement cars designed and engineered for maximum impact.

Love them or loathe them, there was only one way to truly gauge their impact. A journey aboard the Flying Huntsman from Glasgow to Islay.

Much has been written over the years about the role of Anglesey, in Wales, in the birth, development and creation of the Series I Land Rover, but there is another geographical location that played an equally important, if not vital, role in the creation of the Landy – Islay.

The part played by Scotland in the birth, 67 years ago, of what is reputed to be the Queen's favourite country runabout, is little known. Spencer Wilks, then the managing director of the Rover Car Company, owned the 40,000-acre Laggan Estate on Islay, and it was there that he and his brother Maurice adapted a chassis and built a Rover around it in 1947.

According to Roger Crathorne, known as 'Mr Land Rover' and author of *Born in Lode Lane*, the official history of the Land Rover, 'Spencer Wilks brought the Rover (to Islay) and had the suspension raised so it could negotiate the rutted tracks. When his gamekeeper saw it he said "this must be a Land Rover."'

That gamekeeper was Ian Fraser, whose son Duncan recently recounted the family story, that 'My father was supposed to have said "oh aye, a real Land Rover, a great Land Rover."' The name stuck. Renowned for its rugged terrain and vast landscapes, Islay became the unofficial proving ground for production Land Rovers throughout the late 1940s as the Wilks brothers continued to use the island to secretly put the Series I Land Rover through its paces in the build-up to its production. According to Crathorne, 'Despite many of the vehicles being more than 50 years old, they are still adept at coping with the rough and challenging terrain that Islay has to offer, perfectly demonstrating the capability that Land Rover has always been renowned for.'

Islay still plays an important part in the history of the Land Rover, so much so that during the summer, Land Rover made the trip to Islay to celebrate 67 years of Series Land Rover and Land Rover Defender production, and a 1954 Land Rover was included in the party.

So, where better for me to take the not-so-humble Flying Huntsman than to the humble roots of its predecessor? I headed off in this statement car, but soon I found myself wondering what had possessed me!

I feel naked. Like I am on a stage with no clothes. People are straining their necks and rubber-necking. I watch one man nearly walk into a lamppost. A dog walker stops in his tracks, his mouth open wide. I have never been the subject of so much attention. I feel conspicuous and vulnerable.

I am in the Highlands, driving along the shores of Loch Lomond, arguably one of the most beautiful drives in the British Isles. I have driven this route dozens of times before, and on each occasion I have been lost in a reverie of natural beauty as I have twisted and turned along the meandering road.

Loch Lomond has been the starting point for so many of my life's great adventures, but now, today, on a cold, rainy spring day, it feels different. Cars flash their lights and honk their horns as I pass. Now this is particularly strange for several reasons: firstly, behind the body of a moving car I have become accustomed to a degree of anonymity. Now don't get me wrong, I am not insinuating that I am some A-list personality whose life has become a misery as I am stalked by paparazzi, but in the words of that great wordsmith, Ron Burgundy, today, 'I am kind of a big deal', or, to be exact, 'my vehicle is kind of a big deal.'

Now, as you have guessed, given the title of this book, I am of course in a Land Rover. A Defender, to be exact. And herein lies the second mystery. One of the great attractions of the Land Rover Defender is its ability to stand out and blend in at the same time. Let me explain. A Ford or a VW is completely anonymous. It is unlikely to get a second glance. These marques are the epitome of the homogeneous vehicles that swarm our roads. If you were a bank robber on the run from the police, these are the kind of cars you would want. The pigeons of the automobile world.

At the other end of the spectrum is the supercar, the Lamborghini, Ferrari or McLaren. These are cars that beg you to look at them. That is the point. These are not cars driven by shy, retiring types, they are cars driven by successful, wealthy individuals who are asking you to look at them. Their vehicles have become a social commentary on their success.

This need to show our success through objects has spawned the whole luxury market. Clothes, watches, homes, jets, jewellery – the market is driven by ostentatious shows of wealth. By and large – and of course there are plenty of exceptions to the rule – the English are a rather unostentatious society. We have tended to view extravagance as slightly vulgar. The old-school money prefer a derelict stately home and a decrepit old rusting Land Rover over the gold-plated bling of some other nations.

I like to consider myself the consummate Englishman. I don't like to talk about money, politics or religion. I have always preferred to blend in and recoil from shows of flashiness. I don't like to court attention – which may seem a strange statement from someone who has spent a decade and a half in the public eye – but here's the point: the Land Rover Defender has managed to transcend comment. The Land Rover Defender has the ability to be different and independent at the same time as blending in, but today all that has changed because I have abandoned any chance of anonymity by taking to the Scottish Highlands in one of the most expensive Land Rover Defenders ever modified – the Flying Huntsman, a Kahn Design six-wheel-drive monster of a car.

The licence plate alone is enough to make me blush: 2222 V. I suspect this alone is worth more than my house. But this is not the reason why Scotland has come to a standstill, its residents lining the streets in anticipation of a glimpse of this beast. I am exaggerating, but only just …

I broke my journey around the shores of Loch Lomond with a quick lunch in a shoreside pub. As I ate, I counted no fewer than fifty people crowded around her taking photographs. Within minutes of arrival, photos had been posted across social media. A local news photographer even turned up to take a picture.

This was a car that said, 'LOOK AT ME', 'WOOF'. This was a car to suit the hedonistic 1980s excess. It reminded me of Harry Enfield's 'Loadsa money'. With a price tag of £250,000, it was certainly that.

I almost wasn't here. No one would insure me to drive this massive vehicle through the Scottish Highlands. I was only granted the insurance at the last minute on the understanding that it would be kept off-road in a secure car park at night.

Land Rovers have, of course, become covetable vehicles to steal in recent years, but I couldn't help but think that if this one were ever stolen there would be a long stream of social media entries that would enable the police to track it down within minutes. There is nothing subtle about the Flying Huntsman.

I watched, worrying, as the fuel needle moved in real time before my eyes. I mean that. I'm not even exaggerating. It literally dipped before my eyes and within an hour it was time to refuel.

'Whose car is that?' said a gruff-sounding Scotsman as he came into the pub. I slunk into my seat and pulled a newspaper up close. Was I embarrassed? I could feel my cheeks burning. Somehow I had to get out of the pub, past the crowd, into the car and back out onto the road. I took a deep breath and ran for it. An audible astonished silence emanated from the gathered crowd as I leapt behind the wheel. I didn't wait around to explain myself – I just drove off at speed. Or that was the plan … the automatic transmission seemed to have frozen in first. I shuddered out of the car park and back onto the Loch Lomond road. The car wheezed and screamed but the gearing was stuck; it wouldn't change into second. The car trundled along at 30mph with a long queue of cars behind her.

As if I didn't already stand out enough in a quarter-of-a-million-pound, matt-black, six-wheel-drive Defender, I was now holding up several dozen cars. They must have loved me.

Now for the next obstacle. I had to catch the ferry from Kennacraig to Islay. I have used Caledonian MacBrayne ferries many times over the years; they are the lifeline to many of the Western Isles.

'Hello, Mr Fogle,' smiled two Scotsmen at the ticket barrier, 'we weren't expecting you to drive that monster. Did you get it specially made?' I did what will henceforth be known as a Kahn shrug, which I combined with a smirk.

In Lane 1, waiting for the ferry once again, a small crowd appeared. 'That is the most amazing car I have ever seen!' squealed a young boy, begging his parents to get one. Soon the Flying Huntsman attracted the first 'anorak'. I could spot him a mile off. Green shirt. Beard. Dog on lead. He had the broadest grin. 'I know all about you,' he smiled. 'This must be a Kahn.'

He told me that he drove a 20-year-old Defender – or 90 as it is known – and that it was his pride and joy. He had completely overhauled it and was a passionate Land Rover lover. I prepared myself for his disdain at the beast.

'Go on,' I said, 'tell me what you think.' I was prepared for the worst.

'I love it,' he answered without hesitation. He examined the whole vehicle. 'It's like a work of art. I'll tell you what,' he continued, 'I'd trade my wife for that.'

I boarded the ferry for Islay.

Bob and Liz Cunninghame are cattle and sheep farmers. Their hillside farm is hidden along a remote country track far from the distilleries and tourist trails of Islay. Bob had run their 1000-acre farm for 62 years, but of course I wasn't here to see his farm, I was here to see his Series I.

'What a poser,' Bob laughed, before gripping my hand in one of those vice-like handshakes that only farmers know how to do.

'What do you think?' I asked, as he looked around the beast.

'Poncy poser,' he repeated.

Bob's father, William, was one of Land Rover's very first customers. As a farmer he had seen various concepts being tested around the island, and in 1949 he sold his Rover 15 for £150 and placed an order for a Series I Land Rover.

Bob had learnt to drive in that same vehicle, and so began a lifelong love affair with the Land Rover. He remembers taking the Series I around the farm aged just nine years old. 'I couldn't see above the steering wheel,' he laughed.

Bob has owned dozens of Defenders over the years. They were vital to enable him to reach the remote corners of the farm during lambing and calving.

'This is tough terrain,' he admitted. 'I have been bogged thousands of times.' Each time he gets stuck beyond personal recovery he calls his long-suffering wife Liz, who arrives on either another Land Rover or a tractor.

His nostalgic memories of the Series I never left him, so finally, ten years ago, Bob realised his lifelong dream and bought one from an agricultural auction. He painstakingly repaired it and got it back to full working order.

It is now his pride and joy, which surprised me; I had always imagined farmers to be very practical types, not prone to emotional nostalgia, but Bob was different.

'I'm not allowed to drive her,' chips in Liz, serving me a cup of tea and a scone. 'He loves her more than me.'

Bob remains silent. He doesn't disagree.

He remembers as a child when they had up to 13 people crammed into the old Series I because there were very few vehicles on Islay and everyone wanted a lift. As farmers they used to rig up the Land Rover to other farm machinery, such as threshing machines. Just as Wilks had conceived, this vehicle would be a farmer's best friend. A dual-purpose vehicle.

'Shall we take her for a spin?' Bob asked.

'I thought you'd never ask,' I replied, getting my coat.

Soon we were trundling along the narrow single-track roads in his beloved car. It felt good to be back in a Series I. Despite the number of people looking at us and waving, I felt a semblance of anonymity returning. It was like I was finally dressed. Despite the attention, it felt different. Less intense. Less scrutiny and more admiration.

We drove past the whitewashed Hebridean cottages and small farms. Highland cattle grazed in the rich green fields that bordered the turbulent azure waters beyond. We cruised along at 40mph in fourth gear until we reached the island's capital, Bowmore, home to the famous whisky of the same name. People craned their necks as we pulled up near to the little harbour wall that was lined with fishing boats and nodded in appreciation as they snapped photographs of a vehicle that had been born here.

'You can drive us back,' he smiled, throwing me the keys. I was in heaven. Driving a Series I on Islay.

'You should visit Kathy Wills at Kilchoman distillery,' he told me as we drove back to his farm, 'her grandfather was Spencer Wilks, who invented the Land Rover.'

I didn't know whether to be humiliated that I didn't already know this fact or excited at the prospect of meeting someone whose grandpa had invented the Land Rover.

Kathy Wills and her husband Anthony established the Kilchoman Farm distillery in 2005 – the first new distillery on the

island for 125 years. I climbed back into the beast, waved goodbye and headed back across the island.

I only needed to follow my nose towards the smell of hops and
barley to find the farm, and soon enough I pulled alongside a
small distillery surrounded by moorland.

'Hello,' I greeted a woman wearing a Kilchoman fleece. 'Do
you know where I can find Kathy Wills?'

'I'm Kathy,' she smiled.

If angels could sing. It felt like I was in the company of Land
Rover royalty.

Over a dram of Islay's finest, Kathy told me the incredible tale
of her grandfather, Spencer Wilks. She had grown up between
her family home on the Isle of Wight and her grandfather's estate
on Islay.

'When I was growing up we were surrounded by Land Rovers.
Islay in particular was always full of them. We had seven at one
stage.'

She continued, 'Every summer we were here, and when my
husband decided that we should open a distillery somewhere,
Islay was the ideal choice, not only because Islay is iconic in terms
of whisky but for me it was coming home.

'Everyone who knew me remembered my father and grandfather and the strange cars that they brought over and tested on the
island.'

'Are you proud of your Land Rover pedigree?' I ask.

'No, I'm embarrassed, embarrassed that I don't know more
about them; we were always proud to see them on the roads but
they were just part of the furniture. My three sons seem much
more interested,' she admits.

'Do you ever get bored of talking about Land Rovers?' I ask.

'Never,' she says. 'To be honest it was only recently that Islay was put back on the Land Rover heritage map.'

I, like many others, had assumed Anglesey had been the true birthplace of the Land Rover, but as I had discovered, Islay was not only the testing ground to assess its viability for the shooting estates in the Highlands of Scotland, it was also the birthplace of its name.

Kathy naturally learnt to drive in a Series III Land Rover, which is still in the family. I ask her whether she thinks Land Rover have stayed true to their origins?

'My grandfather built utilitarian vehicles, Land Rover have moved too far away from their heritage and into the luxury market,' she concedes. 'The original Land Rover was like Meccano. They were boxy and square and had a silhouette that was instantly recognisable. That's gone today.'

I ask if she uses Land Rovers in the distillery and she shows me a smart long wheelbase Land Rover with whisky decals along the side. Her sons drive them around the globe to help market their whisky worldwide.

'Do you drive a Land Rover?' I ask. She looks a little sheepish.

'I drive a Volvo.

'You must meet Duncan and Anne Fraser,' she continues, 'together they drove and tested almost all my grandfather's Land Rovers over the years.'

I get back into the beast and continue my journey around Islay to meet more Land Rover royalty.

Soon I find myself driving down a small dirt track that leads to a little tin house set amongst a neatly planted garden. As I pull up I am greeted by the smiling bearded face of Duncan Fraser.

'I'm just changing Anne's sheets, she's had a stroke you know. Make yourself comfortable.'

I make my way into the front room, which is brimming with knick-knacks, and the walls are plastered with paintings and photos of Labradors.

There had been no employment after Duncan had left school, so, as Duncan explains, 'I made a few bob killing rats and rabbits'. Then he was offered a job at Wilks' Laggan Estate, a sporting estate which was used for grouse, stalking, fishing and wildfowling.

Duncan's father, Ian, was already a gamekeeper on the estate, and father and son both worked for the Wilks family. Duncan's father was a wild man who didn't suffer fools, according to his son. Anne nods in agreement.

'How do I put this?' says Duncan, in his strong Scottish accent. 'My dad was a bit of a bullshitter, so I never really knew what was true and what was made up.

'The story he told me was that Spencer Wilks turned up one day with a Rover 10 that had been modified to have higher ground clearance. He asked my father what he thought and my father said, "put the back axle on the front and then you will have a decent car, a Land Rover."'

According to many, it was indeed Ian Fraser, Duncan's father, who came up with the name. The Land Rover was born. However, the story doesn't end there. According to Duncan's father, Spencer Wilks had invited the king of England, George VI, to join him in the Series I Land Rover for a test drive. His Majesty was instantly taken with the vehicle and asked if he could have it. Wilks replies, 'I'm afraid, your Royal Highness, I have promised this car to Ian Fraser, my gamekeeper.'

And so Fraser legend has it that the king of England was beaten to the first Land Rover by a man from Islay.

'I still remember that first Land Rover,' he says, 'its registration was GWD 744.'

It never ceases to amaze me, people's ability to remember Land Rover serial numbers and registrations.

I ask about the North Wales connection.

'The first time I heard about Anglesey and its role as the birthplace of the Land Rover, I thought, what bullshit,' Duncan says. 'The Land Rover was born here on Islay.'

Anne was also heavily involved with the Wilks Land Rovers from an early stage. She had to collect all the prototypes from the ferry and drive them to the estate.

'I lived in the bloody things,' she says, 'but I loved them.'

'I'll tell you what,' says Duncan. 'Spencer was a bloody good man. He used to drive his grey Land Rover down to the beach every morning; he loved those cars and he loved to talk about them. He would get very excited if he saw one on the television and he'd be sure to tell everyone about it.

'Spencer was an inventor. He was always making things in his workshop; one day I noticed some little holes on the front bumper of his Land Rover,' Duncan recalls, 'it transpired they were for some mudflaps ... "On the front of the car?" I asked, perplexed, pointing out that mud splatters backwards, so why would you need mudguards in front of the bumper? Apparently they were for brushing sheep and lambs away from the car when it drove around the fields of the estate.'

Islay was used to test almost every marque of Land Rover over the years. Duncan recalls the arrival of the first Range Rover on the island, wistfully remarking, 'they don't make Range Rovers like that anymore.

'In my opinion, Land Rovers got worse as they evolved,' Duncan declares. 'They were bloody good vehicles at the start.'

My time on Islay was coming to an end. I took the beast for one final drive – I still had one vital test to carry out. It was on this island that Wilks and company had tested the vehicles for their off-road capabilities, and so far I had only used the 6×6 on the road.

I drove to a secluded spot with a steep boggy plateau leading to a pebble and sand beach.

'Here we go,' I thought, as I left the tarmac and finally took the Defender where she naturally belonged, off-road.

The wheels gripped magnificently into the boggy peat, as mud and water shot under the arches. I braced myself to get bogged, but she seemed to ride rough-shod over the boggy section and soon she was gripping onto the large pebbles. The engine wheezed as we climbed a steep bank. I breached the summit and soon she was safely on the sand. I edged her closer to the water. Mr Kahn, if you are reading this, look away now. I edged close to the water. Closer. Closer, until I was in the water. An inch, two inches, hell, a foot. We raced up and down the beach, water spraying.

It was the happiest she had been since I had boarded her in Glasgow. I'm sure I heard her sing. The engine had stopped making strange noises. I smiled. We smiled. Gone were any reservations. She might look like something from a Steam Punk festival but underneath she was a Land Rover, and here on a remote Hebridean beach in the Western Isles of Scotland, she could finally be herself.

CHAPTER SIX

WEIRD ROVER

In 2014, nearly a decade after I had said farewell to the Silver Bullet, I had an epiphany while I was travelling through a remote corner of Central America in an old Series II. The family was growing. Marina and I now had two children and two dogs and often more of both on loan from other people. We were leading busy lives and I was starting to film more and more TV shows back in the UK, often some distance away from home, so we were finding ourselves increasingly double-booking the single family car. I had just started presenting ITV's *Countrywise* and the planets, it seemed, were aligned. We needed a second car – and it would be a Land Rover. I would revert to my childhood sweetheart.

But how to broach the subject? I knew Marina would be amenable to a second vehicle. 'What a good idea!' she'd say. 'Let's get a Toyota Prius or a fuel-efficient Skoda.' Marina has always been the practical one in our relationship – where I am drawn by aesthetics and looks, Marina is driven by function and economics.

I knew the suggestion of a Defender would be a long shot. 'Why?' she would ask. 'It's noisy, uncomfortable and not particularly safe.' I love my wife dearly but I have never been able to beat her in a debate. She is deft and ruthless with her argument, borne by honesty and practicality.

I tried rehearsing my argument: 'It would be a practical vehicle that could get us anywhere,' I would explain, 'and it would never get stuck,' I would say with a flourish. 'Besides, it would be a good investment', I would add.

One of the benefits of 10 years of marriage is an instinctive knowledge of how she would reply in such a negotiation: 'But we never get stuck.' And with that she would win the conversation before it had ever really begun.

I could offer my own honest debate and argue my cause with the following: 'Okay, I know it is a noisy, shaky, uncomfortable farm vehicle in which all conversation gets drowned out at 65mph – which is also her top speed. I know it's difficult for us to get in and out of and nearly impossible for the non-athletic, elderly or infirm. I know that children are likely to get sick by sitting opposite each other in the back seats that face inwards. I know that it will either be too hot or too cold and that the windows will be perpetually misted. I know it often leaks and that the seats can be cold and uncomfortable but … it's a fine-looking vehicle.'

It would be perfect. I never considered another vehicle. I also knew I wouldn't win the argument, so I decided to take the brave and honest approach favoured by so many men the world over. I bought one without telling her.

Now, if you know my wife you will know this is a particularly brave thing to do. We have always shared all aspects of decision-making – in fact, Marina runs the household finances. I knew it was a risky strategy, but I also knew that it would be easier to persuade her to my way of thinking once the car had been bought and delivered.

I started looking online and in the various specialist magazines. To be honest, it was slightly overwhelming, there was such a vast array of vehicles to choose from. I liked the idea of a vintage model but worried about the reliability and comfort of long journeys for which I needed the vehicle to be consistent. I didn't want to buy a brand-new vehicle – I had already done that once, and although the vehicle had served me well I had suffered on the massive depreciation.

This would be my third Defender and I had very specific demands, the main one being that I wanted a soft top. I'm not sure what it is about convertibles but I have always loved them. For a short period the family car had been a convertible Mini. We had loved that car; it had the ability to turn life into a perpetual holiday. I would take the roof down whatever the weather. Driving without a roof creates instant happiness, in cold or heat – I defy anyone to sit in a convertible with the roof down and not smile. Perhaps it is the non-conformity of the vehicle, or maybe it is the feeling of the wind in your hair. Possibly it is a sense of escaping to the romanticism and glamour of sun-filled locations such as Hollywood or the South of France, but the lack of roof has the power to bring happiness to mundane journeys.

I wanted a convertible Land Rover. I was looking for the holy grail of the double-smile vehicle. I wanted something that would light up a rainy day and transform a mundane journey into picture-postcard perfection. An idyllic summer's day of a journey.

I have spent an awfully large amount of my life in vehicles of one kind or another; indeed, I'm writing these particular words from a World War II Russian van as I cross Mongolia. Those journeys are monotonous. They are voyages of necessity undertaken in a vehicle of practicality. As I have already explained, cars for me have always been about functionality – the ability to deliver me from point A to point B. The majority of cars on the market cater to this desire for practicality. The environmental sustainability and fuel efficiency, the safety specifications and comfort are all maximised to create the ultimate in homogeneous vehicles. Take a look at any road in Britain and, apart from the badges and marques, see if you can genuinely distinguish one car from the next. The colours and contours merge into a standard bland car catering to those focused on pure function.

I'd argue that was how I was brought up. A car is not for show but for use. We had been a very functional family. Why waste money on a car? Cars were chosen to suit the appropriate needs rather than any narcissistic aesthetic aspirations. I had been brought up to consider it rather vulgar to drive an ostentatious vehicle. To be honest, during my childhood the vehicles in my neighbourhood could probably only be divided into two categories: standard or foreign. The streets were filled with Fords and Austins.

Up until my twenties I never really cared or worried about appearance and aesthetics. By that I mean I wasn't really bothered one way or another. I appreciated nice things, but how something looked wasn't the priority. If it looked good, that was merely an added bonus. As the years have marched on I have found myself driven by aesthetic principles more than ever before. My house, my clothes, my own appearance have all taken on more signifi-cance. I sometimes wonder if it has anything to do with the amount of time I spend away, sleeping in freezing igloos or in stuffy hammocks in jungles, unshaven and often wearing the same clothes for weeks on end. It gives me too much time to dwell on what I have left behind me. I call it my nest syndrome. I want and imagine everything to be perfect back at home. I wonder how much of this perceived idea of aesthetic perfection has affected my life choices.

Heavily armed soldiers and camouflaged army vehicles protected the airport as I made my way out of the arrivals hall and into the balmy warmth of summer. A Chinook helicopter circled over-head as I passed through a police blockade.

Surprisingly, I wasn't in some war-torn country but in Belgium, on my way to see one of the most outlandish Land Rover Defenders ever created.

Following the attack on Brussels airport in April 2016 and the discovery of some of the Paris Bataclan terrorists also in the capi-tal, the tiny European nation had been under lockdown and it felt a little strange driving along the largely deserted streets of Antwerp.

I wasn't actually here to visit Belgium, but its near neighbour, the Netherlands. I must admit it was a relief to cross the border into the land of tulips. I'm sure the threat to the country was by then negligible, but there had been an unmistakable sense of unease across Belgium.

I was on my way to the small town of Tilburg, perhaps most famous as the home of Tesla, the new electric sports cars brought to the world courtesy of Elon Musk. However, I was in town to visit Studio Job, to meet one of the world's craziest artists.

Studio Job was set up by designers Job Smeets and Nynke Tynagel, who met while studying at the Design Academy Eindhoven. The duo wanted to create what they describe as 'Gesamtkunstwerk', which roughly translates as 'universal artwork'. In short, they wanted to combine artwork with everyday objects in a synthesis of the arts.

Their design studio was hidden in a relatively anonymous industrial park; only a tiny colourful sign above the entrance door – 'Fuck Off' – gave away the maverick world within.

Nynke met me at the door; tall and beautiful, she was as striking as her astonishing designs.

I should probably explain now that I am not a great arbiter of art. To be honest, I have quite simple taste. I am certainly an aesthete and I do appreciate beautiful things, but I am rather literal when it comes to art. I find many aspects of modern art completely baffling. Sharks in formaldehyde, unmade beds and giant dots simply don't cut it with me. I need something I can understand.

The world in which I now found myself was one of the most surreal, outrageous, crazy places I had ever been. The designs of Smeets and Tynagel are so outlandish and wacky that it is difficult to know where to begin. So let's start with their Land Rover, because you will learn quite a lot about these designers from their car.

Land Rover Defenders have always been popular with the Dutch, and in 2013, to commemorate the 65th anniversary of the iconic car, the duo were asked to design a concept car.

'For a designer, one of the most prestigious commissions is the design of a car,' explained Smeets. 'We wanted a JOB Land Rover that's here and now. A sculpture of today! It got totally out of hand!'

Let me try to explain the craziness.

The windows of the vehicle have been replaced by stained glass, while one of the four wheels has been replaced by a cart-wheel. One of the mirrors has become a frying pan, while the other has been super-enlarged and covered in Swarovski crystals. The lights have been replaced by glass balloons in a riot of colours, while the space where the front grille was now sports a huge pink tongue. One of the hubcaps has been replaced by an image of Capitol Hill, while the other is a birthday cake. The snorkel has been adorned with a large silver cloud. From one side of the bonnet flies the Zimbabwean flag, and on the other flies the Congolese flag with a gold skull atop the staff.

The frame of the car has been hand-poured in bronze, while sticking out of the bonnet is a huge rhino horn cast out of aluminium and covered in 24-carat gilding. Atop this brass frame are red and blue lights, while at the back is an elaborate 'fuel system' which includes a hose, a trumpet and a meat grinder alongside a large oak barrel.

The interior of the Land Rover is just as crazy.

The dashboard has been recast in bronze and silver leaf. The speedometer has been replaced by a clock, and there is a large egg timer alongside a gold compass. In place of the cubby box or third seat is a gold crate of Duval beer. The seats have all been re-covered in African print called 'L'Afrique', while the floor has been carved from French oak.

To be honest, my description doesn't do it justice. This is a Land Rover to take your breath away.

'As you would expect from someone who knows nothing about making a car, our approach got completely out of hand,' says Smeets. 'The numerous elements kept accumulating. The car literally sticks its tongue out. It wants to be something that it actually isn't. It's become a great concoction, monumental and cynical, but isn't that also true for power and class structures? Those are surely also inventions. A fictive status symbol that other people supposedly look up to. It's a nudge at designers who are asked to design a concept car and who then invent a stylish-looking apparatus that is launched with all the necessary bells and whistles. So we also take aim at the car industry; I can already imagine the chief sitting in this very modern carriage, with his chauffeur in the front and his various wives and children in the back. A Popemobile for an African chief personalised in a bizarre way.'

The Job Defender is an anti-car. A kaleidoscopic riot of layered storytelling.

To the uninitiated the car is a hotchpotch, but having spent so long immersed in the world of Land Rover it all made perfect sense. The gold rhino horn is a comment on conservation and the problem of illegal poaching of endangered species. The Capitol is a nod to North America's abandonment of the Land Rover and its subsequent demise. The egg timer and the clock are symbols of time running out for the vehicle, while the birthday cake is a celebration of the car's 65th birthday. The oversized wing mirror is a reflection of one of the car's most distinctive designs, while the frying-pan mirror symbolises the car's role in camping expeditions. The Congolese and Zimbabwean flags represent the role of the vehicle in dictatorial Africa, while the meat-grinder fuel system perhaps symbolises the car's use by armies around the world and on the battlefield. The colourful Swarovski globe attached to belts that turn the wheels illustrates the car's dominance around the globe and more significantly the importance of the world for the Land Rover, while the ostentatious back of the vehicle is demonstrative of its popularity among the wealthy.

The tongue is curious. It's not so easy to read. Is it sticking it out to society? To conformity? Or to the establishment? I suppose therein lies the beauty of art. Everyone will have their own interpretation.

For me the Job Land Rover was so much more than just a work of art. It was psychedelic storytelling. A vehicle that has become a parody of itself. A multilayered parable that has the power to inspire and confuse.

On the one hand, the Land Rover Defender is a car in the simplest and most basic sense. It is a car stripped of complication and modernisation. This blank canvas has been reimagined countless times over the years by enthusiasts, emergency services, the military, explorers, dictators, musicians, actors, farmers, hunters and royalty. If there were one car that was the summation of this book, however, it would be the Job Land Rover. This car is a contradiction in terms; it is a parody of itself while at the same time mirroring its own meandering life. A Land Rover created from the trip of the light fantastic. A car dipped in a bath of

Ecstasy and born from a Dalí-esque imagination, where everything has been magnified. The volume has been turned up.

I found the Job Land Rover mesmerising – a cacophony of colour and texture. If Lady Gaga, Vivienne Westwood and the late Mr Nice created a car, this would be it. She caused a riot in the senses. Funny, weird, strange, enchanting, captivating. I have rarely been moved by a piece of art as much as by this extraordinary creation.

I explored her wacky chaos with Nynke. Quiet, pretty and reserved, she exuded sophistication and neatness – the antithesis of this Land Rover. Before I left, Nynke wanted to show me some of their other work. One sculpture stood out. It was of a train crash. The bronze and gold-leaf work named 'autobiographical' was a table, the smoke from the two trains merging to create the universal surface.

'Job and I used to be together,' explained Nynke. 'When we split up romantically we stayed together in art, and the train was us.'

It was simple, beautiful and tragic. A little like the story of the Land Rover.

I forgot to tell Marina I had bought a Land Rover.

She found out when I was filming in Newfoundland, when the registration documents arrived in the post.

'You bought a Defender?' she asked quizzically down the crackling line as I battled against the autumn Atlantic winds lashing against the rugged Canadian coastline.

There is nothing like being caught on the back foot. Honesty, people, that is my advice to you.

I'm not sure how I forgot to tell her but I kind of thought that if I asked she would say no, but if I turned up with it she would fall in love with it and everyone would be a winner. Like a dog from a rescue centre; the car would seduce her with those lines and those puppy-dog lights. And once I'd reassured myself, the issue went out of my mind.

Right now, though, as I got a lecture via phone across the Atlantic Ocean on the importance of shared family decisions, no excuse was going to cut it.

Nene Overland is just one of dozens of companies that has sprung up within the rich cottage industry around Land Rover. They started fitting out Land Rovers for overland expeditions and soon discovered a market in modifications that Land Rover themselves were not prepared to do.

In recent years, Nene had tapped into the rich nostalgia market by modifying contemporary Defenders to have a retro and heritage style. Nene had chopped the roof of my short wheelbase Land Rover and converted her to soft top for me. She was the most beautiful Rover I had ever seen – and she was mine.

I couldn't sleep the night before collecting her. My mind buzzed and raced with visions of the fun we would have with her. I got that same shudder of excitement as I hauled myself aboard, too. There is something so familiar about a Land Rover. Despite their variety and their adaptations, modifications and design evolution through the years, there is an unmistakable familiarity amongst all vehicles. It's rather like wearing a comfy sweater, sitting on an old sofa or eating a bowl of spaghetti Bolognese. The smells and the aesthetics have a soothing familiarity.

140   *Land Rover*

Perhaps this is one of the Land Rover's great virtues – its ability to press 'pause' in our lives, to take us reeling back to another time and place. Just sitting in the rigid driver's seat brought memories of old journeys flooding back. It is this nostalgia that captures the emotions, creating an extraordinary bond that we rarely forge with a vehicle.

Like a highlighter pen, the Land Rover Defender seems to have a way of underlining and highlighting events, journeys and periods in time. I can remember trips aboard Land Rovers that would long have been forgotten in any other vehicle. I can remember every journey I have ever done in a Defender. And now a new chapter was starting with her. I called her Polly. I am not alone in creating this personal connection with my car; throughout the country there are dozens of people who have dedicated their lives to the unique world of the Land Rover. In fact, in many ways this has been a pretty easy book to research. I won't give away my secrets, but suffice to say that if you type 'Land Rover' followed by almost anything into Google, you will find something.

'Land Rover' and 'DJ' reveals a mobile DJ who works from his decks mounted in the back of a Land Rover Defender; 'Land Rover' and 'limousine' shows several stretch Land Rover Defenders available for parties; 'Land Rover' and 'Bar' comes up with a mobile drinks Land Rover, in which the back has been converted into a fully stocked bar. There are ice-cream Land Rovers and fish-and-chip Land Rovers, but perhaps the strangest find of all was the Land Rover hearse. I'd like to think it's demonstrative of the level of rigorous research that has gone into this book that I discovered an undertaker who specialises in Land Rover burials.

A line of four beautifully polished Land Rovers of varying marque and age was waiting for me as I reached the end of a long drive. We were in a beautiful farmyard surrounded by stone buildings. Like the Land Rovers, it was clean and neat.

Jacqui was waiting eagerly with her friend, who had an equally excitable black Labrador. Jacqui's eyes sparkled as we got on to the topic of Land Rovers. During the course of my Tour de Land Rover across Great Britain I had met dozens of enthusiasts who all oozed the same excitement, but Jacqui was different. She was properly Land Rover bonkers. A fanatic.

Not wanting to digress from funerals, but if I'm honest I was most excited that she was a girl. A woman who had the same affection for the Land Rover as so many of the bearded men I had met on my journey. I knew that Land Rovers had equal appeal to women – you only need to peer into the driving seat of any Defender you see on the road and you will see a high percentage of women in the driver's seat.

To digress for a moment, I had asked my great friend Caroline Gladstone, wife of Charlie Gladstone, great-grandson of the former prime minister, about her connection to the Land Rover. The Gladstones are probably the coolest family I have ever met. It is not right to covet another person's life, but if I had to do a life swap I would exchange mine for theirs in a flash. Caroline and Charlie have six children, and yet both, in their early thirties, look fresh-faced and calm. They run multiple businesses, including hotels, pubs and shops, as well as festivals – and did I mention they live between a castle in Wales, a house in Scotland, a château in France and a home in London? They do all this with ease and in the company of five dogs in addition to their six offspring.

Their mode of transport is, of course, a Defender. Several, to be precise. Whenever they travel between properties, it is Caroline who fills the Defender with canines and drives the long journey to Scotland or France or Wales. I have often marvelled at this. We are not talking an infrequent journey once a year; these are regular trips, like a school run, only 14 hours long in a noisy, cold, uncomfortable vehicle.

What had always fascinated me about the Gladstones was that although the Land Rover was undoubtedly a family love affair, it was Caroline who was the true aficionado. It is a labour of love to drive five dogs for an hour aboard a Defender without company. To drive for half a day is true, deep-seated love.

'I would never use any other car,' explained Caroline when I asked her why she didn't choose something a little more comfortable. I don't like to pry into others' finances, but they are the kind of family that could probably stretch to a Range Rover if they chose. Only they didn't. They don't. They drive Defenders.

Caroline drives a Defender for the same reason as I do. It is the no-nonsense, classless car that allows individuality with anonymity.

Likewise, Jacqui reassures me that there really are plenty of women who are just as crazy about the Land Rover as men.

Jacqui learnt to drive in a Series IIA Land Rover in Norfolk. Her father loved them and she can still remember the time she persuaded him to take the Landy to Woburn Safari Park, where the monkeys proceeded to trash the entire car.

An undertaker by trade, it took a brush with death for Jacqui to launch her new business venture. A cancer diagnosis made her rethink her life. While she recovered from chemotherapy she had a light-bulb moment. At this point the only funeral option for a hearse was a standard limousine. She wanted to create something different that would appeal to a non-conformist market. It was the beginning of the unconventional funeral and she hit upon the idea of converting a Land Rover Defender into a hearse.

The silver Defender looked like a standard model from the outside, but the interior had been stripped to make way for the wooden hydraulic coffin platform. She had been fitted with slightly oversized tyres, giving it an almost decadent lift.

She got in touch with Foley – specialist Land Rover dealers and producers of bespoke vehicles based in Essex – and asked them if they could convert a standard long wheelbase so that it could accommodate a coffin that was a little over six feet long. They built two; one was shipped to the Falkland Islands and the other went to Jacqui, who began to market her trade to the Land-Rover-loving market.

'We wanted to appeal to Land Rover enthusiasts, but we also appealed to families who had lost young children,' she told me. 'The sight of a small coffin aboard a Land Rover Defender seemed to soften the horrors of a child's funeral.'

I ask what kind of people she transports in her hearse.

'The most common thing I hear when I get to the church and the coffin is removed is "typical", "that is just typical of ..." It makes people smile. It adds an individual's personality to the sad conformity of a funeral process.'

With more bookings, she added another long wheelbase Defender as the sister car to carry friends and family in convoy.

'I feel very honoured to be a part of such personal funerals,' she confesses.

I ask her if she dresses in the smart funeral attire traditionally worn by hearse drivers. 'Sometimes,' she admits, 'but sometimes they ask me to dress more casually, tweed and wellies.'

Today the Land Rovers have been polished to within an inch of their lives. They are sparkling. I ask if she is ever asked to make them muddy.

'All the time,' she smiles. 'We often go off-road with the coffin aboard.' Jacqui explains that on occasion she takes the convoy across fields or through woods, sometimes to reach a remote funeral spot for which they actually need the 4×4, but often just as a nostalgic, emotional journey to the deceased's favourite places.

Gamekeepers, shooters, farmers, former employees of Land Rover – she has buried them all. She even buried her own mother, carrying her coffin in the Defender.

Jacqui admits an unusual feeling of closeness with her clients. The Land Rover is a unifying presence that bonds. She takes the Land Rover hearse to dedicated Land Rover shows and she often finds families of those whom she has buried staring at the vehicle, touching it and even talking to it – 'it's like the vehicle has retained a part of their loved one.'

I ask if there is anything she has ever refused to do.

'No,' she answers, 'but there was once a very strange request. I was burying a man who had used a Land Rover to scout forests for places to hold illegal raves. He had used his Defender to get to remote corners of the countryside from which he could hold the illegal parties. When they delivered the flowers for the coffin for me to take on board, they were made up entirely of marijuana leaves.'

Where most undertakers will stick to a local region, Jacqui and her Defender travel the length and breadth of the country. As we sit in the hearse she explains that she is off to Yorkshire for a funeral. Her husband and she will drive there that night and stay over in a hotel.

'We always ask the hotel if it's okay to park the hearse in their car park, in case anyone finds it uncomfortable,' she reveals.

With the enthusiasm of the Landy fanatic, Jacqui talks me through her plans to upgrade the vehicle. There is already the ubiquitous rust that is so endemic to these much-loved vehicles appearing on the hearse. Unsurprisingly, the families love these little quirks. 'John would have commented on that rust,' one family had said.

When she isn't driving the hearse or the limo, Jacqui, of course, drives her own short wheelbase to transport her dogs around.

'Timeless, classic and British is what I like about the Land Rover. If it's good enough for the Queen then it's good enough for me!' laughs Jacqui.

After the success of her Defender hearse, Jacqui decided to explore the feasibility of turning an older Land Rover into a hearse. Many early Land Rover owners had asked her if she had considered converting a Series I. There was only one way to find out. She purchased a Series I trialler but the problem was that the coffins were simply too big for the vehicle. What's more, the DVLA scuppered her plans with their ban on a Land Rover pulling a Land Rover.

'Can I have a look at yours?' she asks, with that unique Landy twinkle in her eye. Before even waiting for an answer, her nose is pressed close to the window. 'Ooh!'

Back in London, I was about to meet another bizarre and quirky adaptation of the Land Rover, for an equally unconventional business use.

Savile Row, in London's Mayfair, is the home of British tailoring. It has a rich and colourful history that dates back to the 1700s, having dressed everyone from Lord Nelson to Napoleon III, Winston Churchill and Prince Charles.

The 'golden mile of tailoring' has dozens of old-school tailors side by side along it, but among the Palladian architecture lies a modern firm of tailors who have taken their bespoke drapers beyond the limits of Mayfair to the good people of the countryside.

Their means? A Defender, of course. Three Land Rovers, to be precise. The Cad and the Dandy was the brainchild of James Sleater and Ian Meiers, who wanted to create an alternative, parallel business to the old-school stuffiness with which the Mayfair street is often associated.

Their business was founded in 2008 and today they have a turnover of millions.

'We are the biggest tailor on Savile Row,' explains James.

This seems particularly incredible as I am sitting in the passenger seat of his long wheelbase Defender. The Cad and the Dandy wanted to bring Savile Row tailoring to the masses. Their secret ingredient was a modified Land Rover that could get them out into the countryside.

They found a company in Léon, France, that could convert their Land Rover, nicknamed the Cad Wagon. They fitted a tailored canvas roof so that the duo could reach the parts other tailors simply couldn't reach, and the elevated roof meant customers could be measured up in the privacy of the vehicle at big country fairs.

'The car has been responsible for our success,' explains James with enthusiasm. 'It has probably shifted half a million pounds' worth of shirts and suits.'

For Meiers and Sleater, the Land Rover was like a mobile advertisement for their business. The Land Rover is just like Savile Row. It represents British heritage, age-old craft, detail, quality, all the virtues a young business needs to share with an unsuspecting public.

The duo would park their vehicle on Savile Row, and before long the orders were pouring in. Of course, like all good Land Rover aficionados, one was simply not enough for James. He had always wanted a Series II from 1981, his year of birth – 'it was nostalgia,' he admits.

But of course there was a problem – Mrs Sleater. Between every man and his Land Rover there is often an unwilling wife, and Sleater was no exception.

'How did you persuade her?' I ask.

'I told her I swapped it for a suit,' he smiles. He admits it's the same with their customers and their suits. Many of them have two credit cards and buy suits on different cards to pass their wives. And I thought it was only me.

'Underneath we are all kids,' admits James, who couldn't resist adding a third Land Rover to the Cad and the Dandy fleet.

'They get under your skin,' he shrugs. 'I have had motorbike riders and bus drivers stopping me on the road to chat about the car and get my details. I have sold shirts and suits at farm auctions.'

Soon we get down to business.

'I want you to make me a special jacket for me to wear while I drive a Land Rover.'

I walk to the back of the mobile-tailoring Land Rover and he gets his tape measure. It seems appropriate that I am being fitted for a new driving jacket in the back of a Land Rover on the most iconic sartorial street in the world.

HISTORY OF THE
LAND ROVER

PART IV

Back at Land Rover, the company had gone through a series of ownership changes that would have a seismic effect on the fortunes of the company.

The Germans had been in charge for four years by the time of the Range Rover's 1998 launch, but they disappeared two years later, following the sale of Land Rover to Ford in 2000.

The announcement came on Friday 17 March 2000. The price was $2.7 billion (£1.8 billion). It was a huge shock to the Land Rover workforce, who had anticipated that BMW would want to keep profitable Land Rover, even though it was getting rid of the vastly unprofitable Rover and MG brands (to the controversial Phoenix consortium led by ex-Land Rover boss, John Towers, for all of £1). Land Rover and its former parent company, Rover, were now separated for good.

Although Ford had its own 4×4s, they were not in the same class as Land Rovers. Ford knew that, too, which was one of the prime reasons why it wanted to buy into the brand. The boys behind the blue oval would cherish Land Rover's green oval, with all its associated heritage. They wanted to learn how Land Rover built Land Rovers.

Ford had the sense to allow the experts at Lode Lane to get on with their job of building the world's best all-terrain vehicles. It knew that one of Land Rover's greatest assets was its dedicated workforce; Ford provided investment, marketing, strategy and – most important – better quality control.

The break-up of the Rover Group was a sad day for the British motor industry. BMW's role as executioner was questionable, but the truth was that the death sentence had been passed more than 20 years earlier during the dark days of the 1970s by the unlamented British Leyland. Unreliability and defects had been an issue back then and it was still upsetting customers in 2000. The demise of the British motor industry was largely due to poor-quality products compared to those offered by foreign manufacturers. It was an issue that had never been adequately addressed, with the result that British marques that had once been household names had largely disappeared. Land Rover was luckier than most, but it too had suffered – particularly in overseas markets where manufacturers like Toyota could produce 4×4s that were often more reliable.

Arguably the biggest impact of the Ford takeover came in the larger-than-life presence of MD Matthew Taylor. He was a big man, used to making big decisions. Born in Uruguay, and fluent in Spanish and French, Taylor attained an economics degree from the London School of Economics and was a First Lieutenant in the Royal Navy, serving in the Falklands on HMS *Invincible*.

He joined Ford in 1985 and was part of the team that bought Land Rover from BMW in 2000. He became managing director of Land Rover in 2003 and was a hugely popular and charismatic leader of the company until he left in 2006.

These days Land Rover's current owners, Tata Motors, get much credit for their recent aggressive launch strategy, but they are following a path already well trodden by Taylor, who took control at a critical period in the company's history. Other companies, such as Porsche and Volkswagen, were attempting to muscle in on Range Rover territory, and there were plenty of doubters who wondered whether Ford was the company to take Land Rover forward. Taylor answered those critics by leading Land Rover into an exciting succession of new launches – yet he never forgot the importance of the Defender as the natural successor of the original Land Rover that had made all the other models possible.

Rather than worrying about the pretenders to Land Rover's throne, Taylor insisted on concentrating on the company's strengths. As he explained at the time, 'One of the challenges for us, working inside a big company like Ford, is that everyone says, "Why don't you look at what all these soft roaders are doing, because that's where the real sales growth is?" But we stand for something, and if all we do is copy somebody else, then we are losing what we stand for.'

With his strong and genuinely held views on the importance of Land Rover's rich heritage, Taylor was an instant hit with green oval enthusiasts. He was a genuine man of the people, and he knew most of his huge workforce by their Christian names. And they loved him for it.

The acid test for enthusiasts, though, was his views on the Defender. When he took over the reins in 2003, the veteran workhorse was selling in very small numbers: just 27,000 a year worldwide (fewer than the number of cars Ford sold in the UK in a month). To make matters worse, its old-fashioned design meant that it was time-consuming and hugely labour-intensive to build. There was no profit there, and a lesser man could have taken one look at the bottom line and consigned the iconic model to the scrapheap of history. But not Taylor, who, when talking of a future Defender replacement, said: 'I saw the essence of it was the simplicity and the capability, and these really need to come through very strongly. But we also need to give it something so that it doesn't become a Discovery. It has to have a unique appeal – Defender has to come through. The question is, how do you do it looking forward as opposed to looking backwards all the time?

'The Defender is an anchor, which is great in tough times because people keep buying them, but an anchor stops you from moving. It doesn't allow you to become relevant to a wider group of drivers. We can't sell it in the States, for example. And a lot of people shy away from Land Rover as a whole because they see the Defender as rather military.'

The Defender was safe under Taylor, but, like his predecessors – and successors, for that matter – the dilemma of replacing it with a new model that met stringent modern safety regulations in countries like the USA still hadn't been solved. (It still hadn't when production of the Defender ended in 2016, and the new Defender that replaces it won't appear until at least 2018 or 2019.)

Ford never got to launch a new Range Rover of its own. Like BMW before them, they had done most of the development work on its replacement, but Tata Motors were in charge when the fourth-generation Range Rover was launched in 2012. By now, the model had moved so far upmarket that it had little in common with its Defender stablemate, apart, perhaps, from the green oval badge.

Tata Motors is an Indian automotive company, based in Mumbai. Although most of Britain hadn't heard of Tata until its acquisition of Land Rover and Jaguar from Ford in 2008, it is in fact the eighteenth-largest motor-vehicle manufacturer in the world (by volume). It is part of the Tata Group, which also owns companies as diverse as British Steel and Tetley Tea. Tata Motors makes cars, trucks, vans and buses. Worldwide, it is the world's fourth-largest truck manufacturer and second-largest bus builder.

Tata's takeover of Jaguar Land Rover rocked the motor industry. On 27 March 2008, Tata paid Ford $2.3 billion for the two companies, which included the Gaydon HQ and Land Rover and Jaguar manufacturing facilities. It was a controversial move, particularly in India, where many pundits doubted the wisdom of taking on the loss-making company. Although Land Rover was profitable, sister company Jaguar most certainly was not. The stock markets also disliked the deal, which reflected heavily on Tata Motors' share prices.

The 'experts' said that Tata had no experience of luxury brands, nor the European and American markets where most of them were sold. And at first the detractors appeared to be right – by 2009, Tata Motors suffered an annual loss of over $500 million due to a slump in Land Rover and Jaguar sales in their traditional markets as recession bit hard. Yet by April 2012, Tata Motors was able to reveal that more than 80 per cent – or $1.7 billion – of its whopping $2.04 billion annual profits in the previous year had come from JLR.

To put this into perspective, when Tata Motors took over in 2008, Jaguar had annual sales figures of 15,700 cars and Land Rover had sold just under 50,000. But between 2009 and 2012, Tata Motors managed to sell 244,000 cars from Land Rover and Jaguar, despite most of the European countries still struggling in recession.

It was not hard to see where the new sales had come from. In the final quarter of 2011, China overtook the UK as JLR's biggest market, with 17.2 per cent of total sales compared to 16.5 per cent for the UK. Over the same period, JLR made a profit of £440 million – up 57 per cent on the same period the previous year.

Much of this recent success can also be attributed to the sales of the Range Rover Evoque, which sold 32,000 cars in that same quarter. The Evoque went into production in July 2011, with a fanfare of publicity helped in no small measure by the fact that much of its interior was, apparently, designed by Victoria Beckham (aka pop singer Posh Spice and the wife of former England football captain, David Beckham). She had been given the title 'creative design director' in July 2010 and had worked with Land Rover's design director, Gerry McGovern.

The importance to Land Rover of the Evoque/China/Brand Beckham alliance was made clear at the Beijing Motor Show, in April 2012, when Ms Beckham unveiled a new, bespoke, luxurious, hand-finished Range Rover Evoque Special Edition.

The launch of the Evoque might well have sounded the death knell for the Defender, in a move that took Land Rover away from its original utilitarian vehicle completely. But in fact it was very good news for Land Rover – and for the British economy, to which Land Rover and sister company Jaguar currently contribute over £3 billion a year. Currently, 75 per cent of production from JLR's factories in Solihull, Halewood and Castle Bromwich is exported, generating revenue in export markets alone of around £8 billion in 2010 (global retail sales increased by 19 per cent that same year).

Back in 2012, JLR pledged to spend around £1.5 billion annually on product creation, creating thousands of new jobs, investing £100 million in an advanced research facility at Warwick Manufacturing Group, and building a new factory in Wolverhampton to manufacture its own engines.

You can't help wondering what Land Rover creator Maurice Wilks would have made of the latest luxury offerings from Land Rover. Nothing could be further removed from his original 1948 masterpiece, but it is a sign of how the world – and the world order – is changing. Not always for the better, some would say, but remember that in Wilks' era the sun still hadn't set over the British Empire and Rover cars were symbols of luxury to Britain's senior managers. However, there's no doubt at all that Wilks would be very proud of the success of the Defender and the other Land Rover models it inspired.

The Range Rover Evoque was designed to appeal to urban buyers, taking the Land Rover marque a step further from its utilitarian, off-roading roots and firmly into the luxury market. Was this the end of the Defender?

CHAPTER SEVEN

CRUISIN' FOR A BRUISIN'

Hidden behind an industrial estate in Essex is Foley Land Rover, a three-generational Land Rover dealership. Peter Foley Senior started the business, and his two sons, Paul and Stuart Foley, now run it in Essex, while Paul's son Nicholas runs a Land Rover business in Kenya.

Over the years Foley has converted Land Rovers into everything from fire trucks and ambulances to police cars and gun wagons, but they are most famous for their expedition vehicles.

The business was born during the Vietnam War when wealthy Americans sent their children to Britain to escape the draft. These adventurous young Yanks saw the world on their doorstep; after all, the African continent was just a hop and a skip away. 'These US kids wanted to explore,' Peter comments, and went on to explain that their parents would send a telex with instructions to kit out the vehicle to full expedition spec. The youngsters would drive them overland to Cape Town, at which point Peter was told to sell the vehicle, take out whatever costs had been incurred and keep the profit. The vehicles would then be overhauled, upgraded and sold on for a tidy profit in South Africa. The world of Expedition Land Rovers was born.

Perhaps Foley's biggest coup came in 1992, though, when they got a call from the Angolan Police. 'They wanted us to build them 650 Land Rover Police cars,' marvelled Peter. It was a tall order.

'Land Rover didn't want anything to do with it,' he explained, 'they simply couldn't do the order in time.'

And here lies one of the quirks of Land Rover; the company had created their business but it was their intransigence that created a market for others to provide what they couldn't.

'It was a massive order,' remembers Peter. 'We were excited but we were nervous as to whether we could deliver.'

They had two months.

Foley agreed with the Angolan Police that they would divide it into two batches of 325 vehicles. Every one of them needed to be left-hand drive. Where could they find that many vehicles? The answer was, of course, the military. Research led them to Germany, where the British Army had more than 500 left-hand-drive Land Rovers that were superfluous to their needs. The Army had been struggling to sell them as each one came equipped with a trailer. Foley agreed to buy the lot, trailers and all. The deal was signed. Now they had to convert them.

Their tiny yard was too small for the job so they rented another, hired 20 men and ran the workshop 24 hours a day, 7 days a week.

Part of the deal was that the vehicles could be any Land Rover model, but they needed new engines. The Foleys put in an order with Land Rover for 350 brand-new engines. They signed the paperwork but they missed the small print. Although Land Rover accepted the order they insisted on delivering all 350 engines together … in six months' time. The deal with Angola relied on their delivery in two months.

'Land Rover shafted us,' smiled Foley senior, 'and you can quote me on that.'

Their contingency was to put in an order with Land Rover directly for 100 brand-new vehicles to make up for the deficit.

'Incredibly, Land Rover still weren't interested,' he marvelled. 'The order wasn't worth their while, it was only after we agreed to boost it to 105 vehicles, bringing the bill to just over a million pounds, that they agreed.'

But there was another problem. The vehicles would be delivered from Land Rover directly to the harbour ready for shipping to West Africa.

'We had a team of men down on the tarmac fixing jerry cans, light guards and Angola Police stickers as they were being loaded,' Foley senior explained.

They were flying by the seat of their pants. It was a massive job.

'We thought it was the job of our lives. We all bought new cars,' reminisced Foley. But things soon changed. Foley was able to deliver 325 vehicles on time but then the official who had drafted the order was killed and the rest of the order was cancelled. The profit lay in the second batch of vehicles, which were no longer needed.

The Foleys were left with hundreds of trailers and only just broke even.

'It was fun, though,' smiled Foley senior.

It was during the Balkans conflict that Foley hit upon another conversion idea. A friend at ITN had got in touch to ask if he could build an armoured bulletproof Land Rover for ITN journalists covering the conflict. With no experience whatsoever, Foley began to draw up plans for his modified vehicle. He presented his plans. It wouldn't be cheap, but ITN agreed and they built the vehicle.

It was driven to Bosnia, where it joined an assortment of vehicles belonging to other news agencies on the border, where they were stopped by an overzealous Bosnian border security guard. These were lawless times and the guard took it upon himself to use the assortment of vehicles for target practice. The various journalists looked on in astonishment as he opened fire on their vehicles to see how 'bulletproof' they really were.

The Foley vehicle was the only one to stand up to the barrage of bullets. Not one of them pierced the skin – and the calls began. NBC, ABC … all the news networks wanted a Foley armour-plated Land Rover.

Ever the businessman, Foley decided to build a fleet of them and to base them in the Balkans ready to be leased by whichever news organisation would stump up the cash. 'One vehicle brought in £200,000 in car hire alone,' he marvelled.

His greatest moment, though, was when Channel 4 hired one of their armoured vehicles. They were covering a conflict. They were in a convoy on a mountain pass when the car struck the side and rolled off the mountain. The only reason the four men survived was due to the engineering of the Foley Land Rover. 'I've still got the letter of thanks,' he smiled, 'it was the best thing I've ever done.'

Perhaps the strangest vehicle he has ever adapted was in 1980 when he got a call from the president of Zaire.

The story goes that a visiting US government official had met with the president of Zaire and in the middle of their meeting the government official had been interrupted by one of his colleagues with 'there is an important call for you, sir', at which point he was handed a phone. The president of Zaire was amazed. How, he wondered, could he receive a call in the middle of the African bush? This was long before any kind of mobile communication was readily available. The US official had been using a link to a giant dish on a warship offshore. If the USA had a mobile phone in 1980, then so too would the president of Zaire.

Foley was instructed to make one of the world's first truly portable phones aboard a Land Rover. To do this he needed to mount a £250,000 satellite dish on the back of a Land Rover. Remember, this was the 1980s. A quarter of a million pounds for the dish alone?

The problem was that the metal of the Land Rover would affect the efficacy of the dish, so the vehicle had to be made out of carbon fibre. A desk with two permanent telecommunication officers was mounted in the back and the president of Zaire arguably had the first and the most expensive mobile phone in the world. And it all happened in a Land Rover. We shouldn't be surprised.

Foley Land Rovers have been exported all around the world. They were commissioned by the Russian oil industry to make Land Rovers that could be effortlessly lifted by a helicopter. They added some lifting brackets, allowing a strop to be lowered and clipped to the vehicle, and away they could fly.

'We made one vehicle for a potash mine in Cleveland. The vehicle would be used to ferry miners to the depths of the Earth. While the vehicle was largely unmodified, the expertise lay in the fact that the whole thing had to be dismantled and lowered down the deep mine shaft in thousands of pieces before being reassembled many miles below. It was quite scary to watch the axle being lowered into the abyss,' recalls Foley.

'Have you ever made a car knowingly or unknowingly for a mercenary?' I ask. Their connections with Africa and their expertise in tough environments must have attracted the attention of the underworld.

'No,' he replies resolutely. 'The only time we made a vehicle under suspicious circumstances was when we were asked to cut a huge circle in the roof of a Land Rover. We asked the client why and he answered matter-of-factly that he was going to mount a machine gun on the roof.'

'Where was this?' I ask. 'Angola?'

'No. Basildon,' he smiled.

The bread and butter of the Foley Land Rover lay in the overland expedition vehicles.

'We would get one order a week,' he explains. 'It would be a young couple in their late 20s from London, not yet married, no children, wanting to take six months out together to explore the world.'

The London to Cape Town route was the golden journey. The problem was that none of these couples ever considered what they would do at the end of the trip. They would spend all this money on a Land Rover without planning how they were going to sell it later. Once again, Foley's business mind kicked in and he started to rent vehicles for overland journeys.

Business boomed until geo-politics shut down the route – Libya, Syria, Egypt, Sudan, Somalia. It became too risky and, more often than not, impossible to do the journey. It became harder and harder to get the export document to travel overseas with the vehicles, and, before long, one enquiry a week had become one a month.

Today their yard is still bustling with business, with dozens of Land Rovers in various states of repair or disrepair. Half a dozen old army Land Rover ambulances were awaiting conversion into gun carriages for shoots when I visited, while a handful of cars were being upgraded for their loyal owners.

'We often get people dropping off a car worth less than the cost of the changes or repairs,' marvels Foley. 'We get given an old Land Rover worth ten grand with instructions to do modifications and upgrades up to £20,000.'

'Why are people willing to spend so much on something worth so little?' I ask.

'Because a Land Rover is a part of the family, you never get rid of it. Ageless, classless, a Land Rover is like a comfy pair of shoes,' he explains. 'We had one client who asked us to sell an old Land Rover of his for £20,000. We had looked after the car for years and estimated he had spent more than £70,000 on it in its lifetime.'

People really love their cars.

Foleys have adapted numerous cars for a variety of purposes, military and domestic. They have made coffee-machine Land Rovers and hearse Land Rovers, they have shipped cars to St

Helena and to the Falklands, and have made dozens of cars for the Middle East.

'The Saudi Arabians have asked us to make specially adapted "Falcon" vehicles for falconry work. The cars have special rails for the birds, and pop-up seats. One of them got sent back after they decided the rail wasn't comfortable enough for the birds to sit on! We even adapted one Land Rover with a fountain in the back from which people could program their drink to be dispensed.'

Sitting in the yard was one very distinctive vehicle. It was one of the last Defenders ever produced, a limited edition Heritage HUE in mint green. The client had instructed Foley to take the hard top off and replace it with a soft top. The famous iconic vents that had long stopped being produced had been returned for an authentic vintage look, but most surprisingly a beautiful long tube painted in the same colours as the car had been fitted along the body. This was to hold a vintage Indian parasol that would be erected on the back of the car while the owner and his wife sipped sundowners from the back of the vehicle. It was off to India: a throwback to the colonial era when the Land Rover was once the king (or queen) of the roads.

A whiteboard in the office had a long list of current Foley adaptations, and alongside an equally long list of names and vehicle types was one familiar name: the Duke of Edinburgh.

CHAPTER EIGHT

LANDED ROVER

When the Duchess of Cambridge made her front cover debut for *Vogue*, the British fashion bible, the press highlighted the fact that there was a Land Rover Defender in one of the magazine's photos. I eagerly bought a copy of the magazine, keen to see what kind of Defender a future queen had chosen.

I scanned each photograph carefully but I couldn't see a Defender anywhere. I must have been missing something, so I looked again. Still nothing. It was only on a third study of the photographs that I noticed the distinct lines of the car.

Blink and you'd miss it. Only the rear end of the car with its spare wheel was visible in the far left of a photograph of the Duchess, the rest of the vehicle was obscured by a wall. Any other vehicle would have disappeared in the shot. It would have been almost impossible to identify any other marque of car, but the Defender is identifiable by its lines.

Of course, the Duchess of Cambridge is far from the first Royal
to own a Land Rover. Indeed, it was her great-grandfather-in-law
who became the first member of the royal family to drive this
most British of cars. The Queen's father, King George VI, was
presented with the 100th production Land Rover. As a marketing
ploy, it was perfect.

The Land Rover was marketed as the go-anywhere vehicle for
outdoorsmen and farmers, but by including the Windsors the
Land Rover also cemented its credentials as the 'classless' car. A
vehicle that was accepted anywhere.

In 1951 the then Princess Elizabeth was pictured standing in
an open-top Land Rover as she watched her father presenting the
King's Colour to the Royal Air Force in London's Hyde Park. The
Queen took delivery of her first Land Rover shortly before
coming to the throne in 1952 and she has used them ever since.
Of course, the Queen is not required by law to possess a driver's
licence. She learned to drive in 1945 when she was a member of
the Auxiliary Territorial Service (ATS), where she trained as a
mechanic and military truck driver, both rather useful for the
temperamental tendencies of the Land Rover.

Land Rover supplied the first bespoke 'state revue' car for a
six-month, 44,000-mile Royal Tour of the Commonwealth in
1953. It had an elevated viewing area at the rear so the Queen and
the Duke of Edinburgh could easily be seen. The vehicle was
known as 'State IV' and was painted in the familiar royal colour,
'claret'.

Like all state vehicles for use by the monarch, it was not
required to be registered. The vehicle was part of a fleet that
accompanied the royal couple around the world over a route

from London to New Zealand and Australia, then on to Ceylon (now Sri Lanka), Aden (Yemen) and Africa, before returning to Europe through Gibraltar.

When it was not practical to travel by road, the Land Rovers were transported by special air freighters. The varying road conditions and temperatures were a test of the vehicles' resilience. The Australian army provided a 'royal car company' of seven officers who were all given three months' special training in Land Rovers and ceremonial speeds.

Another Royal Revue vehicle was introduced in 1958 and is known as 'State II', also finished in claret with a dark blue leather interior. Land Rover even supplied their own dedicated Land Rover driver, Frank Spalding. The vehicle only racked up 13,000 miles in its 54-year history.

In 1973 a Series III was created for the Queen with a number of regal modifications, including a 'traffic light' system which she could use from the rear to tell the driver when she wanted to stop, slow down or continue the journey.

Land Rover is the only car manufacturer to hold all three Royal Warrants from Her Majesty the Queen, His Royal Highness The Duke of Edinburgh and His Royal Highness The Prince of Wales; the first was granted in 1951, a year before the Queen ascended the throne.

It is difficult to find confirmation of which members of the royal family drive Defenders today, but it is a well-known fact that Sandringham, Balmoral, Highgrove and Anmer Hall all have Defenders for the estate. This being the case, it can be reasonably assumed that most of the royals will have taken to the steering wheel of a Series or a Defender at some stage in their lives.

Her Majesty the Queen is often seen driving around her estate at Sandringham, West Norfolk, in a bronze green 110 Defender (manual). David Viscount Linley (the son of Princess Margaret) has a blue Series III. The Duke and Duchess of Cambridge drive a Range Rover Sport. The late Queen Mother was a Land Rover fan. Prince Charles is also a frequent driver of the Defender, often using them at polo matches, and his former late wife, Princess Diana, was also a fan; there is a famous photograph of her watching the Grand National from the bonnet of a Land Rover in 1982, and she reportedly had her own Defender at Sandringham.

But it is the Queen who has the most well-documented love affair with the Land Rover. My favourite story about Her Majesty and her Land Rovers involves King Abdullah of Saudi Arabia.

Abdullah, then Crown Prince of Saudi Arabia, was visiting Balmoral for lunch in 1998. Former Saudi ambassador Sherard Cowper-Coles told the incredible story of the encounter of the two monarchs.

'You are not supposed to repeat what the Queen says in private conversations. But the story she told me on that occasion was one that I was later to hear from its subject – Crown Prince Abdullah of Saudi Arabia – and it is too funny not to repeat. Five years earlier, in September 1998, Abdullah had been invited up to Balmoral for lunch with the Queen. Following his brother King Fahd's stroke in 1995, Abdullah was already the de facto ruler of Saudi Arabia. After lunch, the Queen had asked her royal guest whether he would like a tour of the estate. Prompted by his foreign minister, the urbane Prince Saud, an initially hesitant Abdullah agreed. The royal Land Rover Defenders were drawn up at the front of the castle. As instructed, the Crown Prince climbed into the front seat of the Land Rover, with his interpreter in the seat behind. To his surprise, the Queen climbed into the driver's seat, turned the ignition and drove off. Women are not – yet – allowed to drive in Saudi Arabia, and Abdullah was not used to being driven by a woman, let alone the Queen. His nervousness only increased as the Queen accelerated the Land Rover along the narrow Scottish estate roads, talking all the time. Through his interpreter, the Crown Prince implored the Queen to slow down and concentrate on the road ahead.'

That the ruler of Saudi Arabia had not only been shown up by Her Majesty, but that it had been aboard a Land Rover, is a testament to these two iconic beacons of Britishness. Land Rover, after all, has held the Royal Appointment since 1948.

One beloved Land Rover that belonged to the Queen was a 1983 110 with a rich green leather interior and a special radio with a hotline to the Home Office. She eventually sold it in 2001, having put 43,000 miles on the clock, averaging 2000 miles a year on the Sandringham estate. Not bad going in a bouncy, noisy Defender.

In 1974 Land Rover built the first Range Rover Royal Ceremonial Vehicle, known as State I. Range Rover had only recently been introduced and Land Rover felt it was a more state-like vehicle for Her Majesty.

State I was delivered in 1974. With just three doors, it was also roofless. Inside the rear compartment were foldaway seats which could be pulled out as supports when the royal party were standing. Over the bulkhead was a lectern and two umbrellas concealed into the vehicle itself to protect the monarch against the inclement British weather. Interestingly, the vehicle was modified to have a maximum speed of 20mph.

As the Queen and her consort have got older, they, like many, have sought a little more comfort in Land Rover's more luxurious vehicle, the Range Rover. When Michelle and Barack Obama recently visited the UK, they were met by the Royals at Windsor. The Duke of Edinburgh, aged 91, leapt into the driver's seat of the Range Rover next to his wife, the Queen, with the Obamas sitting rather nervously in the back. That must rate as one of the most precious cargoes a Range Rover has ever had.

It is no surprise that Prince William chose to collect his wife and new son from St Mary's Lindo Wing in a Range Rover. I used a Defender to pick up my son Ludo from the same place.

Of course, the love affair with the Land Rover does not end amongst royalty with the British royal family. This is the chapter in which I design a Land Rover Defender for a princess. And given that Land Rover ceased production of the Defender in early 2016 and there aren't that many princesses around in the market for a Landy, this was quite a feat.

Isn't it funny how life can sometimes turn full circle? I love how it has a way of turning back on itself. Friends from the past re-emerge on the most unexpected occasions.

Several years ago I was visiting my sister in Dubai. She moved there nearly 15 years ago and she hasn't looked back. I was between filming assignments in Australia and Ethiopia and my wife Marina agreed to meet me halfway in Dubai with our then young son, Ludo, where we spent several days exploring the desert and the beaches. Midway through the trip I was flicking through the national newspaper when I noticed a photograph of someone very familiar. It was my friend Haya.

Haya had turned up at my boarding school, Bryanston, late in our school years. We were 17 and most of us had been at the school from the age of 13, but Haya had come for the sixth form. Picture the scene. It was the first day of term. The new boys and girls sat nervously in assembly, while we looked on suspiciously at our new schoolmates. In the strangely competitive world of childhood friendship, where relationships are charged with adolescent nuance, we sat in our separate tribes.

It was the headmaster's opportunity to welcome us all back after the long summer break. Formalities and welcome speeches over, it fell to a history teacher to deliver the morning speech. He decided to talk on the subject of peace and the Middle East. 'King Hussein has destroyed the peace process,' he began. Without hesitation, Haya stood up, making sure everyone noticed, and she walked out of the theatre. It was an effortless display of respectful defiance.

Perhaps it was a case of deliberate provocation, maybe it was a case of the left hand failing to talk to the right, or possibly it was just bad luck, but the young girl who stormed out of the room was none other than Princess Haya Bint Al Hussein, youngest daughter of King Hussein. She wasn't going to stay and listen to someone slurring her father, and I admired her resolution, so we became friends.

There was no pomp or ceremony with Haya. She didn't flounce around in a tiara with a corgi at her feet. She was just a regular girl with an extraordinary father. And she received no special treatment nor private security. At school, Haya was just one of us.

Pretty, clever and sporty, she was horse mad. I remember her walking around with weights attached to her ankles as she trained for dressage. 'I am going to compete at the Olympics,' she had told me early on. This was a girl who certainly had big goals, but then again, when your father is King of Jordan maybe you are destined for greatness. True to form, after we left school, Haya went on to compete at the Olympic Games in Athens in 2004.

Like many old childhood friends, I had lost track of Haya until I noticed her face peering out from the national paper in Dubai. Next to her in the photograph was a man described as her husband. Of course, being Haya, this was no ordinary man, this was His Royal Highness Sheikh Mohammed, ruler of Dubai and now Mr Haya Hussein. A quick search online and a couple of phone calls, and Marina and I found ourselves invited to the Royal Palace.

Now this in itself creates its own problems when you are midway through two expeditions and you have flown in wearing T-shirt, shorts and flip-flops. But a quick visit to the mall and we were ready for our date with royalty.

Haya's father, King Hussein, passed away in 1999, as the longest-serving head of state in the world. It was a huge funeral, attracting most heads of state. One memorable photograph from his funeral cortège showed a dozen Series Land Rovers – roofs, doors and front screens all removed. It was a breathtaking photograph.

His Majesty King Hussein bin Talal was the father of modern Jordan: a leader who helped guide his country through strife and turmoil to become a relative oasis of peace, stability and moderation in the Middle East. For Jordanians, he represented openness, tolerance and compassion. Of great significance to

Muslims across the globe, the late King Hussein was also the fortieth-generation direct descendant of the Prophet Muhammad.

After completing his elementary education in Amman, he was later schooled at Harrow School in England. He received his military education at the Royal Military Academy Sandhurst, and it was here that his passion for the Land Rover was born.

King Hussein's life was narrowly saved by a medal he had been given by his grandfather after an assassin's bullet was stopped by it. His grandfather, sadly, died in front of him.

King Hussein transformed Jordan, raising the standard of living for his people by building an economic and industrial infrastructure. Throughout his 47-year reign King Hussein struggled to promote peace in the Middle East, though. After the 1967 Arab–Israeli war he was instrumental in drafting UNSC Resolution 242, which called on Israel to withdraw from all the Arab lands it occupied in the 1967 war in exchange for peace. This resolution has served as the benchmark for all subsequent peace negotiations.

While working towards Arab–Israeli peace, King Hussein also worked to resolve disputes between Arab states. During the 1990–91 Gulf Crisis, he exerted vigorous efforts to effect a peaceful Iraqi withdrawal and restore the sovereignty of Kuwait. He persevered in his pursuit of genuine Arab reconciliation, wherever a conflict arose between neighbours or within a country, such as his mediation in the Yemeni Civil War. King Hussein's commitment to democracy, civil liberties and human rights helped pave the way in making Jordan a model state for the region. But above all, His Majesty loved Land Rovers. In short, he was a pretty cool man.

I called Haya to ask about her family connection to the Land Rover.

'My father always had them,' she replied, 'ever since he was at Sandhurst we had them in Jordan.'

A quick trawl through the Land Rover archive showed dozens of photographs of a young King Hussein in Series Is, IIs and IIIs. And the Royal Household in Jordan is still brimming with old models.

Although you can find everything from a beaten up 1970s Series IIA to a fully optioned Range Rover Vogue in pretty much every far-flung corner of the planet, Land Rover's largest markets are the UK, the USA, China, Italy, Germany, Russia and MENA, accounting for over 70 per cent of total retail sales volumes. There is a Land Rover dealer in every single one of the fifty United States of America, including Alaska and Hawaii. One of the first-production Range Rover Evoques was driven in the States, coast to coast, to introduce it to potential customers. But the marque was also important in the Middle East, and it is fair to say that Land Rovers helped shape the Middle East and secure its future. The region's sheikhs and rulers were swift to appreciate their Land Rovers' unprecedented ability to travel to any corner of their territory, no matter how remote.

It was also Land Rovers that helped to discover the oil wealth that underpins the region. Seismic surveyor Edward Cox travelled the length of the UAE studying oil-bearing rock formations, venturing deep into the wadis, prospecting far into the desert in search of likely structures. Their surveying journeys took the team from Abu Dhabi, inland to Liwa, all the way north to Umm al-Qaiwain and Ras al-Khaimah, across the Creek in Dubai and up into the mountains around Hatta. There was no part of the country they could not eventually reach in a Land Rover, and the wheels of these vehicles were often the first to make tracks in the sand in these places.

And where Land Rovers crossed deserts and reached villages once accessible only by camel, so came community and trade. Tracks became roads, oil was discovered in abundance and the nations of the Middle East grew in prosperity. Little wonder then that the region remains a favourite market for Land Rover.

'I don't suppose you have a Land Rover Defender?' I asked Haya.

'No, but I'm about to,' she replied.

And so it was that I was dispatched to Yorkshire by command of Her Royal Highness to choose and design a Defender suitable for a princess, her children and her dogs to explore the deserts of the Arabian Peninsula.

Haya had seen a photograph of the Land Rover limited edition SVX. This is a short wheelbase convertible with black roll bars. To be honest I had also wanted one. She has good taste, does our Haya. She had decided she wanted something similar to drive around the desert and had been advised that the best company for the job was Twisted, based in Thirsk. So I found myself on the road once again travelling to God's Own Country to make a car fit for a princess.

Twisted had purchased one of the last great orders of Defenders from Land Rover before they halted production, 240 to be precise.

Charlie Fawcett started the business in 2001 from his garage. Today they are one of the largest providers of modified Land Rover Defenders. The workshop was a hive of activity when I arrived, as engineers and mechanics worked on half a dozen Defenders. One car had been stripped back to just her chassis.

'What are you making here, Rob?' asked Charlie.

'This is a Spectre,' he smiled. 'We had a request from the Middle East to make them an exact replica of the Defender used in the James Bond film, *Spectre*.'

He handed me a magazine with a handful of photographs of the car on set. In one of them the car is seen launching itself into the air. Incredibly, these few screen grabs from a Hollywood film were all that they could work from to transform a factory-fresh Defender into something worthy of 007.

'We made one white left-hand-drive long wheelbase Defender for a customer in Ibiza,' he says. 'It took six months to build. We sent it out and he decided he didn't want it so he sent the car back.'

That's a £100,000 Defender.

'We had another customer who bought it from us but he wanted it to be silver, right-hand drive. We spent another six weeks converting it, then we delivered it to the customer and his wife went ballistic. She didn't want the thing. It came back a second time.

'Another customer then wanted to buy it but wanted it returned to left-hand drive,' he smiles. They drew the line there.

He showed me one Defender that had had nearly £170,000-worth of work done to it over the years. It had been fitted with three satellite phones and had been used in Africa.

Despite these hiccups, Twisted runs a successful Land Rover business and Charlie certainly has an eye for branding and marketing. As a marketing stunt he signed up three of his vehicles to take part in the Gumball Rally. He also lent one Defender to MTV Brazil and the other, in a stroke of marketing genius, to Tony Hawk, the world's top skateboarder.

They drove the Defenders from Copenhagen to Monaco.

'It was fun,' smiled Charlie, 'crowds gathered across Europe to watch the crazy assortment of vehicles and their drivers.'

Charlie had also managed to buy one of the largest final orders of Defenders before they stopped.

'I put in an order for 240,' he explained. That was nearly £9 million-worth of Land Rover. The order was accepted and signed but then a few days later he got a call from the company. They would no longer honour their agreement. It was too big, they argued.

I have heard time and time again how Land Rover frequently turned down orders, often because they simply couldn't keep up with demand. I still find it incredible that one of the most famous car manufacturers in the world simply couldn't expand the factory line.

'The problem with Defenders,' explained Charlie, 'is that they charged too little. These were handmade cars,' he reminded me.

The dispute became a legal wrangle and Charlie won.

'Suddenly I had to work out not only how I was going to pay for the lot, but also where I was going to store them all.'

In the courtyard outside their warehouse on an industrial estate are dozens of gleaming new Defenders. It was quite a sight.

Now we turned our attention to the real task in hand. I had a royal car to design. We sat in the studio surrounded by swatches of cloth and photographs of various Defenders.

'What would a princess want from a car?' I had wondered. I liked the idea of making her a modern-day Royal Revue car. Similar to the ones made for Her Majesty and the Duke of Edinburgh during their early overseas tours. I had seen dozens of Series Royal Revue cars, painted in a deep blue or purple with white leather seats, royal crest on the door and a Union flag flying from a mast. I liked the idea of creating a modern-day Arabian version.

She had to be convertible. I liked the idea of a sandy-coloured vehicle in a matt or satin with the royal household crest discreetly on the door and white leather seats elevated at the back like a safari vehicle so the good people of the United Arab Emirates could see her. Oh, and a bombproof chassis. I threw that last one in as an attempt to address safety and security. And a coffee machine ... because I've always wanted one in my car. Oh yes, and I stole the vintage umbrella idea from the Foley Defender. This one would have little parasol holders above each seat into which would be slotted beautiful vintage silk parasols to protect the royal family from the harsh sun.

Easy. Job's a good 'un.

The reality was that Haya's needs were a little more wholesome. She needed something big enough for her kids and dogs in which she could travel discreetly. There was another problem; her private security team (she had that since school) were a little more rigid in their suggestions. Although Haya had wanted a convertible, they were more keen on a bulletproof beast with internal roll cage for extra protection.

Killjoys. They are like the health and safety board of the wealthy. Always trying to stop them having fun 'for their own protection'.

I decided that the long wheelbase with double cab and pick up would be the best template to start with.

'What about the dogs?' asked Mark worriedly. 'Would you leave your dogs out in the pick up?' He had a point. 'She wants to take her dogs with her, she's not going to want to leave them outside under the burning sun in the pick up,' he pointed out quite reasonably.

Haya had seen a picture of the SVX. It was one of the very few convertible Defenders ever made by Land Rover, so I suggested stripping off the whole roof.

'The Defender is going to Dubai,' I reasoned. 'It never rains in Dubai, let's strip off the top and replace it with a sun canopy that we can extend to incorporate the pick up. We can include hoops to tie the leads so they won't jump out, and even have a small built-in water dispenser for hydration.'

Next we had to choose a trim. The leather and suede favoured by Twisted felt too stuffy for a dune-bashing princess driving a Defender. A rugged canvas seemed a better option, especially given the presence of dogs and children, who have the ability to make a brand-new car look like a twenty-year-old wreck within an hour. How do children do it? My wife's Discovery looks like there has been some kind of fight or explosion. Every crease, corner and fold is filled with a layer of crumbs. There are wrappers strewn on the floor and chocolate fingerprints across the seats. Dog hair has ingrained itself into the seats alongside the crumbs, and bits of broken toy fill every cup holder and cubby hole. There are old parking tickets and dog leads and shopping bags and half-eaten granola bars and crisp packets and … Aarrrgh! It drives me crazy. 'You try getting two children to school on time and then walking the dogs and try to keep the car clean,' scowls my wife when she sees my disdain.

Haya, princess or no princess, like all mothers will deal with the reality of the above, too. Canvas seats, I reasoned, are easily cleaned.

Next, the colour. I had been particularly taken with Twisted's most iconic vehicle – their Bahama gold retro. It is an awesome-looking car. It's the only Land Rover I've seen in London that made me double back on myself to take a closer look.

I sent Haya a photograph. 'No way. I'll look like a sunflower driving through the desert. Everyone will laugh at me,' she replied. I chose it anyway.

And there we had it. I had designed my first royal car. I wondered whether to ask Haya for a Royal Warrant.

CHAPTER NINE

DEFENDER OF THE LAND

The arrival of the Series I Land Rover had a profound effect on Britain's agriculture. The Land Rover is as much a fixture of Britain's farming community as are the farming folk themselves. Despite the demise of the Defender and the slow creep of the Toyota Hilux, you'd be hard pushed to visit a farm in the British Isles that doesn't have a Land Rover somewhere.

The 1947 Agriculture Act was aimed at making Britain self-sufficient in food and encouraged farmers to be more efficient and productive by mechanising their industry. This was a major influence on the Wilks brothers' decision to produce a 4×4 aimed at farmers. They hadn't focused the development on the military because they knew the British government was already working on its own military 4×4 – the vehicle which would become the Austin Gipsy.

The winter of 1946–7 saw record snowfall, followed by record floods, during which time Maurice Wilks' Jeep on Anglesey had provided invaluable support. Wilks knew that a similar, hard-working vehicle that could endure such conditions and terrain would be popular amongst famers. Right from the offset, early photographs show the centre-steer prototype pulling a plough, a trailer loaded with milk churns and a seed drill, and using its power take-off (PTO) to power a saw bench – all tasks that would appeal to the farmer.

After its debut at the Amsterdam Motor Show in 1948, the next public appearances for the Land Rover were all at agricultural shows in the UK: the Royal Ulster Show, Belfast, Bath & West Show, Cardiff, Highland Show, Inverness, and the Royal Show, York. No region was left untouched. Land Rover unleashed a ferocious campaign to get farmers to buy their new vehicle.

On Tuesday 20 April 1948, the following story appeared in *The Times*:

NEW VEHICLE FOR AGRICULTURE

A special vehicle designed for agriculture and industrial work is to be made at the rate of 200 a week by the Rover Company in Birmingham. Called the Land-Rover, it bears a strong resemblance to the Jeep and is designed to be equally at home on main roads and cross-country.

The *Farmers Weekly* followed with its opinion of the Land-Rover: 'Under severe testing it has been almost impossible to find going or gradients where it loses traction or stability.'

On 30 June 1948, the UK government's Overseas Food Development Corporation (responsible for a groundnuts scheme in East Africa) placed an order of 500 of the new Land-Rovers, to be shipped to the colonies. At the same time, Rover launched an advertising campaign, featuring a farmer driving a Land Rover and towing a trailer, with this caption: 'EVERY FARMER will appreciate the value of this tough little go-anywhere vehicle. Its low-geared four-wheel drive takes it over the roughest going, yet it is a fast and economical vehicle on the road. By using the power take-off it becomes a mobile power unity for rick-building, root cutting and a score of other jobs.'

Early Land-Rover reviews echoed Land-Rover's design brief, and in particular the intention that it be used as a farmer's work and transport vehicle.

In 1948 *Autocar* magazine wrote:

'Land-Rover is a mobile power station, which will tow or do a variety of useful work on the land over rough ground. It can drive a large circular saw and cut up timber for firewood. It can be used with trailers to transport loads over ploughed fields or other hard-going terrain. As a mobile power-source it takes the power to the job and, with the power take-off, it can be harnessed to drive a threshing machine, an elevator or a chaff-cutter, draw a plough, and most other farm implements.'

The Motor Magazine agreed: 'There is no doubt that, in its design, the Land-Rover Company has applied a wide knowledge and experience not only of vehicle manufacture but of agricultural and industrial requirements.' Additionally, they repeated Land-Rover's primary claims that this new vehicle was 'a portable source of power, and an alternative to the light tractor'. Most of this was later realised to lack both realism and common sense!

By July 1948 practically every farmer in Britain and the colonies wanted a Land-Rover, and the company had already received

8000 orders – enough to keep the production lines busy for at least a year. At this stage the directors decided to step up production from 100 to 500 vehicles a week, to try to cope with demand, which was far outstripping supply.

By the 1970s British farms favoured the Series I, II and IIA Land Rovers as workhorses on their land. Of course, they often worked in tandem alongside bigger and more dedicated farm machinery. But despite their popularity, the cars were not without their critics. The ubiquitous rusting and weak engine were despised by farmers, but the ease of repair did lead to their longevity, which made them worthwhile.

The early Land Rovers frequently had to be modified by farmers to improve the power and efficiency of their diesel engines, and as a consequence they became unpopular in farming. By 1985, however, things had begun to change. The new Land Rover reversed this sales trend and farmers started to buy the 90 and 110 Land Rovers, with much-improved diesel engines, which eventually became the Defender range.

Land Rovers have always been present to support tractors on farms and they could, of course, take over some of the lighter and potentially faster power take-off and linkage work, if these features were now available. Realising this to be a fact – and spotting a potential market – two Lancashire-based UK entrepreneurs found the then new 90 and 110 models to be much worthier expressions of earlier Land Rover design thinking than anything from inside Land Rover Ltd and its Special Products Division. So they decided to design their own version of the Land Rover which they named the Agrover.

The Agrover was seen as a way of combining the tasks of the Land Rover and the tractor. In a farming context, early Land Rovers were 4×4 pick-up trucks. As Land Rovers became more sophisticated, with the development of the Freelander, Discovery and Range Rovers, Land Rover's focus seemed to centre on aesthetics and design over practicality as a working utilitarian vehicle.

Land Rover design, including that of the Defender, had centred on passenger-carrying qualities and abilities rather than its potential for farm work, and the Agrover helped return the Land Rover to its original purpose.

It is fair to say that the Land Rover transformed the face of British agriculture, and the vehicle is still a beacon of British farming. You'd be hard pressed to visit a rural community without catching sight of a Defender held together with baler twine and laden with farming supplies.

Land Rovers have a way of teleporting you to another world. I mean that. Not in an actually 'teleporting, beam me up, Scotty' kind of way but in their ability to deliver you to a hidden world of life or work beyond the tarmac. We are so ingrained in the idea of keeping to a boundary that we rarely explore beyond the well-beaten path. Whether we are in a vehicle, on a bike or on foot, most of us tend to stick to the trail. It's part herd mentality and part risk aversion.

For me, the arrival of a Land Rover is the beginning of an adventure, and once more I found myself aboard a Landy in Scotland, in Inverness to be precise, on the edge of Loch Ness. I was a passenger in a long wheelbase Defender with double cab and a pick up on my way to visit a project in the Highlands of

Scotland that could change the very fabric of our environment and our land-management policy.

For half an hour we meandered through the moors, long ago stripped of their trees, the denuded valleys holding a haunting beauty that is quite mesmerising. Finally, though, we left the tarmac and headed off-road and into the Alladale Estate.

I first met the conservationist Paul Lister about ten years ago. We had been introduced by mutual friends at his 23,000-acre estate. Lister had a vision: he wanted to re-wild his huge Scottish estate and offset humankind's detrimental impact on the Scottish Highlands. This landscape was once very different; the Great Wood of Caledon once covered nearly a fifth of Scotland. The Scots pine stretched back 10,000 years to the end of the last Ice Age until people started to destroy these vast wooded plains. These hardy trees can live for up to 300 years and grow to almost 100 feet in height. They have a primeval appearance, but the increased demand for wood for the industrialisation of railway, ship and steelwork construction in the Victorian era led to the decimation of this once-great woodland.

Today just one per cent of that forest remains, leaving much of Scotland with boggy open moorland. Man has tried to redress the problem with plantations of the conifers and heather that are so endemic across the country. A huge variety of key species, from pine martens and red squirrels to the endangered wild cats, rely on these vulnerable remaining pockets of ancient forest.

The trees have been an obvious visual loss, but it is the loss of some of the Highlands' fauna that has had the most profound impact – resulting in the demise of the Scottish wolf and the Scottish bear that once roamed these moors and glens.

The classic 1948 Land Rover Series I, inspired by the US-built Willys Jeep.

© Jaguar Land Rover

Originally conceived as a commercial and agricultural vehicle, Land Rover steered for the masses with its first brochure.

© British Motor Industry Heritage Trust

In the 1960s Land Rover created the Rail Rover conversion by replacing the road wheels on a Series IIA with steel rail wheels. It didn't win the approval of British Rail, though it did pull a train (for publicity purposes). gardenrails.myfreeforum.org

King George VI climbing into his Land Rover, described as 'a new type of British cross-country car' by *The Illustrated London News* in 1948.

© The Illustrated London News Ltd/ Mary Evans Picture Library

A mobile cinema mounted to a Series I Land Rover, as used frequently by governments and charities to show educational films in remote areas.

© funrover.com

'Kam', an elephant from Bertram Mills Circus 'drives' a Land Rover along a road during training for the Christmas Show in November 1959.

© Ron Case/Keystone/Getty Images

A pre-production Series I gets a 30-degree tilt test in 1948.

© British Motor Industry Heritage Trust

Actors Richard Attenborough and John Mills, seen here in an Ealing Studios film reconstruction of the evacuation of the Dunkirk beaches from World War Two.

© Popperfoto/Getty Images

A Royal Air Force helicopter carrying an Army Land Rover moves in to place it on the deck of the Royal Navy's new assault ship *HMS Fearless* during a demonstration of the vessel's versatility off Lee-on-Solent, Hampshire in 1966.

© PA/PA Archive/Press Association Images

In 1955, Land Rover sponsored six students on a trip from London to Singapore – the so-called Oxford and Cambridge Far Eastern Expedition. Here, they are seen fording the frontier river between Burma and the north of Thailand in their Series I Defender. © Antony Barrington Brown

Winston Churchill standing proudly next to his Land Rover on his Chartwell Estate. The extremely rare custom-made Series 1 Land Rover (fitted with wider-than-usual seats) was given to the former prime minister as a gift for his 80th birthday in 1954. © SWNS

A police car escorts the lorry and two Land Rovers believed to have carried much or all of the Great Train Robbery bandits' haul, outside Leatherslade Farm in Buckinghamshire, 1963.

© PA/PA Archive/Press Association Images

The mistress. My pride and joy – a 1949 Series I 'wheels behind the grille' on Red Wharf Beach, Anglesey.

Queen Elizabeth II and Prince Philip wave from an open Land Rover to a crowd in Tobruk during an official visit to Libya in 1954. © Popperfoto/Getty Images

Original unrestored Land Rover Series I 80-inch JAC 165, on show at the Gaydon Heritage Land Rover Show, Warwickshire in 2006.

© Harald Woeste/www.imagerover.com

1950s Land Rover Series I 107-inch recovery truck, part of the Dunsfold Collection of Land Rovers Open Day 2011 in Dunsfold, Surrey.
© Harald Woeste/www.imagerover.com

Actor Idris Elba arrives in a Heritage Land Rover during the opening ceremony for the Invictus Games at Queen Elizabeth Olympic Park on 10 September 2014 in London.
© Paul Thomas/Getty Images for Jaguar Land Rover

By Appointment to the late King George VI
Manufacturers of Land-Rovers
The Rover Co. Ltd.

Tough loads . . . rough roads . . .

the *LAND ROVER* can take it!

MADE BY THE ROVER COMPANY LIMITED · SOLIHULL, BIRMINGHAM ALSO DEVONSHIRE HOUSE · LONDON

Advertisement for the Land Rover as featured in *The Illustrated London News*, 1953, 'by Appointment to the late King George VI'.
© Mary Evans Picture Library

A Land Rover is unloaded from a RAF Short SC-5 Belfast CMk1 at Belize Airport in 1975. © The Royal Aeronautical Society (National Aerospace Library)/Mary Evans Picture Library

Paul and Linda McCartney
with their Land Rover.
© *Life* Magazine

George Adamson, Mara
the Lioness and Virginia
McKenna having a picnic
lunch between filming
scenes from the film *Born
Free*, Land Rover in the
background. © Virginia McKenna,
Born Free Foundation.

Prince Edward on the
roof of the Royal car
watching the Windsor
horse trials in 1972
with Prince Andrew,
Prince Philip and
Queen Elizabeth II.
© Popperfoto/Getty Images

Marilyn Monroe sits in a
Land Rover on the beach
in Amagansett, New York
in 1957. © Sam Shaw/Shaw
Family Archives/Getty Images

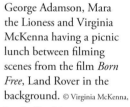

Land Rover Forward Control 110 Series 2B Diesel RHD, belonging to the Dunsfold Collection of Land Rovers. © Harald Woeste/www.imagerover.com

Vickers demonstrate a Land Rover equipped with a special hovercraft conversion kit which partly supports the vehicle over rough territory while its wheels still provide traction, 1962. This one will be used for crop spraying. © Ron Case/Keystone/Getty Images

Legendary reggae musician Bob Marley's son Julian with Marley's Series III Land Rover, which has been carefully restored.

© Bryan Cummings/*Jamaica Observer*

Ian Meiers (left) and James Sleater from Tailors, The Cad and the Dandy with their Land Rover Series III on Savile Row in London. Behind them is the company's 110 'Cad Wagon' with elevated roof for measuring.

A Cuthbertson Land Rover in the Upper Danube Valley in Germany.

© Markus Keller/Getty Images

Driving an old Series Land Rover around the Caribbean Island of Bequia with my paddleboard.

Military Land Rover 110 Wolf on display at a Land Rover show. © TRP/imagerover.com/Alamy

AA Road Service Land Rover Series I 80-inch, on show at the Gaydon Heritage Land Rover Show, Warwickshire in 2006.

© Harald Woeste/www.imagerover.com

Rear view of a 1958 2.0 Litre Diesel Land Rover Series II SWB 88 recovery truck, with Harvey Frost crane in original condition. Light blue and white colour scheme showing the golden company name *Handman & Collis Recovery.* © Harald Woeste/ www.imagerover.com

Arthur, the 1976 Series III Land Rover converted by Grounded into a mobile barista truck.

Bob Hoskins, right, and Lord Winchilsea, founder of the Saharaman Aid Trust, outside the House of Lords in London, before setting off for a long charity drive to Southern Algeria in 1989 to help raise money for Sahrawi refugees.

© PA/PA Archive/Press Association Images

A vintage 'Pink Panther' Land Rover of the type operated by the Special Air Service (SAS). In use with the Regiment between the late 60s up until the mid-80s, these were based on the Series IIA Land Rover. The pink paint scheme was said to be a highly effective desert camouflage, especially at dawn/dusk. They were eventually replaced by the Land Rover 110 series and its more subdued beige camouflage scheme (see plate 11).

www.adrianstomcat.co.uk

The Land Rover rapidly developed into a fashion icon, with many designers featuring the iconic car in prominent advertising campaigns. American designer Ralph Lauren, an enthusiast himself, owns a 1950 Series I Defender. http://paneraiworld.blogspot.co.uk/

The lone policeman patrolling Tristan da Cunha's one-mile road in his trusty Defender, one of only a handful of vehicles on this remote island in the South Atlantic. © Tristan da Cunha Government/Tristan da Cunha Association

The former British prime minister Margaret Thatcher, accompanied by King Hussein of Jordan, stands in the back of a Land Rover to view a parade of tanks at the Qatrana military base in Jordan in 1985. © AP/Press Association Images

Armoured Land Rovers boarding a merchant vessel in Belfast Harbour at the start of their journey to Iraq in 2003. The Land Rovers were all drawn from reserve stock (at the time) thought to be surplus to requirements in Northern Ireland, intended to give protection to army patrols in southern Iraq. © Paul Faith/PA Archive/Press Association Images

The Job Land Rover designed by Job Smeets and Nynke Tynagel from Studio Job. A kaleidoscope of Land Rover storytelling.

A Pink Panther Land Rover desert patrol vehicle of the British Army.
© Stocktrek Images/Getty Images

A Land Rover Santana recovery truck seen in Morocco. © Harald Woeste/www.imagerover.com

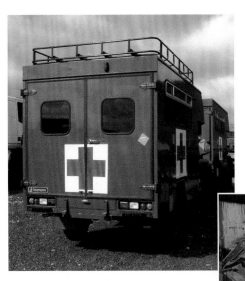

Rex Cross military Ambulance Land Rover vehicle. © Sign/Alamy

Ben in Belfast, Northern Ireland with a PSNI Land Rover.

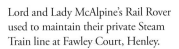

Lord and Lady McAlpine's Rail Rover used to maintain their private Steam Train line at Fawley Court, Henley.

Denis Ferry's incredible amphibious Land Rover off the coast of Donegal in Ireland.

Royal National Lifeboat Institution (RNLI) Land Rover Defender on the slipway in Morecambe, Lancashire. © Stan Pritchard/Alamy

Land Rover Defender 90 TD4 waiting to compete in the ALRC National 2008 RTV Trial.
© TRP/imagerover.com/Alamy

A Land Rover Defender 90 driving down a steep bank during an off-road exercise. © Roger Bamber/Alamy

Camel Trophy Land Rover Defender.
© Harald Woeste/Alamy

Camel Trophy Land Rover Defender 110 camping at a lakeside in Herefordshire. © Jeff Morgan 08/Alamy

The hugely successful 1994 film *Four Weddings and a Funeral* prominently featured Land Rovers. © Working Title Films

A cheetah standing on a Land Rover on safari in the Masai Mara National Reserve in Kenya.

© Manoj Shah/Getty Images

Kathy Wills, daughter of Spencer Wilks, next to her long wheelbase Defender used to carry whisky from her distillery Kilchoman on Islay.

A woman carries her supplies home on her bicycle as a UN vehicle drives out in Vukovar, Croatia, under Serb control, 1992. © Mike Goldwater/Alamy

Fire-and-Rescue Land Rover during floods in York city centre. © Loop Images/ UIG via Getty Images

My wife Marina in Queenie, the yellow Defender, during our camping safari in Tanzania shortly before we got stuck.

The Animal Park Defender used for a decade of filming at Longleat Safari Park.

The Flying Huntsman, the six-wheel drive Defender adapted by Afzal Khan on Islay.

This model was the first and only prototype of the Bell Aurens Longnose variant, built in 2008 as conceptualised by two German Land Rover enthusiasts, Thomas Bell and Holger Kalvelage. They wanted to create a sort of Off-Roadster, a classic British 4×4 with the long hood, rearward cockpit and yacht style rear-end of an old Jaguar. They have since shelved the idea but have been quoted as saying that they'll relaunch the concept if the demand is ever sufficient. silodrome.com

Kenya, Africa 2016. The unmistakable silhouettes of Defender and me.

Lister's vision was simple. Reintroduce these apex predators and restore the natural ecosystem. Perhaps unsurprisingly, his idea has attracted both admiration and derision. However, his argument is simple: without predators, the Scottish Highlands' remaining trees have become further denuded by the unnaturally high number of sheep and red deer populations. Fortunately, many landowners are adopting a more thoughtful approach to the reforestation of Scotland by replanting not only Scots pines but also native juniper.

Lister has argued that, by reintroducing the wolves and bears that were once prolific across Scotland, the ecosystem will restore its fine balance. The idea of these wild animals roaming the Highlands of Scotland has been an emotive subject, and Lister's vision has been further hampered by a bureaucratic contradiction in which the law demands that 'wild animals' be secured with a high fence, while at the same time Scotland's 'right to roam' ensures no barrier. The stalemate has lasted more than a decade.

This is wild country, stretching as far as the eye can see. It was once a hunting and shooting estate just like its vast neighbouring estates. I clambered from the cab into the pick up at the back of the Land Rover to get a better view of the landscape. Exploring the wild moorland and the efforts and work the estate has done to begin the re-wilding project was humbling and inspiring. It seems incredible that anyone would be against such an exciting, visionary project.

The reintroduction of apex predators is not something to be scared of, but something that could put the Scottish Highlands firmly on the map, drawing much-needed tourism and jobs to the Highlands. Lister's vision has already been realised by others, as far afield as Yellowstone Park in the USA and the Argentine Pantanal.

While many of the large Scottish estates cling to the age-old business of the sports of hunting and fishing, the Alladale model could well change land management throughout the UK – if only we would allow it to happen.

'Imagine it,' says Lister, as he joins me in the Land Rover. 'People will come out here in specially adapted Scottish safari Land Rovers with cameras and binoculars. They will be on a Scottish safari; instead of stalking African lions and cheetah with their lenses, they will be looking for Scottish wolves and bears.'

I find Paul mesmerising. His vision is intoxicating. One day perhaps you really will be able to go in search of a Scottish wild wolf aboard a Land Rover Defender.

Land Rovers such as Lister's Highland fleet have served the rural communities since 1948, which tallies with Wilks' original intention for them to be used as an agricultural vehicle and as a gamekeeper's vehicle on the sporting estates.

Whatever your opinions concerning humankind's relationship with the countryside, the Land Rover has been an indispensable facilitator. Land Rovers have performed a vital role in managing our landscape from the beginning. The National Trust, English Heritage, the National Parks … the list of environmental and conservation bodies who have used the Land Rover as the defender of our green and pleasant lands is extensive.

Inspired by my trip to the Highlands, I decided to visit another organisation in the south of Britain to see how their conservation work has been transformed by these steel workhorses. First I went to one of our most ancient courts, that of the Verderers of the New Forest.

Evidence suggests that they date back to the thirteenth century when the Verderers were the legal guardians of the sovereign's hunting ground that we now know as the New Forest. Their powers were altered during the eighteenth and nineteenth centuries when boat construction at nearby Buckler's Hard meant a new role in the legal protection of the forest oak for ship construction. Today, tradition still dictates that the Crown elects the 'official' Verderer while the remaining four are elected by the forest's 'commoners', better known as resident landowners. The Verderers then use a team of Agisters to manage the forest's livestock. And so it was that I found myself exploring the largely empty New Forest with a real-life Verderer and Agister.

Despite their heritage, the modern-day work of the Agister and the Verderer would be impossible without the help of a Land Rover.

I climbed aboard a Landy and our first stop was the ancient court in which the Verderers sit once a month to hear from members of the public. While the Agisters wear ceremonial jodhpurs and hunting gear for ceremonial and court appearances and often patrol the forest on horseback, my introduction was rather more informal in the back of a Land Rover as we made our way around the 219-square-mile park that was once the hunting ground of William the Conqueror.

The New Forest is perhaps most famous for the 9000 or so wild ponies that live within the National Park. These animals are, of course, all owned by individuals who exercise their commoner's right to allow their ponies to roam and graze the forest. They are the resident gardeners, maintaining the vegetation through grazing and their heavy footfall. The Agisters' primary role is to keep an eye on these ponies to ensure they are healthy and happy.

Fallow deer grazed on the open meadowland as we meandered along the Park's highest point. Through ancient forest and across heathland we bounced cross-country in search of the famously hardy ponies. Once a year the ponies are gathered in a series of 'drifts', during which each animal is checked, wormed, vaccinated and their tail trimmed to the pattern of the Agister responsible for that area of the Park. I was lucky enough to join one of these drifts several years ago now, and it remains a highlight of my rural experiences. Sadly, traffic accidents remain one of the biggest problems for the Agisters, who each get called to pony fatalities several times a week. I felt humbled to have shared a little of our rural heritage with the New Forest Verderers.

From the New Forest of Hampshire, my own faithful Landy, Polly, and I drove to another unique conservation project under the vast skies of Cambridgeshire that would be impossible without the help of a Land Rover.

In the Great Fens there is a section of land between Peterborough and Huntingdon that was once a thriving watery wildlife habitat. The Great Fen formerly stretched for hundreds of miles, but in the seventeenth century much of the land was drained for agriculture, destroying 99 per cent of the original wetland, along with its abundant flora and fauna. Woodwalton Fen and Holme Fen (which is nearly 10 feet below sea level) were all that remained, but now one of Europe's largest restoration projects hopes to transform the landscape back to the Great Fen once again.

The plan is to create a series of connecting parcels of land that will eventually encompass over 9000 acres of land. The restoration project has other benefits, too; as long as the peat is kept wet, it acts like a huge sponge for carbon dioxide. It has been estimated that the peat here prevents the release of 300,000 tons of carbon dioxide (CO_2) every year. Without the water, the peat soon dries and crumbles into a fine powder, turning the area into a great dust bowl as well as releasing harmful CO_2. The dykes, ditches and drains that once used to clear the water from the land are now being used to retain the water in a controlled way.

Much of the reclaimed land has in the past been used for agriculture, so the first process is to remove the excessive levels of nutrients in the soil after years of fertiliser use. This will be done over time, by replanting grasses and bringing in grazing livestock that also help to turn the soil with their feet. But much of the work here requires heavy machinery, and I watched in awe as huge diggers landscaped the level plains, digging vast reservoirs and canals which will soon be filled with water diverted from the canals. It was humbling to see the scale of the project. By digging down to the clay base beneath the peat, the water will sit naturally. Soon the reeds will return and the landscape will be transformed.

From reedbeds to meadows, there are now more than 2140 acres of land in restoration, and with it a huge and growing variety of wildlife, from breeding barn owls, overwintering short-eared owls, lapwing and snipe, to rare plants and invertebrates. Beavers, otters and voles were once prolific in the fens, and it's hoped that one day they will again thrive in this unique part of Britain.

The Land Rover has been the custodian of the countryside; not only has she helped protect our green and pleasant lands but she has also always been responsible for transforming our infrastructure. The 1960s and 70s were a period of mass development across the United Kingdom, featuring the widespread construction of our transport networks, power grids and telecommunications, and at the centre of this period of boom was a tiny company on the outskirts of Southampton – SHB Vehicle Hire.

Mike Street learnt to drive in a Series II Land Rover. Like so many people I have met while researching this book, what started as a practicality turned into a lifelong passion, and a fleet of thousands of Land Rovers.

We met on a rainy spring day in a featureless industrial site in Romsey, on the outskirts of Southampton. I had to navigate my way around hundreds of golf buggies to reach the entrance. A huge 'By appointment to Her Majesty the Queen' sign hung next to the door, alongside which were five rusting old Land Rovers which had certainly seen better days.

I waited in a rather bleak, featureless reception room. On the walls were several framed photographs of some Land Rover Defenders and a Land Rover Series I. Street appeared and he walked me into his office. Boxes of documents lined the floor, his desk had disappeared underneath piles of paperwork, and some luminous yellow hazard vests hung on the back of the door.

Street's parents owned a construction hire company, hiring out equipment to building sites. It was a visit to one of these construction sites, in Slough, that changed his life. A friend had invited him up to see the construction of a natural gas pipeline. The construction workers were using a small fleet of Land Rovers but they needed more. They had asked Land Rover, but true to form they had been told there was a six-month waiting list.

'I'll get you one,' blurted Street.

He asked his boss, who declined. 'You buy it,' he said.

Street scraped together the £150 he needed to buy an old 1958 Series II which he duly hired out at £7 a week. 'It broke down once a week,' he recalls. 'I had to make regular trips to Slough to fix it, and it cost me a fortune to repair.' But the hire was a success and he persuaded a friend to invest in a second Land Rover.

It was the 1970s and the oil and gas industry was booming. Britain's infrastructure was in a state of flux and gas pipelines were being laid across the land. In that economic climate, the business grew, and by 1973 he had an order for 40 Land Rovers. 'Land Rover wouldn't even entertain the idea of supplying me,' Street recalls. So he had to find a secondary source. The nearby army base had a huge fleet of ex-service vehicles, so soon he had 200 Landys.

The problem lay in the Land Rovers' unreliability. Street had a huge team of mechanics to keep them running, but, he admitted, 'their unreliability was the reason I had a business; no one wanted to own them themselves. They didn't want the bother with the maintenance.'

The Rovers' gearboxes were so unreliable that he had two permanent mechanics who would go on location to the building sites to replace the entire gearboxes as needed.

'It sounds strange, but the Land Rover's reverse gear was only made with a running life expectancy of 12 hours,' he explained. The problem, of course, was that in gas pipe installation vehicles often had to access thin, remote corners of the countryside, often only wide enough to go one way. The Land Rovers had to reverse as much as they went in first gear. The result was a weekly overhaul of the fleet.

'We had to keep a huge stock of replacement vehicles as they were so unreliable,' he remembers. But there was no alternative, it was still the only 4×4 vehicle out there and there was an infrastructure to build.

Street had a dozen Land Rovers working on the construction of the M4 motorway and a further 30 working on the M27. SHB provided vehicles for the M25, A3 … the list goes on and on. Although Street's memory is fading, he still has a near-encyclopaedic memory for registration numbers of Land Rovers.

'Are you a Land Rover geek?' I ask. 'Outside of business, do you have Land Rovers?'

A smile envelops his face. I've seen that look before. It's the familiar 'Land Rover smirk'. It means you flipping love them.

'How do I put this …?' he stumbles. 'All the Land Rovers I have are a part of the business. They are all for hire.'

I ask which models he has. There is another pause.

'I have an original 1948 Series I and a 1949 Series I 80-inch – two of those,' he adds.

'I also have a 1950 Series I and a Minerva left-hand drive Belgium Land Rover and a 1958 Series I and a 107 breakdown truck.'

That's not it, the list goes on. He has eight Series II and four Series III … he continues to reel off a list before admitting he has bought two of every edition of Defender ever made.

'Okay, you really are a Land Rover nut,' I smile.

'My wife hates them,' he finally admits. 'When we first married I bought her a Series I that I painted bright yellow. I even had the seats retrimmed with flowery fabric. She now refuses to set foot in a Series I.'

One of the earliest customers for SHB was Michael Eavis, a Somerset dairy farmer who planned to hold a music festival on his land. Glastonbury is today one of the biggest festivals in the world, and arguably the growth has all been thanks to the Land Rover, the only vehicle capable of ferrying the artists around the infamously muddy quagmire. Michael Eavis still drives his famous red Land Rover Defender around the site, and SHB has provided all the Land Rovers for the festival since it started in 1970.

During the 1980s the business continued to grow. In 1981 the Army put in an order for 250 Land Rovers. They had a planned Civil Defence exercise called 'Brave Defender', for which they needed the cars on Salisbury Plain. From then on, SHB started to adapt vehicles for all sorts of businesses, including built-in generators and capabilities for the construction of cross-country pylons, or cars with cherry-picker arms that could be adapted for virtually any task. The landscape of Britain is peppered with communications systems that exist thanks to the support of Land Rovers – bypasses, the M6 and the Severn Bridge, as well as sewer systems and even Milton Keynes, built using hundreds of SHB Land Rovers as workhorses. Open-cast mining also led to new contracts, with specially adapted vehicles allowing mechanics to work on the huge wheels of the machines from standing-up platforms in the pick up of the Land Rover. Street confirms that they had 20 Land Rovers at each site in Wales, Derby, the Midlands and Newcastle. SHB Land Rovers also helped with the construction of the Channel tunnel, and at the height of their productivity SHB had a fleet of nearly 2000 vehicles.

SHB continued to diversify their client base, though, and the Balkans conflict opened a whole new portfolio as journalists from across the world descended on the region to cover the escalating war. So SHB began to hire out Land Rovers to all the major news agencies. They also supplied vehicles for the G7 summit in Ireland and for the national parks. British Gas hired a fleet of Landys every winter to ensure staff could get to work through wintry conditions, thereby keeping the nation warm. When Britain was flattened by the great hurricane of 1987, it was a fleet of SHB Land Rovers that set off to rebuild the country's shattered infrastructure. The company have even sent Land Rovers to the Falkland Islands, Ascension and the Outer Hebrides.

Today, it is SHB Land Rovers that are responsible for building wind and solar farms across the UK. They have been hired to build sea defences and power stations. I love the idea that these iconic vehicles have helped shape the very infrastructure of Britain and continue to do so. Without SHB and the Land Rover, the country would be a rather different place.

Shortly before Land Rover ceased production of the Defender, SHB put in an order for 600 brand-new cars, which are all ready to meet the demand over another decade for SHB shaping and maintaining our national grid. In total, Street has a little over 900 Defenders in the fleet – and 1500 Toyota Hilux.

The writing was on the wall as far back as 1979 when the first Hilux hit the market.

'The Japanese vehicles were cheaper and more reliable,' explains Street. 'What's more, they could deliver almost any order. Where Land Rover would more often than not decline an order, Toyota would always deliver huge quantities on time.'

Before I left, Street offered to show me around the site. An army of mechanics was busy welding, cutting and adapting half a dozen trucks and vans for motorway maintenance and construction jobs. Calendars with naked girls hung on walls while mechanics, their hands blackened with oil, bustled from vehicle to vehicle. We walked past spot welders and angle grinders until we reached a small door. Inside lay a handful of Land Rovers in various states of disrepair.

'That's a Series I,' he said, pointing to a pile of rubbish in the corner. I strained my eyes but all I could see were boxes and crates, piles of newspaper and rusted metal. There was certainly no obvious sign of a Land Rover.

Mike carefully moved some of the rubbish, and there, hidden beneath the mountain of refuse, was the unmistakable outline of a Series I. The three wheels that remained on her axle were all flat, and the missing wheel had tipped her lopsided. Heavy rust had spread across much of her body. 'Beautiful,' smiled Mike. 'She's one of the first 1500 ever produced.'

'Beauty is obviously in the eye of the beholder,' I smiled. I like to think I have a good eye. I can usually see the potential, but here in the corner of an oily workshop I failed to see any chance for this old wreck. She looked beyond the scrapheap.

'Come back in a couple of years and she'll be a beauty,' he smiled.

In contrast to this wreck, in the corner stood a brand-new Land Rover Defender.

'Have you heard of the Dormobile?' Street asked.

Dormobile is a conversion for VWs, Bedfords and Land Rovers that converts a normal cab into a camper van with the use of the famous lifting roof. SHB bought the company in 2002 and began converting Land Rover Defenders. The conversion is relatively simple; the roof is cut out and replaced with a unit costing £2500 that hinges up on one side, allowing you not only to stand up in the back but also to add a bunk bed. It is the same Dorma principle made famous on the original VW Combi camper van.

In the back of the long wheelbase Defender before me, the seats had all been removed and replaced by a long bench seat that turned into a double bed on one side of the vehicle and a work surface complete with stove along the other.

Street smiled as he showed off his show vehicle. It was becoming more and more obvious just how obsessed he was with Land Rovers.

In another part of the workshop, a Series II hard cab had been hoisted onto the lifting block for repairs. Street pointed at it. 'That is exactly the same model as the first Land Rover I ever bought to hire.' The car that ignited the fire that flamed the business. The car that he had bought for £150 to hire out for £7 a day.

Who hires all these old vehicles? I wondered. Street had dozens of Series I, II and III Land Rovers, none of which would be particularly reliable or functional for contract work.

'We hire them out for film and photo shoots,' he explained. 'They are hired for fashion shoots and for displays. We'll lease them to anyone, really.'

Like so many of the people I had met along this journey, Mike had managed to turn a hobby into a business. There can't be many people who can claim to own upwards of 1500 Land Rovers. In fact, the only organisation to boast those numbers is arguably Land Rover's biggest single customer, the military.

I love the idea that the Land Rover helped build Britain. It was the Land Rover that helped lay our very infrastructure, from our rail network to our power lines, communications and gas pipes, bridges and motorways. Farming, too, has an awful lot to thank the Land Rover for, as it helped to revolutionise agriculture. The very foundations of modern Britain in the twentieth century were all built under the chassis of the Land Rover.

And today the Land Rover is also on the front line of conservation, both in the UK and around the world, helping environmental organisations to protect our rich habitats.

No other car better deserves the title of Defender – as the Defender of the Land.

CHAPTER TEN

MARLEY AND ME

I have a story about David Beckham; world-class footballer, global icon and arbiter of good taste. I can't validate my tale, but it has given me immeasurable pleasure in assuming it's true, so excuse me if I indulge you with my humble brag.

Living in West London, as I do, you often bump into famous folk going about their normal routine. They often say that Londoners are never more than 3 feet away from a rat, but I'd argue that the saying could just as easily be applied to our proximity to celebrities. We are pretty prolific in the West London area. If you're lucky you'll catch sight of a Hollywood A-lister exploring Portobello Road; if you are less lucky you will spot me driving around in my beloved Defender with a child's or dog's head lolling out of the window.

The Defender affords me just the right amount of anonymity. It is different but it also blends in. It will attract a nod from the Landy aficionado, but for the most part it is ignored.

On this particular occasion I was returning from the park with a Land Rover full of dogs when I drove past one of Notting Hill's schools. Outside were the ubiquitous fleet of black and navy-blue top-of-the-range Range Rovers, and leggy, Lycra-clad yummy mummies pouring from the 4×4s. One individual stood out. With flat cap and black T-shirt, I watched a lone father carrying a little girl to a waiting Range Rover, parked ahead of me in the street with its hazards flashing.

As my car drew up behind the dad, the mosaic of tattoos that coated his body confirmed that I was indeed staring at one of the most famous men in the world.

I rarely get starstruck. Apart from that time I went on holiday with Buzz Aldrin and became a jibbering wreck with 'star' syndrome, I am rarely overwhelmed by anyone. But you'll have to admit that Beckham has that Midas touch. He commands attention.

Our eyes met as he strapped his daughter into her seat. He looked at me and then he looked the car up and down before giving me the thumbs up. 'Nice car,' he smiled, and with that the car in front moved off and so did I. I caught him admiring the car in the rear mirror. I very much doubt he had a clue who I was but he had admired my car. I felt a shiver of excitement. I went home, told the wife and duly forgot about it.

A week later I opened a newspaper, and what did I see? Beckham climbing into his brand-new long wheelbase Defender.

Now this is where the story takes on an individual's interpretation. In my mind, he saw my car and thought, 'that driver looks so cool in that car that I shall get one myself to be just as cool'. In my mind he had taken my style advice on the only car to drive and he had got one of his people to call their people and a Defender had arrived. While mere mortals have to wait up to six months for a Defender, Beckham can obviously make things happen with a click of the fingers.

Now for the benefit of the doubt, it might just have been a coincidence that Beckham had long ago ordered his Defender and his eyes happened to fall upon mine in the week preceding delivery. But I like to go with the story that I introduced Beckham to the Defender.

Of course, Beckham is not the first star to fall for the iconic Land Rover. Indeed, the humble Landy has a long list of aficionados who have been lured and seduced by the boxy 4×4. Although originally targeted at farmers, these vehicles soon became a favourite for stars of screen and stage.

One of my favourite Land Rover drivers was Bob Marley. There is a photograph of Marley at the wheel of his blue 1977 Series III Land Rover. He used to drive his beloved car to gigs around the island, right up until he died in 1981. After his death, his Landy was abandoned in the car port of his house in Uptown Kingston. The former home was eventually turned into a museum dedicated to Marley, while his Land Rover, like thousands of others around the world, sat fading and gathering dust and rust.

A team of Jamaican engineers eventually decided to salvage the car and restore it to its former glory with a few added details. A new engine was sourced from a military Land Rover Series III in Ethiopia, and Marley's daughter Cedella, who designed the Jamaican Olympic Team uniforms for London 2012, designed a new interior that included seats in the Jamaican Rastafarian colours of red, black, gold and green. It took two years to restore the Series III.

Bob Marley had often used the car to transport his large family of eleven children. One of them, Julian Marley, still remembers driving around Jamaica in the pick up.

'I have always loved my father's Land Rover and I remember driving in it,' he confesses, while Julian's sibling, Ky-Mani, recalls, 'I remember my father picking me up and taking me to his birthplace in Nine Miles, me and my brother Stephen. It was built in the year I was born so it's good to see it back up and running.'

Still today there are many Land Rovers working the island's coffee plantations.

Marley's son Rohan lives on the island, where he is a coffee grower, exporting his Marley Coffee brand around the world.

'I love driving through the coffee fields in my Land Rover, and you see farmers driving their 1970s Land Rovers; and these things, you just can't finish them. If you're a farmer you need something to fit the part, and that's why I have a diesel here, that's why I drive a 2001 Defender.'

Of course, Bob Marley is just one of a long list of celebrities who have owned a Land Rover. In fact, it seems that if you are a celeb and you haven't been photographed in a classic Land Rover, you have missed out.

There are iconic photos of numerous legends of film and screen who have been snapped in a Land Rover. Steve McQueen has been pictured with his child asleep on his lap, Virginia McKenna appears in one iconic photo in Africa with a lion (Christian) on the roof, Marilyn Monroe was famously captured in a white bathing suit, her leg dropping out of the door of a

Series I – two icons of the 1950s in one photograph. Paul McCartney was also captured on film with his daughter Mary and his late wife Linda McCartney and their dog on the Mull of Kintyre next to their Series I.

Then there are the celebrities, who, like Bob Marley, are dyed-in-the-wool Land Rover fans and have been spotted driving around in their own vehicles. Fred Dibnah drove an iconic red Series I until his death, and Ralph Lauren has several – I can still remember the first time I saw him with his limited edition black Series I. Amy Winehouse learned to drive a Series IIA around the Caribbean shortly before her death. Bryan Adams loves his so much that he put one on the cover of his 1993 album, *So Far So Good*. Welsh actor John Rhys-Davies has five Series and Defenders. His Land Rover fleet includes a Series II 109 with a roof tent, an ex-RAF 88 Defender, and even a Series III with a built-in welder, all of which he keeps at his home on the Isle of Man. Jim Carey, Kevin Costner and Sylvester Stallone all drive Series III. Jane Fonda and her husband Ted Turner drive around in 110 Defenders, as do Michael Jordan, Oprah Winfrey and Sylvester Stallone. Sean Connery, former Bond, drives a Defender around his Spanish estate on the Costa Brava. Closer to home, Jonathan Dimbleby and Dick Strawbridge have both been photo-graphed in their beloved Landys. Mohammad Ali and Henry Cooper were both Land Rover drivers, as were Johnny Cash and Kate Moss. Hollywood star Clark Gable used his Series I to seduce various leading ladies, as did fellow actors the late Richard Attenborough and John Mills.

As well as being beloved of film stars, the Landy is also a film star in its own right. It has a long on-screen pedigree. It is perhaps best known for its role in James Bond films over the years; from the archetypal Aston Martin DB5 of *Goldfinger* to the sub-aquatic Lotus Esprit of *The Spy Who Loved Me*, James Bond rips through cars faster than he knocks back Martinis, but everyone's favourite gentleman thug broke hearts when he ruined a Land Rover Defender 110 double cab pick up during *Skyfall*. He redeemed himself somewhat by bringing back the hardy 4×4 in *Spectre*. This time, Land Rover Special Operations weren't taking any chances and the vehicles were heavily beefed up for a better chance of survival. For a chase scene in Austria, the Big Foot Defenders were fitted with huge 37-inch-diameter off-road tyres, as well as bespoke suspension and enhanced body protection.

But of course it doesn't end there. The Land Rover has been a matinee idol of many other films. The big-screen credit list for the Land Rover Series and Defender runs long: *Tomb Raider, Born Free, The Italian Job, Gorillas in the Mist, Judge Dredd, Black Hawk Down, Octopussy, On Her Majesty's Secret Service, Buster, A Clockwork Orange, Priscilla, Queen of the Desert, The Wild Geese, The Dogs of War, Cry Freedom, The Gods Must be Crazy, The Man with the Golden Gun, The Living Daylights, Romancing the Stone, Tomorrow Never Dies, Spies Like Us, Stand By Me, White Hunter Black Heart, The World is Not Enough* … the list goes on.

Of course, the Land Rover has also had a significant role on the small screen, too, appearing in everything from *Emmerdale* and *Heartbeat* to *Last of the Summer Wine*, and also, of course, in BBC's *Animal Park*. I spent the best part of a decade making this series, and much of my time was spent driving around the Marquis of Bath's Wiltshire stately home of Longleat in his fleet of zebra-print Defenders. Like the Marquis, these is just one generation in the historic estate. In the house, there is a great old black-and-white photograph of Lord Bath and his late father looking at the lions from the open back of a short wheelbase. Of course, health and safety regulations have changed since the 1960s …

The Land Rover is also a favourite for making an entrance. Idris Elba drove into the Invictus Games in 2014 aboard a blue convertible Series Land Rover, and successive popes have been paraded around in the famous Popemobile, which is a Land Rover adapted to have a glass-roofed turret from which believers could catch a glimpse of His Holiness.

This just serves to prove that the Land Rover has been a constant companion through popular culture and has never shied away from the spotlight, despite its humble nature. Of course, there are some historic moments that Land Rover may not be so proud of by association; notably the legendary Great Train Robbery.

In 1963 two Land Rovers were enlisted to help 15 thieves pull off one of the most famous heists of all time. The mastermind of the Great Train Robbery was Bruce Reynolds. Inspired by the railroad heists of America's Wild West, Reynolds and his gang held up the Royal Mail train travelling between Glasgow and London. Using a false red signal to get the train to stop, they attacked the driver, clubbing him over the head with an iron bar, then took control of the train.

Hidden along the tracks were the rest of the gang – Jimmy White, Roy James, Bob Welch, Buster Edwards, Gordon Goody, Charlie Wilson, Tommy Wiseby, Jim Hussey, Ronnie Biggs and 'Pop', the gang's specially recruited train driver. Dressed in blue boiler suits, the thieves loaded 120 postal bags weighing an estimated two and a half tons and containing £2.6 million in used banknotes – the equivalent of £49 million today.

The only vehicles that could reach the rail line were, of course, two Series I Land Rovers. The robbers loaded the stolen cash into the back of the two Landys and sped off, although I'm not sure if the word 'sped' is appropriate, given that the Series I had a top speed of about 45mph.

The Land Rovers had been stolen from Central London and had been fitted with identical licence plates to confuse the police. The robbers drove for nearly an hour through the winding roads of Buckinghamshire using a VHF radio to listen to police broadcasts from their cars. They stopped at Leatherslade Farm in Buckinghamshire where the Land Rovers could blend into the rural agricultural environment while the gang divided their spoils.

It was a tip-off from a herdsman who had a field adjacent to the farm that led police to the robbers. When the police arrived, the building was deserted. They found a half-dug hole believed to have been intended to bury the money, and they also found a half-painted yellow truck, a Monopoly board, food and sleeping bags, as well as, of course, the two infamous Land Rovers.

The gang became folk heroes to many for their audacious crime on an unprecedented scale. Many in Britain saw it as a case of the laymen against the system. There was a huge manhunt and 12 of the 15 thieves were eventually captured. In all, the gang received a combined sentence of 300 years. Perhaps the most famous gang member, Ronnie Biggs, escaped from prison after just 15 months. He had plastic surgery to disguise himself then fled the country and eluded capture for nearly 40 years until he finally gave himself up in 2001, when he returned from Brazil to serve the 28 years remaining on his sentence.

Of course, the real stars of the robbery were the two Land Rovers, and for a time they were the most wanted cars in the world. They were eventually discovered at the thieves' hideout at the farm. Today the cars are in a private collection.

These two Series I Land Rovers were far from the only Landys to be part of an event that captured the world's imagination, though. Thirteen years later, in 1976, an Air France airbus en route from Paris to Athens was hijacked by two Palestinians and two Germans. The flight had originated in Lod, Israel, and nearly a third of the passengers were Israeli and non-Israeli Jews.

The hijackers were from the Popular Front for the Liberation of Palestine (PFLP) and the Baader-Meinhof Gang initially diverted the plane to Benghazi, in Libya, for refuelling before heading to Entebbe, Uganda, where it landed on 28 June. Here they were joined by three PFLP accomplices, and the 248 passengers and 12 crew were herded into the airport's old terminal building.

The Israeli government were quick to begin their military response to the hijacking. To succeed in liberating hundreds of Israeli nationals, they needed an element of surprise in their rescue mission.

The hostage takers soon issued their demands: either Israel, France, Germany, Switzerland and Kenya release 53 imprisoned comrades or they would begin killing passengers at 2pm on Thursday 1 July. Three days into the crisis the hostage takers released 47 non-Israeli passengers, who were flown to Paris.

Mossad, the Israeli secret service, was immediately dispatched. It transpired that Ugandan soldiers were co-operating with the terrorists. The following day, the hostage takers released a further 101 passengers, leaving only Israeli and non-Israeli Jewish captives and the French crew behind.

With 24 hours' notice, Israeli commandos from Sayeret Matkal special operations began rehearsing a rescue plan conceived by Lt Col Yonatan Netanyahu, brother of the future prime minister, Binyamin Netanyahu. The plan was as perilous as it was audacious; it called for troops to fly into Entebbe airport and drive to the old terminal building, fooling the Ugandan guards into believing Idi Amin was paying a visit.

By a stroke of good fortune, the Israelis got hold of detailed plans of the old airport building in Entebbe, so they built a mock terminal and practised their rescue plan.

Idi Amin had long been a fan of Land Rovers. Not only did he have his own personal collection but, as with many armies around the world, it was his vehicle of choice, and the marque was a common sight when escorting the infamous dictator. Amin also had a white Land Rover that was his communication vehicle, with a Fitted For Field radio (FFR) used as a first-generation mobile phone.

A 29-strong rescue team set off from Israel in top secret on the 2500-mile journey to Uganda in four C130 transport planes. Intelligence suggested the airport was protected by upwards of 1000 Ugandan soldiers. The aircraft took off from Israel in different directions so as not to arouse suspicions and flew at under 100 feet above the Red Sea to avoid Egyptian and Saudi radar.

One of the transport planes touched down at Entebbe airport, and a Mercedes and two Land Rover IIIs, packed with Israeli commandos wearing Ugandan Army uniforms, rolled out of the back.

The Land Rover's manual shift was perfect for the quick start they needed. They could start as they were rolled from the back of the Hercules but the automatic Mercedes was much harder, so they started her engine before the plane had even landed to ensure there were no problems with stalling engines.

The idea was to trick the Ugandan soldiers who were securing the airport into believing this was a surprise visit by Idi Amin and his protection guards. No one was sure whether Idi Amin still drove a Mercedes, so the Land Rovers were used to deflect any suspicions.

The Land Rovers approached the control tower where two Ugandan sentries stopped the convoy. They were shot dead. The surprise was over and the rescue bid descended into a firefight. In the ensuing battle all seven hijackers and their accomplices, as well as two dozen Ugandan soldiers, were killed. Colonel Netanyahu, the creator of the rescue plan, was the only Israeli fatality, along with three hostages.

The rescue team had strict orders not to leave anything behind and the Mercedes and Land Rovers were all hastily loaded, along with the 100 hostages, back onto the transport planes. As they took off, one of the pilots heard Idi Amin on the shortwave radio and attached it to a loudspeaker for all those aboard. Idi Amin announced that he had reoccupied the airport and released the hostages.

On the return journey, one of the planes stopped off to refuel in Nairobi, Kenya, where several more Land Rovers were loaded onto the plane as ambulances for the wounded.

This was not the only significant political event in which the Land Rover has been caught up. Across the Atlantic in the Caribbean Sea, until 2008 the island of Cuba was virtually frozen in time under the iron fist of Fidel Castro. I can still remember my astonishment, the first time I visited the island, seeing such a huge number of American cars from the 1950s in seemingly perfect condition on the roads. Indeed, the cars have become as iconic as the cigars and the socialism, but few people realise that it was the original 'people's car', the Land Rover, that helped Fidel Castro and Che Guevara overthrow the US-backed authoritarian government of Cuban president Batista's regime.

Castro and Guevara are famed the world over for their revolutionary battle against the ruthless Batista regime of Cuba. Theirs was a story of blue-collared workers against the establishment, an ideological purge for a world of equality. David versus Goliath. A tiny band of revolutionary men against a well-armed army of thousands.

The Cuban revolution began in July 1953 and continued until the rebels finally ousted Batista and his cohorts on 1 January 1959. The revolution had powerful domestic and international repercussions; perhaps most significantly it reshaped Cuba's relationship with the United States.

The Cuban revolution followed many years of instability in Latin America, often exacerbated by US military and financial aid. The United States were worried about their neighbours and they often helped engineer puppet governments propped up by the White House and military coups to depose those they saw as a threat to US freedom.

Batista was a former Cuban soldier who had served as president of Cuba from 1940 to 1944, but he became president for a second time in 1952, after seizing power in a military coup and cancelling the 1952 election. The formerly progressive president became more and more radical and he ruled over the rising unemployment and Cuba's limited infrastructure with dictatorial control. He also turned a blind eye to the organised crime that flooded the city of Havana and opened the door to American companies that dominated Cuba's fragile economy.

By now, communist ideology was sweeping in from the East and the leftist ideologists were beginning to take hold across Latin America. Shortly after the 1952 coup, a young lawyer named Fidel Castro began a constitutional 'revolution' against the tyrannical Batista, who effortlessly suppressed any legal insurrection. Fidel and his brother Raul resolved to launch an armed revolution. They founded a paramilitary organisation known as 'The Movement', stockpiling weapons and recruiting thousands of disgruntled Cubans from the working class.

The Castro brothers began their armed campaign with focused strikes against military installations. They were soon overwhelmed by Batista's forces who killed many and captured many more. Fidel was captured. At his trial he spoke for four hours, ending with his famous quote: 'condemn me, it does not matter. History will absolve me', after which he was sentenced to 15 years' imprisonment.

Worldwide political pressure led to release of the Castro brothers in 1955, after which they fled to Mexico where they met the Argentine revolutionary Che Guevara. Che joined the fight and they founded the '26th of July Movement'. Together they returned to the island aboard the yacht *Granma*. Batista's forces were waiting and many of the revolutionaries were killed. The Castro brothers, Che and a small group of surviving revolutionaries escaped into the mountains.

From their remote mountain hideout, the revolutionaries began a sustained campaign of attacks on small garrisons loyal to Batista. Around the same time, support for the regime began to fade and even the USA imposed a trade embargo on the increasingly ruthless and bloodthirsty dictator.

In the rural hinterland of Cuba it became the story of David and Goliath. A small group of 200 revolutionary ideologists against a state army and police force of 37,000. In a final bid to weaken and destabilise Che and Fidel, Batista sent a force of 12,000 soldiers to defeat the revolutionaries. Castro's forces had the upper hand against the mainly untrained soldiers, and a series of skirmishes resulted in the defeat of the junta and the capture of hundreds of soldiers.

By 1958, the ideologists had defeated the army and overthrown the junta. On 8 January Castro arrived in Havana for a victory march.

Not a great deal of evidence remains about the type or quantity of Land Rovers used during the revolution, but it is well documented that Fidel Castro used a long wheelbase Series I station wagon in the last throes of the revolution. Today his vehicle is on show at the Museum of the Revolution, in the former offices of the deposed President Batista.

The museum covers the period from 1895, when Cuban insurgents unsuccessfully rose up against their Spanish rulers, through to the late 1980s, when 50,000 Cuban soldiers fought in Angola against the racist apartheid regime. It also includes items from the Bay of Pigs invasion attempt in 1962, by puppets of the 'Imperialist Aggressors'. And, among the blood-stained uniforms of the martyrs, weapons, photographs, newspaper clippings, wireless sets and flags, are parts of a B-26 bomber, shot down during the Bay of Pigs invasion; parts of a U-2 spy plane shot down during the Cuban Missile Crisis; and the self-propelled, surface-to-air missile launcher that brought it down.

Amongst the vehicles is a red Ford delivery van, completely riddled by what appear to be .50-calibre machine-gun bullets, which indicate there were some contentious issues in Cuba in the late 1950s. But behind the red van, and in company with a post-war Jeep and an old Toyota Land Cruiser, is Fidel's famous Series I Land Rover; roofless, but bearing a badge on the back that labels it as a four-wheel-drive station wagon. This was the car used by President Castro as his personal command vehicle in the late 1950s, and it is still riddled with bullet holes from the Battle of Maffo, which took place in December 1958.

The car is a surprising find, given Cuba's heavy reliance on the American automotive industry prior to the revolution. One wonders if Land Rovers were a more popular choice in South America, because it is known that Che Guevara travelled extensively across South America from his Argentine birthplace before calling Cuba his home.

Bodily straight and bearing a low mileage (in kilometres), its Birmabright body has been painted over many times and the rear seats and centre front seat have all been removed. Writing in red paint on the front passenger door (on the right-hand side) indicated this was indeed the Comandante's vehicle. In its final incarnation it was painted in battleship grey, just like the two other four-wheel-drive vehicles nearby.

Closer to home, the Land Rover was also popular with the leader of Britain. One of the country's most famous prime ministers, Winston Churchill, was never far from his trusty Series I Land Rover. In the post-war years, the Land Rover was the perfect utilitarian vehicle for the victorious prime minister, but perhaps his best-known Landy was the one built exclusively for him for his 80th birthday – the 1954 Series I Land Rover with its famous registration UKE 80. Registered in the name Rt Hon Sir Winston Spencer Churchill Kg. OM. CH. MP. Chartwell. Westerham, Kent, there are many photographs of the PM in and out of this car, cigar in mouth, beloved Airedale terrier at his side.

The Land Rover had been specially modified for the prime minister to enable him to be chauffeur-driven around his Chartwell estate in Kent, and to include an extra-wide seat to accommodate his ample girth. The dark green vehicle also had a heater in the footwell to ensure he didn't get cold feet, to which he was prone in his later years, and it featured leather-covered seats and a roof-mounted grab handle so that he could haul himself in. It also had a padded armrest in place of the standard centre seat. Perhaps the most intriguing feature, though, was a wooden box specially fitted into the pick-up bed, which is believed to have been added to accommodate a trowel and a bag of mortar, so that Churchill could indulge in his favourite pastime of bricklaying.

After Churchill's death in 1973, the car was bought by a Kent farmer for £320. It was used for light farm duties and for towing his daughter's horse trailer until the last road fund licence disc expired in 1977, when the car was put into retirement.

The historic Series I, with nearly 13,000 miles on the clock, was recently auctioned, selling for £129,000, making it the most expensive Series I ever to be sold and proving just how important the heritage of these much-loved vehicles can be amongst true enthusiasts.

CHAPTER ELEVEN

SEA ROVER

In one of my most extraordinary adventures while following the Land Rover story, I crossed the Irish Sea to the Emerald Isle to meet a man who made a Land Rover waterborne.

'This was once a city divided,' Denis Ferry told me as we drove across the bridge in Derry that had once been a military checkpoint. The river here was formerly the boundary between the Catholics and the Protestants. The Troubles here are now, of course, a thing of the past. For the younger generation they have been consigned to history, though for the older generation who lived and suffered through those times, there is still a bittersweet aftertaste.

A mechanic by trade, Denis has looked after an assortment of vehicles, including many Land Rovers for various customers over the years. He recounted the recent purchase by one customer of an ex-military model; the owner was so worried about any connections to the Troubles that he had decided to paint the words 'US MILITARY' across the side, presumably to distinguish it from the UK military – the fact that it was an English-made Land Rover painted in British Army colours to a unique British Army spec seems to have been lost on the young man. The story was made all the more surreal by the revelation that the owner also used to drive around in full army camo.

Soon we had crossed from Northern Ireland into the Republic of Ireland, into County Donegal. A bright sun beat down on the rich green fields that give this island its nickname as we journeyed along the Wild Atlantic Way, a winding road that snakes its way more than 1200 miles alongside the rolling Atlantic Ocean. Huge waves crashed against the vertiginous cliffs as I made my way to Malin Head, at the very top of the Inishowen Peninsula, which is mainland Ireland's most northerly point. Over millions of years the Atlantic Ocean has carved the cliffs into the rugged headland that is visible today. Not far from here is Banba's Crown, from which families once waved goodbye to their families and loved ones as they set out on their long oceanic journey to a new life in North America. In the distance I could make out the unmistakable silhouette of Tory Island, home to Patsai Dan Mac Ruaidhri, better known as the King of Tory. The tiny island has elected its own king since the sixth century, although the current king has no formal duties apart from meeting every visitor off the ferry.

A stiff breeze cleared my lungs with a bracing freedom you only ever experience on the coast. There is a unique warmth in Ireland, borne through close family and community – it embraces you like a warm hug. It is a warmth of generosity and hospitality and I soon found myself in the hearty embrace of a kitchen full of Donegalese, where I was plied with food and drink in a gesture of Celtic charm.

At a little beach next to a little harbour a small crowd of people had gathered around the unmistakable silhouette of a Land Rover Defender. However, this was no ordinary Defender, this was an amphibious Defender lovingly built by Denis to cross the Irish Sea.

This was not the first attempt to make a Land Rover float, though. During the Cold War period, Land Rover had established the Fighting Vehicle Research and Development Establishment (FVRDE). The Soviet Union was making worldwide headlines and Europe was preparing for a land attack from the Soviet Union. The British troops stationed in West Germany, close to the front line of the Cold War, had to prepare for such an attack, but they were worried about the large number of rivers in Eastern Europe that would slow down the movement of troops and vehicles. Bridges would simply take too long to construct. What they needed was an amphibious vehicle, so FVRDE was tasked to develop vehicles that could cross water under their own power.

One proposal involved attaching rubber buoyancy bags to vehicles which were inflated from their own exhaust, then some kind of water propulsion system was added to give forward motion in the water. The APGP (Air Portable General Purpose) Land Rover of the early 1960s was based on a Series II and came with two huge inflatable rubber bags (from the Avon Rubber Company) mounted along its flanks. Twenty-three prototypes were ordered by the British Army, but they were decommissioned in the late 1960s. One of these prototype vehicles is housed at the

Dunsfold Collection, the largest collection of historic Land Rovers in the world.

Another version of the 'floating' Land Rover was developed a few years after the British Army project, in this instance for the Australian military. Since April 1965, the Australians had been involved in the Vietnam War, but they had quickly run into problems, with flooded paddy fields restricting their movement. Even a Land Rover couldn't get across them, but what they decided they needed was a Land Rover that could float. Although Land Rover duly developed a prototype, the Australians were not convinced by the finished article and didn't place an order.

While the amphibious Land Rover never took off, Land Rover also created the Hover Rover, which had a Land Rover body on a hovercraft skirt. It was a bizarre-looking experiment from Vickers which had been intended for the military to use as a mine-clearance vehicle but also for farmers to crop-spray their fields. The problem was that the air draught blew the spray away, so the experiment faltered.

While Land Rover abandoned their efforts to place a Land Rover on or above the water, it hasn't stopped countless others from trying. Sir Ranulph Fiennes was the first to attempt the icy crossing. His failed bid was followed by millionaire property developer Steve Brooks who attempted to drive around the world, including the notorious ice bridge that forms across the Bering Sea between the USA and Russia.

I have long been fascinated by the Bering Sea, the relatively narrow 56-mile channel of water that divides North America from Russia. During the Cold War this was on the front line of the frosty relations between East and West. I can still remember the excitement as a child when *Blue Peter* presenter Peter Duncan attempted to drive a vehicle across the thick winter ice that clogs the ocean each year. That narrow stretch of water has been a magnet to explorers and adventurers ever since. Benedict Allen lost his dog team while trying to cross it and Karl Bushby became the first documented person to walk it. The ever-shifting ice floes and the danger of being crushed between giant icebergs or slipping into the freezing waters have so far defeated all vehicular crossings of the strait.

Self-made millionaire Steve Brooks decided to drive from New York to London heading west. The biggest hurdle in the 18,000-mile trip was the Bering Strait. Brooks needed a vehicle that could travel through all terrain on land, sea and snow. His first choice was a military Hummer that had been customised with a floating skirt, allowing it to glide above the water and ice like a hovercraft, but Alaskan tests soon failed when they found out the Arctic snow was so dry and fine that the air blowing under the 'skirt' passed right through the snow, rendering it ineffective.

The Hummer was abandoned and they focused their attention on converting a snowcat, the type of vehicle used in ski resorts to smooth the slopes. The vehicle needed to be able to float on water and to climb onto the ice shelf. The team added two enormous 16-foot aluminium frames on either side of the vehicle into which huge floats could be added for buoyancy. Once rotated they could be used to haul the car up onto the ice and across the rugged ice floes. The result was Snowbird V, but the vehicle had too little buoyancy and it sat too low in the water. It was too dangerous and the attempt was abandoned.

Undaunted by the notorious stretch of water, it was British farmer Steve Burgess who finally cracked the crossing in 2008 using a Land Rover, of course. A Yorkshire farmer, Steve had grown up around Land Rovers. He remembers his father's Series I. The 50-year-old farmer Steve drove from Yorkshire on a 10,000-mile journey in his Land Rover Defender.

Along with teammate Dan Evans, they modified the Land Rover with giant floating pontoons and set out on the 56-mile stretch of open water. Their Land Rover was stripped of everything but the essentials to make it as light as possible for the crossing. The intrepid Land Rover adventurers set off from Uelen in Russia and, wearing survival suits and rebreather diving apparatus, they travelled 43 miles across the water before a storm forced them to stop and seek shelter on the island of Little Diomede before continuing on to Alaska. The Land Rover Defender used for the crossing is still used on Burgess's farm today.

Denis Ferry's Land Rover was no less impressive, even though it was designed for less inhospitable conditions.

'So why did you build her?' I asked, while examining her mighty pontoons. Denis just smiled and shrugged. I liked Denis. He had a schoolboy mischief about him. I had discovered on the journey from Belfast just how much of a Land Rover nerd he really was. He seemed to know everything. And not only that, but he had also bought one of the last ever Defenders off the production line. This was becoming a theme during my journey around the British Isles – and in this case beyond our shores, too.

The love and passion for the Land Rover is unquantifiable but it glows with enthusiasm. It reminds me of a *Just William* kind of 'boy's own' adventure. The Land Rover Defender, boxy, noisy and uncomfortable, is like a teleportation machine in which grown men can pretend to be young boys.

The car's simplicity means it has an easy adaptability. I had seen this dozens of times. I had seen Land Rovers transformed into hovercrafts, while others had been modified with a similar hovercraft mechanism, but instead of being adapted for use on water, these had been built as crop sprayers for farmers; they were intended to glide over furrows and ploughed fields effortlessly spraying insecticides. I had seen more still adapted into ice trucks with monster wheels in order to navigate the tundra of Iceland and beyond.

There seems to be no end to the potential for modification. Indeed, in all my research almost the only adaptation I couldn't find was a 'flying' Land Rover, even though the British Army came pretty close to making Land Rovers that could fall from the sky – but more of that later.

Denis told me with gleeful excitement of one man's attempt to 'drive' a Land Rover along the sea bed, under water, fully submerged. You couldn't make it up. The Land Rover enthusiast in question had stripped the car down to its body without windows. He had waterproofed the engine and he intended to use scuba gear while driving it along the ocean floor.

This story starts back in the early 2000s when two friends had an idea about an amphibious Land Rover. They started working on a prototype using a 1987 110 ex-military Defender. After a while it was parked up to make way for their new project, a Defender twin cab pick up that they would build and in which they would successfully cross the Bering Strait.

In a farm outhouse lay Stan (they named it this, as the original owners were called Steve and Dan). Stan had stood still for well over a decade and Denis, with his friends Les and Paul, thought that this prototype deserved to be coaxed into life and taken to its natural habitat, the sea. They took Stan to their workshop in Donegal and the work began on recommissioning it. They spent months stripping, rebuilding and converting different parts and areas of the Defender until it was ready for its maiden voyage.

When the time came, though, Denis admitted it was pretty hairy.

'I've driven in a lot of the inhospitable places in the world in a 4×4, from the Dalton Highway in north Alaska to the narrow high-altitude "death road" in Bolivia, but when I drove the Defender into a lake that is only a few miles from where I grew up I must say it was nerve-racking and it felt very wrong sitting in a Land Rover while travelling up a lake.'

Driving in the water was no mean feat. Once all the equipment has been fitted, the driver must enter the water and drive until the water is at doorstep level, then drop the pontoons which lift the Defender. When the road wheels lose traction, the driver must take the Defender out of gear on both gear sticks, pull out the PTO lever and engage fourth gear, then let out the clutch before the Defender transfers drive to the propeller. Then the driver has to set the pontoons at a height. While all this is happening, the driver has to keep the steering wheel straight and the rudder in the middle (straight position), then use the third lever in the cab to steer the rudder. Once the car is out on the open water, it can be steered by keeping the rudder straight and turning the steering wheel, which moves the road wheels. The

Defender will change direction, but at a much slower rate than when using the rudder.

When on the water, the Defender has to be kept in fourth gear and can travel at a speed of around 5 knots. Launching and landing on a beach is, according to Denis, quite easy after a bit of practice, but using a slipway at a pier with other boats, sea walls, and so on, so close can be tricky, especially if the sea is choppy, because then the 3-ton Defender often wants to go with the flow. Literally.

Denis's Defender is a vehicle that can take you anywhere over land and sea. I bet the Wilks brothers never thought that their drawing on the sand could someday cross seas and go along the Thames under Westminster Bridge, tooting its horn at Big Ben.

There were a few details in his floating Land Rover that Denis failed to resolve, though – weighting and buoyancy. The air in the wheels acted like a flotation device, but the vehicle wasn't weighted down enough to be able to be driven along the sea or river floor. The result? The Defender floated and the project sank.

Regardless, I love this story because it is symbolic of the Land Rover and the dreams that this legendary car creates. And it really is a dream maker. Here is a vehicle with which you can do virtually anything or go pretty much anywhere.

For me it is the car's adaptability that is truly astonishing, but here, on a windswept harbour in Donegal, I think I had finally met my match. Here was a Land Rover that exceeded expectations. Bonkers. Eccentric. Silly. Funny. I defy you to look at Denis's creation and not smile.

That was certainly the mood on that spring morning when Denis offered to show me how the car moved in the water. The crowd of locals who gathered to see us off were, of course, used to the famous 'floating Land Rover', but they had turned out nonetheless – perhaps the draw this time was the prospect of watching a minor celebrity get soaked.

With childish enthusiasm and charm Denis showed me around the vehicle. My eyes glazed over as he did the prerequisite Land Rover nut 'engine check and description'. What is the attraction of engines? Every Land Rover book I have read included exact details of every engine. In the course of my journey to meet Land Rover enthusiasts, each one had, at one stage or another, drifted into a form of Land Rover mechanical proselytising, like priests who start to quote passages of scripture, they would lose me in the minutiae.

With the 'geek' inspection over we moved on to the more interesting and practical stuff, such as, how do you turn a Land Rover Defender into a boat? The starting point was pretty obvious: two huge orange floats had been secured to the side of the vehicle with removable stainless-steel bars so that the car was still fully roadworthy and, more importantly, road legal. A pneumatic arm had also been attached to the side to allow the floats to be lifted and lowered according to the conditions.

At the back, or should I say the stern, of the Land Rover, was the propeller that had somehow been connected to the gear shaft so that it could be controlled within the normal working framework of the car.

To be honest I have absolutely no idea how it works, so for those 'nuts' out there I got Denis to write the technical details for you:

'Attached to the chassis are 4 box sections on either side and these are permanent and don't protrude or affect the vehicle when it's in normal road mode. Two removable hinged frames then slide into the box sections and are secured with bolts through the box sections to prevent them from sliding out at sea. Then the orange inflatable pontoons are attached to the frames, which are in turn attached to a hydraulic ram in the middle, housed in the original army side lockers. The rams are controlled inside the cab by levers, thus allowing the driver to raise and lower the pontoons so that we can float in the water.

'As with a lot of Defenders, Stan has a PTO system. There is a removable shaft fitted to the PTO that comes out at the rear of the vehicle and then a propeller is fitted to that. So when you engage the PTO and let the clutch out the propeller turns via the gearbox using the Defender's engine, allowing us to move in the water.

'Attached to the towbar is a pole that a removable rudder slides on to, and the rudder is attached to a hydraulic ram that again is controlled by a lever inside the cab to allow the driver to steer.

'Under the bonnet is a 200 Tdi engine but without the turbo – there are enough things to go wrong without blowing a turbo as well. The engine has a hydraulic pump fitted that is turned with an industrial-type toothed fan belt (toothed to prevent slipping in the water) off the crankshaft. The pump is piped to 3 levers inside the cab; 1 for steering right and left and 1 for each pontoon to move them up and down. A breakwater checker plate board is attached to the front bumper to help with waves and steering.

'All of the convention equipment to turn the Defender from road mode to sea mode is carried on or in the vehicle, and it takes approximately 1 hour for three people to make the transformation.'

There you go. Job's a good 'un.

You climb into a Land Rover, but you clamber into an amphibious one. The floats are too close to the doors, rendering the doors useless. To get in, you need to climb over the bonnet and then into the cab, which has had its roof removed. Rather amusingly, the ubiquitous bonnet wheel had been replaced with a bright orange life ring. Nice touch, that.

Once aboard, we settled into the seats. Denis became captain, I was the passenger, while Leslie was the navigator in the pick up or stern of the car, or, as I should now call her, boat. Slowly we edged our way into the tepid Irish waters. The wheels were still firmly on the sand as water started lapping at the wheel arches.

'Lowering the floats,' smiled Denis as the hydraulic ram settled the giant orange floats onto the water surface. 'We are now afloat,' Denis confirmed, as he swapped from the gear stick to the stick-operated inboard engine.

Slowly we edged our way to the harbour edge. I write 'slowly' advisedly here – that should probably read *very slowly*. We could probably have paddled or even swum faster. I'd estimate she was doing about 1 knot (one mile an hour).

'She's a little slow. Not made for the water,' chuckled Denis as we literally drifted towards open sea. She was so slow that I was worried a single gust of wind would send us hurtling back to shore, but she ploughed on into rougher waters.

'Where are we heading?' I asked optimistically.

'Over there.' He pointed to a beach in the far distance.

'This is about as big a sea as she's been in,' Denis said rather unreassuringly. More comforting was the presence of a support boat, 'just in case'.

After 30 minutes we neared the beach. Huge rolling waves were crashing against the sandy bottom. 'Don't worry about driving ashore if it's not safe,' I offered nervously.

To be honest, I really didn't think we would make it. The waves were huge and would easily swamp the vehicle from behind if they broke close to her, which they invariably would. My uncertainty wasn't helped by the very near capsize of the rigid inflatable boat next to us. She had been hit by one of the breaking waves and had accelerated rather than decelerated into the surf. The boat had gone perpendicular – 90 degrees straight up. I was sure she was a goner, but luckily the helmsman had cut back at the last minute and she had come crashing down flat.

Now it was our turn. Denis waited for a break in the waves and then used the smaller surf to race towards the beach. We picked up speed and before I knew it our wheels were back on hard sand, the floats had been lifted and we were cruising up the beach past dog walkers who looked on in astonishment. I swear I even saw the dogs do a double take.

'Now for the really interesting bit,' smiled Denis mischievously, as we turned towards the water and made for a re-entry. I cannot emphasise enough how big the surf was – by my rough calculations it would be impossible to break it without being enveloped by a wave.

Denis didn't wait around long. 'Here we go,' he smiled as we nosed into the surf. This seemed like a suicide mission, but, as they say, 'in for a penny, in for a pound'. As the waves scooped us into their clutches, Denis lowered the floats. I looked on as a giant wave gathered momentum.

I closed my eyes and waited for impact as the full force of the water hit the bonnet of the car before ricocheting up and tumbling down on us. This wasn't a spray. This was, as they say in the navy, green water. A full soaking. The footwells were swamped.

For the first time I was grateful for the gaps around the door as the Irish Sea escaped through the openings. Denis was dripping wet and laughing hysterically as smoke billowed from the bonnet.

'That was fun!' he hollered above the wind as I wiped the salt water from my eyes.

We had made it through the breaking surf and suddenly the sea that had previously appeared rather choppy seemed calm and benign.

'I'm not sure, is that smoke or steam?' he asked Leslie. Like a monkey on a climbing frame, Leslie worked his way along the outside of the vehicle before standing on the bull bar at the front and lifting the bonnet.

Of all the eccentric sights, the vision of a mechanic lifting the bonnet of a Land Rover while ploughing through the sea was certainly one of the most surreal. We were relieved to discover that it was just steam, though. Unsurprisingly, the cold soaking had swamped the hot engine. Despite the onslaught of sea water, Stan still worked effortlessly.

I looked around the beautiful scenery and marvelled at the ingenuity with which Land Rover enthusiasts like Denis had embraced these unique cars. Like Lego, they have adapted them into things from our imagination.

The crowd had grown as we pottered back to the harbour entrance. Once again the floats were lifted and slowly we edged our way out of the water and back onto the safety of the beach and the Land Rover's natural habitat: land.

Before I left Ireland, Denis was keen to show me his latest acquisition: a brand-new, end-of-the-line Defender. She was black and shiny and lovely.

'Seven miles on the clock,' he smiled, 'and look at that …' he pointed to some rust around the back of the vehicle, 'and they forgot to put a footplate on.'

He was still smiling. Denis, like so many others, forgave Land Rover their foibles. He forgave them the rust on a brand-new car, because this was true love. Just as in marriage, we forgive one another our shortcomings and embrace the positives.

'Shall we take her for a spin?' he asked. 'You'll be my first passenger.'

I climbed aboard. She had that indescribable 'new' smell that is so hard to regain once it is lost. He started her up and we climbed the road that zigzagged towards the Atlantic Way. There were four of us in the vehicle now. The two passengers in the back sat hunched in their seats, their knees around their noses, their heads brushing the roof. To my knowledge there was no need for them to be in the car and it looked pretty uncomfortable as we bounced along the rough track.

Soon it was time to head back to Belfast.

'Shall we go in the Defender?' he asked, smiling.

'Hell yes,' I answered. The two passengers also nodded.

We began the two-hour journey back along the winding coastal roads through the Republic of Ireland before crossing into Northern Ireland. We all sat there in silence, listening to the hum of the Defender. We were all lost in the undefinable world of the Land Rover.

I looked around at Denis and our two passengers. All of them were staring at the road ahead, that huge 'Land Rover' smile etched across their faces.

CHAPTER TWELVE

LAND ROVER HEAVEN

Dunsfold Aerodrome, near Cranleigh in the south of England, has seen some of the world's most impressive cars racing on its circuit. In fact, the sleepy Surrey track is home to the most popular motor show in the world, *Top Gear*. However, few people know that just beyond the perimeter fence there is housed arguably the biggest and most important collection of Land Rovers in the world – the Dunsfold Collection.

The collection was begun in 1968 by Brian Bashall, who had become obsessed with unusual prototype and pre-production Land Rovers. Land Rover weren't interested in keeping these prototypes, which are part of Britain's transport heritage, so without Brian's foresight and enthusiasm many of these historic vehicles would have been lost forever.

Over the years, the Dunsfold Collection has expanded to include not only prototype and pre-production vehicles but examples of almost every model made by Land Rover from 1947 to the present day, including military vehicles, record-breakers, royal cars, limited editions and display vehicles. The collection – now containing over 130 vehicles – is managed by Brian's son, Philip, who has become an internationally recognised expert on the Land Rover.

Sadly, the collection is only open to the public on a couple of days a year, when the vehicles are driven out and displayed on the grounds of the neighbouring estate, although the family are working hard to raise funds to be able to establish a permanent museum that will be open to enthusiasts. Until then, the shop-front of the Dunsfold Collection is a Land Rover workshop.

A handful of mechanics were busy dismantling engines as I pulled up on a late winter morning and Phil greeted me with a cheery smile. He had the blackened hands and stained clothes of a working car mechanic.

The collection has now outgrown the garage and the vehicles are currently stored in a series of barns, lockups and garages across Surrey. An anonymous barn on a nearby farm was our first stop. Phil fumbled with a key to open a heavy padlock on the enormous doors. He pulled them open to reveal twenty Land Rovers of every shape, size and colour, all carefully parked with just a few inches between them.

The first car to catch my eye was a striking yellow Land Rover. To be honest, this was the car I had really come to see – it was the world-famous elephant Land Rover. Back in the 1950s and 60s, the arrival of the circus was a time of great excitement for chil-dren and the circus companies would make sure their proces-sions of vehicles into town were as colourful as they could be. The most colourful of all was Bertram Mills Circus, whose procession was led by Nelly the elephant (real name Kam) 'driving' an open-top Series I bearing the near-personalised numberplate, LLY 920. Actually, Kam wasn't driving at all, but merely grasping the fake centre-mounted steering wheel with her trunk.

The real driver, of course, would sit in the box-like structure at the rear and control the vehicle from there using extended controls. To make room for the driver it was converted to left-hand drive so that their feet would miss the rear diff and prop shaft (the elephant didn't seem to mind where the wheel was located so his wheel was placed in the centre of the dash). The car had extra suspension and the chassis was extended so that Kam could climb aboard, and there were coloured lamps on the bonnet which were used to send messages to Kam, instructing him which side of the Land Rover to get off.

We carried on to another barn where I met another famous vehicle I had been hoping to see, a 1957 Series I 88-inch SAS vehicle. It is one of only two genuine SAS specification Series I vehicles known to exist, having gone into service in March 1957. Ten were built, including the prototype in late 1954 which was on an 86-inch wheelbase (the other nine were built on the 88-inch wheelbase). The collection's vehicle was sold in 1967 to Joe Hirsts of Andover, then sold on to a film and theatre hire company, but it made its way back into the collection again. The car is fitted with weapons, including two Vickers K .303, a Bren light machine gun .303 by the driver and a .30-calibre Browning machine gun on the rear tailgate, much as it would have had when in service.

Another unusual Land Rover in the collection is the 1958 Series II 109-inch Moy Elevator. With its long belted elevator it was intended to be a baggage-handling vehicle that could be driven straight to a plane's cargo door to unload. According to Phil, the elevator makes the car all but impossible to drive, due to the high centre of gravity. It also has a ramp at the front that can be used as a crane by clipping on a custom-made hook.

Next to these cars was the famous 'Forest Rover', a 1964 Series IIA. This odd Land Rover was built by Roadless Traction of Hounslow (who mainly converted tractors to four-wheel drive) for companies that needed a vehicle with superb traction and ground clearance, such as the Forestry Commission. Most of the twenty or so of these models which were built went overseas, but a few stayed in the UK. This vehicle was bought brand new by the Central Electricity Generating Board, and was driven on purchase in 1964 from Hounslow, in Middlesex, 200 miles to where it was put to work at Rhayader, in Wales. And there it spent its life on dam maintenance work until it made its way into the collection.

The collection really is an assault on the senses. I had never seen so many Land Rovers in one collection and certainly not in such wide and varied forms. There are some truly unique vehicles gathered together, such as one of the three Defender Td5 110 driven by Lara Croft in the 2000 film *Tomb Raider*. Phil informed me, 'The car was fitted with a 3.5 V8 carburettor engine and automatic transmission and given a custom paint finish with lots of chequer plate and accessories, because the idea was to create a "fantasy" expedition vehicle.'

Another short journey away and I finally saw my first Pink Panther, a 1968 Series IIA 109-inch – one of the 72 converted to SAS specification by Marshalls of Cambridge in 1968. When new, it was painted bronze green but it would later have been painted to suit whichever theatre of operation it was sent to. The list of its many special features includes extra fuel tanks, smoke grenade launchers, bead breaker on wing, radios, GPMG machine guns, SLR rifles in wing boxes, flare gun, axle guards, oil can stowage, water cans and bladders, sun compass, search lamps and blackout lamps.

Still reeling from this impressive Landy, Phil drew my attention to another striking military vehicle – a 1991 Land Rover Perentie 6×6 Omani. It was built in 1991 by Jaguar Rover Australia Limited, and because it was constructed on a galvanised chassis to 6×6 axle configuration, it is considerably wider than a standard Land Rover. The Perentie was based on the Defender 110 and was introduced in 1987 to replace the ageing fleet of Series IIA and Series III vehicles, produced as both a 4×4 and a 6×6. For the Land Rover geeks amongst you, I am informed that they were powered by an Isuzu 3.9 four-cylinder 4BD1 or a 4BD1-T turbo-diesel. This impressive-looking vehicle proved itself both in Australia and on operations overseas, including Somalia, Timor, the Solomon Islands, Iraq and Afghanistan. The car in the Dunsfold Collection was previously owned by the Omani military and used as a supply vehicle for some ten years. After its withdrawal it was acquired by Land Rover along with three others, with the intention of being upgraded to 6×6 heavy duty trucks.

The collection is most impressive too for its array of unique vehicles, and one that caught my eye, after my very wet but nonetheless exhilarating experience with Denis in Ireland, was the 1965 OTAL One Ton Amphibious Land Rover, which was based on a Land Rover One Ton with a six-cylinder petrol engine. The cab, wings and rear body are made from aluminium watertight compartments, and every possible bit of space on the vehicle is stuffed with expanded foam for buoyancy. The vehicle went to Australia for trials but it was never accepted by the army there, so it was returned to the UK where, in the early 1970s, it lived at Eastnor Castle, on the edge of the Cotswolds, then by 1983 it was in the hands of the British Motor Museum at Gaydon, before landing in Phil's collection.

A personal favourite amongst the sea of Landys was a 1969 Shorland Armoured Patrol Car. It looks like a mini tank, though it retains the unmistakable Land Rover form, and is one of the six Shorlands delivered to the Royal Ulster Constabulary in 1969, following the original ten that were delivered between 1966 and 1967. The Shorland was issued to 3 Platoon (Glenravel Street), Reserve Force RUC, on 4 October 1969, but was withdrawn in January 1970 and stored at Thorburn Road with other RUC vehicles, then issued to 5th Battalion, Ulster Defence Regiment, with service registration 27 BT 69.

According to Phil, the Shorland was based on a Land Rover Series IIA 109-inch chassis cab and was built by Short Brothers and Harland of Belfast. Later types used the six-cylinder engine with consequent improvement in performance. The crew of three had a .30 Browning machine gun (later replaced with a GPMG) in the revolving turret, radio installation, and the armour had hinged door top flaps and drop-down windscreen visors.

There was a slight sadness seeing so many Land Rovers cooped up in damp barns, but then I suppose that is all a part of their charm. These are not vehicles to be buffed and polished and placed in museums. These are working cars. Each one of them has its own unique story to tell.

We headed back to the workshop, where Phil took me to look at the store and office. Every inch of space was piled high with Land Rover paraphernalia: log books, manuals, posters, adverts and model cars. The Dunsfold Collection has become the unofficial archivist of Land Rover. What was astonishing to me was that, without the passion, drive and determination of the Bashalls so much of Land Rover's history would have been consigned to the scrapheap. That the private Dunsfold Collection holds more Land Rover treasures than JLR themselves speaks volumes about a company that never truly understood the importance of their heritage.

The problem with the Dunsfold Collection is that, by Phil's own admission, it has outgrown its space. The sight of dozens of cars parked cheek by jowl gathering cobwebs and rust in largely unheated barns is enough to bring most Land Rover enthusiasts to their knees.

The shortcomings are not through a lack of love; on the contrary, the passion borders on the obsessive, but the cost of keeping and maintaining all the cars is the realm of the super-rich. Nick Mason, Jay Kay or Jay Leno could probably house the collection, but the Dunsfold Land Rovers are in serious need of space: a place where they can be enjoyed and shared with all enthusiasts of this legendary marque.

HISTORY OF THE LAND ROVER

PART V

Although largely the Land Rover has remained unchanged since the early days, there have been some notable adaptations over the years. Many are one-offs, but some were special editions that were produced for a limited market – or simply didn't always catch on.

Land Rovers not being known for being exactly luxurious, the first attempt to create a modicum of comfort in a Land Rover came very early in the life of the original 80-inch Series I in 1949, when special conversions were built by Tickford, a coachbuilder known for their work on Rolls-Royces and Lagondas. The bodywork was wooden-framed and aluminium-skinned, with seating for seven on leather seats. There was even a heater! Unfortunately, the vehicle was much more expensive than a standard Land Rover – about double the price once Purchase Tax was added – and so only 641 were ever sold.

In 1954, a one-off commission was requested, for HM the Queen and the Duke of Edinburgh as they embarked on a tour of the Commonwealth. For this, Land Rover constructed seven open-backed state review conversions on the Series I 86-inch chassis. So successful were these, that six more were built in 1958, on the 88-inch chassis, in time for the Queen Mother's tour of Australia.

Of all the Land Rover conversions, perhaps the one most often discussed is the famous Cuthbertson, which was put together between 1958 and 1972. Indeed, it is one of only five Land Rovers on display at the company's Heritage Museum in Gaydon.

The Cuthbertson is a very odd-looking vehicle. Its modifications – replacing the standard wheels with tracks – were intended to help the Land Rover cross boggy ground. The wheels were removed from standard Land Rovers and replaced by demountable tracks, which lowered the ground pressure to 1.9lb per square inch and allowed the vehicle to travel across boggy ground where standard vehicles would get hopelessly stuck. The conversions were by the car's namesake, Cuthbertson of Biggar, Scotland, and a total of 15 were built – mainly for the forestry industry.

In the 1960s Searle of Sunbury-on-Thames built sleeper/camping conversions on 109-inch Series from the 1960s through to the 1980s, under the approval of Land Rover. The elevating roof of these carwagons allowed people to stand up inside the vehicle. The converted Landys were used mainly as campers, although the Army ordered 34 to be used as Tactical Command Posts.

Land Rover fire trucks had been available since 1948, but it wasn't until the arrival of the Range Rover in 1970 that the Rover Fire Truck really took off. A six-wheel-drive conversion with an extra axle was adapted so that the car could cope with the extra weight of the water. The 6×6 conversions were perfect for small airports and as quick-response fire engines at larger airports. When a British Airtours Boeing 737 bound for Corfu burst into flames on the runway of Manchester Airport in 1985, it was a Land Rover fire engine that was first on the scene. An engine failure had led to an aborted take-off, and 55 holidaymakers lost their lives, but the swift arrival of the Land Rover, some minutes before the other rescue vehicles, helped save a further 82 passengers. As a testament to the endurance of Land Rovers, that same vehicle is still operating today at Peterborough Business Airport near Glatton, Cambridgeshire.

Rover attracted worldwide publicity during September 1960 when it provided the support vehicles for Donald Campbell and the Bluebird team during their World Land Speed Record attempt at Bonneville Salt Flats, in Utah. Land Rover supplied four 88-inch and two 109-inch vehicles, together with a fleet of nine Rover saloons.

Another Rover-approved conversion, the Roadless 109, was one of the oddest-looking Land Rovers ever, setting a 109-inch model on four huge tractor wheels and tyres. It was introduced at the same time as the Series IIA in September 1961, and the last nine production examples were probably built in 1966. It was arguably the first of what has since become known as the Monster Truck.

The conversion had its origins in a Forestry Commission requirement for a vehicle that could cross deep ditches and climb over fallen logs. By May 1959 the Commission had put together its own experimental prototype with ten 28-inch tractor tyres on a long wheelbase Land Rover, which gave a ground clearance of around 17 inches and seemed like a good basis for a working vehicle. With a few tweaks and adjustments and further trials, Land Rover finally approved the conversion. However, the Roadless 109 was probably an expensive vehicle and sales never made it a viable production car. Of the nine production examples constructed, only two went to the Forestry Commission; two more went to the Institute of Hydrology for use in Wales and Scotland; and one each to the Central Electricity Generating Board, to a Scottish shooting estate, to Gibraltar, to the Snowy Mountains Authority in Australia, and to a sheep farmer in the Falkland Islands. The Roadless prototype, the only one with a diesel engine, was also eventually sold off to a hill farmer in Wales. Several still survive, and the one on the Falkland Islands was still in regular use in 2006.

During my research I also saw a photograph of another bizarre adaptation – a Rail Rover. Literally, a Land Rover on railway wheels pulling a trainload of Land Rovers.

In the 1960s Land Rover created the Rail Rover conversion by replacing the road wheels on a Series IIA with steel rail wheels, so that it could be used for rail inspection purposes. It didn't win the approval of British Rail, though it did pull a train (for publicity purposes). It was a stunt the company repeated in 1989 at the launch of the original Discovery, when a Disco equipped with train wheels pulled a short train of passenger coaches into a Devon station to surprise the assembled press.

I was desperate to see one of these bizarre modifications, but I just couldn't track down a Rail Rover. In exasperation I sent an email to my friend and neighbour, Lady Judy McAlpine. As the wife of Sir William McAlpine, a rail enthusiast, it was my last bid.

'I don't suppose you know where I could find a Rail Rover?'

'We have one, my darling,' came the immediate reply. Isn't it strange how we search far and wide for something, only to find it, quite literally, in our back garden? I shouldn't have been surprised; the McAlpines have quite a pedigree.

The McAlpines live next to my mother- and father-in-law in the pretty little hamlet of Fawley on the hill above Henley. A scion of the McAlpine dynasty, William had two passions in life: wild animals and trains – both of which he used to fill his rural estate. Not content with the meercats, wallabies, llamas, alpacas, reindeer, lemurs and some of the other 1000 exotic animals that roam wild across the estate, he had built a full-gauge railway line across his land, complete with tunnels, bridges and full-scale station platforms. It is as eccentric as it is wonderful. Quintessentially daft and crazy and brilliant.

On our visits to my parent-in-laws' home we would often find strange animals in our garden at weekends that had made a bid for freedom through a gap in the fence, and we'd see the unmistakable streak of the full-sized steam train that ran around the estate.

And so it was that I found myself clambering over the fence that separates my wife's parents' cottage from their estate and walking through fields of deer and alpacas down to their private railway station. There, parked on the tracks next to the station platform, was a bright yellow, long wheelbase Land Rover.

These Land Rover trains never took off as locomotives, but industrious engineers discovered that the vehicles had exactly the right width to be mounted to the track using a simple set of track wheels mounted on the axles of the car.

I clambered aboard and we drove along the rail concourse in normal Land Rover mode until we reached the raised tracks that disappeared into the estate. We carefully lined up the wheels with the track and then, using a lever, the heavy metal railtrack wheels were lowered onto the rails.

The steering is locked and the wheels themselves provide the traction using the accelerator for propulsion. It is a very strange feeling. The noise of the rail wheels scraping along the track with a click every time we reached the gap between the tracks gives the sound and feel of being aboard a train. Wallabies and alpacas looked on as we drove, or should I say chugged, our way along the railway line and through the forest, perhaps seeing nothing unusual in a Land Rover travelling by rail. It may not have been notable to them, but to me it was another Landy trip that I shall not forget in a hurry.

CHAPTER THIRTEEN

LANDY WORLD

This was my first Land Rover 'fair', The Great British Land Rover Show. 'Britain's only indoor Land Rover show', boasts their marketing material. I wonder whether this is really something to be shouting about. It seems a paradox that a vehicle made for the outdoors should be celebrated indoors.

Of course, this isn't the only oxymoron. I have visited many shows – from camping and caravanning to any outdoor show – all of which seem to think it's a clever idea to take an indoor venue, more often than not at the NEC.

It has always seemed like such a disingenuous thing to do. I realise we live in the UK which is prone to rotten weather, but surely THAT IS THE POINT? Maybe I'm missing some other point, but it strikes me that a Land Rover fiesta, like an outdoor show, would be better suited to a muddy field rather than a sterile exhibition hall.

To be fair to the Great British Land Rover Show, they had at least chosen a rural showground, Stoneleigh Agricultural Halls to be exact. I drove past the offices of the Kennel Club and *Farmers Weekly* and pulled up alongside a pallet of brightly coloured Defenders.

Ashamed and worried about losing any kudos, I waited quietly until the road was clear before making a run from the car. I couldn't be seen in a white Discovery with no expedition modifications. It didn't even have spare jerry cans or a roof rack.

Around me were hundreds of Defender 90s, 110s, Series I, II and IIIs of every shape and size, and spilling out of the vehicles were hundreds of men in khaki trousers and green tops. With some of them were long-suffering wives. More surprising was the number of dogs. I had noticed on the show information a large announcement that dogs were welcome. This had stood out because of the number of times I have been to shows where dogs have been very unwelcome. A little like the juxtaposition between having an outdoor show indoors, I have long been amazed at the idea to ban dogs from Crufts or the National Pet Show. Surely the point is to celebrate your pet dogs … with your pet dogs?

And now here, at a Land Rover show, dogs were welcome and they came in their droves. There seemed to be almost as many dogs as people – and most of them were Labradors. And I had left mine at home. What was I thinking? Thank goodness for the green T-shirt, was all I could think as I paid my entry fee of £10 and entered the world of the Land Rover fanatic.

Don't bite the hand that feeds you is a mantra I often repeat. I am fully aware that many, perhaps most, maybe even all of you who have parted with hard-earned cash to read these rambling tales are Land Rover fanatics. This book, after all, is about you and for you. But for those who have never been to a dedicated Land Rover fair, it is quite a sight. Lined up like sentry vehicles at the entrance was an assortment of Landys, and around each vehicle were gathered small crowds who were snapping selfies with the rugged-looking 4×4s.

Of course, this is only the tip of the iceberg when it comes to the world of the Land Rover. A long line of Defenders snaked as far as the eye could see. Like a packet of Refreshers they were dressed in an assortment of colours – yellows, greens, blues, reds. Some had big aggressive wheels, others were sporting technical roof racks, while some wore cumbersome-looking roof tents.

Once again I was reminded of the individuality of the Defender; no two cars are alike. However, that is more than can be said for their drivers – each one seemed to be sporting a beard and a green fleece. I looked down at my top – a green T-shirt – and then my hand involuntarily reached for my chin, where a week's stubble had turned into a short beard. I was becoming one of them.

Except today there was a big difference: a massive difference that left me feeling vulnerable and fraudulent. I was in a DISCOVERY. Aaarrrgh! As if that weren't bad enough, it was a white Discovery. A car better suited to Victoria Beckham or TOWIE than a rugged outdoor 4×4 fair. Where were my bleached white teeth and my sprayed-on V-neck T-shirt?

Now don't get me wrong. The Discovery is an excellent car and a vital component in the evolution of Land Rover, but to a true enthusiast (and, let's be honest, the majority of those heading to the show were dyed-in-the-wool enthusiasts) there is only the Series and Defender.

There were no admiring looks. No Land Rover waves or finger nods. No requests to look around her. I was completely anonymous. It was like I was wearing an invisibility cloak. All around me Defender drivers were rubber-necking to cadge a glimpse of one another's Defenders; in the car parks, noses were pressed against windows as the Land Rover fraternity admired their brothers' work, but in my white Discovery I was no one.

Finally, I spotted another Discovery. I wasn't alone. It was bright orange, which made me feel a little better, until it turned into one of the car parks and pulled alongside a dozen other identical Discoverys. These were G4 expedition cars.

I continued on past the cars towards the cottage industry of products for Land Rover aficionados. First was a luxury company that would re-upholster your Defender in anything from white leather to snake skin. Next to the assortment of leathers, crocodile and python skin seats was what to the uninitiated looked like a load of junk from the scrapheap, which in essence is exactly what it was. There was a pile of old doors, next to a heap of roofs, as well as old bonnets and dozens of seats in various states of disrepair.

The stand wouldn't have been so jarring if it wasn't next to the luxuriousness of the leatherworkers. But herein lies the key to Land Rover's success and our abiding love affair with the Landy. It is Everyman's car.

Men in work overalls and tweed caps sold old spades alongside old engines. Men wandered around in T-shirts saying things like 'One Wife Livid' next to a picture of a Land Rover, another said

'I was born to be Awesome, not Perfect'. This latter shirt seemed to sum up the exhibitors rather well. People were here to perfect the imperfections of the seemingly perfect vehicle.

You see, the true reality of the Land Rover Series, and latterly the Defender, is that the design had evolved over such a long time that, despite our enduring love affair with them, their quirks and foibles have created, and sustained a thriving market around them.

My favourite exhibitor, who offered to solve one of those issues, was a dedicated company called Defender Demister. Land Rovers have an ability to mist. Misting happens, of course, where there are temperature variations and moisture. The fact that Land Rovers are barely sealed, leak and have a hairdryer as a heater leads to some pretty spectacular misting. While Land Rover engineers seemed to work out how to demist the windscreen, the rest of the car was liable to resemble the great fogs of London.

I have lost count of the number of times I have sat in an old Land Rover, often in some of the most beautiful corners of the world, my view completely obscured by a perpetual layer of condensation on the inside of the window. The layer of mist would return faster than I could clear it with my elbow. Many Land Rovers even have dedicated rags of chammy leathers to battle the ubiquitous mist.

Defender Demister was the invention of one disgruntled Land Rover driver fed up of years spent driving with condensation. The heating on a Land Rover, as described previously, is freeze or fry. A direct pipe from the engine ensures that either scalding-hot air or ambient air, which more often than not means freezing cold, is piped up through what is little more than a hairdryer into a vent onto the windscreen. The Defender Demister is a simple plastic pipe that takes that hot air along the front dashboard and redirects it towards the side windows, clearing them of mist, too.

It is a simple technique, and the most puzzling thing about it is, why, after more than 60 years of production, has a designer at Land Rover never thought about including this? Even with my basic understanding of engineering and manufacturing it is easy to see how such a simple bit of kit could have been incorporated into the car in the factory, and yet it took them until 2007 to do it themselves. The millions of cars made in the 50 years prior to that all have to make do with a Demister.

I wandered past companies selling rubber matting for the floors and soundproofing material for the engine. There were companies selling everything from engine components to lights. For every exhibitor selling something to improve the Defender, there was another offering the chance to modify it.

There were stands selling Land Rover books and others selling Land Rover magazines, and even holiday companies offering Land Rover safaris in Africa and Iceland. One company, Toylander, was even offering £3000 pedal-car versions of the Series I for children.

One of the biggest cottage industries surrounding the Defender is that of security and theft. When Wilks first designed the Series I, theft was not of primary concern, but the escalating value of Land Rovers in recent years has created an unhealthy market in both the vehicles and their parts – and not just among Defenders: prices have peaked for Series cars too.

Since Land Rover halted production of the Defender there has been a massive spike in the number of thefts. The cars are often pushed silently out of barns and garages and onto trailers or into containers where, more often than not, they are stripped and cannibalised for their parts. So as a result, there are all sorts of anti-theft gadgets now available, marketed directly to the Defender driver, which include everything from gear, pedal and steering wheel locks to immobilisers and alarms.

One Gloucester-based Land Rover specialist had been broken into twice. The thieves had physically moved three different vehicles in order to steal the prized Defender. Frustrated at this repeated assault on their vehicles, the specialists had worked with some former soldiers to create the ultimate Land Rover anti-theft device. The system not only monitors the car's movement but geo-circles the Land Rover, sending you a text if it is moved. The tiniest of vibrations is enough to alert the system. Most impressive of all is the ability to remotely cut off the fuel to the engine.

The fair was an educational experience and a fascinating insight into the world of the Land Rover enthusiast, but, of course, through the course of researching this book I had realised that the love of Land Rovers isn't restricted to bearded individuals. In many cases it is a family affair. My next trip was to meet one such dedicated family.

Not far from Her Majesty's Sandringham Land Rovers live the Hammond family, the self-proclaimed RSPCA of neglected Land Rovers. Hammond Senior was a car mechanic who had become obsessed with Land Rovers at an early age. The handful of rusting Land Rovers parked outside their home gave away the address of the Hammond clan. However, as I was about to discover, this was merely the beginning. Nigel Hammond had ten Land Rovers, while his son Liam had a further three, his other son Tim had

more than 25 cars and Mrs Hammond, not to be outdone, also
had a handful of Land Rovers.

'She's the biggest Land Rover nut of all,' smiled Tim.

The walls of the kitchen were covered with Land Rover clocks,
paintings and photographs. On the floor was a giant Land Rover
showroom floor mat. There were Land Rover models, Land Rover
biscuit tins, mugs, plates, sculptures and tea towels.

'Why the passion?' I asked over a steaming cup of tea.

'Because they are all different,' Tim replied, his hands blackened with grease and oil, 'and you can go anywhere in them,' he
added in his Norfolk drawl. 'They make me grin when I get in
them.'

And this reaction is not just the preserve of Everyman, it seems
to be one shared by even the most critical of car experts, too.
Three generations of BBC *Top Gear* presenters have all owned or
own a classic Land Rover. Richard Hammond has a Series I, as
does the most recent presenter in the driving seat of the world's
most popular motoring show, Chris Evans. But another former
Top Gear presenter, now host of *Fifth Gear*, is motoring expert
Quentin Willson – who is also a serial Land Rover owner.
Quentin is arguably one of Britain's top motoring journalists, but
despite having spent decades surrounded by some of the fastest
and most expensive cars in the world, he is a die-hard Land Rover
aficionado.

His first car was a Series II that he named Georgia, after an old
girlfriend. 'She was enigmatic and mysterious,' smiles Quentin,
his eyes twinkling at the memory of his beloved Land Rover. That
car was the start of a long love affair that has included dozens of
Land Rovers. Another favourite was a Java green Land Rover 109

with a V8 engine. 'She was so powerful that she came with speed limiters for safety,' he told me, 'so the first thing I did was to remove them. I used to race her at 120mph against BMWs.'

A father of three, Quentin soon traded it in for a much-loved family Land Rover 110. 'We used to drive her to France regularly,' he recalls with genuine nostalgia. 'Five dogs and three children,' he adds.

'And Mrs Willson?' I wonder.

'Mrs W preferred to fly,' he chuckles. 'She was never a fan. Can you imagine? Ten hours in that noisy, uncomfortable vehicle? But the children loved it. We used to return with cases of wine on the roof. It was the only vehicle the left-wing French would tolerate. They hate anything with posh pretensions. Can you imagine turning up in a Range Rover?'

Despite its British pedigree, the French would tolerate this work vehicle. Like the iconic French blue work jackets, the Land Rover had stayed close to its working roots.

'My daughter Mini had her own viewing platform on the roof. She loved that car.'

But Quentin eventually sold her. He didn't tell the children. 'One day they noticed she had gone. "Where's the Land Rover?" they asked.' When he told them, they all ran off in tears, inconsolable. 'It is the only car with which you have a genuine emotional connection. There is a period of mourning, like losing a friend.'

I am not surprised to hear these sentiments about the Land Rover, but it seems incredible to hear them from such a respected car journalist. We often anthropomorphise animals, but the Land Rover seems to have a similar bewitching hold over us. Individual and unique, they develop characters and personalities.

'My children never forgave me,' he adds honestly, then went on to try to explain why he believes this car has such a hold over us.

'The Land Rover helped us reach the farthest corners of the Empire. We have an emotional engagement with it. We forgive it its failings. It is part of our roads and furniture, like a listed building. And all of this from Birmingham,' he marvels, 'arguably their most famous export.'

'Apart from Jasper Carrott,' I add.

'And UB40,' he smiles.

There is a weirdness about the Land Rover. It is the unimprovable car that is universally acknowledged by almost everyone who has ever had one as 'shit' – they break down frequently and yet we forgive them.

Of their current popularity, Quentin believes it confirms our 'impulse to preserve'. He repeats the oft-heard mantra of its classlessness.

'It says top bloke. It has retro charm. It is simple, friendly and non-threatening,' he adds. 'It is a car that can turn you into a country squire or farmer. It is safe and solid and dependable. It has saved thousands of lives. It is in the same league as the hovercraft and Concorde. An icon of British engineering.'

Quentin insists it was the progenitor for every SUV, Utility and 4×4 vehicle since, adding, 'It is undoubtedly the most influential car in the world.'

Quentin Willson's long association with Land Rover made him a natural choice to run the proceedings at the ceremony when the final car rolled off the production line in 2016.

'I wasn't paid. I did it for the love of the car. It was a simple ceremony for the staff and employees, many of them second generation for whom Land Rover Series and Defender had been their livelihood and their life.'

In the week leading up to the closing ceremony, the interest in Land Rover reached near-frenzied proportions as the world suddenly realised that we were about to lose part of the architecture of the roads.

Quentin did dozens of interviews, declaring that 'the world had a lump in its throat' as Land Rover prepared to switch off the car's life-support machine.

'Land Rover were completely unprepared for the global reaction,' he revealed.

'Really?' I ask cynically. Surely Land Rover realised the huge affection for this iconic vehicle?

'They have always been a homespun, family type of business,' he explains.

Quentin recalls one of the most extraordinary and saddest days in his motoring career. Where most car ceremonies were well-orchestrated multi-million-pound launches of new vehicles, this was the antithesis; 'no other car marque would have done a final car ceremony,' he insists. This was for the staff.

Men and women were openly crying. The red-eyed audience was moved to tears.

'They played "Jerusalem" and the world wept,' recalls Quentin. I'm sure I see his eyes moisten at the memory. Vicki Butler-Henderson, his television co-host, was at his side. A farmer's daughter, the Land Rover meant as much to her.

'Vicki wobbled as she talked,' he admits. 'It was one of the most moving occasions I have ever witnessed and I feel honoured to have been there.'

Quentin was driven out of the factory in the last car off the line. Incredibly, he was offered the chance to buy one of the last cars off the line, but 'I turned it down because these are cars to be driven, used and loved, not stored away for investment.' Too true.

CHAPTER FOURTEEN

THE CONQUERER

In my travels I have seen what is arguably the most remote Land Rover in the world. In 2003 I set off on a 100,000-mile odyssey around the world in search of the last pink bits on the map, the remnants of the Empire. My journey took me to some of the most isolated islands in the world, spanning the Indian, Pacific and Atlantic oceans.

One that I visited was the Southern Atlantic island of Tristan da Cunha, often described as the most remote inhabited island in the world. 'Inhabited' is key here; while there are plenty of other more isolated and remote isles and islands, it is the permanent population of 267 at the last count that makes this island so unique. It also happens to be an overseas territory of the UK, which means they drink tea, use the pound and celebrate the monarchy. As is often the case with Britain's overseas territories, they are in some ways more British than the British.

To get to Tristan da Cunha is no easy feat. Without an airport or a harbour, the only way to get to the island is to hitch a lift on either a fishing boat or, until 2015, onboard one of the annual sailings of the Royal Mail ship, *St Helena*.

The ship began the long journey to the remote isle from Cape Town, in South Africa. The tiny island made headlines in the 1970s when the volcano on which the settlement is built erupted. The whole population was evacuated to England where they were treated like Victorian circus freaks, oddities from the Southern Ocean. People would come to gawp at these 'lost' people. Unsurprisingly, once the island was deemed safe enough to return, that is exactly what the majority of the population did.

The settlement of Edinburgh of the Seven Seas (to avoid confusion with Edinburgh of Scotland) is built on the relatively flat plateau at one end of the volcanic island. Here there is one single road that leads from the city to the potato patches, about a mile away.

At the time of my visit, the island policing fell to Conrad Glass, and according to recent reports he is still the sole policeman. His vehicle is a Land Rover Defender. On an island 2000 miles from Africa, Inspector Glass is able to patrol his beat with the formidable 4×4. He must be a good deterrent because he has only made one arrest in his 25 years on the island, which is just as well, as there isn't a prison or even a cell.

'It's hard to remain aloof on such a small island, but that's what I try to do. I only go to the Albatross Inn [the only pub] once or twice a year. I'm not much of a drinker and I'm much happier at home with a book.

'I don't want to do this forever. Neither of my special constables wants to take over and nobody has come forward. I'd be very happy for an officer from the UK to come and do the job and I'd love to arrange for somebody to come out here for a month and see if they like it.'

What is most incredible about this story is how a Land Rover managed to find its way to one of the most remote corners of the world, and how unique its presence is there. On mainland Africa, though, it is another story. There the Land Rover is a familiar, reassuring presence – viewed with love and frustration in equal measure.

'The death knell for the Land Rover,' opined Tanzanian bushman and naturalist Rob Glen while we bounced through the Ruaha National Park in Southern Tanzania, 'was the Td5. How can you expect bush people to perform electronic diagnostics on a car when we don't even have electricity?' he added in frustration.

'Then they gave us the Puma engine with six gears. Six GEARS!' he repeats in incredulity. 'Why does a bushman need six gears, boy? Land Rover started chasing the wrong market. They abandoned their rural roots long ago and focused on the luxury city market. They abandoned the working market, the farmers, the conservationists, the scientists and the bush people.'

It amazed me that a 60-year-old Tanzanian could feel such emotions for a car produced thousands of miles away, but the Land Rover had become a significant part of African life.

The Land Rover has helped define Rob's life more than any other vehicle. A natural historian and explorer, Rob has spent the best part of 50 years exploring the continent in search of new species of bird, mammal and reptile.

'We were in our Land Rover, at the base of the Ugandan mountains, collecting bird specimens for the Natural History Museum when we found ourselves under mortar attack from the Ugandan military who had mistaken us for rebels. They had heard gunshots and assumed we were armed militants. It was nightfall so we rushed to our Land Rovers and turned on all the engines and lights to make sure we were visible. If it wasn't for my Land Rover we would have been shelled again and killed, boy.'

My favourite story from Rob was when he was returning from an expedition in Gabon. His Land Rover was laden with sackfuls of snakes when they were stopped by suspicious border patrol police. Their Land Rover was impounded along with the three explorers.

'We had grown straggly beards,' Rob admits ruefully, 'the telltale sign that we were mercenaries.'

The prison was already full, so they were held in a small garden next to the police station. After a couple of days, Rob became concerned about the health of the snakes in the Land Rover so he decided to 'take them for a walk'. He opened the bags on the grass and 'aired' the dozens of horned vipers and Gabon vipers, some of the most venomous and feared snakes in Africa.

'You should have heard the police scream!' chuckles Rob at the memory.

Meanwhile, half the village had turned up to stare at these suspected mercenaries, only to witness their extraordinary display of snake handling. Realising they were snake collectors, dozens of locals proceeded to arrive at the police station clutching bags of venomous snakes.

The police chief, terrified of the serpents, eventually had enough and released Rob and his Land Rover of vipers. Rob, like the Land Rover, came from a different era when men were men and cars were cars.

I discovered Africa late. I was 27 when I first set foot in Zambia. I was in the Luangwa Valley on a walking safari and I fell head over heels in love with the dark continent. Having previously shunned Africa for Latin America, I spent the following 15 years trying to make up for that lost time.

I travelled and worked extensively from Namibia and Botswana to Uganda and Kenya. The safari lifestyle still had echoes of *Out of Africa*, frozen in a nostalgic epoch of charm and beauty. I can remember my resolve to one day return with my children in tow, and it was while filming my year-long natural history series, during which I followed the migration of the wildebeest, that I finally brought my wife and children to join me in Northern Tanzania.

The Land Rover has a rich heritage in Africa. Its sturdiness and long presence on the continent is why the Defender is a car that became synonymous with Africa. The UK was still a colonial power at the time of its inception and so the car spread throughout its colonies. It was quickly snapped up and used by government officials, for expeditions, safaris and hunting.

From the beginning, Land Rover produced specialised vehicles for non-governmental organisations (NGOs). Its original specification as a go-anywhere vehicle made it ideal for the many functions required by NGOs. Its rugged capability and durability had made it popular with the military, police and rescue services, ambulances, missionary and aid organisations, and the mining industry around the world.

Right from the start, Rover made bespoke vehicles from its Solihull plant, tailoring vehicles to specific requirements. This would later become known as Land Rover's Special Vehicles Operations, which in recent years was renamed Land Rover's ETO (Engineered to Order).

Until the end of Defender production early in 2016, the ETO produced numerous adapted vehicles. While retaining the legendary characteristics of the standard Defender, the AVM range was tailored to a number of civilian, industrial, emergency response and security roles in which the vehicle's strength, reliability and performance were key factors.

The AVM range differed from other post-manufacture conversions undertaken by firms like Foley's, Nene and Twisted by virtue of having been engineered to the same high levels as Land Rover's standard vehicles. Whereas modifications by non-approved converters would not be covered by Land Rover warranties and could in some cases actually invalidate them, the AVM range also carried the full weight of the company's service support network and enjoyed the benefits of the same warranties as unmodified Land Rovers. To qualify as an AVM, converters had to abide by rigorous design, purchase, quality and manufacturing standards. All designs and finished products were tested to ensure that the conversion elements did not compromise the vehicle's capabilities.

During the 1980s, aid flooded in to Africa following the worldwide reaction to Live Aid and Band Aid. Non-governmental organisations swamped Africa. The British Red Cross, Christian

Aid, Oxfam, Save the Children, Water Aid, UNICEF and the UNHCR, to name just a few of the thousands of charities to descend onto the African continent. They needed sturdy vehicles to allow them to access those previously inaccessible communities ravaged by disease, famine, war or social unrest.

The Land Rover was the perfect vehicle, having long been adapted as the ideal car for the rich and varied terrain of Africa, and an abundance of parts, and mechanics knowledgeable in the workings of the simple, uncomplicated engine, meant that cars could be easily repaired.

In recent years the car has become indispensable to environmentalists and conservationists – WWF, Tusk, Born Free and Save the Rhino have all used Solihull's most famous car in their efforts to protect the natural world. Over the years I have been fortunate enough to tag elephants, track lions, follow poachers and even go on safari with Princes William and Harry, all from the back of a humble, loyal Land Rover.

In the last decade and a half, though, Land Rover's ubiquitous presence has been replaced by its Japanese opposition, the Land Cruiser. Many have wondered how Land Rover lost its foothold in Africa, and indeed other parts of the world. It is unquestionably a part of the reason for the end of production. Worldwide sales simply did not make economic business sense to JLR.

But how did a car once so prolific lose out to what many argue was technically an inferior car?

Price, ease of repair and quantity of parts seem to have been responsible for the flood of Land Cruisers and Hilux across Africa that quite literally left Land Rover in their dust. The Land Rover simply became too expensive to buy and its maintenance was complicated by the advent of the high-tech, electronic engine that required expensive diagnostic machines where once a mechanic and a pair of stockings had sufficed.

It had always saddened me to see the demise of this iconic vehicle. Over the years they had become more and more elusive. They were always there, but they had become the cheetah to the more prolific lions.

Marina, Ludo and Iona had arrived in Tanzania to spend a couple of weeks with me while I was working out there. We planned a road trip to explore the rich wildlife of the East African nation. There was only ever one car I could consider for such a family expedition: a Land Rover Defender.

Fortunately for us, a Bristolian had spotted this niche market long before the arrival of the Fogle family and had gathered a fleet of Birmingham's finest at a workshop on the outskirts of Arusha. It was certainly a brave commercial gamble in a country that had all but fallen to the lure of the Toyota. To make matters worse, we were off to join a group of British expats and their convoy of Land Cruisers.

'What is that?' asked Paul, one of the expats, as we pulled up in our bright yellow Land Rover nicknamed Queenie.

The comment contained a double barb, given that it came from a Brit himself. Where was his patriotism? I wondered.

'You won't get far,' he winked as we headed off into the wilderness with a Land Rover laden with camping gear and the family.

His patriotism had merely been replaced by practicality, as I soon discovered as we bounced and lurched along the rough tracks. His choice of vehicle soon made sense when we left the track and headed across country. The rains had turned the

ground to a boggy quagmire and the wide tyres on the Land
Rover hung beyond the mud rim coating the car in a thick layer
of muck and slime.

Windows obscured, I proceeded to drive into a warthog hole
where we came to a shuddering halt.

Now, I had some experience of driving a Land Rover off-road,
but even that did not prepare me for what I had to attempt here.

In fact, the first off-road course I had ever done was back in
2001 at Eastnor Castle on the edge of the Cotswolds, as part of
the Land Rover Driving Experience. This was followed by a
slightly bizarre experience, when, for some inexplicable reason, I
found myself agreeing to do a show for BBC1 called *Stars in Fast
Cars*, taking part in an assortment of car challenges alongside
Edwina Curry, Reggie Yates and DJ Spoony.

The first competition was to drive a white Transit van around
a race circuit which was filled with hundreds of pieces of crockery, the winner being the driver who smashed the most crockery.
Next up was a race around the track in a Lamborghini ... towing
a bath full of water. The winner was the car that spilled the least
water. Have you ever tried driving a sports car at 5mph? It's agony.
But it was the final challenge that I enjoyed the most, an off-road
safari in a Land Rover Defender.

A Land Rover only really comes alive when it embraces mud,
water, hills and gradients, and in this challenge we had to drive
along steep cantilevered slopes that threatened to topple the vehicle, through deep channels of water and up seemingly impossibly
steep climbs. We drove over seesaw bridges and across boulders
and deep sand in a course that was designed to test the driver as
much as the car.

The fear of losing to Edwina Currie was too much to bear and somehow I pulled through and won the heat, but in the end I lost the competition to Reggie Yates, who beat me in one final challenge of car darts, in which we had to fire full vehicles from a huge cannon towards a giant 'car dart' board.

My next off-roading course in a Land Rover was in 2012 when I teamed up with the comedian and actor Hugh Dennis for the BBC's *World's Most Dangerous Roads*. We were put together for a car journey that would take us from the high Andes of Peru down to the muggy tropical rainforest of the Amazon far below. But before we embarked on our South American adventure, we had to master the skills required to cross one of the toughest roads in the world, which we attempted to do in rural Wales. Hugh and I took turns to navigate through thick mud and across deep reservoirs, and what stays with me about that challenge is the image of Hugh in a pair of waders in water up to his waist holding a stick to test the depth of water, looking slightly ludicrous.

This time, it was my turn to look ridiculous. I used all the off-roading skills that I had learnt on these experiences to extract us from the hole, but Queenie wouldn't budge. It got worse, though. To my utter horror and humiliation we had to be towed from the bog by a Land Cruiser. The Japanese car saving the Brit ... Even worse, this was only the beginning. Over the week, much to the amusement of everyone else, we had to be rescued half a dozen times. Hugh, I shall never laugh at you again.

However, despite my mishaps on that trip, I still believe that the Land Rover is Africa's car. Kingsley Holgate agrees with me.

According to him, Africans see it as their car, as much a part of the African landscape as the acacia and the elephant.

Kingsley Holgate is a South African explorer and humanitarian who has been described as 'the most travelled man in Africa', and who is, by his own description, a modern-day David Livingstone. Holgate's expeditions are rarely completed on his own; notably they usually involve him travelling with other members of his family, including his wife Gill and son Ross.

He has crossed Africa from Cape Town to Cairo following the lakes and rivers of the continent in open boats, then circumnavigated the globe using various methods of transport following the Tropic of Capricorn. He has also re-created Livingstone's 1862 expedition up the Ruvuma River, which separates Mozambique and Tanzania, to Lake Malawi or the 'Lake of Stars', circumnavigated Lake Victoria in an open boat following in the footsteps of H.M. Stanley and his boat the *Lady Alice* and tracked the Rufiji River in tribute to explorer Captain Frederick Selous. Most recently, he has crossed 33 countries promoting malaria awareness, and he has founded the Kingsley Holgate Foundation, which aims to save and improve lives through adventure, with the mantra 'humanitarian expeditions that make a difference'.

This has been the focus of his more recent expeditions such as the Africa Rainbow Expedition and the Outside Edge Expedition, in which he handed out thousands of mosquito nets to help prevent malaria; and the Right to Sight campaign, which provides glasses to assist the hard of sight, allowing them to resume simple tasks such as sewing, reading and beadwork to help them contribute to their community. The third campaign, Teaching on the Edge, a scheme supported by Centurus Colleges and Rotary

International, aims to provide teaching resources and mobile libraries to remote communities to provide education and improve literacy.

When I met Kingsley at the British Motor Museum in Gaydon, he was admiring the Series I hard top and he spoke for a generation of Africans. 'Beautiful, eh?' he commented in his African lilt, his mouth hidden beneath his huge beard. 'These cars are really something, they have saved thousands of lives, eh. You might think of them as your car, but they are Africa's car, they helped open up the whole continent.'

Kingsley's comments were a sobering reminder that a vehicle that has done so much for British society has affected lives way beyond our borders and beyond the wildest dreams of the Wilks brothers, too, when they etched their diagram in the sands of Anglesey all those years ago.

But we should not forget that from the very beginning Land Rover realised the importance of overseas sales and the global nature of this go-anywhere car, so providing regional-spec vehicles that were tailored towards specific environments and geographies was a crucial part of their marketing strategy.

No two countries are the same, and many require specific models to suit their own specific landscapes and environment.

For Sweden, where most parts of the country have long, bitterly cold winters, they produced a special vehicle with climatic characteristics not found in many other territories where Land Rovers were sold. The standard Land Rover had no heater at all, and even the 1949 update did little more than burn the legs of whoever was sitting in the passenger seat, so a small specialist company in Stockholm developed a special cab and high-output heater to deal with the problem. Their solution was to build a fully enclosed and insulated driving compartment onto the standard Land Rover bulkhead which overhung beyond its edges, giving the grip-converted vehicles a very distinct appearance.

In the spring of 1951 the Rover company allowed Minerva to build Land Rovers under licence for the Belgian army. The Minervas had a unique specification that included a locally made steel body with sloping wing front, a unique grille and a fixed rear panel in place of a drop-down tailgate.

After deliveries were completed in 1956, the Belgian army stockpiled many vehicles, so it was not until the 1960s and even the 1970s that large quantities entered service. Some were kitted out as assault vehicles with pedestal-mounted machine guns, armoured front wings and windscreens, while others were fitted with Milan guided-missile systems.

Brazil was another country to request specific adaptations, the locally made Land Rovers were cheaper than their equivalents from Solihull, with better ventilation, particularly through opening vents towards the back of the hard tops' sides. The doors were single-piece items that had their own interior trim panels.

Australia soon followed suit with its own CKD made from local materials. The vehicles were originally made for the Snowy Mountains' hydroelectric scheme in New South Wales.

There were many other CKD operations around the world during the Series II era, but one of the most interesting was the Santana one in Spain. The name 'Santana' came from the name of the company, Metalurgica de Santa Ana (MSA), which ran the Land Rover operation at a factory in Linares. In the early 1950s the Spanish government had erected trade barriers to protect and encourage local industry, and these made the export of Land Rovers to Spain prohibitively expensive. However, the Spanish were prepared to approve the manufacture in Spain of Land Rovers from CKD kits, on condition that the proportion of Spanish-sourced components gradually increased over the years until the whole vehicle was actually made in Spain.

There were endless delays in establishing the Spanish CKD operation, which was initially run with Rover's Spanish importers, Tabanera Romagosa, as intermediaries. Agreement in principle was reached during 1956, but the assembly lines were not ready for operation until November 1958. So the first Santana Land Rovers were Series II models.

In all important respects these were identical to Solihull's own series IIs; the Spanish-built vehicles had locally sourced instruments, trim, glass and probably tyres. In addition, the Santana Land Rovers incorporated the Santana name below the oval Land Rover grille and tail badges. In due course, Santana introduced locally manufactured options, such as chromed hubcaps and body edge trim, and these appear to have been available before the end of Series II production. The very first vehicle was presented to Generalissimo Franco, the Spanish Head of State, in a gesture that attracted welcome publicity for the new venture.

Series II Santanas were built at a rate of more than 500 a year, which would give a production total of around 1500. All of these were sold on the Spanish home market, and over the years Santana produced several Land Rovers, making its Series IV, or 2500, as it was known, from 1983 until 1994. But then the entire production line and tooling were sold to Morattab and shipped to Iran.

For years Iran had been under tough global sanctions and had been forced to manufacture its own vehicles because the draconian embargo meant they couldn't import Western vehicles. Morattab, based in Tehran, has been making Series clones since the 60s, based on an original from the CKD kits sent from Spain. In fact, Iran is now the only place in the world where you can still buy a version of the Land Rover Defender, known locally as the Morattab Pazhan.

Versions of the Series Land Rover have been made under licence in a variety of countries over the decades, including Germany, Belgium, Spain and Turkey, but the Iranian model is a version of the Series IV Land Rover, and its production in Iran came about as a result of a partnership with Santana Motor. Santana signed an agreement with Land Rover in the 1950s to produce a version of its famous off-roader and production started with a Spanish version of the Series II in 1959.

It is the descendant of that vehicle that is still produced today in Tehran. It was based on the Land Rover Series III but it had suspension with leaf springs rather than the coil springs used by Land Rover. Morattab started full production in 1970. The Iranian Land Rover was originally powered by a 1.8 cylinder petrol engine and then a Nissan engine. In 2004, in an effort to match the Land Rover Defender, the Morattab was completely redesigned with selectable four-wheel drive. At a cost of around £13,000, it was only sold as a double cab pick up. Restrictions in Iran meant that only petrol engines were offered. Today, of course, the Morattab Pazhan could well be the holy grail for those wanting a new Land Rover Series.

But it wasn't just a need for adaptability to climate that brought about these internationally tailored vehicles. In many countries the

Land Rovers were being asked to cross terrains and work in industries that the designers in Solihull might never have dreamed of.

The mining industry required vehicles that could carry heavy loads while providing access to wild and remote regions, and from this need the Mine Site Defenders were born. The cars featured roll-over bar protection as standard, front nudge bars for greater impact resistance, and underbody skid plates that helped to protect key areas of the underside, such as the sump and steering mechanism.

For safety around the mine environment they were fitted with amber roof lights, reversing buzzers, top and bottom reversing lights and a flagpole mount, which provided improved visibility when operating in the vicinity of larger mine vehicles, and a roof-mounted LED light bar that could be programmed to display signals to drivers of other vehicles. Each car was also fitted with fire extinguishers, battery isolators, first-aid kits and vehicle recovery kits.

Even below ground, the mining industry soon realised that Land Rovers could be the perfect vehicles to shuttle miners down to the bowels of the Earth. Some Land Rovers were completely disassembled before being rebuilt beneath the ground; indeed, today there are hundreds of Land Rovers inside abandoned mines across the globe.

The Defender also had a role in protecting valuable commodities across the world, as well as people.

Land Rover offered a protected cash-in-transit (CIT) vehicle as part of the AVM range. The Defender's payload capability allowed a high level of protection to be provided without adversely affecting the vehicle's excellent performance.

These vehicles were built to withstand armed attacks. These security vehicles had armoured cabs and a transparent armour system to deter would-be attackers. The cash vault was in a compartment that used multi-layered anti-intruder materials in its construction, and was equipped with a secure drop-chute and protected electrical system. The vault could be reconfigured to carry everything from coins to gold.

A number of options were available to increase protection levels. They included an armoured security guard compartment and a transparent armour upgrade to give better protection against ballistic threats, and there were gun ports and racks in the compartments for the driver and the security guard. Additional seating for two more guards could be provided in the rear compartment, and the front and rear areas were linked by an intercom system, rear-view camera system, anti-blast three-point security lock system, an escape hatch for the rear cabin occupants and GPS tracking systems.

Land Rovers were popular cars in some of the more remote regions of the world, but perhaps one of the most interesting markets that the marque reached was North America. The USA is often referred to as the land of the car. It is a nation that has built its infrastructure around motorised transport. It is almost impossible to explore, live or work in the United States without a car.

Of course, we know that the Land Rover itself owes a great deal to its American cousin, the Willys Jeep, and the United States has arguably dominated the world in the market for SUVs and 4×4s. It is a nation in which bigger is better. This is the land that gave us the commercial Hummer.

It was always a natural market for the Land Rover; indeed, Rover themselves had once arguably taken the suicidal decision to focus on the American market rather than that of the Middle Eastern market with their choice of diesel over petrol. They wanted a piece of the North American market, but the ascent of America's strict and draconian safety legislation, and a notoriously litigious population which thrived on blame culture, led to the death of the modern Defender.

Perhaps the most infamous event featuring a Land Rover in the USA was that of the 'kidnapped Defenders'. In 2015, The Department for Homeland Security (DHS) impounded 25 Land Rover Defenders on the grounds that the imported Defenders were younger than the 25-year exemption and as such did not meet US DOT and EPA regulations.

One of the first owners to have a visit from DHS was Danny Harrington, from upstate New York. Ten DHS officers stormed his garage early one July morning demanding the seizure of his 1983 One Ten. Treating the Land Rover enthusiast like some drugs junkie, the armed officers claimed the vehicle was a year 2000 model and towed it away. Just a few weeks earlier Danny had replaced the clutch himself in a 10-hour marathon. As a friend of Danny's said: 'All the dude ever wanted was his hunk of junk truck back!'

It seems pretty astonishing that the Department for Homeland Security had focused their attention and resources on a Land Rover enthusiast and his 'hunk of junk', but perhaps it is testament to the overall power of the Land Rover to create overwhelming sentiments both for and against.

The story became a cause célèbre. What the government failed to investigate was the total make-up of the chassis number. They only referenced the numeric vehicle identifier, which vehicle manufacturers recycle on a regular basis based upon production volumes. In short, the vehicles were classics from 1995 and therefore perfectly legal.

Another owner of a 'kidnapped' vehicle, Will Hedrick, became known in the press as the Defender of the Defenders. He gave up his regular law practice to work full time on the liberation of the Defenders and the rights of Americans to drive a Land Rover.

It took him nearly 10 months to reach a settlement with the Department of Homeland Security, in which it was agreed that all the vehicles were to be returned to the owners within 30 days at no cost to the owners. A celebration party was organised for all the Defender owners, with Will (Defender of Defenders) as guest of honour.

It has always thrilled me that a vehicle born to serve the farmer in war-torn Britain went on to conquer the world. The humble Land Rover in its various forms from Series I through to the powerful Defender had captured the hearts and imagination of people around the globe. Everyone from dictators and humanitarian relief agencies to mercenaries and missionaries had seen the benefits of this robust utilitarian vehicle with its no-nonsense, go-anywhere capabilities.

The Land Rover was able to reach remote regions that were otherwise inaccessible, providing aid and relief to those dispossessed and displaced by war, famine and disease. The Land Rover has undoubtedly been utilised in plenty of the world's dirty conflicts and civil wars, but there is also no doubt that the humble vehicle from Solihull has helped save thousands, if not hundreds of thousands, of lives across the globe by providing medical aid to the planet's most remote regions.

While the Land Rover may have lost her dominance around the world, her legacy is as rich and emotive as the day the first Series I began exploring the furthest regions of the Earth.

CHAPTER FIFTEEN

THE AFFAIR

I have heard the effect Land Rovers have over us described variously as a creeping tide of fungus and as an affliction. Rarely on
my journey have I met anyone with just one Land Rover. Land
Rovers seem to have this power to make even the most rational
person begin to collect and hoard. Maybe it's because a Land
Rover never really dies. They may rust and eventually fall apart,
but their parts live on; they become donor vehicles.

Farmers have always been resourceful folk. Visit any farm and
you will invariably see the decaying frame of a Series or Defender
in a barn or a corner of a field. The usefulness of the donor vehicle has given many an excuse to hoard and collect vehicles and I
have visited dozens of people with huge collections of Landys in
varying states of decay.

I am not a natural petrol head. Cars have always been very
practical items in my mind. The Defender was the perfect car for

me and I never had need of anything else. But over the course of my journey, something had happened. Something had changed. A small flame had become a burning fire.

Like an affair, I had been seduced by another vehicle. I know I shouldn't. My Defender, Polly, gave me everything I needed and more. She was loyal, dependable and great on the road. She was pretty and outgoing and we had fun together, but another car had caught my eye. An older model. She had a charm and a wit that I found beguiling. She wasn't so much beautiful as she was handsome. She had weathered the years with magnificence. She had a regal sophistication.

At first I found myself sneaking looks at her in photographs from magazines and books, but soon I started searching online. I found one site which agreed to rent her by the hour or even by the day. My heart would skip and my stomach fluttered as I pictured a new life together. Exploring the countryside together. Going topless around London.

I became captivated and smitten by the idea. I needed her in my life.

After a few weeks of online flirting, I finally made the decision to make the call, the call that would seal our fate together forever. We talked about the legality. Would she be allowed to come to live with me in London? Where would she live? How expensive would she be? What kind of maintenance should I expect? Was she reliable? Would she let me down?

It was a huge decision to make, both emotionally and financially. I already had a beautiful wife, two incredible children and a car I had always longed for. Did I really need to do it? Was it worth the risk?

Sometimes you have to give in to your animal instinct, you have to go with your heart rather than your head. I settled on a fee and we agreed to be together.

And so I found myself aboard a train racing north to Thirsk, in Yorkshire, to meet the object of my desires. She had been the subject of many sleepless nights and arguments/debates with my wife.

'Here you go,' smiled John, as he walked me up a track towards a big barn. My heart was racing in anticipation.

He pulled a heavy gate and we walked into the gloom. Sunlight cast shadows across the rough floor as we walked towards a dark silhouette. With a flick of a switch, the lights illuminated the room and there she was.

I had to catch my breath. I felt that kind of tummy knotting that you get when you are excited and nervous at the same time. I couldn't help staring at her. She was beautiful. Much more beautiful than I had expected. She had aged well. Her body was sun-kissed and weathered, her wrinkles and dents were evidence of a life well lived.

Her body was trim and she was shorter than I expected, but she was neat and trim and ... perfect. Absolutely perfect. Suddenly Polly was a thing of the past. Here was my future. She was older, but she bore the wisdom of her age well.

'Here you go,' John said again, handing me a key. 'She's yours now.'

I was finally the owner of a Series I Land Rover, a 1949, lights behind the grille in green. I stuck my hand through the little hole in the tarp and opened the door. Inside she was even more perfect. A broad uncontrolled grin had taken over my face. I couldn't believe she was mine. This was one of the progenitors, a car from which all other SUVs and 4×4s have adapted and evolved.

This was the car that helped transform the face of agriculture. It helped farmers mechanise their farms. This was the car that spread across the world, becoming part of the African savannahs and the Welsh hills. The car that helped build the infrastructure of this whole country. The car that had helped save millions of lives around the world delivering aid and charity work for NGOs in some of the least hospitable and wildest environments. The car that has policed our streets, protected our shores and rescued the lost. The car that has become the symbol of safety, discovery and durability.

And now I was a part of that rich heritage.

This car had been in service for 67 years and now she was going to be a part of mine and my family's lives.

I was surprised by my emotions. Not in a weepy way, but in a harder-to-define sentiment. It was overwhelming to take possession of a vehicle that had plagued my days and nights while I researched this book. In doing so, the Series I had become slightly mythological. Folkloric. This was a car that people talked about with reverence in slightly hushed tones and now she was mine.

I wanted to get to know her, to understand her quirks and her foibles. I'm not sure why, but there had never been a question of where I would take her first. I wanted to take her on a pilgrimage to where it all began. Like a beautiful poem, I wanted to take her to Anglesey in Wales, where, in 1948, Wilks had drawn that iconic image in the sand.

Perhaps unsurprisingly, having never spent much time in such an old vehicle, I felt the tiniest bit of apprehension in embarking on such a long road journey on my own without support. So I enlisted the help of two Land Rover experts, John Brown and his mechanic Ben. They would both share the journey with me. Besides the fact that it would be enjoyable to have company, it was also somewhat reassuring to have someone who actually knew what to do if she broke down.

I turned the engine and she hummed into life. Soon we were cruising west towards the northwest corner of Wales.

She was noisy, bouncy and clunky, but I couldn't wipe the smile from my face. Where in my Defender the 'Landy wave' was restricted to other Defender drivers, in my Series I, everyone waved and nodded.

My co-driver, John, was a one-time school teacher who has now become one of the most respected names in vintage Land Rovers. As a teacher he had been plagued by debilitating headaches and at 30 his deteriorating health forced him to abandon teaching for something less stressful. While on a trip to California, he had come across an old Land Rover and the obsession was born.

He came back to Yorkshire and bought an ex-military light-weight. 'I did it up nice,' he explained, and before the paint had dried he had found a buyer. He repeated this and found he couldn't keep up with demand.

Together with his wife, childhood sweetheart Lisa, they set up John Brown 4×4 (due to copyright laws they had to change their original name, John Brown Land Rovers), and they now have some of the best vintage Land Rovers in the country, regularly hiring them out for fashion shoots. 'We recently hired one for a

Ralph Lauren shoot in London,' he smiled with pride. 'Ralph Lauren wanted to buy it but it wasn't for sale,' he adds. 'Another went to a Belstaff shoot with David Gandy.'

John talks of each of his Land Rovers as if they were his children. He knows them intimately and often talks potential customers out of a sale if he doesn't think it's the right car for them, 'a vintage Land Rover is like a bespoke suit; it has to be right for you,' being his fervently held belief.

His customers are wide and varied and they often have an immediate emotional bond with the cars. 'One customer had bought a Series II, then, when he came up to collect her, he slipped into the driver's seat and he realised his girth was too large. The steering wheel wedged against his belly,' he told me. 'The poor man sobbed his eyes out. He had always longed for a Series II, and now that he was in it he realised he couldn't ever drive it. He and his wife both left in tears.'

One of John's favourite projects was when he discovered the remains of Hugh Fearnley-Whittingstall's gastro-wagon Land Rover that he had converted for his very first series of *River Cottage*. The car had largely been dismantled by its previous owner, and John and his team had meticulously reassembled her by watching the old series and taking screen grabs to work out where all the pieces belonged.

Land Rovers still run deep within the Brown family. His son, also named John, recently passed his bar exams to become a lawyer, but instead he is set to take over the family business because 'Land Rovers run in the blood'.

When John's daughter Meg recently got married, they ferried the bridesmaids to the church in a Series II while the ushers and best man all arrived in a mighty forward-drive 101; 'we use her once a year to collect the Christmas tree'.

People have very different requirements from their Series Rovers. Some want them rebuilt to perfection, and it is not unknown for people to spend upwards of £60,000 on a mint condition Series I, but according to John 'the trend from North America is for the Rat Rod look, whereby the engine, brakes and chassis are all overhauled but the body is left rusty and rough. They want it mechanically sound but visually imperfect.'

Before we reached Red Wharf Bay, where it had all begun, I wanted to visit David Mitchell of Landcraft 4×4. Dave is one of the country's top off-road instructors, having spent many years teaching courses in Bala, but he is better known for his collection of toy Land Rovers.

One of the benefits from doing this book is that I always know if I have come to the right place when meeting people as there is always at least one Land Rover parked nearby. In Dave's case, true to form, there were half a dozen Land Rovers parked outside his house.

Inside the garage was another Land Rover, this one a Defender SVX, perhaps Land Rover's most 'aggressive' model. When his parents passed away, in their will they insisted Dave bought himself a new Land Rover. It is certainly one of the most striking Defenders; indeed, it was the same one that had inspired Princess Haya to buy a Land Rover.

But I wasn't here to see full-scale Land Rovers, I was here to see one of the world's largest collections of Land Rover toys.

To say the garage was stuffed would be an understatement. Boxes and boxes lined the walls and the floor, their little Perspex windows revealing Land Rovers of every shape and size. There were radio-controlled Land Rovers and ride-aboard Land Rovers, but these were only the tip of the iceberg.

'Are you ready?' his eyes twinkled mischievously.

The door opened to reveal an Aladdin's cave of Land Rovers, hundreds and thousands of them, but this wasn't the only reason for the diversion. Dave began his career selling Land Rover parts. He was then taken on by Land Rover to train staff in how to use the vehicle. He would use and test the various models on off-road tracks. He ended up putting on shows for Land Rover and even launching new models. His off-road business in Bala (the same place where I had done my off-road course with Hugh Dennis) had taken off, but then life took a downturn. His wife was diagnosed with cancer and he had to take time off work. He reneged on a contract and he lost the business. His eyes moisten as he recounts how he saw his life's work 'stolen' from him.

He turned to his other great hobby: model cars. What started as a hobby soon turned into a business. He diversified and began to sell belts until Land Rover instigated one of its periodic copyright clampdowns. I had heard about these legal onslaughts by dozens of people during my Land Rover tour. The lawyers forced him to burn and crush his entire stock of Land Rover belts and he returned once again to model collecting and selling.

He discovered there was a huge market at the Land Rover shows for people to buy models and replicas of their vehicles, and business boomed. He estimated he has 5000 different models: 'by different, it might just be the packaging or the colour or a licence plate alteration. This is where I become quite mad,' he admits with candid honesty. 'You see, if there are two identical cars, but the font of the writing is slightly different on the box, or there is a different texture cardboard, I have to have both. I know it sounds ridiculous, because it is.'

The room was bursting with Land Rovers of every conceivable colour and size. I recognised many of the unique vehicles I had discovered along my journey. It struck me that I could have done a great deal of research here in this cluttered room of Land Rover history. Every toy Land Rover is modelled on the original car, leaving behind a wealth of information about the history of the car in miniature. It was like my pilgrimage had been shrunk to miniature proportions.

Of course, miniature proportions certainly didn't mean miniature prices. Many of the cars in the collection still had their boxes and price tags, and most of them seemed to be priced between £20 and £30. Given that his personal collection runs at over 5000 items, not to mention the stock for sale, he has many hundreds of thousands of pounds tied up in toy cars.

Some of the models can fetch massive prices, too. 'There are about 10 big collectors like me out there,' Dave confirms. 'One limited edition Land Rover model recently sold for £16,000.'

And of course the models don't stop there. The world of miniature-scale drivable Land Rovers for children is also booming. One Chepstow-based company is offering replicas of Series I, II and III for up to £5000 for a pedal car, while Land Rover themselves manufactured a £10,000 pedal car version of the Defender.

'There are scale models of the Range Rover complete with petrol engines that sell for the same price as a brand-new Range Rover,' marvels Dave. Sixty grand for a children's toy car seems excessive, but I shouldn't be surprised by the power of the brand.

Dave had agreed to join our merry little convoy of Land Rovers on the pilgrimage to Anglesey. I love the way the Land Rover has the ability to bring together such a disparate group of individuals who would never normally meet.

We stopped for lunch in a pub, and John entertained everyone on the piano while young Ben listened to Dave's tales of his adventures.

Slowly we meandered through the mountains and hills of Snowdonia. The beauty was enough to make angels sing. John and I sat in awe as our little convoy snaked past lakes, over mountain passes and moorland and past cascading waterfalls. This was true Land Rover country.

The undisputed birthplace of the Land Rover is a remote corner of Anglesey in North Wales. The island, separated from the mainland by the Menai Strait, is a beautiful place, perhaps best known currently as the place in which the Duke and Duchess of Cambridge spent the first few years of their marriage away from the prying eyes of the world. For me, though, it has a rather different meaning. It was the place in which I ended up on the front page of national papers under the memorable headline, 'TV Star in Helicopter Crash'.

I had been working for BBC's rural affairs programme *Countryfile*, a show in which I cemented my love affair with the Land Rover. We had our own *Countryfile* Land Rover and we would explore the country visiting farmers and country folk. I have lost track of the number of times we bounced across a field or got bogged down in mud as we explored our green and pleasant hills and valleys, but for this particular episode we had parked the Land Rover and replaced her with a ship.

The *Patricia* belonged to Trinity, the company responsible for lighthouse maintenance around Great Britain. Since the last lighthouse was automated, her role had become even more crucial, replacing light bulbs and carrying out maintenance on some of the remotest lighthouses around our coastline. I have long been fascinated by lighthouses, and this was my first experience visiting a tiny unmanned station off the coast of Anglesey.

It was a typically windy, overcast day as we boarded the *Patricia*. We were a small film crew of just four and soon we were rocking and rolling on the Irish Sea. The weather had taken a turn for the worse and our director was horizontal with seasickness – even my rock-solid constitution was being tested as we bucked and yawed in the ever-increasing winds.

Force 7 became 8 and then 9. Unpleasant conditions for anyone. To be honest, it seemed highly unlikely that we would get a chance to go ashore, so you can imagine my surprise when we were instructed to get ready for a helicopter transfer.

Obviously, working the relentlessly stormy coastline of Britain had hardened the crew of the *Patricia*. If they waited for benign conditions their work would never be done.

We were talked through the emergency drill and had to practise getting into the large orange 'once only' survival suits. Soon we were ready and we swayed and stumbled our way out onto the aft deck where the helicopter was tethered. The wind was howling and saltwater spray was breaking over the side of the ship. We boarded the helicopter as the pilot carefully lifted us off the bucking deck.

The helicopter jumped and jostled as we fought into the wind towards the remote isolated island offshore. Once again, the pilot slowly lowered the chopper to the ground and we all hopped out. We ducked down and got as far from the helicopter blades as we could before the pilot took off back to the ship.

So far no crash. We were safely on the island and we began to film our tour of the lighthouse with the last resident keeper of the light.

However, the weather continued to worsen and in the distance we could occasionally make out the silhouette of the *Patricia* being battered in the storm. We had a VHF radio for communication with the ship, and it was during our tour of the light at the top of the house that we heard the unmistakable words 'SOS' echoing from our radio.

We froze to the spot. 'Mayday, mayday, mayday', we heard, 'the helicopter has ditched'. My heart was in my mouth. The helicopter had crashed into the ocean. Shocked, we were unable to do anything. We didn't want to disturb the frequency by asking what had happened so we just sat and waited and prayed.

It seemed a lifetime until we finally got a call from the ship. The helicopter had returned after dropping us on the island, but as it landed on the deck, the ship hit a huge wave that twisted it, and it literally got flipped off the back of the ship into the drink. Incredibly, the pilots were both able to get out of the helicopter and were hauled aboard by a rescue team. End of story.

Except that we were now marooned on a wind-lashed island off Anglesey. The RAF and the Coastguard were scrambled and it was at this point that the story got a little out of hand. Soon we were getting back into the emergency 'once only' survival suits while a Coastguard helicopter hovered above and lowered a strop to winch us up, one by one.

I certainly wasn't worried or scared; to be honest, it was the most excitement I had ever had on a *Countryfile* shoot. Once aboard the chopper, we all settled back and enjoyed the ride. I posed for some selfies with the crew and we were dropped off in a field where a Land Rover Defender was waiting to take us back into town.

We diverted to the pub. These were the early days of celebrity, and to be honest it never occurred to me that there might have been larger interest in a story that had gained its own momentum through Chinese whispers. It was only after I checked my phone and noticed dozens of missed calls, including a tearful answerphone message from my mother, that I realised something was up.

Journalists had heard that a helicopter had ditched and that I had been rescued, and they concluded that I had been in a near-death helicopter crash. My mother had been called to comment and had naturally become a little tearful at the revelations.

The next day, newspapers ran with the story. I still have a framed copy given to me from the *Countryfile* crew.

Those were happy, eventful days, but now I was back on the beautiful isle for a pilgrimage of my own. We had crossed the Menai Strait and we were heading towards the hallowed sands, but before we reached them I had one last trick up my sleeve. I had heard about a local girl, Sera Owens. Not only did she drive a 'Rat Rod' Series I but she had also written a song about it. So Sera joined our merry little band as we drove around the bay and out onto the sands. It was low tide and a flat expanse of sand that stretched out to the horizon.

Our convoy of Land Rovers, young and old, drove out onto the hard sand.

'Here,' smiled Dave, 'is where Wilks drew his vision of the first Land Rover.'

It was here, too, that the Series I was put through its paces.

I sat on the bonnet of my Series I next to Sera. Under a clear sky pockmarked with cartoon-like fluffy clouds she sang her ode to the Land Rover Series I.*

Occasionally the wind would steal her words. We all sat in silence. It struck me that this remote Welsh landscape itself has echoes of the Land Rover characteristics. It is a tough, no-nonsense, rugged, adventurous place, but more significantly it has a simple honesty about it. I'm not saying that the Land Rover was born out of its environment, but it must have played a part in the car's design.

It had been a surprisingly emotional experience, but there was one final ironic twist to come.

On the journey home, not far from the Menai Strait on the outskirts of Llandudno on the North Wales coast, my Series I failed me. Just as I reached an elevated section of motorway with no hard shoulder, the clutch collapsed. I had no way of getting into gear and so she came to a halt. The ocean glinted below while cars swerved to avoid me. Young Ben the mechanic swung into action, reversing his Defender carefully down the road to provide some protection as he squeezed himself under the chassis.

He reappeared sometime later, grease streaked across his face, his hands blackened. 'We're gonna need to take the gear apart,' he lamented in his thick Yorkshire drawl.

---

* https://m.youtube.com/watch?v=ky3N5KhtVwc

We were stuck on a busy road, unable to fix it there. We had been stopped for barely 10 minutes and hadn't even summoned help or road-side recovery when a Land Rover Discovery screeched up behind us. 'A customer called saying he'd seen a broken-down Series I,' he explained. 'We're only around the corner, we're a Land Rover specialist.' And with that we hitched up a tow rope and pulled her to the workshop, where I had to leave her to be fixed and John and I jumped into young Ben's Defender for the long drive home.

My Series I experience can be taken as a metaphor for Land Rover as a whole: a business and a car that have shifted and evolved dramatically over time. It seemed ironic that it was a new-generation Discovery that came to our assistance. Maybe it is a metaphor for the changing times. It is symbolic on many levels in my mind. The arrival of our Land Rover recovery saviour is testament to the rich and caring community bonded by the Land Rover. There can be few if any other marques of car that would stop for one another on a busy road simply because they share the same brand?

Many have lamented the fast-changing face of Land Rover. The loyalist will argue that the manufacturer has lost its way. Indeed, the purists will argue that the Series, 90, 110 and Defenders were the only true Land Rovers that remained close to their origins.

There is no doubt that the evolution of the Discovery, and more significantly the popularity of the Range Rover, have affected perception of a vehicle once valued exclusively for its off-road capabilities.

No one is underestimating the 4×4 abilities of either of these vehicles, but it's fair to say they are more familiar in an urban context than a rural one. How many farmers do you see driving a Discovery, or a Range Rover?

The result is that, for many, and particularly for the younger generation, the Land Rover has become synonymous with luxury rather than off-road capability.

CONCLUSION

To paraphrase the words of Winston Churchill, 'Never have so many owed so much to one car.'

Before they ceased production, Land Rover produced several special editions of the Defender. These were often little more than standard models fitted with certain option packs and equipment, although some creations were more ambitious. They started to appear after the Defender's Discovery stablemate had established that there was a lucrative lifestyle market out there in addition to the utility Defender's roles in agriculture and industry.

In 1992 the first special edition Land Rover Defender was produced. It was the 90SV (SV because it was finished off by Land Rover's Special Vehicle department). It was painted turquoise-blue and fitted with a black canvas soft top and alloy wheels as well as disc brakes all round (standard models still had drum brakes at the rear), with a standard 200Tdi turbodiesel engine. Only 90 were made.

Two special editions were later built for Land Rover's 50th anniversary in 1998. The first was the Defender 50th, which was influenced by the earlier NAS (North American Spec) Defender 90 and was powered by a 4-litre V8 petrol engine coupled to an automatic gearbox. This model was fitted with roll cages, and 1071 were built – 385 of which were sold in the UK, the rest abroad.

The other 1998 special edition was the Heritage, available in 90 or 110 wheelbases, both with a distinctive retro look: finished in either dark bronze green or light pastel Atlantic green. A metal mesh-effect front grille, body-coloured alloy wheels and wing mirrors and silver-painted door and windscreen hinges echoed the original Series I of 1948. But the powertrain was the standard Td5 diesel.

In 1999 the X-Tech followed, a metallic silver 90 hard top fitted with County-style seats and alloy wheels, but the most popular special edition Defender was the Tomb Raider of 2000, built to cash in on Land Rover's role in the Lara Croft film of the same name. The Tomb Raider was painted metallic grey and designed to look like an off-road expedition vehicle, with a roof rack, additional spotlights, winch, bull-bar and snorkel. They were available as either a 90 hard top or a 110 double cab, with standard Td5 turbodiesel – even though the actual Defender used in the film was powered by a V8 petrol engine.

Following the first G4 Challenge event in 2003, G4 Edition Defenders were produced in the Tangiers orange finish of the actual competition vehicles, as well as yellow and black. Defender 90 and 110 4×4 versions were available, with roll cage and front spotlights as standard. This was followed by the Defender Black

– a 90 or 110 County with metallic black paint, leather seats, air con, roll cage and dark-tinted rear windows – and the Defender Silver, with silver metallic paint, front A-bar and spotlights, chequer plates and winch.

Then in 2008 Land Rover's 60th anniversary was marked with three SVX models: available as a 110, a 90 hard top or 90 soft top, a 110, a 90 hard top or 90 soft top model County with metallic blue front grille design was also produced.

In 2011 Land Rover unveiled the DC100 concept car at the Frankfurt Show. The official line was that the company was gauging reaction, but nothing has been heard of the DC100 since, even though it was believed Gerry McGovern had championed the concept. Although seen as a possible Defender replacement, it had a lukewarm reception with enthusiasts.

A year later, in 2012, Defender got its final major upgrade, with a more refined and powerful 2.2 Puma engine. Meanwhile, the ever-increasing number of independent Defender specialists launched more new takes on the old model, on a seemingly weekly basis. Some added luxurious interiors, others dramatic exterior styling. There were – and still are – plenty of specialists who drop in big engines and automatic gearboxes, and who tune Defenders to a level unheard of just a decade earlier. Some are said to be capable of 140mph-plus, if you happen to be looking for a very expensive and messy way of ending it all. Travelling at over 100mph in a vehicle with the aerodynamics of a brick outbuilding isn't everyone's idea of fun.

In 2015, with Land Rover insisting that production of the Defender would end in December that year, it declared that 2015 would be a year of celebration. Its stunts included a giant drawing in the sand of Red Wharf Bay, Anglesey, where Maurice Wilks sketched that first Land Rover back in 1947. Simultaneously, the company launched three new special edition Defenders – the Heritage, Adventure and Autobiography, priced from £27,800 to £61,845. I dribbled when I saw them. They all sold out within hours. Land Rover also asked British fashion designer Paul Smith to produce a one-off version of the Defender in 27 different colours.

It was a fitting tribute for a vehicle that had meant so much to so many.

The rumour mill had it that Land Rover would end Defender production with a special run of V8-powered models and that the whole production line would be shipped out to a country in the developing world where Defender production would continue for those parts of the world where safety and emissions were less of a concern. But it didn't happen.

Production actually finished on 29 January 2016.

So what does the future hold for Defender? First of all, even though the most iconic Land Rover of all ceased production in 2016, it is far from finished. Even in the worst-case scenario – if the unthinkable happens and Defender is not followed by a new model and is never built again – you can sleep easy, happy in the knowledge that enthusiasts will keep the existing ones on the road for as long as the world has roads and tracks. It is estimated that 70 per cent of all Series Land Rovers and Defenders ever built are still out there, so that's about 1.5 million of them!

The value of secondhand Defenders has increased dramatically in recent years, due to the huge demand. There is no sign of this demand abating, which means that even tatty old ones which would once have gone to the scrapyard will now be restored. They will be too valuable to lose. Just like Series Is are now.

Even Land Rover itself is getting in on the act. When Defender production ended, Land Rover revealed that it is setting up a new Heritage Restoration programme. Based at Solihull on the site of the existing Defender production line, a team of experts – including long-serving Defender employees – is now breathing new life into classic Series vehicles and Defenders that they have sourced from around the world.

What about spares availability? Well, that too is a simple case of supply and demand. If there's enough demand, some entrepreneur will supply it. And with Land Rover itself now gearing up to supply classic parts for its obsolete models, it's a healthy situation that will steadily get healthier.

For a couple of years, Land Rover insiders had insisted that once Defender production ended at Solihull the whole line would be dismantled, put into shipping containers and reassembled somewhere else in the world – no doubt in a country where workers were paid less, making such a labour-intensive model as the Defender a cost-effective exercise. This intention was confirmed back in March 2015, when a Land Rover spokesman admitted: 'We are investigating the possibility of maintaining production of the current Defender at an overseas production facility for sale outside of the EU, after we cease building in the UK.' At the time of writing (August 2016), this new Defender is believed to be going into production, for delivery in 2018 or 2019. Jaguar Land Rover already has factories in Brazil and China, plus parent company Tata has ample production facilities in India. And just to add a little spice to the mix, JLR has announced that it is building a new factory in Slovakia. Could this be the place where the old Defender continues in production? Probably not. Should this be the case, though, it will be a shock for traditionalists as well as Solihull employees. A Defender built anywhere other than Lode Lane? Doesn't sound right, does it …?

So what about the new model? The company has tasked itself with making the new model every bit as versatile as the outgoing one. In April 2015, Land Rover's design director, Gerry McGovern, said: 'The Defender is all about durability – that indestructible, durable vehicle which is what a family of Defenders should be. In its core form it can be something that can be quite elemental up to something incredibly luxurious. When you see the new Defender, people will know it's worthy of carrying the badge. It will be able to do everything it says on the tin.'

Land Rover believes that the company should be split into three distinct families: Luxury (Range Rover), Leisure (Discovery) and Utility (Defender). Luxury sales should reach 2 million units per year globally by 2017, Leisure should hit 8 million vehicles, while Utility should achieve 3.3 million units once the new Defender is launched. But the latter is a tough task, because the existing Defender has sold in tens of thousands per year, not millions.

It's unlikely the new Defender will look anything like the DC100 concept vehicle of 2011. The company has distanced itself from that model and insists that the replacement is nothing like it – which is gratifying. The DC100 looked too much like a Skoda Yeti for most enthusiasts.

There has been plenty of conjecture that the new Defender will use the T5 platform that currently underpins the Discovery 4 and first-generation Range Rover Sport, but with the Sport already superseded by the second-generation model on a new platform, and the Discovery, too, due to be replaced soon, this is looking unlikely. Who would launch an all-new model on an obsolete platform? The days of make-do-and-mend and raiding the parts boxes for Morris Marina door handles and Austin Maestro light clusters are long gone.

Land Rover has witnessed the paying public's astonishing appetite for customised Defenders and can see a new generation of the model being hugely popular, particularly since the company's new SVO (Special Vehicles Operations) is now on stream and could create an infinite number of personalised Defenders, each created to cater perfectly to its owner. The ultimate working machine, in other words.

So exactly what does the future hold? Defender fans will probably be pleasantly surprised by the newcomer, but can it replace the old model in our affections?

Many say it will be impossible.

Back in 2005, journalists were told that Ford was already working on a replacement for Defender and that full-scale clay models 'looking something like the slab-sided Discovery 3 but with a Defender-like front end' already existed, locked away at Land Rover's development facility at Gaydon, Warwickshire.

Journalists were informed that as long ago as the early 1990s Land Rover was involved in talks regarding assembling Defenders in CKD kit form in the former Soviet Bloc countries soon after the Iron Curtain had fallen. There was also talk of moving some Defender production to Turkey, where some military models were already assembled. There is nothing new about building

Land Rovers under licence: as we have seen, it has been done since the days of the Series I and continues today, with factories in India and China (albeit with Range Rover Evoques, not Defenders).

Either way, this is an exciting time to be a Land Rover enthusiast. Even if you prefer the older models – the 'proper' Land Rovers, according to enthusiasts – you can't help but be fascinated by the incredible success story that the company has become. Huge economic growth in Asia has seen the emergence of a new upwardly mobile class who seemingly all want to drive Land Rovers. It is this new market that is fuelling the amazing sales figures that Land Rover is enjoying.

How much of this is down to astute new owners Tata and how much to events – namely the eastward seismic shift in world power – is debatable. Would Land Rover under Ford have recognised the potential and acted so quickly and decisively as world events unfolded? Probably not, because Ford has had well-documented problems of its own in the past few years and would have been too busy putting its own house in order in its heartland, the USA, where the big auto-makers have struggled to a degree that nobody could have predicted.

Land Rover is a lucky company. Otherwise how would you explain the sequence of events that have shaped it and turned it into the hugely successful manufacturer it is today? From the accident of its birth, brought about by the rationing of the post-war years and the availability of aluminium, through to its acquisition by Tata at just the right moment to take advantage of hugely lucrative new markets in the East, Land Rover has been very lucky indeed.

As recently as 2010, as recession took a hold on Land Rover's traditional markets, workers at Solihull were afraid that owners

Tata Motors would be closing down the factory that had been the company's historic production facility since 1948. But suddenly a host of new orders from new customers in the emerging economies of Asia put a very different complexion on matters, and within a year Land Rover was announcing that it was taking on 1000 new staff at the Solihull site! Meanwhile, of course, Halewood on Merseyside has the new Range Rover Evoque and Land Rover is currently busy signing up agreements to build Land Rovers elsewhere in the world. Factories in India and China have already been agreed.

Why is the Far East suddenly so important? It's all down to the most populous country in the world (nearly 1.5 billion – 60 times greater than the population of the UK) rapidly becoming prosperous enough for its citizens to afford to buy cars. In 1985, car ownership in China was virtually zero. A decade later there were an estimated one million cars on China's roads. By 2005 that figure had reached 15 million – and was growing fast. By 2011, when 18 million cars were sold in China, ownership had reached 75 million. By 2019, the number of cars sold is expected to rise to 30 million a year. It is estimated that there will be 200 million cars on China's roads by 2020.

Only a small percentage of all those cars will be luxury SUVs like the Range Rover family members, but that segment of market is forecast to climb 49 per cent in China to 265,200 vehicles by 2015. That's one heck of a lot of 4×4s. No wonder Land Rover is concentrating on China … and no wonder it's on a launch spree.

Do the top brass at BMW and Ford ever regret selling off Land Rover? Actually, that's a rhetorical question: of course they do!

They probably wake up in the middle of the night in a cold sweat over it. They most likely gnash their teeth in frustration at letting such a priceless gem slip from their grasp.

This book tells Defender's story since 1948. But this is only the start of the story. While the last 67-odd years have been very eventful, there's much more to come. The Defender story is unfinished.

As the years have passed, the old-school Defender has been left behind as new Land Rover models have appeared with ever-increasing levels of sophistication and technology. However, Defender enthusiasts would argue that this is exactly why Defender has become so popular in recent years – that refreshing simplicity that you simply cannot find in modern cars.

There is now a huge gulf between the old and the new. Recent years have also seen the launch of multiple 'luxury' cars from JLR, none of which has anything in common with the Defender, apart from the badge.

My journey revealed a world of passion and obsession driven by the simplicity of the Series and Defender Land Rover. It is a vehicle that has defied fashion and transcended time. The Defender gave people the chance to regress to a different era, a simple boxy world in which we still have to wind down windows with a handle. It was, and is, an antidote to the high-tech world around us.

In a world where everyone is trying to be Everyman and where every product is trying to be everything, the Land Rover has remained true to its roots. It has never strayed far from the utilitarian vehicle it was originally designed to be.

Enigmatic and mysterious, the Land Rover has an ability to camouflage our national obsession with stereotyping. Here is a cartoon-like vehicle that plays into our psyche, allowing us all to be children again. It allows us to forget our responsibilities and regress to the care-free days of simplicity and unstructured freedom. Like Alice in Wonderland, it is a portal to a world of make believe where anything is possible. We can go anywhere and we can transform it into whatever we want.

A coffee shop, a tailor, a bar, a DJ booth, a riot van, a Popemobile, a carriage fit for a queen, a hearse, an expedition vehicle … the Land Rover has become a beacon for adaptability. Like Lego or Meccano, it can be tailored and built to suit our individual needs and our dreams.

Few cars or objects have that ability to connect with our emotions like a Land Rover, and that is because of its individuality. No two vehicles are ever the same. Over the years and during my research for this book I have been in hundreds, perhaps thousands, of Land Rovers, but no two vehicles have ever been the same. Each is defined by its unique quirks and foibles. These nuanced charms are often only visible to the owner who has forged a unique bond with their vehicle.

Quirky, weird, adaptable, solid and loyal, we smile at her imperfections. Like our national stereotype for bad teeth and apologising even if it is someone else that bumps into us, the Land Rover is us. The Land Rover really is the British people's car. A living, driving embodiment of Britishness.

The Land Rover is a metaphor for the British in general. It is like a mirror to our nation. A small nation that hits way above its weight. I have often marvelled at the global power such a tiny island nation wields.

Like David and Goliath, the Land Rover has survived the might of global car manufacturing. It has dodged the wrecking ball for nigh on 67 years. An icon of design, durability and function.

Like Britain, the Land Rover has never felt comfortable showing off. Modest and reserved, it has always preferred to keep a low profile. Honest, robust and stubborn, it has soldiered on with its chin held high and a stiff upper lip.

Sometimes, though, we need to celebrate our achievements. We need to remind the world what we have done and to give ourselves a pat on the back.

If the Land Rover had a sport it would be the heptathlon. It is multi-talented: town, country, rescue, police, ambulance, fire, utility, construction, conservation, exploration, military, coastguard … the list is endless.

In this world of increasingly homogeneous rigidity, we have become a society set by boundaries. We have become risk-averse. We have wrapped ourselves in cottonwool and created overly cautious safety parameters around us.

We have become a society that has set self-imposed artificial boundaries. We are driven by conformity and comfort. The Land Rover has never been conformist, though. It is the eccentric Brit that has become an integral part of our DNA. A part of our fabric and our psyche.

For 67 years the Land Rover has provided the antidote to this rigidity. It has set us free from conformity and the modernisation of society. It has bucked trends and fashions.

In it we can all be adventurers and explorers. We can all step back into a simpler, less complicated time. It allows us to be children again.

The Land Rover has allowed us all to be dreamers.

EPILOGUE

'Junction 12 is closed' read the giant sign above the motorway.

I was heading towards Gaydon on the M40, and the warning of the slip road closure was symbolic of what has happened to Land Rover. While the end of Defender production was lamented and mourned by many as a final chapter, Land Rover itself has boomed since then.

They don't have enough space and capacity to keep up with demand. The Range Rover collection and the Discovery alone have turned the business around. The massive investment in construction of new plants has meant the need for a whole new transport grid between the two sites to ensure the thousands of workers can reach the factories. New roads and roundabouts have been built to cope with the increased 'Land Rover' traffic.

Much has been discussed about the 'end' of the Defender, but of course this isn't really the case. In reality it has merely reached another crossroad in its rich evolution, in much the same way that the basic Series I of 1948 evolved into the comparatively sophisticated Defender.

Land Rover had always made it very clear that this was merely a punctuation mark in the tale of the company, not the end of the story by any means. The narrative is ongoing. It's still being written.

Of course, there are many writers but there is only one author, and that man is Gerry McGovern.

I had first met Gerry several years ago when I was seated next to him at a dinner. I was intrigued by him. He, after all, had been responsible for saving Land Rover with the Range Rover collection, turning the brand into one of the most covetable marques in the world.

In the hope of some closure for this book and perhaps some insight into the mysterious evolution of the Defender I sent him an email. And now I was here at the glass tower, summoned to meet the man who bears the responsibility of the future.

My Land Rover journey had taken me along the fringes of the vehicle as I met the cottage industry and cult that surrounds the vehicle. The periphery had been laden with love and passion, and to be honest I was always worried about meeting the beating heart itself. This, after all, was a multinational business, no longer called Land Rover, but JLR (Jaguar Land Rover) incorporating the two marques and owned by Tata, the India Steel company.

Land Rover had become a vast multinational organisation, accountable to the markets, who had to deliver profit margins. Wasn't that the reason for the end of the Defender? As the last Defender rolled off the line, the company blamed a relatively small market with antiquated production lines and a safety record that didn't meet twenty-first-century requirements. The car, Land Rover argued, had simply not kept up with the times.

I was at G-DEC, which stands for Gaydon Design and Engineering Centre. This huge complex is home to 4000 individuals, busy designing and engineering the Land Rovers of the future.

It is like stepping into another world. This was a far cry from the line outline drawn in the sand on a beach by Wilks all those years ago. The beach has been replaced by banks of high-tech computers, as an army of designers and engineers pore over every single component. No aspect of the modern Land Rover is left to chance as designers labour over the smallest of detail and design.

The Design studio was like Cape Canaveral meets Savile Row. I entered a virtual reality hub, where I was able to walk around a projected 3D view of an imaginary car. I could sit in it and even take it apart with the click of a button. I could examine the engine and sit in the back. It's incredible how technology has advanced in a relatively short period of time and I couldn't help but wonder what Wilks would have made of this new high-tech world.

Times change. It is an inevitability of life that things move on. The much-loved noisy, leaky, rattly Defender is being reimagined. The man responsible is Land Rover's Design Chief, Gerry McGovern. Above his desk is a large photograph of the Range Rover, but more significantly the only other two photographs are of the Defender. One is an archive picture of a young Queen Elizabeth with a dashing Prince Philip standing next to a Series III, and the other is a picture of the actor Steve McQueen next to his Series I Land Rover.

'What do these images mean to you?' I asked.

'Icons and heritage', he answered unhesitatingly.

'Do you feel the pressure? There is so much expectation,' I said.

'Not really, more of an honour. It's the greatest automotive challenge left. The time has come to create a new Defender and it will be created in a manner where function and form go hand in hand. It is all about creating a cohesive form that will have all-terrain capability coupled with design excellence.'

'But why the delay?' I pressed, 'why didn't you release the updated Defender as an immediate replacement?'

'Because we want to get it right. The evolution of the Land Rover brand is important. People change, the world changes. We have to create a vehicle that is relevant to today's customer needs.

'Can you imagine how an original Defender tests in a wind tunnel?' he asked.

'Like the vehicle development stage itself, environmental standards and vehicle safety have also moved on from those heady days of 1948 when the Series I rolled into the world. Previously a car was built to fit the engine, but things have changed, now the engine is built to fit the car,' he explained.

As I left the Design studio Gerry reminded me of his passion for the Defender, remarking 'It is important that the successor to the Land Rover Defender is a worthy one because the Defender has been the anchor of the Land Rover brand. It is still the spiritual core.'

Iconic is often an overused term, but the Land Rover Defender has managed to transcend the world of ever-changing fashions while remaining relevant. It is much more of a people's car than the Volkswagen ever was. It is a car that has survived the shifting sands of time. A car that has become a national treasure, subliminally etching itself onto our national consciousness.

INDEX

ACKNOWLEDGEMENTS

Special thanks to Dave Phillips for all his help with the complex tangled history of the Land Rover.

To my very tolerant assistant Polly Arber.

To my agent Julian Alexander and all at LAW.

To my editor Myles Archibald, Julia Koppitz, Helena Caldon and everyone at HarperCollins.

Special thanks to everyone who helped me along the way.

Phil Bashall – Dunsfold Collection
Kate Carver – Great Fen Project
The Hammond family in Norfolk
Roger Crathorne/Mr Land Rover

Afzal Kahn, Victoria Stapleton, Suzanne Celensu and Steve
   Whitaker at the Chelsea Truck Company
Barry Dowsett, New Forest Verderers
Mike Street, SHB
Denis Ferry and Paul Doherty – amphibious vehicle
Jacqui Whinnett – Alpha 4×4 funerals
John and Pam Simpson – Strawberry Fields, Lincs
Rosie – Grounded coffee
Liz and Bob Cunninghame, Islay
Bruichladdich Distillery
James Wright – Twisted, Thirsk
John and Lisa Brown
David Mitchell, Anglesey
Sera Owens
Drew Bowler and Jon Chester – Bowler Manufacturing
Sue Cummings – Charlesworth & Sons
Garrath McCreery
Lorraine McLearnon – Northern Ireland police riot squad
Nynke Tynagel, Alyssa van der Heijden, Maarten Statius
   Muller, Job Smeets – Studio Job, Netherlands
James Sleater and Ian Meiers, Cad and the Dandy
Colonel Blashford Snell
Ant Anstead
Quentin Willson
Gerry McGovern
John Edwards
Ros Brassington, PA to John Edwards
Kamila Guzowsk, PA to Gerard McGovern
Paul Owen

Kim Lawrence Palmer

Martin Sullivan, press officer for GLASS (the Green Lane
Association)

Gemma Glover, PA to the Chief Executive and Commercial
Director – YHA hostel, Black Sail, Lake District, Cumbria

Rewfus Browde – Mobile cocktail bar

Stuart Webster – Prescott Speed Hill Climb, Gloucestershire

Errol Wright – Defender camper vans

Jez Hermer – Ovik

Stephen Laing – Curator, British Motor Industry Heritage
Trust

Jim Lawn – Toylander

Lady Judy and Lord Bill McAlpine at Fawley Hill

William Hindmarsh

HRH Princess Haya Bint Al Hussein

And to everyone one else who helped me along the way.

BEN FOGLE
LABRADOR

THE STORY OF
THE WORLD'S FAVOURITE DOG

WILLIAM
COLLINS

To all the Labradors who have loved
and been loved.

CONTENTS

Labrador – noun \\\'la-brə-ˌdôr-\\ *any of a breed of medium-sized strongly built retrievers largely developed in England from stock originating in Newfoundland and having a short, dense, black, yellow or chocolate coat and a thick rounded tail – called also Lab.*

PROLOGUE

THE BEGINNING OF THE END

'Don't cry because it ended,
smile because it happened.'
Dr Seuss

I called Dad.

'What do *you* think?' he asked.

There was a pause. Not because I was thinking, but because I knew. I knew the answer but I couldn't bring myself to say it.

'Then we know the answer,' he replied.

I burst into uncontrollable tears.

The twenty-four hours following that phone call were some of the most painful of my life.

The knowing. The feeling of betrayal.

Inca, my beloved Inca.

We took Maggi and Inca to the beach one final time. I carried

Inca from the car to the shore so she could lie with her paws in the water. Here we were on a beach again, just as we had been on Taransay when her life was just beginning.

I watched as her ears flapped in the wind and she lifted her nose to smell the sea air. Then, her belly covered in sand and seawater, I carried her back to the car and we began that torturous journey back to London. I couldn't look anyone in the eye. In the rear-view mirror I could see Inca's snout on Maggi's back.

Dad was waiting when we arrived home. I lay on the floor and sobbed uncontrollably into Inca's fur.

'One more night.'

I carried her up to our bedroom, put her bed next to mine and lay there listening to her deep snoring. I didn't sleep. I felt sick with panic and in the morning my pillow was stained with tears.

At 6am I carried her downstairs and fed her, then picked her up and took her into the garden.

'Give Inca a big hug,' I said to Ludo, who threw his arms around her.

'Where's she going, Daddy?'

'Up into the sky,' I said, turning away to hide the tears falling down my cheeks.

I carried Inca to the car, taking Maggi with us, too, and drove 10 minutes up the road to my parents' house. I don't remember much about that journey except that I cried uncontrollably all the way.

'Thank you, Inca,' I sobbed as we drove through the empty streets of Notting Hill. 'Thank you for being my best friend. I owe everything to you.'

I carried her from the car into the house, burying my face into her fur, and laid her on the kitchen floor. Mum, Dad and my sister were all there.

Canine blood flows through the Fogle blood. Dogs are family.

I lay on the floor, hugging Inca while Dad injected her. Her breathing became heavy. I could feel her heart pounding and the warm blood beneath her skin. I breathed the familiar scent of her fur as I nuzzled into her thick coat. I have never sobbed like that in my life. It was a primal, uncontrollable, guttural sob as I felt her heart stop beating.

I lay there on the kitchen floor clutching my best friend, unable to move. Wishing, hoping it was a dream, I held her lifeless body.

Maggi came and sniffed Inca. I wanted her to sense that her friend had gone.

'Where's Inca?' asked Ludo, as I returned home with Maggi.

'She's gone up into the sky.'

'Hello, Inca,' he said, waving to the sky.

I had lost my best friend. It felt like losing a limb. My shadow was gone. A flame had been extinguished.

I had loved and been loved. Now I had lost and I was lost. I needed to find a way back. Thirteen years is a long time.

It's been quite a trip, Inca and me.

CHAPTER ONE

SALTY SEA DOGS

The tiny boat yawed and bucked in the mighty ocean. Huge Atlantic rollers crashed against the vertiginous cliffs as seagulls wheeled above. A lone lighthouse stood sentry, ready to warn shipping of the hazardous coastline.

My salt-encrusted hands gripped tightly to the oars as we, too, heaved into the surf. A rogue wave caught the front of the tiny boat, sending green water spilling in.

We were a pinprick on a tiny ocean.

I had come to Newfoundland and Labrador on the eastern-most point of Canada – often described as Atlantic Canada. This is frontier country; a tough, rugged coastline where the people are as hardy as the geography. It holds a lot of similarities with its counterpart on the other side of the Atlantic Ocean, the Western Isles of Scotland. The flora and fauna reminded me of Scotland, only larger.

I was with local rower – Pete – on one of the original

fishing skiffs, a tiny two-man wooden boat that looked like it would be better suited to a pond than an angry ocean. These were the craft with which the fishermen had, in better times, caught the cod that were once so prolific in these waters.

Like a detective following a trail, I had come here in search of the Labrador. It seemed wrong, coming to a place that was also named after a different breed altogether, but all the evidence seemed to conclude that Newfoundland did play a role in the evolution of the Labrador Retriever.

Despite a lifetime of travels to Canada, this was my first visit to this part of the country. A Canadian father had ensured plenty of summers on the lakes of Ontario, where I spent my time canoeing, swimming and fishing. Of course, there was also a dog. A mutt called Bejo that had somehow been rescued from the streets of Marrakech, in Morocco, by a family friend and had been flown to the Canadian lakes.

I had long wanted an excuse to visit this remote corner of one of the least-populated countries on Earth, and now here it was . . .

My journey to Atlantic Canada began in the rather inauspicious surroundings of Dublin, in Ireland, from where I caught my transatlantic flight to St John's, which must surely be the shortest hop across the Atlantic Ocean. We had barely taken off when we were landing again, just four hours later.

St John's is a rugged working port. I'm sure it had once been a very beautiful harbour, but the heavy industry and the presence of dozens of offshore supply ships servicing the oil industry give it a gritty industrial feel. The supply ships tower above the small buildings of the city.

St John's is considered by many to be the 'big smoke', but even with the majority of the region's employment opportunities and, therefore, population, it has a small-town feel. Colourful, clapboard-style houses dot the streets as reminders of the city's heritage. This is pioneering country.

Labrador and Newfoundland are collectively one state. Bordering Quebec on the west and the rugged Atlantic to the east, it covers more than 29,000 kilometres of coastline. At nearly 150,000 square kilometres, it is the same size as Japan.

I had come here, not for the landscape, nor the people, but in search of a dog famed for its fierce loyalty and ferocious love of food. A dog intricately tied to British culture. A dog beloved of families across the world and championed by countless prime ministers and presidents. A dog both used to sell loo roll and owned by royalty: the humble Labrador Retriever.

The story of the Labrador is as intriguing as it is complex. It is estimated that there are between 300 and 400 different breeds of dog in the world – the exact numbers are disputed by various kennel clubs which have yet to recognise certain breeds that have been crossbred over time. Of course, all breeds began with some sort of crossbreeding, but how did the Labrador evolve?

Breeds of dogs are variously broken down by the English Kennel Club into Hound, Terrier, Gundog, Utility, Pastoral, Toy and Working. While many will class breeds according to what they were bred to do, you can also categorise them according to geography: Welsh Corgi, Yorkshire Terrier, Afghan Hound, Bernese Mountain Dog, the Maltese, Rhodesian Ridgeback, English Setter, Hungarian Vizla, German Shepherd,

Irish Setter, Spanish Water Dog, Manchester Terrier, Norfolk Terrier . . . The list of dogs with a geographical tie is long so I won't bore you, but you get the gist.

The heritage of the Labrador, however, is much more complex and confused. Indeed, dozens of books have been published over the years with conflicting stories about the history of the world's most popular breed.

While it is widely accepted that the Yorkshire Terrier, for example, was developed in the nineteenth century to catch rats in the clothing mills of the historic county in Northern England, and the Border Collie was a working dog cultivated to herd live-stock in the borderlands between England and Scotland, the Labrador does not actually originate from Labrador, the bleak northerly mainland region of Canada. I, like many, had always assumed it was named after its geographical namesake in Northern Canada, but in fact the breed has its roots, by way of Europe, in the Atlantic island of Newfoundland where, in the late eighteenth century, fishermen relied on a working sea dog of similar appearance to retrieve fish. In researching this book and the history of this humble breed, I have ventured from Portugal to Labrador, Newfoundland, and then full circle back to Europe.

The origin of the Labrador is a slightly confusing issue, not least because 'Newfoundland and Labrador' is the umbrella name given to the vast easternmost province of Canada. The two distinct land masses that make up the province are separated by the Strait of Belle Isle, a hazardous, ice-choked, fog-wraithed, treacherously tidal channel approximately 125 kilometres long and ranging between a maximum width of 60 kilometres to 15 kilometres at its narrowest.

In all probability, the nineteenth-century Britons lumped the far-flung area and its associations together just as writers of that era indiscriminately use the words retriever and spaniel. But there are two distinct territories under one geographical title and – just to complicate things – two dog breeds associated with the province, each named after the wrong region. The short-coated Labrador is actually from Newfoundland; and the shaggy-coated Newfoundland emerged at about the same time in Labrador.

The early settlement of Labrador was tied to the sea by the Inuit and Innu people. It is widely assumed that the Vikings were the first Europeans to sight the land but it wasn't until the Portuguese explorer João Fernandes Lavrador mapped the coast that the region was settled. Today the region is sparsely populated, with around 27,000 residents, most of whom work the land for its iron ore.

So how did this popular family dog, with its lust for food and cuddles, come to live in such an inhospitable terrain and climate?

To further confuse the mystery, another 'geographical breed', the Nova Scotia Duck Tolling Retriever, comes from Nova Scotia, just south of Labrador and Newfoundland. All three dogs have distinctive webbed feet, a water-resistant undercoat and incredible swimming abilities – they evidently share some genetic stock. Most historians agree that the native inhabitants of Newfoundland, the Beothuks, did not have dogs. Nor did the pre-Inuit settlers, the Dorset Eskimos. Others insist there would have been Inuit, Innu and Mi'kmaq dogs left by the region's Aboriginal peoples, as well as descendants of the Norse dogs.

We must assume therefore that the Labrador descends from a mix of genes from the various dogs taken on board ship by fishermen from Spain, Portugal, France and England when they set sail to fish for cod in the waters off Newfoundland.

Dogs were needed to guard the camps, to hunt for game and to kill rats and mice. They were a useful bit of kit. Breeds traditionally taken on ships from the early sixteenth century onwards included mastiffs, bloodhounds, spaniels and terriers. It is probably fair to assume there would have been a number of cross-breeds. Residents of Newfoundland kept no records or census of the dogs on the island so there aren't many clues for breed enthusiasts to mull over. In a footnote in his *Variation of Animals and Plants under Domestication* (1868), Charles Darwin states that the Newfoundland dog is believed to have originated from a cross between an Esquimaux dog and a large, black St Hubert hound. Others point out that Inuit dogs thrive in cold weather, but not cold water.

It still seems amazing to me that some of the world's most prolific swimming dogs came from some of the world's coldest water. But then maybe that was the point. The people had to find an alternative to getting in the water themselves.

But the Labrador is a dog that loves to curl up on the sofa or sprawl on the bed. They are never happier than with their heads lolling out of the open window of a Land Rover speeding along a country lane. Newfoundland and Labrador? Surely this was the land of the hard-working pastoral collie – a dog happier outside and often without human contact. There seems to be a great contradiction in provenance and character.

Today it is very fashionable to mix breeds together; the

Labradoodle is a Labrador and Standard Poodle cross, the Puggle is a Pug and a Beagle, but what breeds might have mated to create the Labrador as we now know it?

Many canine historians believe their genetic make-up owes something in particular to the Spanish Black Pointer (the aptitudes of obedience to a master and of being hard-wired to follow a scent) and to the Basque or Portuguese Shepherd Dog, which is notable for a herding instinct and a close sense of territory. But it was from a very large gene pool that dogs were bred on an ad hoc basis and trained over 300 years to meet the specific needs of the fishermen. 'There were many ways in which they could be useful,' wrote Wilson Stephens, in an article entitled 'The Lost Years of the Labrador' in *The Field* in December 1989. 'The slippery decks of trawlers, heeling when the nets were being hauled overside on the cod banks of Newfoundland, sent many a hard-won fish sliding into, and often through, the scuppers. Retrieving out of water may have been the ships' dogs' first and basic role. Not retrieving fish only. A sailing ship's rigging included many small components also likely to be washed overboard – blocks, pins, lines, and so on; a fetcher-back was more than worth his keep. Who ever saw a better dog in water than a fit and confident Labrador? It is bred into them.'

The harsh, rugged isolation of Newfoundland and the specific traits required of the dogs allowed the ancestors of the Labrador to evolve into fine, shapely dogs. The terrain and climate required them to be sure-footed on land and broad-chested to swim strongly and surf the strong and choppy Atlantic waves. They needed to be sturdy enough to haul wood on land and drag fish nets ashore, yet small enough not to overpower a fisherman's two-man dory craft. The fishermen bred these dogs, presumably matching sires with exceptional traits to dams of a similar calibre. Or maybe it was more rudimentary, simply monitoring the accidental intermixing. Whatever the technique, it somehow produced the much-loved, distinctive, water-loving retriever of today.

Like their namesake, the people of Labrador bear a unique mix of cultural heritage, borne of their historical roots. Their accent and language is a mix of Scottish, Irish and a mid-Atlantic drawl. On first hearing I was sure they were from Southern Ireland. To be honest I couldn't make head nor tail of what my cab driver was saying on the journey from the airport to St John's, with his heavy Irish drawl spoken in a kind of pidgin twang. Indeed, there are more varieties of English spoken in Labrador than anywhere else in the world. No wonder I couldn't understand a word.

The Aboriginal population of what is now Newfoundland and Labrador can be divided into three ethnic groups – the Inuit (once called the Eskimos), the Innu and the Beothuk – but the current-day population owes more to its European roots, being largely the south-west of England. Fisherfolk from Dorset and Devon emigrated in the hope of making their fortunes with the cod banks, but it is more likely the small number of Highland Scots and the Southeastern Irish settlers who had the most profound effect on the culture and heritage of Newfoundland and Labrador's current-day population. They bear the ruddy cheeked, wind-weathered appearance of island folk. Having spent so much time in Canada as a child, I was struck by how un-North American this region was. It felt they had more in common with Europe than with their Canadian brothers.

The mix-up between the names and geographical roots of the Newfoundlands and Labradors occurred once the dogs were imported into England and the Americas. The dog more commonly associated with Labrador became the Newfoundland – the giant, shaggy, bear-like dog beloved of poets Lord Byron and Emily Dickinson and immortalised as Nana in *Peter Pan* – and the smaller, close-coated dog (also known as the St John's Water Dog, the St John's Dog, the Lesser Newfoundland or the Little Newfoundler) became known as 'the Labrador'.

The word *labrador* has dual Portuguese associations. For a start, the region of Labrador in Canada was named after the explorer João Fernandes Lavrador, who in 1499 and 1500 mapped the coastline, labelling the vast, scarcely imaginable area 'Labrador' on topographical charts that circulated during this period. *Labrador* or *lavradore* also means 'labourer' or 'workman' in both Portuguese and old Spanish.

The Portuguese predominated other European fishermen during the opening decades of the sixteenth century, and the men who subsequently undertook hazardous voyages to these inhospitable waters would have been gritty, rugged sea hands inured to working the sails around the clock and enduring cramped conditions. So the word was 'in the air' in any contemporary consideration of the nature of the venture. Both in terms of the region and of the prevailing sailing-cum-fishing nation which set an example of reliance on its sea dogs, the name 'Labrador' was wholly appropriate for a hard-working dog valued by generations of fishing crews trawling the chilly waters for bumper cod harvests.

It seems indisputable that there is a Portuguese connection, but the earliest references all seem to originate in Newfoundland. One of the earliest mentions comes from J. B. Jukes in his book *Excursions In and About Newfoundland,* written in 1842:

> *A thin, short-haired, black dog, belonging to George Harvey came off to us today. This animal was of a breed very different from what we understood by the term "Newfoundland Dog" in England. He had a thin tapering snout, a long thin tail and rather thin but powerful legs, with a lank body and hair short and smooth. These are the most abundant dogs of the country. They are by no means handsome, but are generally more intelligent and useful than the others. This one caught its own fish and sat on a projecting rock watching the water.*

Could this have been one of the early forms for the Labrador? The breed that has become one of the most popular in the world? Loyal, handsome and hungry?

Newfoundland is still a rugged, bleak land. It is hard to imagine the hardships of those early settlers. This is a place dominated by the weather. Trees grow crouched and bowed to the curvature of the prevailing winds. The ocean bites into the coastline, tearing away at the cliffs. It is a region of natural wealth; where once the fish was king, today minerals and fossil fuels are the main export. The offshore oil rigs provide employ-ment to those who still eke out a living here.

In one of the small working fishing harbours, a number of boats were tied alongside the quay – the *Mystic Voyager,* the *Cape John Navigator,* the *June Gale* – all weathered by the cruel ocean. Their nets lay on the harbour side, ready to be repaired.

I have spent time with trawlermen in the North Sea. It was one of the most miserable experiences of my life. A week being tossed around a mighty ocean, like a rubber duck in a washing machine. Cramped and stuffy. Hot and humid. I can feel the nausea returning just thinking about it. The sleep deprivation. The smell. The blood. The oil. The rust. The diesel fumes. It's like groundhog day. Haul. Gut. Eat. Haul. Gut. Eat. Haul. I wouldn't go back out on one of those trawlers if you paid me. Here, 4,800 kilometres away, on the opposite side of the ocean, are the same ships. The same fishermen. The same hopes and dreams. The same wild, violent ocean.

The skipper of my trawler had been capsized alongside his father and brother when he was just 18. They clung to one another in the frozen, black waters. Rescue came, but in the process he lost hold of his father. He was lost to the ocean – one of the many fisherfolk to perish in the cruel sea.

This part of the world holds many parallels to the Western Isles of Scotland where I have spent so much of my life. Indeed, it was here, on a remote island, that my love of the ocean and Labradors began.

The American novelist Annie Proulx gives a measure of the bleak landscape in her bestselling novel *The Shipping News*, which is set in Newfoundland. One of her characters muses on the landscape:

This place, she thought, this rock, six thousand miles of coast blind-wrapped in fog. Sunkers under wrinkled water, boats threading tickles between ice-scabbed cliffs. Tundra and barrens, a land of stunted spruce men cut and drew away.

*How many had come here, leaning on the rail as she leaned
now. Staring at the rock in the sea. Vikings, the Basques, the
French, English, Spanish, Portuguese. Drawn by the cod, from
the days when massed fish slowed ships on the drift for the
passage to the Spice Isles, expecting cities of gold. The lookout
dreamed of roasted auk or sweet berries in cups of plaited
grass, but saw crumpling waves, lights flickering along the
ship rails. The only cities were of ice, bergs with cores of beryl,
blue gems within white gems, that some said gave off an odor
of almonds. She had caught the bitter scent as a child.*

*Shore parties returned to ship blood-crusted with insect
bites. Wet, wet, the interior of the island, they said, bog and
marsh, rivers and chains of ponds alive with metal-throated
birds. The ships scraped on around the points. And the lookout
saw shapes of caribou folding into fog.*

Walking along the coastal paths of Newfoundland, the vegetation and trees had become a vivid red, orange and yellow. I
wandered among the fishermen's pots and nets. Traditionally
this is fishing country and the dozens of trawlers moored along
the harbour were now wrapping up for the season, hunkering
down for the winter. It wouldn't be long until the snow and
ice arrived; freezing the harbour and isolating the tiny communities further. The locals I met on my travels in the region had
told me of 'black dogs' that still roamed these beaches; wild
and untamed, some believed these were the ancestors of the
Labrador.

Beyond the city limits, the weak late autumn sunshine illuminated the cliff edge on the most easterly tip of North America

– Cape Spear in Newfoundland. Huge rolling waves crashed against the rocky foreshore below as flocks of gulls feasted on a passing shoal of fish. The next stop due east of here was to be Cabo da Roca, in Portugal, the most westerly point of mainland Europe, on which I had stood many times and wondered what its North American opposite looked like. Now I knew.

The mighty lighthouse is a reminder of the treacherous nature of the ocean that has cost many ships and their crews their lives. This is a hard, tough land. Newfoundland itself is a huge island, almost twice the size of Great Britain, and for many months of the year the island is buried under 3 metres of snow, but during the summer months, the islanders have a brief respite from the cold. Although even in the summer months, Atlantic Canada is reminded of its Arctic geography, as swarms of icebergs descend on the island. Locals make good use of these icebergs, though, by making iceberg water, iceberg beer and iceberg vodka. They even collect washed-up shards which they then use in their gin and tonics.

Perhaps the most astonishing industry, here, is that of the iceberg 'movers', those individuals tasked with either blowing up or tugging away mighty icebergs that are blocking harbours or are in danger of damaging property. There is even a website called Iceberg Finder where 'iceberg ambassadors' track the movement of these mighty bergs, which are more than 10,000 years old and can weigh in excess of 10 million tonnes. Icebergs also bring polar bears – which use them as ocean rafts, sometimes depositing the fearsome predators close to human habitations – which has given rise to another local expert, the polar bear 'relocator'. Today, though, there are no signs of icebergs, polar bears or the sperm whales that migrate through these waters, just a vast grey ocean.

In another strange twist in the tail and connection to yet another country, the Labrador – now the most popular pet dog in the United Kingdom, the United States, Canada, Israel and Australia – ultimately owes its status to John Cabot, the famous Italian navigator and explorer whose name is honoured in streets, towers, academies, universities and golf courses around the world. Cabot's 'discovery' of parts of North America under the commission of Henry VII in 1497 is believed to have been the first European encounter with the shores of North America since the Norse Vikings landed in around 1000 BC. Some historians think that either Nova Scotia or Maine was the location of his landfall, but the official position of the Canadian and British governments is that Giovanni Caboto – to give him his proper Italian name – landed at Cape Bonavista, a rugged headland on the east coast of Newfoundland. He found a Utopian land of plenty and his discovery heralded an era of heavy European fishing traffic which, in turn, brought about the development of the versatile sea dog we know today as the Labrador.

On 24 June 1497, Cabot set sail from the port of Bristol, then the second most important seaport in the country. About 3,500 kilometres later, his ships gingerly negotiated the rugged sea stacks and steep cliffs of a *terra nova* to touch land at Cape Bonavista. By all accounts, he made a quick turnaround, excited to share the news back in England that his expedition had indeed found, discovered and investigated something unknown to all Christian folk – an incredible wealth of fish stocks off these shores. His crew reported 'the sea there is full of fish that can be taken not only with nets but with fishing-baskets'.

Today the cod or 'baclau' is still the regional dish. Fish and brewis, which is pronounced 'brews' is the most popular. The meal consists of cod and *hard bread* or hard tack. With the abundance of cod it became synonymous with many Newfoundland households as a delicacy to be served as a main meal. The recipe may vary, but the primary ingredients are always the same. Typically baclau uses salt fish which is soaked in water overnight to reduce the salt content, and hard bread which is also soaked in water overnight. The next day, the fish and bread are boiled separately until tender, and then both are served together.

The traditional meal is served with scrunchions, which is salted pork fat that has been cut into small pieces and fried. Both the rendered fat and the liquid fat are then drizzled over the fish and brewis. It tastes like . . . fish. Very, very salty, chewy fish. I had eaten the same on the island of Taransay when I was marooned there for a year. It was the only fish we ever caught. We were hopeless. We were living on what the local fishermen described as a fish roundabout. But we had no boat; no nets and no rods. All we had was a crate of salted fish. To be honest, I hated it and I still do. It makes me retch. The last time I had it was in the deserts of Oman; we took it in homage to the old explorer Wilfred Thesiger, who took salted shark meat. It was foul, but I ate it nonetheless.

I made my way through a hearty bowl of baclau as I sat looking out over a tiny harbour. A colourful, wooden-stilted fisherman's hut stood out against the gunmetal waters, the hard granite cliffs towering behind it. It was at once utterly beautiful and hauntingly severe. The view certainly helped the digestion.

The abundance of cod would be a turning point for the region and the emergence of the Labrador. Word spread quickly about the new-found lands and their bounty, and by the early sixteenth century, fishermen from Europe were regularly setting sail in a north-westerly direction and converging in the harsh and squally North Atlantic waters to fish for cod. The French, Spanish and Portuguese fishermen tended to fish on the Grand Banks of Newfoundland and other banks out to sea, where fish were always available. They carried an abundant store of salt and processed their fish on board ship, laying it down in layers strewn with salt to cure the fish. They did not attempt to dry it until they returned to their home ports. Without access to an indigenous source of salt, the English fishermen – travelling in fleets of vessels from West Country ports in Devon, Dorset, Somerset and Cornwall – sailed each spring and brought home a harvest in autumn. To eke out their meagre salt supplies and preserve their hauls, they developed a custom of salting the fish with a light paste, washing and drying it on long wooden racks onshore. This process required fish-curing stations to be set up on land. This meant they concentrated on fishing inshore (where the cod were only to be found at certain times of the year, during their migrations) and used small boats to return to the Newfoundland shore every day. In their chosen seasonal loca-tions, English fishing captains at the turn of the seventeenth century reported cod shoals 'so thick by the shore that we hardly have been able to row a boat through them'. Some even talk of walking across them – during my short stint as an offshore fisherman I once saw a net of cod pulled from the North Sea, so full of fish that the trawler men could walk between the two trawlers on the fish.

Once dried, the fish were then loaded on board the ships and sent back home. A winter crew was left behind each year to stake out the shore, maintain the curing facility and protect the fragile and lucrative toehold that England had established in the cod-fishing industry. Permanent settlements were discouraged, so it is easy to imagine how those left behind would have relied on their dogs not only to hunt for food and guard their base, but also for companionship.

The cod moratorium of 1992 nearly devastated the region. The Canadian government declared a halt on the northern cod fishery, which for nearly 500 years had shaped the lives and communities of Atlantic Canada. The biomass of cod had fallen to just 1 per cent of its early levels and was in danger of complete extinction. Better fishing technology and trawlers had decimated stocks. It was a brave and bold decision by the Canadian government, and one that caused untold misery and hardship for the local people. More than 35,000 fisherfolk from 400 communities were left unemployed overnight.

Some communities never recovered. The effects of the moratorium are still obvious; there is an air of sadness that clings to the region like an Atlantic fog. A large imposing museum that soars into St John's skyline like an ugly carbuncle is symbolic – like a giant fish factory, there for all to remember. The museum is crammed full of fishing gear and boats. Photographs of weathered faces hauling, processing and salting cod. Huge piles of fish.

Nostalgic photos of a bygone era when the cod was king and the community thrived.

By the 1620s, tiny, isolated settlements on the coast of Newfoundland became home to fishermen and their ship dogs – mainly from England, but also from Portugal, Spain, France and the Basque Country – as competition over the best waters hotted up and everyone was eager to stake their claim on the fishing rights.

The first sightings in Britain of the 'St John's Dogs or Little Newfoundler Dogs' were in the late eighteenth century. They had been brought back across the Atlantic aboard the ships carrying their precious cargoes of dried and salted fish.

In 1785, Robert Burns's poem, *The Twa Dogs*, refers to a creature, 'His hair, his size, his mouth, his lugs/Shew'd he was nane o'Scotland's dogs/But whelped some place far abroad,/ Where sailors gang to fish for cod.' Could this have been the loyal Labrador?

In 1814, Colonel Peter Hawker, a well-known sportsman, watched Labradors at work on the trawlers in Newfoundland, describing them as the St John's breed of Newfoundland. In the first published account of a Labrador, his diary describes the dog as 'by far the best for any kind of shooting. He is generally black and no bigger than a Pointer, very fine in legs, with short, smooth hair and does not carry his tail so much curled as the other [meaning the Newfoundland, which had a rough coat and a tail that curved over its back]; is extremely quick and active in running, swimming and fighting . . . The St John's breed of these dogs is chiefly used on their native coast by fishermen. Their sense of smelling is scarcely to be credited. Their discrimination of scent . . . appears almost impossible . . . For finding wounded game of every description, there is not his equal in the canine race; and he is sine qua non in the general pursuit of waterfowl.'

Eight years later, in 1822, the Scottish-Canadian explorer William Epps Cormack, who was born in St John's, crossed Newfoundland by foot. He was the first European to journey across the interior of the island and it was during this expedition that he noted small water dogs, writing in his journal: '[they are] admirably trained as retrievers in fowling, and are otherwise useful. The smooth or short-haired dog is preferred because in frosty weather the long haired kind becomes encumbered with ice on coming out of the water.'

The earliest known depiction of the St John's water dog – owned by a Mr Alsop – was on the canvas of the famous animal painter Edwin Landseer in 1822. Initially entitled *Watchful Sentinel* and known now as *Cora. A Labrador Dog*, the commissioned portrait of a much-loved pet shows a black dog with white paws and chest lying inside a stable yard or carriage house, with horses and grooms working in the background and, interestingly, no water in sight. (The earliest portrait of a yellow dog is believed to be in the Bowes Museum at Barnard Castle in County Durham – a portrait in oils of Mrs Josephine Bowes painted in the late 1840s with a yellow dog called Bernardine at her side.) This seems to be the moment these early 'Labradors' made the transition from sea to land. These dogs, seen and admired for their eye-catching skills in West Country ports and harbours, were being purchased for use on land.

For a land famous for two world-class dogs, there was a

distinct lack of canine activity as I wandered the tiny fishing ports. I spotted a single working Collie. In the absence of either of the region's namesakes, I arranged to meet two of the region's living mascots. Gus the Labrador and Felix the Newfie are both employed by the State to greet people arriving in the remote territory, predominantly by cruise ship.

We arranged to meet in a tiny harbour that is now home to an artisan collective where artists produce paintings and knit-wear. It was a picture-postcard, perfect location. Bright yellow fishing houses with faded red piers were reflected perfectly in the calm waters. Here, away from the rough Atlantic surf, I could image Labradors plying these waters collecting fallen fish and fishing tackle.

As instincts required, Gus belly dived into the clear waters. It was like an echo of an earlier time as I imagined his early cousins swimming in these very waters for the fisherfolk.

The extraordinary twist in this furry tail is that Gus's prov-enance owed more to England than it did to those early pioneers. Indeed, his distant relatives had come up from Portugal to this remote land, only to traverse the Atlantic Ocean once again, back to Europe.

For the fortune-hunting fishermen, dog trading had become a lucrative subsidiary. The sale of fish was the main business, but canny sailors also sold the ice used to preserve their catch and, increasingly, established a dog import trade. The dogs' water skills were much talked about. They feature in old stories as near-mythical water dogs, as fetchers of sailors' hats in icy waters and blustery gales, big-hearted, eminently trainable and intelligent. They could swim with ropes in their mouths and sometimes – so the stories went – paddled out to the aid of ships in distress. They retrieved whatever their master bade them. The proud seamen put on a remarkable show of human–dog teamwork for the quayside crowds.

Wilson Stephens wrote in *The Field*, 'No wonder that the deck dogs on the ships off-loading in Poole Harbour caught the eye of passers-by. Perhaps the crew men entertained the locals by throwing overboard things which the dogs would retrieve, demonstrating their expertise at diving in and swimming back with a load. Perhaps bets were struck. No wonder, either, that the impression they made caught the eye of the local gentry – strolling, as all men do, on the quaysides . . .'

One spectator was the second Earl of Malmesbury, an MP and sportsman, born in 1778. He kept detailed records of the game he shot and of local and national weather. A large part of his estate at Hurn, in Dorset, included the floodplain between the River Stour and River Avon, north-east of Bournemouth. Hurn is listed in the Domesday Book as 'Herne'; the name comes from the old English '*hyrne*', meaning a disused part of a field or the land created by an oxbow lake. The Earl was fascinated by these amazing water retrievers. Until drainage operations in the mid-twentieth century, the River Stour had been habitually liable to winter overflow, spilling over its banks so that water spread over the countryside, creating large watery meadows a metre or more deep. The land was crisscrossed with carrier channels to control the annual floodwater; for half the year it was, as one observer put it, 'a minor Venice'. The quantity of water was such that a raised causeway had been built around a 16-hectare floodable meadow so that the ladies of the house could continue to enjoy their carriage drives before stopping for afternoon tea.

I know the River Stour well. I spent much of my childhood navigating, rowing, paddling and swimming in its meandering waters. My school was built on its floodplains. A distinctive memory was of flooded sports fields; the river often burst its banks, creating a watery world. How many times I found myself wading through this very water.

So could this have been the very same river that helped give rise to the most popular dog on Earth? Was the answer there all along?

The early nineteenth century was the golden age of wild-fowling, and the sporting pride and glory of the Malmesbury Estate was the duck. With such expanses of swampy waterlands there were always plenty of ducks – but many a shot duck would fall where only a swimming dog could retrieve them. The Earl of Malmesbury and a neighbour, Major C. J. Radclyffe, who lived close to the watery hinterland around Poole Harbour, saw these Labrador dogs as the answer to their sporting problem. There is mention of 'the Earl of Malmesbury at Heron Court' using his St John's dog for shooting sports as early as 1809.

And here lie the crucial links between Poole in Dorset and Newfoundland . . .

The Newfoundland fishing fleet docked regularly at Poole Harbour, with its catch of cod and other fish kept on ice in the hold. After the fish had been sold, the ice was sought by local squires for their ice houses (typically a brick-lined hole in the ground, covered with a domed roof, and used to store ice in the years before the invention of the refrigerator). The Hurn

Estate had two such ice houses that needed regular re-stocking with blocks of ice. According to the late sixth Earl of Malmesbury, 'It was usual for each ship to carry at least one dog on board. My great-great-grandfather on occasions rode over to Poole Harbour, and saw these dogs playing in the sea and retrieving the fish that had not "kept", so had been thrown out. He thought to himself that these water dogs, who retrieved so naturally in the water, were exactly what he required for his wildfowling. In 1823 he acquired two couples and built kennels on high ground for them, near a bend of the River Stour, known as Blackwater, which was only a quarter of a mile above the official tide end of the river, and bred from these dogs.'

The genesis of the breed began as a private whim. The dogs so impressed the Earl with their skill and ability that he devoted his entire kennel to developing, stabilising and pioneering the breed in Great Britain. He was the most influential person in keeping the Labrador breed alive and kept his kennel well stocked until his death in 1841.

Poole? It seemed such an incongruous place for this pivotal moment in the adaptation and creation of the Labrador. Poole, the home of millionaires, Harry Redknapp and the RNLI. Poole, where not only had I spent much of my childhood but also the last two years filming an ITV series about the history of the place and its people. In all that time I had never heard any mention of Labradors.

The only way of finding out how this connection had come about was to leave Labrador and Newfoundland before the weather marooned me for the long winter, and head to Dorset. But before I left Newfoundland, I wandered down to the harbour side in St John's. There, in pride of place, are two life-sized statues overlooking the sea passage. The bronze statues stand proudly, their heads held aloft, a reminder of this region's most famous inhabitants, not some great explorer nor a political goliath but two humble dogs that left these shores. Today, there are now estimated to be nearly 30 million Labradors across the world.

CHAPTER TWO

FISHY TAILS

Despite her outdoor life, Inca hated the rain. In fact, the only thing she hated more than the rain was getting her paws muddy. She also detested anything uncomfortable under her paws: rocks, pebbles, pine cones, pine needles, mud, even puddles could sometimes stop her in her tracks. But rain was the worst for her. If it was raining outside and she was inside, she wasn't going anywhere. She hated getting her coat wet almost as much as her paws.

Like most Labradors, she lived for her stomach. Inca *loved* food. She loved food as much as she hated stepping on pine cones.

Rather contradictorily, although she hated rain and puddles, she loved swimming. Like a moth to a flame, she was often left completely unable to stop herself. She would sleepwalk, like a zombie, into the water.

I will never forget the first time I met the TV presenter Kate

Humble. We had been teamed up by the BBC as a 'TV couple' to present a new series, *Animal Park*, following life behind the scenes at Longleat Safari Park.

I had just returned from Nepal when I picked up a voice message from Kate suggesting I come to dinner at her house so that we get to know each other ahead of filming. Naturally, I arrived with Inca in tow. Kate opened the door, and before I had time to introduce myself, Inca had barged past, down the hall, through the kitchen and belly flopped into the large fish pond in the back garden.

She re-emerged above the water line with pond weed on her head. I half expected a goldfish in her mouth. What's more, she couldn't get out. I had to kneel and haul her out by the scruff of her neck, at which point she shook the stinky water all over Kate, her kitchen and me.

It gets worse . . . Inca then discovered Kate's beloved rats. Yes, Kate kept several pet rats. She's since got better taste and keeps dogs of her own, but back then she had rats and Inca loved them. She sat next to their cage, staring, drooling and singing.

Inca had the best singing voice of any dog I know. Some might describe it as a kind of whine, but a whine is like a whinge – it's a negative noise. Inca sang. It was a happy, positive noise. I liked to think she was serenading the rats, but the rats weren't so sure. They hid in the corner as this giant, dripping wet, black dog sang to them.

Kate eventually intervened, worrying that the canine song might lead to cardiac arrest on the rats' part. And so we ate dinner to the smell of wet dog. It was the beginning of a long friendship, though, so it wasn't all bad.

Another time I remember visiting the late Duchess of Norfolk at her home, Bakers, in Berkshire. I was dating her grand-daughter, Kinvara, and we had both been invited for Sunday lunch. As always, I arrived with Inca. It was a glorious summer day and once again Inca made a bee line for the water. In this instance, it wasn't a fish pond but an immaculately clean swimming pool. Before I could stop her, Inca was sailing through the air into the azure waters.

We weren't invited back.

Over the years I lost count of the number of times I hauled Inca from rivers, canals and even cattle troughs. And all this from a dog that didn't like to get her paws wet. It was all or nothing with Inca.

It is perhaps unsurprising, given its coastal place of origin, that the Labrador began its life as a Water Dog. 'It was as a water-dog that the Labrador came into Britain. Regarded as a water-dog only, except by the few who treasured them, and ignored by most, Labradors spent the next 50 years in the well-cushioned obscurity which is the privilege of specialists,' wrote Stephens.

It was in Dorset that the Labrador was first treasured and ignored in Britain. I have always loved Dorset. I even lived there for four years, in the army town of Blandford, which I remember used to be called 'An Interesting Georgian Town'. Perhaps it was because I spent some of my formative years there that I can feel my whole body relax when I arrive in the county. It has that unique ability to combine happy memories with a largely unchanged landscape.

Often described as Thomas Hardy country, Dorset is defined

by its rolling green farmland and its famous Jurassic coast. I have since returned many times both for work and pleasure. Indeed, I have spent the past few years based at Poole Harbour, making a series about one of the world's largest natural harbours.

Poole really is a place of contradictions, where hard-working fishermen moor their ships alongside Sunseeker super-yachts. There can be few places in the United Kingdom where there is such a jarring clash of the 'haves' and the 'have nots'.

Sandbanks peninsula is often described as the most expensive real estate in Great Britain, and even one of the most expensive in the world. Here, million-pound glass and steel structures look out onto the working waters where fishermen still ply their trades. That it was here that the Labrador was first discovered seems incredible.

The harbour wall has changed very little in the last century. Close your eyes and you can still imagine the hubbub of trawlers emptying their holds of cod after their long voyage across the Atlantic. This would once have been a bustling place. It must have been quite a spectacle.

Today, the small fishermen's harbour is largely ignored. A handful of small boats still work the harbour and the ocean beyond, but Poole is as much a location for pleasure craft as it is for working boats.

Next to the old harbour pilot office, overlooking the estuary and the Sunseeker factory beyond, is Poole Harbour's museum. The museum is full of old artefacts covering the harbour's rich history, where old, faded black-and-white photographs offer a small porthole into the bygone era. I asked the curator if he had ever heard about the harbour's connection with the Labrador.

Nobody in the museum knew anything. There were no records. No photographs. No documents or accounts. The only inference was the large section dedicated to Newfoundland and the Dorset families who emigrated in search of wealth.

I sifted through hundreds of old photographs hoping to find the famous performing 'black dogs' that had captivated Lord Malmesbury, but there was nothing.

It seems that Poole has long forgotten its part in the story of the evolution of the world's most popular breed. So while the connection between Poole and Newfoundland is strong, Poole's role in the import of the Labrador as we know it today remains a bit of a mystery. Back in London, at the British Library, I read the first page of the leather-bound *Stud Book of the Duke of Buccleuch's Labrador*. The book names Ned (1882), sired by Lord Malmesbury's Sweep (1877) and dam Lord Malmesbury's Juno (1878), and describes him as 'of a different category to any of the other dogs' at the Duke's kennels. According to the book, Ned was followed by Avon (1885), hailed as even better than Ned – sired by Lord Malmesbury's Tramp, with Juno again the dam dog. The carefully kept stud book represented the start of an official record of the Labrador, but in retrospect, it is a rare and valuable document which highlights some of the events in the development of the breed. Another entry describes the time Buccleuch Avon is said to have sired 'liver-coloured' pups: in 1892, the record states that two 'liver colour' Labradors were born at the Buccleuch kennel. Labrador enthusiasts then began to demonstrate a desire to preserve and safeguard the 'new breed'. Records also show that in 1899 the first registered yellow Labrador was born at the kennel of Major Radclyffe and named

Ben of Hyde. Was this the first time the breed deviated from the traditional black?

The colour of the breed has long divided Labrador lovers. Many still believe that black is the true original colour and that yellow and brown are mere anomalies that caught on. Certainly as a dog to blend into the landscape during a shoot, black is undoubtedly the best colour, although yellows can blend in well in some wildfowling situations.

Throughout the second half of the nineteenth century Labradors were carefully bred but still remained 'rarities if not eccentricities' in the sporting and domestic scene. Traded exclusively among the landed gentry, they proved themselves the most versatile of working dogs: hardy, reliable, efficient, gentle, clean and undemanding. The same traits that define them today.

The Field once wrote, 'One of the countryside's riddles is how and why a race of dogs, so dominant for only 10 years short of a century, could also have been so dormant for so long, a clear case of unrecognised talent.'

There is a truism here. In 1886 – 75 years after their arrival on these shores – J.H. Walsh, in his *Dogs of the British Islands: Being a Series of Articles on the Points of their Various Breeds and the Treatment of the Diseases to which they are Subject*, described the Labrador or Lesser Newfoundland Dog as a mere accessory to a certain lifestyle: 'As his use in this country is almost entirely confined to retrieving game, he cannot be included among the non-sporting dogs.'

How did the Labrador go from being a specialist wildfowl retriever prized by a small elite circle in Britain to being the world's most popular domestic dog? The answer begins with another milestone in history: the wide-scale development of the breech-loading gun in the late nineteenth century. Up until then, shooting was by muzzle-loaded guns, *i.e.* a firearm into which the 'shot' and the propellant explosive powder are loaded from the muzzle of the gun (the forward, open end of the gun's barrel). To go shooting usually meant several guns (people with guns) walking through a woodland, copse, moor, waterland or field, shooting the birds their dogs put up. This style of 'walked up' shooting (sometimes called 'shooting over dogs') remained customary until the introduction of the much more efficient double-barrelled, quick-loading shotgun.

Thanks to the revolutionary refinement in precision engineering and machining in the nineteenth century, breech loading – whereby a cartridge or shell is loaded into a chamber integral to the rear portion of a barrel – became the norm. It meant a significant reduction in reloading time and gave rise to the popularity of driven game shooting, where beaters are employed to walk through woods and over moors or fields (dependent on the quarry and the season) and drive game over a line of standing guns spaced about 50 metres apart. In driven shooting, the head count of shot game is much higher than in walked-up shooting, requiring pickers-up with dogs to make sure all shot or wounded game is collected. The advent of driven game shooting was the cue for the Labradors to come into their own. Only dogs could keep up with the guns.

But it didn't happen quickly. Wilson Stephens described the evolution in *The Field*: 'Although those to whom it had become second nature no doubt learned to reload them safely in half the time that we would take, the pouring in of powder, the

ramming of the wad, the charging with shot and further
ramming, all processes duplicated for each barrel, made driven
game as we know it pointless. All shooting was over dogs, and
those which quested or hunted up the game also retrieved it, as
spaniels still do . . . With so little game on the ground at any
time, and with no need to hurry because of the time taken to
reload after every second shot, specialist retrievers were unnecessary . . . When the shooting scene changed with the development
of breech loading, the Labrador was not only present in Britain,
but was the only retriever available. Yet it was not widely adopted
to meet the new situation. Instead, the flatcoated retriever
became supreme. Perhaps the strictly functional, workworthy
Labrador seemed plain beside the more elegant flatcoat. But
beauty is in the eye of the beholder, and is not necessarily
synonymous with usefulness. The flatcoat had, and still has, an
unlosable handicap.'

Stephens continues to press their claims in comparing the
retrieving processes of both dogs – the flatcoat's tendency to
cast widely, downwind of a target, and then work slowly towards
it, dependent on air scent versus the Labrador's 'direct line to
the mark, followed by a tight-patterned working-out of a limited
area around a fall'. Stephens notes, 'The extra distance covered
by flatcoats not only takes longer but inevitably moves other
game off the ground, to the detriment of the sport. When
Labradors worked, more game remained . . .' He triumphantly
concludes: 'Realisation of the average Labrador's superiority was
sudden, positive, and has proved permanent.'

So when did the Labrador become popular away from the
field? Perhaps unsurprisingly, the gundog was now known not

just as the Labrador but as the Labrador Retriever, and it had become the gundog of choice for the British aristocracy.

The Victorian love of both dogs and pastimes led to the incredible popularity of field trials and dog shows. The first conformation dog show – a show to assess how well individual dogs conform to specific breed standards – was held in the town hall of Newcastle upon Tyne in June 1859. The only breeds scheduled were pointers and setters. The first organised field trial – a competitive event at which hunting dogs such as retrievers, pointers and flushing dogs compete against one another in a series of tasks – took place at Southill, in Bedfordshire, in 1865. Both sports gained a large and fashionable following.

In April 1873 the Kennel Club was founded to provide a set of rules and standards for the popular new pastimes. The very first sport recognised by the Kennel Club was the sport of Field Trials, which in this era particularly tested the skills of working gundogs and attracted large and appreciative audiences. In 1886, Charles Cruft, a general manager at a dog biscuit manufacturer, founded Crufts Dog Show. Billed as the 'First Great Terrier Show', it began with 57 classes and 600 entries. By 1891, the show was known as Crufts Greatest Dog Show. The venue was the Royal Agricultural Hall, Islington, and it was the first at which all breeds were invited to compete, with approximately 2,000 dogs and almost 2,500 entries.

As a young boy, I used to visit Crufts with my father, when it was still held in central London, at Earls Court, and it helped define my childhood. I loved going to Crufts – the noise, the smell, the dogs. My role in the show became tighter in 2006, though, when I was asked to present the BBC's live coverage of the show. I presented Crufts for two years. I can't say those years were as happy as my childhood recollections; the pressure of presenting a live prime-time TV show, and the interaction with a significantly haughty group of breeders who didn't like my style of presenting, inevitably led to a bumpy ride.

I co-presented the show with Inca, my black Lab, at my side. The show was dropped several years later, after the BBC ran a panorama exposé that revealed the slightly murky world of the Kennel Club and their breed requirements that often lead to long-term health complications for many breeds. In fact, Inca was a case in point. Her epilepsy was more than likely to have been caused by a limited gene pool. In short – incest.

I digress.

Back at the late turn of the last century, dog ownership was booming, and with it an appetite for specialised breeds that ordinary people could 'discover' as the dog that best suited them. Labradors had come to Britain as sea dogs. They were spotted and cultivated as wildfowling water dogs. As gundogs to the gentry, they acquired a fashionable social status attractive to the aspirational classes. Eager to please and eminently trainable, loyal and lovable, playful and energetic, the Labrador gradually became a great all-rounder, a symbol of social status, a valued working dog to some and a treasured family pet to millions. Once the development of breech loading revolutionised the shooting scene, the breed's gundog expertise was its passport to the millions.

I left Poole and headed to meet Lord Malmesbury's son on their old estate. The Malmesbury Estate itself was broken up and sold several decades ago, with the great house turned into apartments and flats. Driving through the gates and along the drive, however, you still get a sense of the estate it once was.

The River Stour meanders through the land, through fields that were once flooded from the heavy rain which had made the river burst its banks. The Stour had memories for me from my school days, just a short way upriver from where I was now.

My first port of call was the small keeper's cottage. Over tea and scones, the keeper explained to me how important Labradors still are for the shoots. We piled into a battered pickup and drove through the old estate to the remains of the kennels. They had long since fallen into disrepair, with just a couple of walls remaining, largely overgrown. Looking at what remained of them, it seemed incredible that the dogs that had once been kept in these kennels were more than likely to have been the progeny for the millions and millions of Labradors across the world.

It was about the same time that the Earl of Malmesbury was beginning his breeding programme in his kennel on the south coast of England that the fifth Duke of Buccleuch (1806–1884) and his brother, Lord John Scott, imported dogs for use as gundogs on the Queensberry estates, in the Scottish borders, from a Newfoundland fishing fleet which sailed into the River Clyde. They had also realised what an extraordinary dog the Labrador was and so established a kennel in around 1835. One of the Duke's dogs, Brandy, earned his name on his journey across the Atlantic. Having been sent overboard in a heavy sea to fetch the cap of one of the crew, the young dog spent two hours in the water before he could be picked up again, by which point he was so exhausted that the sailors had to revive him with brandy.

The brothers loved their dogs so much that when they went

on a yachting holiday to Naples in 1839, they took their favourite Labradors – Moss and Drake – with them: something that was unheard of back then.

According to records, in 1871, the Earl of Malmesbury's neighbour, Major Radclyffe – who had patrolled Poole Harbour with the Earl admiring the fishermen's sea dogs – imported a dog direct from Newfoundland. He was called Turk and would go on to sire the line that included Ben of Hyde, the first yellow Lab to be registered.

By the early 1880s the original Buccleuch strain had died out, just five or six decades on from the original purchases from the fishermen on the Clyde. This could well have signalled the end of the Scottish lineage of the Labrador Retriever, were it not for our friend the sixth Earl of Malmesbury who 'gave them a pair, descended from our own imported dogs'.

It is probably fair to say that a chance meeting between the third Earl of Malmesbury (at the age of 75) with the sixth Duke of Buccleuch (1831–1914) and the twelfth Duke of Home (1834–1918) saved the Labrador from extinction. The two Scots were visiting a sick aunt on the south coast of England and while there accepted an invitation to participate in a waterfowl shoot at Hurn. Precisely where I was heading now.

The Hurn Estate is another old estate that was broken up long ago, but what remains is managed by the current Earl's son, James Fitzharris. In an old pickup truck we drove through what was left of the estate that had once been the family seat to James's ancestors. Hurn Court is now apartments, and there was an air of sadness as we drove along the road that had once been the drive to the grand house.

It was hard to imagine what this place must have been like when it was still the thriving seat of the Malmesburys, in the family's heyday, when aristocracy had money and power.

'That's all that remains of the kennels,' pointed James from one of the misted windows of the pickup. There were some simple foundations and the skeletal remains of one of the walls. The remains had been largely consumed by the encroaching Dorset countryside.

It struck me that these sad, unloved, anonymous ruins were symbolic of our amnesia as to the provenance of the world's most popular breed. James explained that he still kept Labradors, but that his father, the current Earl of Malmesbury, 'couldn't stand them'.

It was lucky that the current Earl wasn't seated back in 1887 when the two Scottish visitors were impressed by Malmesbury's eager-to-please, efficient water dogs and recognised they were the same Little Newfoundler dogs as their father's. Malmesbury generously offered them some of his dogs to carry on the breeding programme north of the border, and the pair of dogs, Avon and Ned, that he entrusted them with are now considered to be the ancestors of all modern Labradors: the legendary progenitors.

And so it was that the Earls of Malmesbury and the Dukes of Buccleuch were instrumental in developing and establishing the modern Labrador breed.

In a letter written to the Duke, dated 1887, the Earl first used the name 'Labrador' in print. 'We always call mine Labrador dogs and I have kept the breed as pure as I could from the first I had,' he wrote. 'The real breed may be known by their having a close coat which turns water off like oil, and, about all, a tail like an otter.'

Inca had the fattest tail you have ever seen; it was more like an otter's tail – thick with coarse hair. It had never occurred to me that this was part of her heritage – the powerful motor and rudder to propel her through the water.

As I said, Inca loved water.

CHAPTER THREE

BANCHORY BOLO AND BEN

In 1999, I had been languishing in the offices of *Tatler* magazine in London and I was now looking for an escape. A way out. I wanted adventure. I was 24 and still living at home. I wanted an opportunity.

At that time the BBC were looking for people to be marooned on a deserted island in the Outer Hebrides for a year, beginning in January 2000. The project, *Castaway*, would later become one of the first reality shows to be broadcast in Britain. I applied and was chosen as one of 36 people to be shipwrecked on the Isle of Taransay for a year as part of a social experiment to see if we could create a fully self-sufficient community.

We reared our own livestock and grew our own crops. We built a slaughterhouse, a school and our living accommodation.

Each of us castaways had been asked to choose a luxury item that we could take with us. One couple had chosen a bed, another asked for a piano. Someone even opted for a home-brewing kit.

A dog. That was what I'd take. My own dog. A puppy.

Until that moment in my life I had led a relatively selfish existence. The previous 24 years had largely been about me. I had never had to think about anyone else but myself; the family pets were still the responsibility of my parents and I had never had to do an early morning walk with a hangover, or worry about a late night because the dogs were hungry.

This would be the moment that I made the sacrifice and took on a canine responsibility of my own.

But what breed?

I had grown up with Golden Retrievers; I liked Deer Hounds but they were too big; I liked Newfoundlands but they were too hairy; I liked Pugs but they had too many health problems. To be honest, I would have been happy with most breeds, but in reality there was only ever one breed of dog I ever really truly wanted: a Labrador.

Why a Labrador? Well, that is a complicated one, and it will take more than a chapter to explain.

Growing up above a veterinary clinic, I had more than my fair share of encounters with a wide variety of breeds. To be honest, growing up, I loved all dogs – irrelevant of breed, but I knew three Labradors in my childhood, two of which belonged to my late friend Alice Benkert. Alice lived in Esher, and the two dogs, Poppy and Oscar, would come with her parents to collect her from school. I would spend hours with them. I remember the time we came back to her home and the dogs had found several boxes of freezer bags that they had scattered like confetti around the kitchen.

The other Labrador belonged to an English teacher at my

school, called PJ. He had a beautiful black dog and a Land Rover – and I coveted both. Now I think about it, I wonder whether getting to know Labradors at the same time that I went to boarding school and was separated from my childhood Golden Retrievers was the seed of my obsession. I cried for a year when I left home. My homesickness was debilitating. It wasn't just that I missed my home, but also the dogs, Liberty and Lexington.

Lib and Lex, as we knew them, were my best friends and my confidants. They were what really made our house a home. They soothed and settled me. I decorated the walls around my bed at school with photographs of the dogs, but that only made things worse. I would sob into my pillow each night, wishing, longing for that warm, hairy body stretched out on my bed.

When my parents finally understood how much I missed the dogs, they decided it would be a good idea if they came along with us when it was time to drop me off at school. But the fleeting appearance of Lib and Lex only made matters worse – tears would stream down my cheeks as I watched my parents drive away, a small tuft of blond fur visible through the back window.

I'm getting homesick just thinking about it!

Lib and Lex were the first constants I really knew in my life. Both my parents would come and go, depending on work commitments, but the dogs were always there – tail wagging at the door, tongue lickingly happy to see me.

Throughout the term I would find their blond hairs stuck to my clothes. A reminder of my two friends waiting for me at home. Boarding school was the only time in my life when I was forcibly separated from dogs and it was then that I promised

myself I would get my own dog at the first opportunity. Young
naivety assured me this would be on the day that I left school,
but then travel and girls got in the way and my plans got put
on a back burner.

Until now. This was the perfect opportunity. The problem
was that neither the production company nor the BBC wanted
me to take a dog. To be honest, I never really understood why.
I think it might have had something to do with the landowner
who was leasing the island. While there weren't many ground-
nesting birds on the island of Taransay, there was plenty of
livestock.

The makers of the show argued that there were already three
dogs, all Collies, coming along, and that a fourth dog would tip
the balance. Not only would it be a drain on our limited
resources, but it would also affect the fragile human-to-dog
ratio.

I set about on a campaign to change their mind. I found as
many cute pictures of Labrador puppies as I could and then got
my father to draft a letter outlining the human benefits of having
a puppy within the community.

We argued that a puppy would be a cohesive addition, helping
to bond strangers and bringing peace and harmony to the newly
created community. Bringing 36 men, women and children
together in the extreme circumstances of a windswept, uninhabited
Scottish island was bound to create tensions but, we argued, the
presence of a young puppy could help to diffuse any emerging
conflict and arguments. Maybe that's why they didn't want the
puppy . . .

I promised that I would train the puppy to be a working dog

so that she would be an asset to the community. I was sure she could be trained to work with the sheep. And as for a drain on resources, I argued that she could quite reasonably live off scraps. She would be a Labrador, after all. They eat anything, I reasoned.

I'm not sure what clinched the deal for me, but the programme makers eventually relented and I set about finding my perfect puppy. A Labrador, of course.

Dad offered to help. For more than a week, we toured the country looking at litter after litter.

We drove as far north as the Scottish borders to look at puppies. Too thin, too fat – none was quite right. Eventually, detective work led us to a tiny kennel near Heathrow airport. There we saw a litter of black Labradors that stuck in my mind, in particular one of the puppies who was the last to be picked, probably because she was a rather scrawny-looking thing with a large swollen eye.

'Wasp sting,' the woman explained.

I examined her carefully.

'No thanks,' I said, rather heartlessly, handing her back.

As we pulled away from the yard, I caught a glimpse of her sad, dark eyes. Why was I turning my back on this lone pup? Suddenly I wasn't sure, but as with love, I wanted to be certain. How would I know she was the one?

For the next few days I couldn't stop thinking about her. It had been more than a week and I was certain she'd be gone.

'She's still here,' said the woman down the phone.

I raced back. We pulled up to the house and were led into the living room, where the puppy was alone. She had been weaned from her mother, which meant separating the dogs.

Immediately she ran up to me and licked my face. The swelling on her eye had subsided and, away from her greedy siblings, she was now much rounder, with a bulging pink belly.

She gazed up at me with her hazel eyes as I ran my fingers through her thick black hair. I nuzzled my nose behind her ear and inhaled her scent. It was instant love. I had always been told that I'd find her, and now I really had found 'the one'. I named her Inca.

I held her close as we walked out into the crisp winter night, but as we approached the car I heard a commotion in the background.

'Get back here!' cried a voice.

The puppy's mother had broken free and came bounding over. She jumped up and licked Inca clean across the face, then lifted her ear. I am not one to over-anthropomorphise our animals, but I swear she was wishing her luck. She was whispering something into that little dog's ear, and I'd like to think she was telling her to look after me.

As quickly as she had appeared, Inca's mother vanished back into the darkness. Her owner looked on in astonishment, a tear in her eye.

And so began a friendship that would change things forever. Little did I realise then how much this little dog would form, shape and create my life. She would change it in ways I never thought possible. The story of Inca is, ultimately, the story of me.

Inca and I became inseparable. I was still living in my childhood bedroom in my parents' house, and I can vividly remember setting up her little crate at the foot of my bed, feeling both fear and excitement at the journey that lay ahead.

My life of blissful selfishness was over and a new one of selflessness was beginning. I genuinely think that those two words separate dog owners from non-dog owners.

I guess, on the face of it, it is a little strange that we invite this hairy animal into our homes. We share our lives with a creature that was once undomesticated and wild. I've always been fascinated as to why we keep dogs. Why we love dogs. Why we mourn our dogs when they go. Of course, it varies from culture to culture and from country to country. Some argue it is a sign of development; the more developed a country the higher the number of pet dogs. The sharp spike in the number of pet dogs in China, with its emerging middle-class population, seems to back that up.

By the very late nineteenth century in Britain, the popularity of the Labrador was on the rise and it wasn't long before the Royals got in on the act, in a connection with the breed that has endured right up to the present day.

The first Labrador kennels were established at Sandringham by King Edward VII, then Prince of Wales, in 1879 to house a hundred dogs, and the Sandringham kennels and the Labradors that are bred there have become firm favourites of the Royal Family as a whole. In fact, it may come as a surprise to many that the Queen is as fond of her Labradors as she is of her infamous Corgis.

In many ways the Corgis are the public face of the Queen's canine companions, but the Labrador is the private love of her life. I was once told a story that the Queen has several Land Rovers custom-made with windscreen wipers on the inside. Apparently these were specifically adapted for her Labradors, who have a tendency to steam cars up from the inside out.

The Queen takes a very great interest in the Sandringham kennels. Since her accession to the throne in 1952, the breeding programme there has gone from strength to strength, culminating in the training of five Field Trial Champions. All the puppies born at Sandringham are named personally by the Queen and are registered at the Kennel Club with the prefix Sandringham.

At any one time, the kennels are home to about 20 dogs of all ages, including Labradors and Cocker Spaniels – ranging from the older and more experienced gundogs used by members of the Royal Family during the shooting season to the younger dogs under training as gundogs.

In addition to providing dogs for the Royal Family, the kennels also supply the Estate gamekeepers with working Labradors and Spaniels.

In a bout of hopeful optimism I sent a note to Her Majesty's equerry asking if it would be possible to visit the Queen's Labrador kennels at Sandringham. I was politely informed that the kennels are extremely private and that a visit would be impossible. While the Corgis are frequently photographed at the Queen's side, her Labradors are rarely seen and it appeared that was the way she wanted it to remain.

Records of the breed were kept by the Buccleuch estate in Scotland at around the same time that Edward VII was beginning his Labrador breeding programme, and it is these that note the arrival of two chocolate puppies or 'liver pups' in 1890. Could these have been the progenitors for the future of chocolate Labradors? The royal household would undoubtedly have given the liver pups the ultimate royal seal of approval.

But while the Labrador was finally establishing itself on our shores, across the Atlantic a problem was looming that threatened the strength and integrity of the breed in Britain. In 1885 the Newfoundland government, worried about the number of dogs in the region, passed the Sheep Protection Act which gave local government the right to impose a dog licensing tax as well as the right to prohibit dogs completely.

Inevitably, dog importations were affected. Colonel Peter Hawker wrote in the *Instructions to Young Sportsmen* that, 'Poole was, till of late years, known to be the best place to buy Newfoundland dogs; either just imported or broken in; until they became more scarce, owing (the sailors observe) to the strictness of those tax gatherers.'

The 1885 Act was meant to encourage sheep raising by reducing the number of potential predators, but the result was to kill the Labrador export trade. The Quarantine Act of 1895 created another barrier to the importing of dogs. The Act prohibited dogs from entering Great Britain without a licence and without first undergoing a strict six-month quarantine to prevent the introduction of rabies.

The future of the Labrador hung in the balance.

Between 1890 and 1930 the multiple taxes, restrictions and paperwork meant no new dogs were imported to Britain and the results were quickly felt. This was the moment when 'breed mixing' began. Some breeders began mixing Labradors with Setters and Pointers. 'Bearing in mind the high qualities attributed to pure Labradors, it is somewhat strange that the breed should have been allowed to degenerate by the various crosses of Setter and Spaniel blood,' wrote Hugh Dalziel in his 1897 publication,

British Dogs, Volume III, referring to new problems such as a hard mouth and sulky temper.

Within the tight circle of enthusiasts there was a move to preserve the purity of the breed. In 1903 the Labrador Retriever was recognised by the Kennel Club. In 1904, it was granted breed status and listed separately as a member of the Gundog Group. The breed standard was written, and it was almost identical to the one that holds sway today.

During the first decade of the twentieth century, Labrador Retrievers rose to prominence in the show ring and in field trials, and were also much favoured gundogs. By 1913, they were so well entrenched in the world of dog ownership that their qualities as working dogs were causing an emotive debate. The criticism that was voiced that they could be a 'bit hard in the mouth' was queried by Frank Townend Barton in his authoritative volume, *Gun Dogs*. The ideal retriever is a 'soft-mouthed' dog, a fetcher which picks up game softly but firmly to bring back birds that are fit for the table. Dogs that unnecessarily drop, crunch on, chew or even eat the bird before delivery to the handler are considered 'hard-mouthed'.

'If the Labrador possesses the qualities assigned to it by James Craw (at one time gamekeeper at Hirsel and Netherby), viz sagacity, stamina, perseverance, quickness and nose, then no other variety can come up to the Labradors,' he wrote. 'The only fault that he had to find with some of them – a fault common to all other varieties of retriever – was that they were a bit hard in the mouth. Gamekeepers and shooting men required a dog that could retrieve birds and game without piercing the skin with their teeth. I have always thought

Labradors have one of the softest of bites; indeed, I have even seen Labradors carry fresh, unboiled eggs in their mouths while running.

Controversy, however, has frequently arisen concerning this matter, but supporters often point out that this trait spans the retriever group as a whole. Sometimes hunger just takes over.

Townend Barton reasoned 'the Labrador was one of the best dogs in existence for a gamekeeper, most of which like their dogs to look 'well and fit' at the opening of the shooting season, without needing to devote much attention to them during the busy time, which necessarily precedes it on estates where hand-rearing of pheasants is carried on to any extent.'

Barton gives his 'strong recommendation of the breed to shooting men' on the eve of the First World War. The sixth Earl of Malmesbury recalls the estate keeper, Mr Beech, being called up into the Royal Artillery and '. . . the [Labrador] bitch he left behind pined so much that she sadly died. As a child I just remember her. She was the last of the direct descendants of the dogs imported in 1823.'

In the middle of the war, in 1916, the Labrador Retriever Club was founded by Lord Knutsford (then the Honourable Arthur Holland-Hibbert) and Lady Howe (then Mrs Quintin Dick), with a Mr T. W. Twyford of Staffordshire, to champion the breed, and Labs suddenly became the fashion. In 1916 the club authored the first Labrador Retriever standard. In the 1920s and 30s, King George VI and Queen Elizabeth promoted Labradors at shows through their kennel, and the King entered dogs in Crufts. In 1938, King George became Patron of the Labrador Retriever Club. In 1952, on the death of George VI,

Queen Elizabeth the Queen Mother continued as patron. Today, the Her Majesty the Queen is Patron of the Club and the Duke of Wellington is President.

The Hon Henry Holland-Hibbert, great grandson of the 3rd Viscount Knutsford, still has the stud book that traces the foundation of the famous Munden line of Labradors and, according to records, the original kennel is still intact on the Munden Estate.

It's strange how trails can lead you in circles. I had already traversed the Atlantic Ocean in an effort to understand more about the breed I love so much, and now I found myself navigating the North Circular around west London towards Munden House, a 30-room eighteenth-century mansion located in the suburbs of London, just off the M1. The seat of the Viscount Knutsfords since 1874, the estate is an oasis of rural calm in the embrace of one of the most urbanised parts of the United Kingdom. There is no great gatehouse, pomp or ceremony; a tiny gate leads the way through barley fields to the manor house.

Henry Holland-Hibbert moved into Munden in 1992, where his father, Michael Knutsford, is the current 6th Viscount Knutsford. Henry's wife, Kate Holland-Hibbert, met me at the top of the drive. She was wearing an earpiece because the house has become popular as a film, television and fashion shoot location and an army of film coordinators had temporarily taken over the grounds. Kate was keeping an ear on proceedings. She invited me into her warm kitchen where a black Labrador was stretched out next to the Aga. On the walls were paintings and portraits of various breeds of dog.

Both Henry and his father, Michael, then welcomed me warmly, as did the Labrador. Under strict Knutsford folklore, every Labrador belonging to the family must be given a name beginning with S. For the current Labs, the family had voted on Smudge and Scooby Doo.

There on the kitchen table was the stud book that I had come to see. Saucy, Sarah, Scottie, Sahib, Sober, Sceptre, Sermon, Sandfly . . . the list went on into the hundreds. It was an impressive list of 'S' names.

No one remembers why the tradition began, but the family dutifully continues it into the present day. What was more telling, though, was the straightforward approach that had been taken towards the estate's dogs in previous decades. Next to each entry was a comment box, and several struck me in particular: 'Picked up poison and died' read one entry; 'Distemper' read many more; 'Died, Swallowed a bone'. Others were a little more brutal. 'Well shot' and 'dead and not mourned for' read several entries – clearly a reference to dogs that were not popular.

The stud book records tell us that the first Lord Knutsford acquired a Labrador in 1884: Sybil, a bitch closely bred back to Netherby Boatswain. The book records a description of her being a 'wonderful good bitch, nose, pace, endurance and marking'. She was mated to a dog from Lord Malmesbury's kennel and thus the Munden line began. Munden Sixty, the result of a mating between Munden Sarah (a Sybil granddaughter) and the Duke of Buccleuch's Nith (a Malmesbury Tramp grandson), was born in 1897 and by all accounts was a much-loved dog. When he died ten years later, it was Lord

Knutsford himself who wrote those words in the stud book that had affected me so much: 'To the everlasting grief of all who knew him, this splendid dog died in August 1907'. Sixty was the sire of a bitch who was to become perhaps the most famous of all the early Labradors, for it was she, Munden Single, whose impact on the field trial world would change the pattern of working gundogs for all time.

Munden Single was born in 1899 to Munden Scottie, who had been bought from the Duke of Buccleuch's kennel. Her breeding was therefore almost pure Buccleuch and Malmesbury. Single was destined for a success in field trials and shows that all others have sought to follow. Single had already won prizes in the show ring, including a CC* at the KC Show, when, in 1904, she was entered in the IGL† field trial at Sherbourne. As the first Labrador ever to appear at a field trial, she attracted much interest. The newspapers of the day recorded:

Only those who were at the Meeting know how very nearly the Stake was carried off by the finest Labrador bitch ever seen on or off the bench. We refer to the Hon Mr Holland-Hibbert's blue blooded Munden Single – up to a certain point nothing could have stopped her winning the highest honours at the trial. One of the best shots in England, a man who has handled retrievers all his life, declared to us that Single was the best game-finder and the steadiest retriever he had ever seen.

---

*The 'Challenge Certificate' is what the judge signs stating that in his or her opinion the dog is worthy of becoming a Champion.

†The International Gundog League.

Sadly, she didn't win because she mouthed a bird when bringing it to hand. Lord Knutsford wrote in his record book, 'she was too gross and I was to blame for not getting her finer. She was out of breath after a strong runner and resented its struggles'. Single had, however, done enough to ensure that Labradors were now well and truly on the map. She won a CoM (Certificate of Merit) at that trial, then went on to win others and continued to win well on the bench. When she died in 1909, her body was preserved and put on display, and it is believed still to be held in a museum vault. Lord Knutsford wrote: 'It is a bad representation'.

In the early days of owning Labradors, Lord Knutsford regularly showed his dogs and enjoyed some considerable success with them. In 1904 he won the first bitch CC ever awarded with Munden Single, and Munden Sentry won the only dog CC, awarded in 1905. In 1909 Munden Sooty won two CCs at Crufts and Darlington. In fact, during the first six years of ownership, when a total of 29 CCs was available, dogs owned by Lord Knutsford or bred from Munden dogs won 15 CCs.

In 1923 Munden Scarcity was mated to Dual Ch Banchory Bolo. There were six surviving puppies; Lord Knutsford kept two: Solo, a dog, and Singer, a bitch. Another bitch was given to His Majesty the King and a dog went to Lady Howe. Lady Howe's puppy turned out to be Ch Banchory Danilo, a dog described by Lord Knutsford as 'winning more championships than any dog ever known – or nearly so'. Munden Solo also did well at shows; at Crufts in 1927 he was entered in ten classes, won six, was second in two and third in another. The judge wrote of him, 'if there had been a little more of him in size, I think he would have been very near perfection.'

Michael explained to me that, alongside his great grandfather, it had been Mrs Quintin Dick, as she then was, who had been instrumental in the formation of the Labrador Retriever Club in 1916, becoming the first Secretary and Treasurer – offices she held until her death in 1961. She also became the Chairman in 1935 when Lord Knutsford died. She was in every way the driving force of the club and the champion of the breed in its formative years.

Lady Howe owned some of the most influential Labradors of all time: dual champions Banchory Bolo, Banchory Painter, Banchory Sunspeck and Bramshaw Bob; champions Ilderton Ben, Banchory Trueman, Banchory Danilo, Bolo's Trust, Ingleston Ben, Orchardton Donald and field trial champion Balmuto Jock, to name but a few. Lady Howe purchased many of the dogs she made famous, her keen eye quickly spotting the potential of any young dog.

Her undoubted favourite was Bolo, though, a dog that did so much for the breed. Born in 1915, sired by Scandal of Glyn (a FT Ch* Peter of Faskally son), Bolo was an eighth generation from Lord Malmesbury's Tramp (1878), through Munden Sixty and Sentry. His start in life was not a happy one and until Lady Howe took him on at the age of three, he showed no sign of the greatness that was within him.

Lady Howe worked tirelessly for the club, and by her example and encouragement the Labrador attained a position as the most popular retriever – which it still holds to this day. In the early days dogs were expected to be dual purpose and most of Lady Howe's dogs achieved success both in the field and on the bench.

---

* Field Trial Champion.

Served well by her trainer/handler Tom Gaunt, Lady Howe ensured that her dogs performed their task successfully at the highest levels. It is very significant that four of the ten dual champions in the breed were owned by Lady Howe.

Together, Lady Howe and Lord Knutsford were great protectors of the breed. He frequently went into print to defend the Labrador. There were constant disputes as to the breed's origins and Lord Knutsford was tireless in his endeavours to get to the true beginnings. There are notes of conversations with Major Radclyffe and Mr Stuart-Menzies, and letters to and from other early breeders. His kennel records describe dogs variously as being Newfoundland-type, Labrador-type, long- and rough-coated, smooth-coated, and frequently they had white markings.

Like so many other kennels, Munden had to endure a number of serious distemper outbreaks. Many promising puppies, and indeed some good adults, were lost. Lord Knutsford worked very hard to find a solution to the scourge. Having had little success in his approaches to the Ministry of Agriculture and the Royal Veterinary College, he finally persuaded the editor of *The Field* to set up an investigation into the disease. Funds were raised, the research was successful and a vaccine was eventually produced in 1929. *The Daily Telegraph* in that year reported that two vaccines were now available, albeit in very small supplies. The report went on: 'dog owners have every reason to be grateful to Mr Holland-Hibbert for the idea and to the great sporting newspaper for the manner in which it has been made possible.'

Michael is a charming man, oozing passion for Labradors. He has personally supplied many dogs to Her Majesty, and the

Queen has often lamented to him how much she wished she could spend more time with her beloved Labradors. Indeed, Michael told me the tale of one such of her dogs. The Queen had a particular soft spot for one Lab and decided to bring it to Windsor Castle so she could spend more time with it. She fed it and walked it herself, but the poor dog pined for its mates back at Sandringham and so she eventually sent it back for the sake of the dog. Even the Queen thinks of her dogs first.

It's another anecdote of the powerful emotional command that Labradors have over us all.

Smudge nuzzled my knee in an effort to gain my attention. Labradors do this; they try to lift your hand in an effort to encourage you to stroke them. Smudge had a litter of eight puppies. Michael recounted how horrified his wife had been to discover that only four were black. Of the two yellows, she exclaimed, 'what a shame', and of the two chocolates she lamented, 'how disappointing'. Colour is still an emotive subject amongst the purists. It seems that, despite the Queen's approval, many still agree with the old fashion adage, 'any colour as long as it's black'.

'Would you like to see the kennel?' asked Kate, as she led me outside.

Nat Parker, the actor, sidled past me, as a director in a clichéd leather jacket and aviator sunglasses barked orders to the hundreds of foot soldiers. They were in the midst of filming *Outcast*.

Next to the house was an anonymous empty kennel.

'There it is,' smiled Henry.

'It's not much to look at,' he explained. 'We don't use it any more.'

Like the Hurn Kennels, it was a forgotten, neglected part of the Labrador's history.

Before I left, Michael told me a little about his great-grandfather.

'The greatest anecdote about my great-grandfather, really, is from when he was speaking in his capacity as Chairman of the Labrador Retriever Club at the end of a field trial at Idsworth in 1935. He spoke, sat down with a drink in hand, collapsed and died. They carried him out in a box but everyone agreed it was the happiest way for him to go.'

Before leaving, I asked Henry about the provenance of their current Munden Labradors. He told me the story of a chance encounter.

'When we got our Lab, who's now 12 years old, my wife went to a breeder whose dogs she'd admired out walking. Knowing the family history, we explained that we were particularly keen to find a puppy that came from the Munden line. "That's easy," the breeder laughed. "Almost all Labradors are descended from the Munden line." We thought we'd be unearthing something really special, but it turns out the Munden dogs are not dissimilar to Adam and Eve for humans!'

The breeder's name was Sussie Wiles, someone I would later meet myself.

Across the Atlantic at the end of the nineteenth century, things were picking up for the Labrador, too, although it wasn't until the late 1920s that the American Kennel Club recognised the Labrador Retriever as a separate breed. The first registration of Labradors by the AKC was in 1917, and in the early 1920s an influx of British dogs had begun to form the backbone of the breed in the United States. Distinguished Long Island families began to compete them in dog shows and retrieving trials, but they were an elite presence. A 1928 *American Kennel Gazette* article, entitled 'Meet the Labrador Retriever', ushered in a wider recognition of its traits as both game finders and water dogs. Up until those words were written in the United States, the American Kennel Club had only registered 23 Labradors in the country.

By the 1930s the 'St John's dog' was rare in Newfoundland, and the 6th Duke of Buccleuch was only finally able to import a few more dogs between 1933 and 1934 to continue the line. The advent of the Second World War in 1939, with six tough years of food shortages and rationing, took its toll on breeding kennels. In many cases, dogs had to be fed on meat that was unfit for human consumption. Soon after the war, an epidemic of hardpad distemper killed significant numbers of dogs; a high proportion of the survivors were left with crippling chorea, a nasty disease of the nervous system also known as St Vitus's Dance. Nevertheless, a core number of top-quality Labradors remained. Over the next four decades, the number increased by 300 per cent. After the war, there was a marked increase in the popularity of yellow Labs, and in 1960, the first chocolate champion was hailed.

The temperament of Labs and their abilities were perfect for all sorts of roles as working dogs; so much so that by 1952, the dog formerly prized solely as a sea dog, then wildfowling retriever, then gundog, became the popular all-round dog of today and the ultimate family pet.

'The Labrador Retriever is without question the most popular retriever breed today, both for work and show,' wrote P. R. A.

Moxon in *Gundogs: Training & Field Trials*. 'A comparatively "new" breed, Labradors have won the esteem of shooting men by their outstanding ability to be trained, find game and become companions and guards. The Labrador, as a breed, can be said to be both fast and stylish in action, unequalled in water and with "trainability" far above that of other breeds, and a devotion to master or mistress that makes them ideal companions. The smooth, short coat has many advantages readily appreciated by the housewife and the car owner. Dogs from working strains almost train themselves to the gun.'

As Wilson Stephens concluded in his definitive paper on the lost years of the Labrador, 'Their versatility stems from a stolidity of temperament which makes them neither exciting nor excitable. It combines with an inherited eagerness to do what is expected of them. Their family tradition of jumping into a rough and icy sea whenever ordered to do so has now been transferred to many other functions outside sport.'

The wide-ranging usefulness of the Labrador sees them valued as guide dogs for the blind, by Customs officers for drug detection, by the police and the military for mine and explosive location, by rescue services, security guards and counterfeit detection experts as well as in a new field of medical detection. They carry out their duties with a sense of decorum. 'Labradors set a tone for the occasions they grace. Their presence means that serious business is going on. The hazardous, often grim, North Atlantic scene seems a strange origin for these omnipresent participants in typically British occasions,' wrote Stephens.

I love that sense of decorum that is prevalent in Labs. It isn't a nose-in-the-air kind of arrogance that some breeds exude, it is more humble. They hold up their heads with pride, assured of their loyalty and ability. Perhaps this is the reason why the Labrador Retriever has been declared the most popular breed in the United States for nearly 24 consecutive years. More than 60 years on, Labradors hold universal appeal which makes them the most popular breed of dog by registered ownership not just in the United States, but also in Australia, Canada, New Zealand, the United Kingdom and Israel.

CHAPTER FOUR

THE INCREDIBLE JOURNEY

Inca, Inca-pinka, Incala pinkala, Pink, Pinky, Stink, Stinkalot, Incapotamus, Stincapotamus, Inca bazinka, Ink, Inky. Like most dogs, Inca had many names.

I had thought about calling her Tatty when I first got her, but I eventually plumped for Inca, in part because I had known one other dog called Inca, a large black mongrel I had met while studying in Costa Rica. She had belonged to an English family that owned a macadamia nut farm in the rainforest.

Dog names are a funny business. Does the dog grow into its name or does the name affect the behaviour and temperament of the dog? Maybe we project a personality according to name. I've always found it comical to meet dogs with human names, like Gary, Charlie or Kevin. There is something comedic about it.

In my mind, she was only ever really an Inca. Having studied Latin American Studies at university and spent the best part of three years living in Central and South America, I liked the nod towards my own travelling heritage.

In fact, her pedigree name was Camilla, but she was NEVER a Camilla. Camilla was far too feminine for Inca. She was more of a tomboy; masculine in both her appearance and her personality. This was helped by her early obsession with humping anything and everything – there was a teddy bear that she would grab onto by one ear and hump for hours on end, or she would scrunch up towels and carpets and dry hump all day.

Despite her masculine build, Inca had the prettiest face. She had a thin stripe of fur down the centre of her nose where two directions of hair met like a wave. I liked to call it her honesty stripe. It really defined her face. If you don't have a dog, and you ever wonder how you can distinguish one dog from another, it's often these little features. I always recognised Inca by her honesty stripe – that and her enormous thighs.

She also had the biggest paws you have ever seen. They were like lion's feet. Huge. They weren't in proportion to the rest of her body. She had long tufts of fur that would stick between the pads. If you came across her paw prints on a beach or along a muddy trail, you would be convinced it was some kind of big cat.

As a puppy she was lean and trim. Her coat was glossy and black, but as the years marched on, both her body and her coat filled out. Just like her paws, her coat began to resemble a lion's mane. It was thick and wiry, so much so that people would often mistake her for another breed.

Inca was, and still remains, the funniest dog I ever knew. She could make me laugh just by looking at me. Maybe it was some of the nuances mentioned above, or just because I knew her so well, but she could make me smile with a flick of the eye or a bound of the legs.

Dogs have that effect on us. They get beneath our skin; we live, breathe and smell them. We are more like care-home nurses than owners. We are responsible 24/7. A dog relies on us for everything – food, walks, warmth, affection, company. We in turn begin to recognise every little quirk and foible. We recognise the smell of their farts and the colour of their poo. We can recognise their gait and bark from a long distance and we begin to see traits that would be invisible to anyone else.

It is with this familiarity that a deep, powerful flame of love begins to glow.

It is also the foundation for the anthropomorphism, the process whereby we give our dogs, or any animals for that matter, a voice. At first it starts as just baby talk, but as you get to know your dog, it progresses to an all-out personality, complete with voice.

I always imagined Inca would have a deep, rasping voice. It was probably a little unfair, but probably quite accurate. In my mind she sounded like a cross between Dame Edna and the Queen. When no one was around, I would find myself having full conversations with Inca and would give her answers in this slightly ludicrous voice. I would love to know what Inca thought of these bizarre, rambling conversations.

My father had suggested I get Inca a few months before we headed for the island in an effort to get her used to urban life before we headed into the wilderness, so that it would help her reintegration to the city at the end of the year. To do this I took her on buses, the Tube, into pubs and even to work. I was still working for *Tatler* magazine, so I took her into the office with me each day. Suddenly I found myself more popular with the girls. There were several office Pekingese dogs that belonged to two of the writers and Inca joined them. I can remember Inca falling asleep on my desk, hidden in a vast pile of paperwork.

Then, on Boxing Day morning, my parents drove us to Victoria coach station, where Inca and I would embark on the journey of a lifetime. I can remember waving as the bus pulled away, my mother in tears. But I didn't feel so sad saying goodbye; this time, as they turned away and left, I wasn't alone.

When we arrived on the island of Taransay, Inca and I largely kept to ourselves – and later more so. Without Inca, I'm not sure how well I would have fared for the whole year. She was my reason – and excuse – to go off and explore the island; indeed, we rechristened one of the hills Inca Ra because she and I spent so much time there. Inca and I shared a cold little room together in one of the eco pods in which we lived. A tiny, inefficient woodburning stove was used to heat each room. The problem was that it was only large enough to burn tiny twigs in it. Ice would form on the inside of the windows. I built Inca a little bed on stilts to keep her off the freezing ground.

Inca enchanted everyone she met on the *Castaway* island of Taransay and soon she became an integral part of our community. Having her was not without its mishaps, though. Just a week into the project, she had to be helicoptered off the island to the local vet in Stornoway after cutting her foot open on a shard of glass. Months later, she was caught in flagrante with a visiting shepherd's dog and once again was helicoptered away for the morning-after pill.

In the beginning she was allowed into the communal 'steading' in which we would all gather, but after a heated debate about dogs on the island, she was banned. Dogs had become a divisive issue on Taransay. For the first time in my life, I found myself living alongside people who disliked dogs. Having been surrounded with dogs all my life, it seemed incomprehensible that anyone could dislike the animals, but the numbers of this group had recently swelled dramatically due to an unforeseeable event . . .

One of the Collies, Fran, that had come along with her canine sister with Trish Prater and her two children, had, unbeknownst to Trish, arrived on the island pregnant, and nine weeks after we settled on the island, she gave birth to a litter of puppies. Not everyone was happy about this, particularly when two of the Castaways decided to keep puppies for themselves. Suddenly the number of permanent doggy inhabitants within the small community rose from four to six, which further irritated the dog dislikers amongst us.

I recall one particularly noisy and passionate community meeting in which the doctor and his family threatened to leave if all the dogs stayed. Not only were they concerned about a rise in the amount of dog shit around the island, but they were also concerned about the safety of their children.

Although I knew the dissatisfaction wasn't specifically directed at Inca and me, I felt guilty as a dog owner and the two of us began to retreat from social gatherings.

Another time we found a sheep that had been attacked. It was bloody and wounded. Apart from the odd stoat, the island had no predators and it was reasonable enough to assume that one of the dogs was responsible. But which one? I would have put my life on the line to guarantee it wasn't my passive Inca, but once again the eyes of suspicion fell on all of us.

Every time something happened involving any of the dogs, Inca and I would be summoned to a meeting to explain ourselves. It was slightly exhausting and, if I'm honest, I slightly resented those additional dogs. Inca had come with me as my luxury item, and only after a long campaign to justify what she would bring to the community, but the two new pups were like stowaways who had gatecrashed the party and added tension rather than diffused it.

During the year we had to keep video diaries to document what we were feeling or what had happened to us. One of the rooms in the little farmhouse on the island had been converted into the diary room. It consisted of a chair and a camera mounted on a tripod. One day I thought it would be funny if Inca left a diary message. I lifted her onto the chair and made sure her face was in shot, then I stood behind the camera and acted as her voice. I even waved some bread around to get her to move her head for emphasis! It was Inca's take on island life, and the viewers loved it.

Inca and I spent our year on the island hidden away in our icy little room, huddled under a blanket together, or walking together for hours on end. We knew that island better than most. We knew every boggy patch, each break in the fence and every loch. We walked and walked and walked. As summer approached, Inca would swim in the azure waters. Seals would pop up to see her. I often wondered if they thought she was one of them, or vice versa.

If I close my eyes I can smell the machair and the salty air. I can see Inca's black body bounding across the island, leaping like a spring lamb. It still makes me smile. Those were some of my happiest memories. Ever. Just me and Inca.

I would wrap up in my waterproofs and we would set off to one of our favourite spots. I had so many, but my absolute favourite was the north-west side of the island. There, we would settle into the soft grass. I'd lean against Inca's body and we would spend hours staring out to the ocean beyond.

I will never forget those views. Fear, happiness, frustration, hope and excitement all at the same time – that view presented such a conflict, such a contradiction. It was the watery moat that imprisoned me on that windswept island, but it was also the open ocean that led to exciting new opportunities.

I would stare at that horizon and imagine where my life was going to take us. My little black dog and I had a whole life ahead of us. The thought filled me with fear and excitement at the same time.

Inca's lifelong obsession with food began on that island. Labradors love food but Inca *loved* food. In fact, it didn't even have to be food, it just had to be consumable – and even that was open to negotiation. Sheep poo and seaweed were always a sure bet, but it was the discovery of the compost heap that had the most impact. Inca disappeared one day, only to reappear an hour later looking like a barrel. Or rather, she didn't so much look like a barrel as look like she'd swallowed a barrel. All of her features were in proportion except for this hideously distended stomach, at the end of which was her tail, wagging furiously.

I couldn't work out where she had found so much to eat, and then the next day it happened again – and then again. I began seriously to worry and even contemplated asking the production team if they could send a muzzle over. I worried that she was eating herself to death. The source of all this food remained a mystery until one day I found her chewing on an old tea bag. I followed the tea-leaf trail to the enormous compost pile where we would throw all of our leftovers, which was a not inconsiderable amount of food, considering there were 36 of us.

But soon the compost heap became a distant memory for Inca, as a thoughtful gift from a stranger became all consuming – and consumed. Unbeknownst to us, both Inca and I had been getting rather a lot of media coverage back on the mainland. The first we knew of it was when the monthly mailbag arrived, brimming with letters from complete strangers, addressed to me and Inca. In fact, there were some deliveries in which Inca received more fan mail than me. She was sent bones and chews and little knitted booties to protect her feet, and even dozens of photographs of other dogs sent by their owners.

One of these parcels contained a dog toy in the form of a squeaky lemon. It was nicknamed Mr Lemon and Inca loved it. Mr Lemon went everywhere with her. If I ever spotted the yellow toy lying around, I could be sure that Inca wasn't far.

I didn't need to worry, though, because Inca never went far. Until one Saturday, when she disappeared. I searched in all the usual places – the kitchen, the storage shed, the compost heap the abattoir. I looked everywhere. No Inca.

I didn't panic at first. An hour passed and there was still no sign. None of the other castaways had seen her. After another hour, I began to worry. Inca wasn't anywhere to be seen, so I organised a small search party and we spread out across the island to find her.

'INCA!' I yelled, with increasing concern.

It was so out of character; she had never wandered off like this. Despite being on an island, my mind began to wander. What if she had fallen into a ravine or been swept out to sea?

Daylight was beginning to recede, the light was failing and night was approaching. She'd been missing for several hours now and I had no lead on where she might be. I walked further and further from our little settlement. Still no sign. My heart began to race with panic. It was the first time I really understood what this little dog meant to me. She was my everything.

'INCA!' I hollered. Nothing.

As darkness enveloped the island I reached the old bothy, half an hour's walk from our little community. Bothies are little stone houses dotted across the highlands of Scotland, located in pretty remote spots over the landscape, and can be used by walkers and hikers to shelter and sleep. There in the window I could see a flickering candle light. Someone was inside; it wasn't one of us, so it must be a visitor to the island.

I walked up to the door and knocked gently. 'Hello?' I said as I pushed open the door.

I could hear the gentle hubbub of conversation. A small flame of a fire flickered in the corner and there, in the middle of the room, was the unmistakable silhouette of Inca . . . being handfed Italian prosciutto.

She turned to look at me and then immediately back to the hand that was feeding her.

Once we had made our introductions and I'd explained that the greedy dog at their feet was my dog, the visitors revealed that when they had arrived they found a yellow squeaky lemon at the entrance to the door. It transpired that Inca had left it at the bothy during one of our previous visits and she had somehow remembered and made the long journey back to collect it. At which point she discovered the Parma ham and had decided to stay.

I didn't know if I was angry that she'd disappeared or ecstatic that she had been found safe and well. Dogs have that ability to tug at our emotions. I wanted to be cross with her for the worry and anxiety, but I was so relieved to have found her that it was all forgiven.

And all for Mr Lemon.

Mr Lemon was eventually lost to the ocean, but there lies one final tale – or tail . . .

When we eventually returned to London we moved into a little flat with my sister. We had been there for some time when one day Inca appeared at my bed, wagging her tail furiously. There in her mouth was the unmistakable yellow form of . . . Mr Lemon.

I was flabbergasted. It was a complete mystery – how had he got there? I knew we had long since lost him on the island, so how could he now be here, in a flat in central London? It was impossible. But there he was, in her mouth.

I struggled to comprehend what I was looking at. It was only after I got her to drop it and I had examined it that I discovered what had happened.

One of the castaways, Tanya, knew about the lost toy. On her return to civilisation she had been in a shop and discovered that they sold them, so she'd bought one, popped it in an envelope and sent it to me. Inca had got to the post first. Much to her delight, she had discovered the yellow lemon and quite rightly assumed it was hers!

Inca certainly set the tone for *Castaway*. Marooned on the opposite side of the North Atlantic to her forebears, maybe it was fortuitous that Inca was in her natural element. Maybe it's why she was so at home there, surrounded by rough ocean. Whatever the reason, Inca was my anchor on that island. My leveller. The whole island experience was so overwhelming, but for me, Inca was the consistency I needed.

Castaway thrust me into the public eye and stripped me of my anonymity, so much so that I had suddenly become a household name. But I wasn't alone; it was me and Inca. Every photograph of me from that extraordinary year includes Inca. She became an extension of me. She was rarely far from my side. My loyal companion.

I can still remember my heartache when the time came to leave Taransay. It wasn't just the loss, but also the fear of the unknown. What worried me, too, was how Inca would cope away from the island. It pained me to think that I had to drag her from this dog paradise and take her back to a city.

She had spent the first year of her life in this wonderful environment. She had never worn a collar or been on a lead. She wouldn't remember what a car was or what it was like to live in a centrally heated house. She had adapted to island life; her paws were toughened to the rock and bog, her coat was like a polar bear's, thick and curly to keep out the cold wind. She was a Hebridean dog, not a London one.

There is a photograph that was used on the front page of the *Times* on the day we left Taransay; I have a copy of it hanging in our bathroom. It is of me with three other castaways and Inca. I am opening a bottle of champagne while a helicopter hovers behind. It was the first time Inca had worn a collar and lead, and she had contorted it so it was pulling at her neck. It is a sad photo.

A funny thing happened the day after we left the island – I had a wobble. Freaked out by the strange new world in which I found myself, I woke Inca in the middle of the night, packed her into a Land Rover Defender that had been delivered to the island ready for our departure a few days later, and we fled.

I'm not sure what happened or why I did it. I certainly worried quite a few people, and it even made it onto the news. I was eventually tracked down by a *News of the World* journalist. I don't remember much about those few missing days; it was just Inca and I driving through the Scottish highlands.

The month following *Castaway* was a maelstrom of interviews and TV appearances, and Inca came to every single one. She was even part of a fashion shoot for *Vogue* magazine. When I was a guest on *So Graham Norton*, Graham pleaded with me to bring Inca. As promised, we turned up together, only to discover that the other guest, Sophia Loren, was absolutely terrified of dogs, so Inca was consigned to her own dressing room throughout.

She came along on photo shoots for magazines like *Heat* and *Hello*. In this bizarre new world, Inca represented consistency. She, too, had experienced that crazy year and now she was with me for the second part of the journey. We were more than just a man and his dog. We were a team.

Shortly after returning to London, I found myself an agent to help me deal with the tidal wave of requests. They had a smart office in Covent Garden and I used to take Inca in with me.

'Is that the famous Inca?' asked a pretty woman one day,

who was holding a young child's hand. 'Can I introduce my daughter?'

'Sure,' I replied with a smile. It was only later that my agent pointed out that Inca had just been cuddled by Kate Winslet and her daughter. Not bad going for a *Castaway* dog.

Soon after this I met with the then-controller of the BBC, Lorraine Heggessey, who took me to lunch.

'You have a dog,' she said, 'and you seem to love animals. Would you like to present some shows about them for us?'

Apart from being an offer I couldn't refuse, it was proof that Inca had helped me get a job. I have often wondered if I would even have been noticed on *Castaway* had it not been for Inca. I certainly doubt my career would have taken the twists and turns that it has since without her.

Just a month after leaving the island, Inca was packed into a crate and sent by plane to Southern Ireland to help me film a *Holiday* show for the BBC. It was a feature on fly fishing, and together we explored the Connemara coast. It was the start of many, many filming assignments together. During our shared career, Inca arguably became one of the best-travelled dogs in the United Kingdom; she came to Whitby to make a show about Dracula, where she had a starring role as the wild black dog reputed to have run up the steps and into the church. She came to Scotland to make films about dog mushing and the Loch Ness Monster. She came sailing with me around the Cornish coast, and she came along to the World Stinging Nettle Eating championships.

A year after I left Taransay, I was asked to make a *Countryfile* special about the island for the BBC. I was working on the rural affairs show at the time and Inca had become a regular fixture.

We drove up to Inverness in our old Land Rover Defender, where we caught a helicopter to the island. Not for the first time in her life, Inca found herself tucked between my legs as we flew low over the stunning Scottish highlands en route back to the island.

Some people say you shouldn't return to a place in different circumstances; they argue it will never live up to your memories or expectations. For us, it was a little like returning to a ghost town. The pods in which we lived had been removed and all that remained was the skeletal structure of the once-thriving village. What was more heartbreaking, though, was how easily Inca settled back to island life. She remembered every break in the fence, every gate and door. Not only did she look comfortable, she was so happy. Her tail wagged uncontrollably as she headed straight back to where her beloved compost heap had once stood. I felt terrible for having torn her from this canine paradise to live in the concrete jungle where her life was restricted to a small garden and a park. Of course, I know that is a simplistic and unfair portrait of an urban dog's life, but that was how it seemed as I watched Inca bound across the wide-open spaces of Taransay.

We spent several days on the island filming, and when it was time to leave, Inca and I volunteered to stay on. I had no idea how we were going to get back to Inverness, and we had very little food, but I didn't want to leave. I felt at home there; just me, Inca and our island. We spent a week there, until our food ran out and we had to start the long journey back across Scotland.

I had a small flat in London with an even smaller garden, but I was spending more and more time away working so it didn't matter. At that time I was making a series called *Animal Park* for the BBC which was based at Longleat Safari Park, in Wiltshire. My co-presenter, Kate Humble, and I shared a tiny cottage on the estate, and it was a perfect place for Inca to spend her days wandering the woodlands and exploring the parklands. The production office was based in a small wooden building next to Longleat's maze, which was surrounded by a fence. There Inca would spend her days, lazing on the lawn, while we went off to film with various animals around the park.

From there Inca could hear the wolves and the lions, but that was nothing compared to the smells that I would come back with. One of my strongest memories of Inca during that time was as we pulled through the gate to the production office to see her sitting on the lawn, waiting loyally.

Of course, like any dog, Inca had a great ability to get me into trouble, but not always in the most obvious ways. Inca became my shadow, a part of me. In the years of so many changes and so much uncertainty, Inca remained a constant. Reassuring and loyal.

Unless you have ever had a dog, it is difficult to explain the unique bond between person and animal. It is one of mutual dependency. If truth be told, I probably relied on her more than she relied on me. She was my crutch in an often wonky world.

My relationship with Inca was far from unique. On the contrary, as we will discover, mine was the simplest and most basic of relationships compared to others who owe their lives to their Labradors.

CHAPTER FIVE

BLUE-BLOODED HOUND

They say dogs look like their owners, but it's more likely that owners look like their dogs. I'm not sure if we consciously choose a dog because it reminds us of our own appearance or personality – it's much more complex than that – but there is something in it.

When I presented Crufts, you could invariably tell what day it was according to the owners. Of course, I'm using broad brush strokes here, but the more preened the dog, the more preened the owner, the softer the dog, the softer the owner, the harder the dog . . . you get my point.

I've lost count of the number of times I've been compared to a Labrador. Let's compare our personalities.

A Labrador is an intelligent breed; they have a good work ethic and steady, even temperaments. Kind, curious and outgoing, they love to explore and they love company.

Loyal, loving, happy. It seems a little too egotistical to describe my own personality, so I got my wife to do it for me.

'Ben is kind, loving, thoughtful, loyal, considerate.' I can add that I love food and a good party.

Hmm. They're her words, not mine. I'll take the ego trip and add some more thoughts about myself.

I love to explore and I'm curious. In fact, the only difference appears to be in intelligence. I'm not that intelligent, though to be fair I'm not sure Labradors are either.

In broad brush strokes I would describe a Labrador as an eager-to-please, smiling, waggy-tailed friend which is exactly the way I'd like to see myself.

Enough about me, though, let's talk about Labradors . . .

A Labrador has an extraordinary sense of smell and can sniff out food from a huge distance. Of course, this isn't a unique trait to this breed of dog, but their love of food puts them at a distinct advantage; where other dogs, blood hounds in particular, have a superior scenting, the Labrador has the distinction of following a scent for their own benefit.

I'd be walking in a deserted park with Inca when she would pick up a scent. She would place her nose close to the ground and sniff deeply. The sniffs would become intense as she lifted her nose to the air to find out where it lead. Then, like a heat-seeking missile, she would place her nose to the ground and gallop towards the source of the scent. Sometimes it would be a tiny piece of ham dropped from a picnicker's sandwich, or perhaps some bread left for the birds, maybe some feathers from a fox kill or even just an old crisp packet. Inca was always able to sniff out food, however small the remains. I've always thought litter pickers should have a Labrador to help them with their work.

Perhaps one of the unique traits that really marks out Labradors from other breeds of dog is their instinctive love of holding objects in their mouths. Socks, shoes, letters, soft toys, cushions, pillows, towels, books, pants, I've been greeted with them all. The key in the door seems to be the command to pick an object up and bring it to the hall. Our chocolate Lab Maggi is never without a tennis ball. Over the years, her teeth have been worn down into the shape of a ball. I've even caught her fast asleep in her bed with a ball in her mouth. I've even been woken in the morning by a happy Labrador holding my wife's bra and my children's shorts. For a Labrador, nothing is sacred but everything is special.

Apart from coating a carried object with a little slobber, a Labrador will rarely damage it. They hold on with great gentleness, being known to have a very soft feel to the mouth, and it is this gentle hold for which they have become coveted hunting and shooting companions, as they are ideal carriers of birds without breaking the skin or damaging the fallen game. A Labrador can carry an egg in its mouth without breaking it.

Labradors are not famed for their athleticism or their sporting prowess, although in the field many are very athletic. On the contrary, the caricature most associated with this breed is usually of a rather rotund dog who has eaten all the pies. It's a fair depiction; Inca loved food more than anything else in life – she would have eaten her own leg if given half a chance – but she also never knew when to call it quits. She was lacking the sensor to tell her when she was full. A Labrador is never full. I've heard stories of Labs that have eaten themselves to death – admittedly I've only ever heard them secondhand, but I've no reason to doubt they're true. Inca once ate a whole marzipan cake – she looked like a walking barrel afterwards and couldn't walk for three days, but it didn't put her off eating.

However annoying such greediness may be, this insatiable appetite is what makes Labradors so very trainable. Offer a Lab some food and they will literally do anything.

Of course, all this is to tar all dogs of this breed with the same, slightly uncomplimentary, brush. There is such a thing as an athletic Labrador – some lines, particularly those bred specifically for their field working skills, are particularly fast and athletic. They can also be further divided by continent. Across the pond, our North American cousins tend to favour a stockier Labrador, but then, everything in America is larger. But in my mind a Labrador's build is roughly divided between working and non-working. House dogs like Inca tend to be a little less athletic than their working brethren.

Yet one of the reasons for the Labrador's universal popularity is the fact that they are equally good as working dogs or as family dogs. Their gentle, eager-to-please temperament means they are great around children and other animals. If I think of Labradors, I think of children. Ludo and Iona used to sit on Inca. They would inadvertently pull her tail and her ears and place their hands in her mouth to examine her gums and her teeth and she would just lie there. I trusted her implicitly with them.

It is perhaps for that reason – dependability – that Labs have become the most popular family pet across the world. In a world where there is so much distrust, a Labrador offers the opposite. It is this unwavering trust that is so appealing.

According to the Kennel Club's Labrador Breed Standard, the characteristics and temperament of the ideal dog are as follows:

Characteristics: Good tempered, very agile (which precludes excessive body weight or excessive substance). Excellent nose, soft mouth; keen love of water. Adaptable, devoted companion.

I would agree on all of the above except for agility. I don't think the build of a Labrador, however trim, is that conducive to agility. When I think of an agile breed, I think of a Collie or a Greyhound – thin, lithe, streamlined and quick.

Temperament: Intelligent, keen and biddable, with a strong will to please. Kindly nature, with no trace of aggression or undue shyness.

All true. Labradors are the opposite of shy. It is the one big difference between me and the breed. I am integrally shy. People are often surprised to hear that, but I am not naturally confident.

A Labrador, on the other hand, is shy of no one, although early Labradors were quiet dogs who knew their place because the breeders preferred them to know their place. They are naturally outgoing and will greet all strangers with a pair of socks and then sit confidently next to them. I'm not too sure if this is done in the hope of food and affection or it is simply their nature to please, but it is a universal trait.

Other breeds are naturally more shy. The Greyhound or Whippet, for example, is much more timid.

It is this happy-go-lucky, bouncy, tail-wagging personality that attracts me to the Labrador. In many ways it is the antithesis to the modern world in which we rarely talk to strangers and don't know our own neighbours. Again, I'm talking in broad brush strokes, but generally society has become more cynical and suspicious. When was the last time you said good morning to a stranger on the Tube?

A Labrador wouldn't dream of missing the opportunity to say hello.

Where humans tend to be naturally suspicious, 'why did he just say hello?', 'he must be an axe murderer/mugger/psycho/ nutter . . .', a Labrador will give you the benefit of the doubt. They make the assumption that you are good and kind rather than entertain the possibility that you are bad.

It's an attractive trait. A glass half full; an optimism that is quickly becoming a rare commodity in modern society.

'Biddability' is a word used by many to describe a Labrador. It's an odd word; I don't think I have ever used it before, but I've heard it used countless times by people when describing the humble Labrador. I think it's much more simple; a Labrador is a happy dog, a Labrador always has a smile on its face. They project happiness – the tail wagging and the overall body language project a euphoria that as an owner I find contagious.

I have lost count of the number of times I have returned home after a hard day's work and my spirits are lifted by the tongue-lolling, tail-wagging greeting I receive at the front door. It has also been scientifically proven that stroking a dog can have a calming, soothing effect on people – blood pressure drops with each stroke of the head. Suddenly, all is good in the world.

The easy trainability and superior intellectual capacity of Labradors make them fast at learning tricks and being able to 'perform'. This is why Labradors, as we will discover later in this book, have been trained for all sorts of jobs, from truffle hunters to drug sniffer dogs. It is the combination of all the above traits that makes them so perfect as working dogs.

While Labradors are fun-loving, fearless, often boisterous, and loyal, they can also be quite independent. Interestingly, according to my father, females may be slightly more independent than males.

I have always kept females – or bitches, to give them their correct scientific terminology. In my experience I have found the males to be a little more boisterous. I don't like their habit of cocking their leg to mark their territory, and I have always preferred the slightly more elegant female over the swaggering male. But I wonder now whether my preference is also down to their sense of independence.

Generally, most dog owners stick to the same sex with their animals. I wonder if it's a case of sticking with what you know, or if it is down to the nuanced behavioural differences – because they can be undoubtedly subtle.

Up until maturity, at the age of three, Labradors can have buckets of puppy-like energy which some people misinterpret as being hyperactive. Thanks to their heritage, even the average pet Labrador loves to retrieve things endlessly, obsessively even. Sticks, balls, frisbees, you name it and a Labrador will fetch it.

Inca and I used to spend hours in the game of throwing things. The key was getting her to drop it afterwards, though. Inca would have made a terrible gundog – she'd have eaten the duck.

Labradors sometimes indulge in alarm barking (i.e., they bark at a noise coming from an unseen source), though they are generally not noisy or territorial – unlike a terrier. But because they are easygoing and trusting with strangers, the one job a

Labrador would not be good at is as a guard dog. I used to joke that if a robber ever broke into our house he would be greeted by a Labrador holding an old pair of pants and then he'd be helped by the same eager-to-please Lab, who would most likely show him where all the valuables were hidden, perhaps helping him with the safe and even holding the swag bag to make life a little easier for him. In a Labrador's eyes people are like food. There is no such thing as bad food; some of it, like nuts and bolts or balloons, just tastes a little different, but in the end it's all food.

It was when the Labrador became the fashionable companion to aristocrats with large shooting estates at the turn of the twentieth century that the breed acquired its unbreakable status as a social icon.

On one level, this remains today. A Labrador-owning father of a boy at Radley, a top English public school, joked that parents collect the compulsory black Lab at the school shop when their boys first get kitted out with their uniform. There is indeed this caricature of the green-welly-wearing, Barbour-jacketed, tweed-capped, Land-Rover-driving owner of the Labrador. (I have all of the above, but would never wear/walk and drive them all at once.)

Perhaps it is their aristocratic, Royal-warranted roots that have made them a middle- to upper-class icon. *Tatler* magazine recently did an article on new money versus old money, and in it they included a section on the dogs kept by the different sectors of the moneyed establishment. All of them include the Labrador, the only difference being the colour. Old-school, old-money aristocrats were firmly in the black Labrador camp, while the middle class was placed with the yellow and the new money with the chocolate Lab.

It's a simple generalisation, but while it's true that no stately home would be complete without the obligatory Labrador, these dogs do span the socio-economic spectrum.

Of course, as I've already mentioned, it was the obvious versatility of the breed as a working dog that made its appeal universal to people in all walks of life. In the world of gundogs, a gamekeeper was as likely to have had a prized Lab as was the lord of the manor. Looking back at its origins, you have to wonder how one type of dog could be so adept at such a wide variety of jobs, be capable of working under very harsh conditions and also have one of the friendliest, most affectionate personalities around. Labradors have been valued equally by rough and often seedy sailors and by the grand landowners who refined and preserved the breed in the nineteenth century. It's not one man and his dog; it is everyman and his Labrador.

Snob appeal for Labs came via gundog circles. By the time *The Official Sloane Ranger Handbook: The First Guide to What Really Matters in Life* by Ann Barr and Peter York was published in 1983, Labrador ownership was deemed a badge for a particular social type. The handbook dissected the Sloane Ranger lifestyle through a portrait of the archetypal Henry and Caroline, and the Labrador features large in the section on The Sloane Dog:

The faithful Labrador. Sloane children have all the usual pets – hamsters, gerbils, guinea pigs, tortoises, cats, white mice – but the mark of a Sloane is a Labrador. The noble yellow fellow (or big black beautiful blackamoor) is Caroline's

secret love, the one she can give all her thwarted affection to,
the one whose smell she dotes on, the one she knows naps on
the beds and hopes Henry won't catch.

It is a myth that Sloane Labradors are well-trained
shooting dogs. Three-quarters of them are the indulged squire
of the woman of the house, dangerous on even a country
road, won't come to heel, and roam (males) when there's a
bitch on heat, or just because they feel like it.

A few even steal, making off with the first course while
the guests are having cocktails. ("The sloberador has eaten
the game terrine!"). Sloanes are amused by their own and
their friends' dogs' naughtiness . . .

In the United States, too, the Lab attained 'must-have' status, a
position which in itself breeds admiring, affectionate and teasing
portrayals of dogs and their owners. One of the most popular
posts on a satirical website called thedogsnobs.com (whose blog-
gers bill themselves as 'canine specialists with a passion for
judging others') sums up the good, the bad and the ugly aspects
of the Labrador Retriever.

We've been harsh on Labs in the past, we can admit that.
We may have called them dumb, over friendly, oafish. There
is no denying it, though, America loves them. They've been
the number one breed in America for . . . a long, long time.

The Good:
1. *Labs are genuinely nice dogs. The vast majority of the time,*
   they're pleasant to be around. They're that iconic bro dog, sort

of easy going but ready to go when you are. They make great exercise partners, love to play fetch and they can be great family dogs. They're pretty much the dog everyone thinks about when you hear 'I want a puppy' from the mouths of children. For an active family or individual there is a Labrador for all seasons from the heftier plough horse Labradors to the sleek seal-like field-breds.

2. *If you want a general bird-retrieving buddy, there's no reason to look any farther than a good Lab. Even the worst bred among them still has that instinct, even if he's destroying what passes for his hips doing it. We're kidding. Labs actually have better hips than a lot of breeds, but given the sheer number of them out there . . . Good luck telling that to your vet. There's a reason the go-to dog for most hunters is a Lab. They do the job, they do it well and they do it with a good attitude.*

I love the idea of the 'bro' dog. I'd never thought of them like that. The Labrador had always been a loyal companion, but the idea of a 'bro'?

It's true. A bro is someone as happy to go for a muddy run as they are to chill on the sofa. A 'bromance' is one in which there is mutual respect without the emotional ties that often come with a relationship between the sexes. There is very little confusion when it comes to a 'bro'; it is a straightforward, uncomplicated friendship.

This is exactly the relationship I have had with my dogs. There is rarely confusion or misinterpretation. There are no arguments, there's no sulking, no jealousy or suspicion. It is as simple and honest a relationship as you could get.

It's true, too, what they say about hips. *Everyone* will tell you that a Labrador has bad hips but I have never experienced one.

The Bad:
1. *Popularity comes with a price. See the above-mentioned lousy excuse for hips. Also, do us a favor. Open a new tab. Go to your local shelters page. Now look at the breeds. How many of those are Lab mixes? Hell, how many of those are purebred Labs? The shelter is overrun with black Labs and mixes. Indiscriminate breeding has been hell on the breed. If you just want a companion, please do not pay $300 via Paypal for a 'purebreed Silver Labrador'.*
2. *We did call them dumb, yes. Really, though . . . it's more . . . oafish. Herding dog people may find this particular quality more obnoxious than others. Labs assume everyone is their best friend and it can get them in trouble, most notably with other dogs but also with cows, vehicles, electric fences and car interiors.*

True enough. They *can* have bad hips and yes they do want to be everyone's friend – but that's the quality I like in them (well, not the bad hips!). Inca was indeed once zapped by an electric fence, nearly trampled by a cow – and a horse – and been bitten by 'less-friendly outgoing' dogs, all in her unfailing trust and confidence that everything in the world is equally good, happy and safe. That's what makes their behaviour enchanting. If they were just nice, they'd be like the Canadians.

The Ugly:
1. *This is the part where we talk about breed splits again. Labs are the original split breed. You have your blubbery show-line*

Labs that can sort of waddle around the ring, you have you crazy high as a kite field line Labs that are like living with a Border Collie with an oral fixation, and then you have something in between that is mostly produced by BYBs, and that's the Lab that lives in most of America's living room.

2. *There's a solid chance your Lab will eat your house in the first two years of his life. Seriously, they are notoriously naughty puppies who must taste everything . . . and we mean everything.*

All true once again. Inca destroyed everything when she was a puppy. In retrospect, it was lucky I was living on a remote island in the Outer Hebrides for most of her 'chewing phase'.

So the love affair with these dogs is about far more than just social status. The point is that the presence of a loyal and friendly Labrador adds warmth – heart, soul and wagging tail – to any home, even a large, draughty stately home.

Having said that, Labradors really are the aristocracy of dog breeds, for Labradors and stately homes go together like Jeeves and Worcester. According to Simon Jenkins, the former Chairman of the National Trust, there should be a compulsory Labrador in the front hall of every National Trust house. Indeed, he once quipped that he would leave money in his will for a Labrador and a pushchair for every Trust property 'to give the illusion that the family are still in residence'.

A lovable dog known for its quiet obedience, trotting at the heels of an estate owner, also projects values of decency, decorum, status and order. When the global luxury Four Seasons Hotel brand opened a country-house resort in a Georgian manor house in Dogmersfield, Hampshire, the finishing touch to the lavish refurbishment was the arrival of a black Labrador puppy called Oliver Beckington, named after two bishops who once lived on the estate. The hotel has been done up as the ultimate English country estate with an equestrian centre and outdoor activities such as fishing, shooting and falconry. A welcoming dog with wagging tail completes the ambience and makes guests feel at home, part of the family. Oliver Beckington is ranked number one of worldwide guests' favourite thing about the hotel in their comments book.

The Labrador is still a fixture of the seated stately homes of Britain. Over the best part of a decade I filmed at Longleat, in Wiltshire, the seat of the Marquess of Bath. Lord Bath may have a reputation for his renaissance, liberal approach to life – and love, with his wifelets – but his true 'mistress' was his beloved dog Boudica, or 'Boudy', the yellow Lab. He loved that dog. You always knew where Lord Bath was as Boudy was never far from his side, leaving a trail of destruction in her wake.

The housekeepers would follow the pair around. It reminded me of that scene from *Mary Poppins* where they brace everything in the house in preparation for the daily cannon explosion. The housekeepers and stewards would cling on to the priceless vases as the pair tore through the house.

For dramatists such as Julian Fellowes, casting a dog in a period drama ticks lots of boxes. In the case of *Downton Abbey*, the Earl of Grantham's Labrador is an iconic canine: a social symbol, a canny plotting tool and an emotional touchstone. Just as Hollywood movie industry veterans swear by a 'save the cat' scenario early in a screenplay to engage the audience emotionally with a storyline's hero, so Fellowes uses the Earl's relationship with his companion Lab as a siphon for his feelings. The Earl is the sort of stiff-upper-lipped aristocrat whose moods can be better interpreted through the prism of his relationship with his yellow Labrador Retrievers, first Pharaoh, and then, in later series, Isis. A dog is always beside him and features in the show's introduction, walking at their master's heel. The *Downton* Labs are an integral part of the look of the show and of its storyline, and are so popular with viewers they even have their own Facebook account. The page has 5,386 likes, and counting, and is a forum for fans to post sentiments such as, 'Isis is the reason why a lot of us dog lovers watch *Downton* each week – with our dogs!' As Viv Groskop wrote in a blog posted on the *Guardian*'s website: 'She is the queen of the opening shot, the unofficial ruler of the roost and the most loved and consistent character through five long and interminably rambling series of *Downton Abbey*. Forget man's best friend. She is the audience's best friend, the only sane patient in the asylum.'

Groskop was writing about Isis, but the Earl first had Pharaoh. In all, the Earl's two Labradors have been played by three actor dogs. Pharaoh was played by a dog named Roly, who had impeccable thespian pedigree, having come to *Downton* from the set of *Midsomer Murders*. Lady Carnarvon's dog did not like other male dogs in his territory, though, so Roly was replaced by a female dog named Ellie to play Isis. The yellow Lab that took over the part of Isis later, during series three, is named Abbey. Hugh Bonneville, the actor who plays the Earl of Grantham, told me that in real life Isis (Abbey) is 'a moody bitch' on set: 'She rarely comes out of her trailer and demands snacks at all times.'

— * —

A blustery wind battered the trees as the torrential rain enveloped the countryside. Through the course of the car journey, Britain had gone from Indian summer to English autumn. The first of the leaves had scattered the fields as I headed west. I drove through some simple, nondescript gates and into the rolling hills of the estate. Huge oak trees towered above as I made my way along the long windy driveway.

Highclere Castle is an impressive sight. As the fictional *Downton Abbey* it is arguably the most recognisable house in Britain. Even for a relative *Downton Abbey* novice like me, Highclere has a striking familiarity. Whether you have watched the show or not, you will be familiar with the photographs of the iconic building from countless billboards, magazines and posters.

The Jacobethan facade bears a striking resemblance to the Houses of Parliament, unsurprisingly given it was designed by Sir Charles Barry in 1839, following the completion of Parliament. It is certainly a grand building, and even on a rain-soaked autumnal day, it shone like a beacon amidst the Capability Brown-designed gardens.

Most excitingly, it was to here that the 5th Earl of Carnarvon brought many of the Egyptian artefacts with which he and Henry Carter returned from their archaeological excavations – most notably that which led to the discovery of Tutankhamun. The peer would later succumb to the bite of a mosquito, often attributed to the curse of Tutankhamun. While the castle fell into disrepair, it seems to have escaped the curse and survived the years; indeed, the castle has since found fame thanks to Hugh and co.

As I approached up the drive, there, out of the gloom and mist, loomed arguably one of the most famous houses in the world. But of course I wasn't here to see the Egyptian artefacts, or even the *Downton* cast. I was here to meet the real Lords of the manor, the Labradors.

Lady Carnarvon had invited me to tea, to chat about our shared passion for Labradors. She met me at the door with what can only be described as a herd of dogs. A group of Americans were sipping tea in the main hall – one of the upsides of the estimated 150 million worldwide visitors was the increased number of people coming to visit the house. For North Americans, Highclere has become more iconic than Buckingham Palace.

On my arrival at Highclere, there was no doubt about who was boss there. The Labradors marched around the house; 'we had to shut our dogs away when the film dogs arrived,' smiled Lady Carnarvon over tea. When the opening three-second shot of the Abbey's Labrador's rear view first appeared on screens on 26 September 2010, it showed Pharaoh, the first *Downton* dog. But Pharaoh/Roly's problems with Percy, the Labrador belonging to the real-life owners of Highclere Castle, the Earl and Lady Carnarvon, meant he was 'killed off' as a fictional character between series one and two. In keeping with the historical accuracy, the Earl needed another Labrador in series two, which covered the years 1916 to 1919 – for the breed was not only the gundog of choice for the landed gentry at the time, but also fashionably celebrated in the founding by, among others, Lord Knutsford in 1916 of the Labrador Retriever Club. Enter Isis, real name Ellie, and, from series three onwards, the appropriately

named Abbie. I love the way the Labs embedded themselves in
the affections of television viewers and reviewers. As Viv Groskop
wrote, 'As for Lady Carnarvon's Percy, he died shortly after
Roly's forced retirement. I make no comment. But we've all
heard of the Curse of the Pharaoh.'

They say Maggie Smith gets the best lines, but in the Christmas
special of 2011, Isis is central to the plot. Scheming footman
Thomas decides to kidnap the Earl's beloved dog, locking her
in a woodshed. His plan is to reappear dramatically with her,
as her rescuer, just when all hope lost, in a bid to ingratiate
himself with the Earl and win promotion to a position as head
valet. The scheme hinges, of course, on the Earl's unquantifiable
affection for his Labrador. In series five, Isis again wins a good
storyline. A visiting art historian played by Richard E. Grant
makes overtures towards Cora in full view of Isis, but typically
the blinkered Earl sees only advances towards his beloved
Labrador: 'Tell your friend Bricker to stop flirting with Isis,' he
barks at his wife. 'There is nothing more ill-bred than trying to
steal the affections of someone else's dog.'

Despite being a fictional drama, the *Downton* Labrador made
front-page news in November 2014. There was speculation that
the dog, which had become listless in one episode, was being
bumped off in response to discomfort about the dog's name
being similar to that of the terrorist group, Isis. This was a ridiculous idea, as the dog was named long before the terrorist organisation began its campaign, in a nod to the real-life *Downton
Abbey*'s connection to Egyptology (the fifth Earl of Carnarvon
financed the expedition that led to the excavation of the tomb
of Tutankhamun in the 1920s). Hugh Bonneville gave a rather

more plausible excuse that, according to the chronological time-line, Isis was nearly 30 years old and so therefore his longevity was becoming less and less plausible. But just to show how embedded in the soap opera the whole dog saga is, Hugh Bonneville was moved to post a comment on his personal website: 'To clarify recent speculation, the Labrador that appeared in series one (1912–14) was a dog called Pharaoh. From series two (1916–20) onwards, the Labrador has been a bitch named – in keeping with the Egyptian theme – Isis. Anyone who genuinely believes the series five storyline (1924) involving the animal was a reaction to recent world news is a complete berk.'

So there.

— * —

The Duchess of Devonshire, chatelaine of Chatsworth, is Deputy President of the International Gundog League Retriever Society (IGL) and a long-serving committee member. The IGL organises the Retriever Championship – a three-day event, recognised worldwide by field trailers. The Duchess sits on the Kennel Club's Field Trials Sub-Committee with distinguished names of the gundog world, including Alan Rountree, John Halstead (five times winner of the Retriever Championship), Graham Cox, Joan Hayes and Wilson Young. She is also president of the Yorkshire Retriever Field Trials Society.

According to an article in *Field Sports Magazine*, the Duchess had seven Labradors in training with John Halstead, most of which she brought up as puppies.

The Duchess's late mother, June Heywood-Lonsdale, became a successful field trialler with a rare gift for training dogs, and was a well-known and popular figure on the gundog scene. The

Duchess's own gundog training started with the gift of a Labrador as a wedding present from the much-respected field trial owner Charles Williams, whose trainer Dick Mayall taught her how to get animals to respond on ground near the Duke of Bedford's Woburn estate. She then had further advice from Arnold White Robinson at Stratfield Saye, the home of the Dukes of Wellington.

I was lucky enough to have met the late Dowager Duchess of Chatsworth, Deborah Cavendish, a number of times, too, and we always got on to the subject of Labradors. The first time I met her, I had Inca in tow. The Dowager Duchess doted on her. She wanted to know if I had ever trialled her? She asked if she was greedy, which I took as an insinuation she might be a little 'large' for field work. We both laughed.

The Duke of Westminster also has a handful of handsome black Labradors for when he goes shooting pheasants at his Abbeystead Estate, in Lancashire, or grouse shooting on his Scottish estate, as does the Duke of Norfolk, who keeps a brace of dogs at the family's seat at Arundel Castle, in West Sussex.

The Labrador, it seems, is part of British society, but not just as a status symbol. Pets create a wider family unit, and a Labrador in the picture adds distinctive personality and an extra emotional dynamic under a roof. For me, on *Castaway* all those years ago, the presence of Inca the black Labrador at my side added to my personality. I benefited from her character traits.

A dog is about so much more than just their physical appearance and even their personality. A dog is an extension of you. In the 90s there was a trend towards owning Staffordshire Bull Terriers within urban areas where young people were looking for a dog as a social symbol. A Staffie, which, incidentally, is a wonderful dog and a great family pet, has the reputation for being a tough, muscly, no-nonsense dog. By walking around with a Staffie straining at the lead, the owner was saying 'look at me', 'I'm tough, don't mess with me'. The dog, in effect, was a subtitle for the owner; 'I'm hard', it says.

The same goes for many other breeds. The trend for the Chihuahua (arguably started by Paris Hilton) says I'm dainty, thorough and high maintenance.

A dog is a metaphor for how the owner wishes to be perceived, and the Labrador must surely be the most dependable metaphor for anyone. It is uncontroversial (perhaps the reason so many presidents and prime ministers have chosen the Lab); they say, 'look at me', 'I'm nice'.

It still seems so wildly fantastic that a hard-working, ocean-going, fishing dog from one of the harshest environments on Earth has transformed into such a solid, dependable dog, but again if we think of a solid, dependable, hard-working person, we could do worse than a fisherman.

A fisherman is what I would call a salt-of-the-Earth kind of person. They work hard and toil under difficult conditions to provide fish for our tables. They do it, not for the financial returns, but largely because they love it. They enjoy the ocean, the weather, the outdoors, the land. They are a wholesome bunch, largely unchanged by modern technology. Indeed, the main difference is that boats have become a little safer and they no longer need a four-legged companion.

I would also describe a Labrador as a 'salt-of-the-Earth' dog. The Labrador is 'everyman's' dog. I should probably rewrite

that to 'everyperson's' dog. It is the Volvo of the dog world –
dependable and arguably a little boxy. And here lies the big
question: big or small? Most dog breeds have a pretty standard
appearance but Labradors really are defined by their size. It can
be quite a controversial topic – opinions on which differ from
person to person and also from place to place.

The most important thing to establish is that you should
never, ever comment on another Lab's size. It is a subject of
much sensitivity. When I visited Newfoundland to establish the
early links of the Labrador, I met up with a local Labrador who
was something of a local celebrity, used to greet passengers off
passing cruise ships as they came ashore.

I'd arranged to meet down by the harbour. A vast pickup
truck arrived and out fell Stan. 'Whoa!' I found myself saying
uncontrollably, 'He's a BIG boy'. It was as if I had just told the
owner that she was fat rather than her dog. She was completely
flummoxed and taken aback. 'He is not fat,' she admonished
me. 'In fact, he meets the exact breed standards,' she continued.
'He's one of the top dogs in North America.'

That will teach me. It reminded me of the time I mistakenly
assumed that a rather famous TV presenter was pregnant.
'Congratulations,' I smiled, pointing to her tummy. 'When's it
due?' I asked. 'I'm not pregnant,' she replied, deadpan. I'm going
red just remembering it. My point is, never ever comment on
girth, be it foetaly or food induced.

Let's be honest, our North American neighbours prefer most
things to be a little bigger. I think it is proportional to the
continent and its population. Think about it – the highways,
the cars, the houses, the portions of food, the chocolate bars,

the people, they're all 25 per cent larger. I'm not sure if it's part of consumerism and the American Dream or whether it's something more complex, but let's not kid ourselves, the US of A loves things BIG. Generally I have found that Labradors in North America tend to err on the larger size though the general definition seems to negate this.

Though not an 'official' differentiation, Labs are often given one of two definitions: 'Working' (or 'American') and 'Show' (or 'English').

The terms Working and Show are commonly used and widely known and accepted nicknames in the United Kingdom for Labradors bred either to work at field trials, agility trials or to the gun, or simply to snooze on the sofa dreaming of chasing rabbits. In the United States and Canada, the terms American and English are often used to differentiate dogs that have been bred either primarily for work (the former) or exclusively for companionship (the latter). More confusingly, some Working (or American) Labs enter conformation dog shows, while some Show (or English) Labs compete in field trials and are used for hunting.

Officially there is only one Labrador breed standard, although there are slight differences in permissible heights between the American Kennel Club and (English) Kennel Club standards:

the American breed standard allows a height of between 21.5 to 24.5 inches while the English breed standard allows a height of 21.5 to 22.5 inches.

Apart from this, the two Labrador breed standards are essentially the same. So why do people say there are two types?

You only need to look at Working-type and Show-type Labs side by side to see the differences.

The Show Labs are stockier, heavier and more solid looking. They have wider heads and fuller faces with shorter muzzles, thicker coats, thicker necks, wider, thicker, straighter tails than their Working (or American) cousins and also shorter legs – and hence don't stand quite so tall. Essentially, Show Labs are bred primarily for their looks, to conform to written breed standards. Working Labs, on the other hand, are bred for athleticism.

By comparison, the Working type has a lighter, slimmer-looking body with a more athletic build; lithe and finer boned, they look more agile. The muzzle is sleeker, the face narrower, the coat is thinner, as is the neck and tail, and the legs of American-bred Labs are longer, which is why they can be up to 5 cm taller than English-bred dogs. In combination with their slimmer build, this further adds to their overall look of athleticism. They are the Olympians to their modelling cousins.

Temperament can vary, too, but before I say anything about temperament differences between Working and Show Labs I want to say something about nature and nurture, about what's inherited and what's learned. I don't think you can separate one from the other. When I talk to Lab breeders they tell me that in a litter from Working parents there may be pups with both low and high activity levels, and in a litter from Show parents some pups may pay attention and others can act like hooligans.

Then look at *our* behaviour and how we nurture our Labs. If you're planning to work your dog, and so you get a pup from a Working line, is it not likely that you'll watch its weight more, give it more exercise, make sure that it's fully obedience trained? If that's so, Working Labs might be a bit leaner and more active because that's the way you've raised your dog. That's what I mean when I say you can't really separate nature and nurture; they're embedded in each other.

That said, and talking about populations, Working Labs tend to have higher energy levels and more 'drive' than their Show cousins. They're noticeably more active. The higher energy levels and drive have earned them the label of being more highly strung, as they are always active and need constant exercise and attention. I've met some that behave like Border Collies in disguise. The Working type, and again I'm talking about populations not individuals, is more suited to an active outdoor life than the Show type.

Both types are gentle and kind but Show types are more likely to mature (if any Lab ever really matures) into relaxed and mellow individuals. Show types are probably better for busy families; although still 'driven' and suitable for life as a working dog, if a family pet is what's desired, the Show or English lab is far more likely to slip into this role as they're less demanding when it comes to activity and will more readily chill at your feet at the end of a hard day. Let me put it this way; any young Lab is inclined to have a mad half hour, but when he indulges in these hoolies, it's generally easier to get him to snap out of it if he's from a Working Lab line.

Regardless of type, when it comes to being loving, affectionate and having an immense desire to please, both the Working and Show Labradors are equally matched, and both the Working and Show types share characteristics of being highly intelligent,

keen and biddable. (There's that word again!) Bold and confident, they are optimistic and rarely show any sign of aggression
towards people.

The reason for the difference between the Working- and
Show-type Labs is due to many decades of specialised breeding.
Labradors that are wanted for hunting and for competing in
field trials are selectively bred for their working abilities; they
have higher drive and energy, and are more athletic, slimmer
in build and agile dogs. These are the most desirable traits in a
Working Labrador. They're bred not to the fickle and ever-
changing interpretations of the Kennel Club conformation, not
simply to come Best in Show, but to succeed at field trials or
retrieving game birds.

Labradors bred for show in conformation competitions are
selectively bred for their looks and temperament alone, with the
Labs most closely matching the judge's interpretation of breed
standard, winning awards in the ring, going on to be used in
breeding programmes. Their ability to perform in hunting and
field trials is secondary, at best.

In dog shows there's also an interesting compromise between
Working and Show dogs. At combination shows, a Labrador's
conformation and working ability are equally important, with
breeders aiming for the prestigious 'double champion' – Labs
that can win in both the show ring and out in the field.

For a shooting or hunting companion, the Working or
American Lab's your dog, but if it's a family pet you're after,
I'd argue it's a Show or English Lab all the way.

In the United Kingdom most of us want well-rounded family
dogs, and what's better than the happy and loyal Labrador? The

ideal family pet. I hate the name pet; a dog is so much more complex than that, but it is probably the best way to explain the differences. A pet is more often than not indulged, and if it is not indulged, then it certainly likes to indulge itself. As we know, the Labrador's appetite is legendary and, by and large, family or house Labs tend to be a little more indulged. Some people mistake it for love, but there is no love in overfeeding your dog – it only leads to an early onset of arthritic pain. We all do it, though. We cave into those pleading eyes. The eyes. Those laser beams that say 'put the digestive biscuit in my mouth'.

If we look at the historical provenance of the Labrador, it seems they began life as slightly more lithe dogs, capable of leaping overboard and being hauled back on by the fishermen. Their dense, waterproof coats protected them from the freezing waters, but as they have evolved, so too has their shape. As they became shooting dogs, they needed more power in their hind-quarters.

Whatever the shape, I have learnt you should never comment. Just assume that it is genetics and smile approvingly. Personally, I have always preferred a slightly stockier look. Inca was stocky. Perhaps that is a little unfair – she was solid.

The most important aspect of a Labrador's personality is that it 'needs' a job. That doesn't mean in a hunting/shooting/fishing/ life-saving kind of way. It needs to have a role. How many of us have been 'mouthed' by our Labs. This 'mouthing' is a form of work. They are merely doing what they have been bred for . . . to carry things. If they can't carry a duck or a fish they will make do with a shoe, a pair of socks or a bra. Failing all of that, they will try to carry us. I have lost count of the number of objects I have pulled from Inca's bed over the years. She was like a canine hoarder. It's blood instinct.

Many dog behaviourists will argue that the obsessive chewing displayed by Labrador pups is a result of being 'unemployed'. They need a job; it's the reason Labradors have excelled at so many roles over the years. Inca used to creep up to the children's bedroom at night to be close to them – it was as if she knew that her job was to protect them. Pat White, the animal behaviourist, explained to me that all dogs need a role, but it is a Labrador's diligence that ensures that if they aren't given a job, they will find one. So Inca became the children's nanny, although I've no doubt it might have also had something to do with the trail of food that follows a young child. Inca would often relieve them of their biscuits, sandwiches – and even ice creams.

It isn't just the body that is affected by the size of the Labrador. Size can completely transform the appearance of their face. The nose of a Labrador is one of its most defining features, which can broadly be described as wide or snipey. To my eye, the long thin noses have always looked a little wrong, but what do I know?

The colour of a Labrador is also an emotive subject for the loyal Labrador aficionado. The three recognised colours are black, yellow and chocolate. A little like the shape and size of a Labrador, opinions on colour can be broadly attributed to the various owning communities. Notably, some within the hunting and shooting world feel that the black dog was the original colour, perfect for blending into most landscapes and therefore the most suitable colour for working. Although I can see the logic to this I have also seen plenty of all three colours on estates across the country.

There has long been a debate as to whether different-coloured Labradors have different temperaments. Some theorise that yellow Labs are lazy, chocolate Labs are hyperactive and that black Labs make the best hunters. There's just about as much logic in that as there is in saying blondes are ditsy and brunettes are studious, though.

There is a commonly held belief that a Lab that has any mismarks, brindling or mosaics of other colours represents a non-purebred mixed Lab, but, again, I'd dispute this on the grounds that there are plenty of Labradors with white patches. Even the Kennel Club accepts patches.

Jack Vanderwyk has been able to trace the origins of all choc-olate Labradors to just eight bloodlines. Although the colour was not recognised until the twentieth century, these bloodlines go back to 1880, to Buccleuch Avon and his sire and dam, Malmesbury Tramp and Malmesbury June. It is, as we say, a small world.

Recently a new colour has become fashionable, although as old as the breed: Red, or 'Fox' as it's now usually called, which is a dark variation of yellow. They fetch a premium over all other colours. (I saw the reverse happen with Golden Retrievers, the dogs I grew up with. When I was a child, most Goldens were the colour of honey. In fact, that was the name of my family's first Golden Retriever. Today, as a consequence of which dogs win at conformation dog shows, most Golden Retrievers are as white as driven snow.)

I will admit to a bout of excitement when I first heard about the possibility of a red Labrador. The reality is a little less red as it is golden. To my eyes they are merely Labradors that look like Golden Retrievers.

I have also heard of black and white Labradors with Dalmatian spots, but more controversially there is the Silver Labrador. The colour is much the same as that of a Weimaraner; indeed, it is thought that the genes that produced the silvery coat originated from cross breeding. No one is really sure how the Silver Labradors have evolved; it may have been due to a spontaneous genetic mutation or outbreeding.

A little like the Red Labs, Silver Labs command a premium on the market; however, a great number of breeders have complained about the Silver Labs and the internet is rife with 'Say No to Silver' campaigns. But why the controversy? Surely all breeds had to begin somewhere? Well, some say that pedigree Labrador breeders are worried about the competition, but I suspect this is not often the case. However, most pedigree breeders are very committed to the concept of closed registry breeding and are angry that what they believe is most likely to be an outcross has been sneaked into the breed dishonestly. As they are in favour of a permanently closed register, they object strongly to what they see as tampering with tradition and the contamination of the Labrador genetic pool.

With so many concerns being raised over the last few years about closed registry breeding this is a contentious subject with strong opinions on both sides.

Perhaps of more concern to the average pet owner, though, are issues of inbreeding in silver Labradors. In order to establish their Silver lines, breeders will have had to breed quite closely, so it would seem likely that the silver Labrador gene pool is very small. On this basis, accusations of inbreeding in Silver Labs may be well founded, and of course inbreeding increases the risk of health problems arising or becoming exacerbated. However, I'd argue that this is a trans-Labrador issue, not one restricted to Silvers.

Ultimately, though, what colour you choose comes down to personal preference. Each to their own. Unless it involves the Kennel Club . . .

This leads us to an uncomfortable topic: pedigree. Not the food, but the provenance of the breed. When I was a small boy, it was all about the pedigree – that is the parentage, the lineage. A quick look through the stud books over the years and it will become apparent that the gene pool of the Labrador, as with many other breeds, has become thinner and thinner, which has inevitably led to inbreeding. It's what we call incest, but it isn't just a case of two first cousins getting together; this is a slow cobweb of interrelations in which the bloodlines have slowly merged, with inevitable health consequences. Hip dysplasia, a loose and painful fit in the ball-and-socket hip joints, and OCD (Osteochondrosis dessicans), where a fragment of cartilage peels away from bone and causes pain in the elbow joint, are common problems that now affect many, many pedigree Labradors.

Some have argued that the genetic 'closed shop' of the Labrador needs to be loosened up, the blood thinned a little, that some healthy genetic variety is added. This has led to one of the most popular changes now occurring in pedigree dogs – cross breeding.

While the Labradoodle is the cross breed that has received all the press, it is far from the only mix to include the Lab. The list of Labrador cross breeds is extensive. The Abrador is an Afghan Hound/Lab, the Boxador is a Boxer/Lab, the Chabrador is a Chow Chow/Lab, the Double Doodle is a Goldendoodle and Labradoodle, the Corgidor is a Corgi/Lab, while the Lab Pei is a Lab and Shar Pei Mix. The Labradbull is a Lab/Bulldog and the Labrottie is a Rottweiler and a Lab. There is the Matador, a Mastiff and a Lab, the Labraheeler, an Australia Cattle Dog and a Lab, a Labradinger, which is a Lab and an English Springer Spaniel, and my favourite, a Wolador, which is a Timber Wolf and a Labrador.

The names are genuinely funny, but are the crosses really an improvement on the original model? I don't think so. Take hip dysplasia, for example. Now that there are enough Labradoodles around to compare the health of their hips to that of Labrador hips, it turns out their hips are worse than those of Labradors. That is because conscientious Labrador breeders worldwide only breed from individuals whose hips (and elbows) have been x-rayed and are shown to be as well made as possible. Labradoodle breeders don't.

There are more than half a million registered Labradors in Britain, and worldwide the estimates range in the millions. They have overwhelmingly topped the most popular breed list in the United Kingdom, United States, Canada and Australia for decades. The humble Labrador is certainly spreading its genes, but what about the future for the Labrador?

The breed has survived and indeed thrived for more than a hundred years, resilient and adaptable. For a breed that has endured for so long, I have little doubt it will continue to thrive and adapt for another century.

At heart I am a Labrador traditionalist. Like an old Land Rover, I love its simplicity. There are no secrets. I suppose on the one hand Labradors and Land Rovers are really quite basic, but on the other hand it is that simplicity that makes them so popular. No hidden catches. What you see is what you get: happy dogs with a strong attachment to people.

The rights and wrongs of continuing the pedigree lines will be argued for many decades to come, and while my brain tells me it's wrong to encourage and support the pedigree spiral, my heart still wants the classic Labrador.

CHAPTER SIX

ROCK AND ROLLOVER

Inca and I became one. We were always together. Like Ant and Dec, we were a unit.

I lost track of the number of photo shoots we appeared in together. It must have been hundreds over the years, but there was one that stands out for all the wrong reasons.

The late Lord Lichfield had asked if I would take part in a calendar for a dog charity. I naturally agreed, and Inca and I duly visited his studio in west London where he took a series of portraits of the two of us. I was away in Canada when I realised something was wrong. I was up in a remote corner of Muskoka, on one of the many lakes in north-eastern Canada, with one of my great friends, Jake, and although mobile coverage had been limited, I had found a good location for a signal and switched my phone on one morning and it went ballistic. It beeped and beeped and beeped. Text message after text message and voicemail after voicemail. My heart sank. Something terrible must have happened. Someone must have died. My heart raced and I felt sick. My voicemail had more than 80 messages – another message from my network provider informed me to call them immediately as they couldn't cope with the volume of calls and messages.

What on earth had happened?

I picked up the first message. 'Hello, Ben Fogle,' said a female voice, before breaking into laughter and then hanging up. The theme of messages continued in a similar vein and it took some basic detective work to get to the bottom of the mystery.

Unbeknownst to Lord Lichfield, hidden under the voluminous black fur of one of the photos, scrawled across Inca's tag, was my mobile phone number. When viewed on a small contact sheet it was unreadable, but when blown up to a full page of a gossip magazine it was there in its full glory. Much to the delight of the magazine's editor, the photo was blown up and published. This was then exacerbated by a mention of it by Simon Mills on Radio 1, which created a mini-avalanche of callers across the country. Thousands of messages later, I changed my mobile number.

Some dogs are plain naughty. Inca was certainly no goody two-shoes, but I do remember a happy, loyal dog rather than naughty one. Of course she had her moments, usually instigated and encouraged by her stomach. There was the time she stole a cake my mother had made for my father. She ate the whole thing. Another time she stole a chicken and a whole family bag of Dime bars. There was also the time when she chewed up the advance I received for my first book, *The Teatime Islands*, and the time she stole someone's pint of Guinness – she sipped half the glass of an unexpected drinker in a pub while he wasn't looking. But by and large, Inca was a pleaser.

As overseas travel became more frequent in my career, Inca had become a firm fixture in my parents' house. To be honest, she was as much their dog as mine. They loved Inca. They had their own dog, a Golden Retriever called Macy, and the two of them spent a great deal of time together.

But not only was I wracked with guilt at my increasingly long absences abroad, I then worried that Inca missed other canine company when I was back at home and she was with me. I liked the idea of having another dog, but the practicality was far less realistic. It was easy to travel with one dog; to stay in hotels, travel on trains and visit friends was relatively simple with a little planning, but even I knew that two dogs would change the whole dynamic, and make life harder rather than easier.

As I mulled over the idea of being a two-dog home, my sister Tamara confessed that she was desperate for a Lab of her own. She often looked after Inca and loved her, so it seemed silly not to breed from her. To share the Inca love. But whom to mate her with? Without Tinder or dating websites it was difficult to know where to begin.

Mating was a subject we had skirted round before, although not in any serious way! Previously, Inca and I had taken part in a doggy speed-dating night. We had been asked by Disney Films to help promote the release of *A Hundred and One Dalmatians* and the idea was an event at which singles and their dogs would meet. The humans above the table – the dogs beneath it. It was a hilarious night, but neither Inca nor I found love.

Mating! It's such an emotionless description, so prescribed.

Not that I had ever really expected Inca to meet a dashing young dog and fall in love, but it seems so mercenary just to choose her suitor and expect her to have his babies, or puppies even. Once again, Dad came to the rescue in the search for a dog in shining armour. He vetted some of his eligible patients and before I knew it we had found a suitable dog and they had been introduced in London's Hyde Park. A neutral territory where they could get jiggy.

To be honest, I couldn't bring myself to go along. It was like sending my own daughter off, and no one wants to think about that. Dad chaperoned her and a week later she was pregnant.

As with so many important moments in my life, I missed the birth. To be fair, I was supposed to be around, but a diving course in Florida for an upcoming BBC project overran and she gave birth to the first puppy as I was about to board my flight home. My parents carefully helped each of her eight puppies into the world. Even so, I was like a proud parent.

My parents had agreed to look after Inca and her litter for the first eight weeks, until they left for their new homes. My sister wanted to take one and the rest were given new homes with friends and acquaintances. It had never appealed to me to 'sell' any of the puppies; I just wanted them to go to loving homes.

For two months my parents' home became the most popular house in Notting Hill, as people flocked to see the puppies.

My mother cried when the first puppy left . . . and the second, and the third . . . until we were left with a little girl called Lola who went to live with my sister. I can't say Inca was as sad to see them go, though. She was finally free of the pain of razor-sharp teeth on her nipples and she had our full affections once again. Despite that, Inca and Lola became best friends. Inca mothered her – she licked her ears clean each time they were together and she looked out for her when they were in the park.

While no Lassie, Inca had attained a reasonable level of celebrity during her life. *Castaway* had made her a household name; she used to receive more post than me from adoring fans during our year of isolation. She received dog toys, bones and even photographs of would-be suitors. One elderly fan knitted her a jumper, while another admirer sent her some winter booties.

During my early career, Inca was a permanent fixture by my side on most of my television work.

She appeared on the sofa next to me on almost every breakfast show and most chat shows. We did photo shoots together for magazines and newspapers, including a cover shoot for *Heat* magazine, which must surely secure her place in the history of canine celebrity.

On BBC's *Countryfile* she sailed the coast of Cornwall and the Western Isles of Scotland. She accompanied me at the Brambles cricket match in the middle of the Solent and at the World Worm Charming championships in Cheshire. She came hound trailing with me in Scotland and lawn-mower racing in Sussex. She flew out to the west coast of Ireland to make a film about fly fishing for the *Holiday* show and appeared alongside Kate Humble and me at Longleat for more than a decade in the BBC's *Animal Park*.

We also presented two seasons of *Heaven and Earth* together, in which we explored everything from mermaids in Cornwall to the Loch Ness Monster in Scotland. She appeared as the canine apparition of Dracula in Whitby, where she ran through a church, and the famous Black Dog in Suffolk. She even appeared alongside me in adverts for P&O and Nature Valley and had a starring role in a *Vogue* fashion shoot.

Perhaps her biggest roles, though, were on *Crufts* and *One Man and his Dog* where, once again, she joined me on the sofa. It is obviously an exaggeration to call Inca my co-presenter, but you must not underestimate her importance as a calming, reassuring friend.

I suppose I shouldn't really be surprised; everyone loves a cute dog, and a Labrador arguably has the ultimate cute factor. But Inca certainly wasn't the first Labrador to become a household name, and she won't be the last.

Think of a puppy – any puppy – and the chances are you'll think of a Labrador pup. They have been a staple of our cultural landscape for decades. They have featured in films, books, cartoons, TV series and advertisements, usually in the role of a solidly lovable, faithful, heart-in-the-right-place kind of character – even as a bit of a goody four-paws (as opposed to a human goody two-shoes). But the absolute game-changer for the breed in terms of cultural definition was *Marley & Me.*

Suddenly the Labrador had Character with a capital 'C'. Originally a pet-owner memoir penned by journalist John Grogan and subtitled *Life and Love with the World's Worst Dog,* the book became an international bestseller and was soon adapted for film starring Owen Wilson and Jennifer Aniston. *Marley & Me* gave the Labrador a personality, depicted ownership of such a mutt as a roller-coaster ride of high emotions and drama, and spawned a whole industry based on cheesy, life-affirming quotes about the newly glamorous emotional dynamic between a pet dog with a 'big personality' and its long-suffering/long-loving family. The book is laced with beautiful quotes such as:

A person can learn a lot from a dog, even a loopy one like ours. Marley taught me about living each day with unbridled exuberance and joy, about seizing the moment and following your heart. He taught me to appreciate the simple things – a walk in the woods, a fresh snowfall, a nap in a shaft of winter sunlight. And as he grew old and achy, he taught me about optimism in the face of adversity. Mostly, he taught me about friendship and selflessness and, above all else, unwavering loyalty.

Animal lovers are a special breed of humans, generous of spirit, full of empathy, perhaps a little prone to sentimentality, and with hearts as big as a cloudless sky.

It's just the most amazing thing to love a dog, isn't it? It makes our relationships with people seem as boring as a bowl of oatmeal.

Give him your heart and he'll give you his. How many people can you say that about? How many people can make you feel rare and pure and special? How many people can make you feel extraordinary?

He taught us the art of unqualified love. How to give it, how to accept it. Where there is that, most other pieces fall into place.

Slightly saccharine, but then, who isn't soft about their dog? The winning theme of the bestseller, however, is best summed up in Grogan's line: '*Dogs are great. Bad dogs, if you can really call them that, are perhaps the greatest of them all.*'

Grogan relates a cameo-filled story about the thirteen years that he and his family spent with their boisterous, neurotic, destructive but utterly big-hearted yellow Labrador Retriever. For a central character that does not speak, Marley – a dog that never acts as expected of him – holds the story well. The tone is one of exasperated hilarity underpinned by deep-rooted mutual affection. It is a charming evocation of the contrast between the problems caused by a lovable, uncontrolled, clumsy dog and the unswerving devotion and love he shows towards his human family. It celebrates the way in which a pet becomes part of a family's DNA. As Grogan and his wife settle into married life, have children and grow older, Marley gradually slots into his role in the family. Their grief when he dies in old age is heart-rending. Grogan later revealed that the eulogy he wrote in *The Philadelphia Inquirer* following Marley's death received more responses than any other column he had written in his professional life.

The book spawned a whole industry of doggy tales, from *The Art of Racing in the Rain* to my own father's *Travels with Macy*, in which he travelled around North America with his Golden Retriever, Macy.

Traditionally in films and cartoons the Labrador was always the good, quiet, dependable dog. In the 1961 Disney adaptation of Dodie Smith's novel *The Hundred and One Dalmatians*, the Labrador tries to protect all the Dalmatians as they attempt to flee from the clutches of Cruella de Vil and her sidekicks, Jasper and Horace. The Labrador is first mentioned by the Collie at the dairy farm, who comments that the Labrador's human is a grocer in Dinsford. When the Dalmatian family (including all 99 puppies) arrives in Dinsford on their hopeful trek back to safety in London, they are greeted by the Labrador, who, keen to help, informs them that his owner has a truck that will take them to London as soon as it is repaired. But almost immediately the three grown-up dogs notice that Cruella, Horace and Jasper are scouring the village for the pups. Cue lightbulb Labrador moment! In their hiding place, Pongo rolls in a pile of soot and gets the idea that this disguise might distract the villains – they can all pretend to be Labradors rather than Dalmatians.

The Labrador confirms this is a good idea. Who could be suspicious of a common old Labrador? After all the puppies are covered in soot, the real Labrador helps Pongo and Perdita escort the puppies to the truck in groups. As soon as the truck is fixed, Cruella discovers the ruse and orders her minions to catch the puppies. The Labrador – a good egg to the end – attacks Jasper and Horace, giving Pongo and Perdita enough time to get in the truck with all of the puppies.

The film worked on the principle that a Labrador is such a trustworthy dog that it would never do anything wrong. It was above suspicion. I'd partly agree with that sentiment, but only until it involves food, in which case a Labrador would happily sell its own tail, or even its mother.

The Labrador gained further traction in popular culture when a particular book was published in the same year – 1961 – as the Disney animated adaptation of *The Hundred and One Dalmations.*

24

The book was *The Incredible Journey* by Scottish author Sheila Burnford, the children's book which tells the story of three pets as they tramp nearly 500 kilometres across the wilds of Canada in search of their beloved masters. It depicts the hardship and stress of a tough expedition in which the emotional dynamic stems from the unwavering loyalty and courage of the three animals – two dogs and a cat – and the chemistry they have as a trio. The story is simple . . . the animals' owners, a family called the Hunters, have had to leave them for several months over the summer with a friend, John Longridge, because Jim, the father, is obliged to deliver a series of university lectures in England. Longridge himself goes away for a two-week duck-hunting trip, leaving the animals in the care of a drop-in housekeeper Mrs Oakes. Feeling the lack of human companionship, the animals decide to set out to try to find their owners. Mrs Oakes assumes Longridge has taken them with him, so the animals are truly alone as they follow their instincts and embark on their incredibly perilous journey home.

As a unit, they are an appealing gang. There is a young Labrador Retriever called Luath, who, with a rich golden coat and warm brown eyes, is the strong, brave, eager leader of the pack – but really only in the physical sense. As the most recent addition to the Hunter family menagerie, he channels his natural exuberance into a determined path home, but respectfully defers in all matters to the original family dog, Bodger. Again, we see the Labrador as an easy-going dog who instinctively knows his place.

Bodger is an old English Bull Terrier whose full pedigree moniker is Ch. Boroughcastle Brigadier of Doune. His fur is white with a skin-pink tint and his demeanour shows him to be a brave, loyal, determined, stalwart, elder statesman-like companion. At eleven years old, his left eye is nearly blind and he tires easily, but his tenacity remains unquestioned. He bears the hallmark of his breed in being prepared to fight his way out of trouble, but he is very fond of humans, particularly children, and whenever the group comes across humans on their adventure, he uses his charm to get food and affection. He hates all cats except for Tao – the third Hunter family pet – who is a slender, seal-point, blue-eyed Siamese cat who earned his respect by standing up to him when Tao first joined the Hunters as a small kitten. They bond over the fact that Tao, like Bodger, despises other cats; in fact, before Luath's arrival, dog and cat shared many outings, terrorising the other cats in their 'hood'. Tao serves as an interesting contrast to the two dogs. He can open doors; he is hardier and better equipped to survive in the wilderness, and he has no difficulty surviving on his own when separated from his canine chums. The Bull Terrier and the Siamese are described by Burnford – who modelled the fiction on her own pets – as being 'closer than any other cat-and-dog relationship I have ever seen'. The Bull Terrier and the young Lab also enjoy a close relationship.

The tale is set in the north-western part of Ontario, a landscape characterised by isolated farms, small towns and lots of lakes and river formations. The animals have to fend off ferocious feral animals and cope with freezing conditions, hunger and fast-flowing water hazards. Though it has been pigeonholed as a children's story, the book has universal appeal – particularly to pet lovers – and Burnford herself maintained that she did not write it specifically for children. Clever old Disney saw its potential, and in 1963 it was released in movie form. Thirty years later, in 1993, it was remade for another generation and released as *Homeward Bound: The Incredible Journey.* If you haven't read the book or seen either of the films, I'm sure you can guess how it ends . . . Yes, a warm and fuzzy happy reunion of animals and humans – signalled by the Labrador's bark.

I can still remember reading the story as a child. It was the first time dogs were given real, relatable characters. I saw myself in Luath. I empathised with him. It was the first story I read that made me cry.

By the 1990s, the Labrador had achieved such iconic status as a dependable hero that the brown mongrel described by Ludwig Bemelmans in his *Madeline* series, written between 1939 and 1961, was changed to a golden Labrador in the 1998 live-action film adaptation. For those unfamiliar with the illustrated *Madeline* tales, the opening page gives the essence:

> *In an old house in Paris that was covered in vines lived twelve little girls in two straight lines. In two straight lines they broke their bread and brushed their teeth and went to bed. They smiled at the good and frowned at the bad and sometimes they were very sad. They left the house at half past nine in two straight lines in rain or shine — the smallest one was Madeline . . .*

My little daughter Iona and my boy Ludo both love Madeline. Genevieve, the dog, became Madeline's canine saviour and friend in an early adventure. Seven-year-old Madeline, the boldest and most outgoing of girls at her Catholic boarding school in Paris, stood on a bridge over the River Seine to make a speech to the other girls and in her excitement fell into the waters below. She was duly rescued by a stray, Genevieve, who jumps into the river and saves her. Madeline brings her rescuer back to school and hides her. Miss Clavel, the nun who runs the school, says Genevieve must stay in a kennel outside, but Lord Cucuface, arriving for an inspection, says the dog must go because it is against the rules to keep her there. In the course of a subsequent adventure, Madeline is reunited with Genevieve and they become friends.

When Warner Brothers set out to create an animated television series based on the DC Comics character Krypto the Superdog, they chose to depict the main protagonist as a white Labrador Retriever. Clearly we are in the realm of fantasy here. Although Krypto's breed is never specifically described in the comic books, he was drawn as a white dog of generic Labrador pedigree – presumably because he shares Superman's moral values in being champion of good and righteousness in society.

Krypto was originally Clark Kent/Superman's dog on Krypton before the planet was destroyed. Like his superowner, he has the same powers, but, in a nice creative touch, some of those powers are heightened as you would expect in a dog, such as his super hearing and sense of smell.

Sitcom writers, when creating the perfect family or set of families, often fall back on the addition of a fun-loving Labrador as a universally recognised symbol of the ideal domestic quota.

Take the Australian soap opera *Neighbours*. *Neighbours* was a huge part of my childhood, and the importance of the Aussie soap cannot be overstated. At 1pm every day, the whole school would race from lunch to the television room to keep up with the hottest TV show of the time.

There was never any question in my mind as to the real star. It wasn't Kylie or Jason but Bouncer the yellow Labrador. Bouncer added complexity, humanity and bemusement to the plot for six years. From the time he made his first screen appearance as a cute golden-coated puppy acquired from a shelter during an episode broadcast Down Under on 4 February 1987, until the day he left the series, six years later on 12 February 1993, Bouncer lived at three addresses on Ramsay Street, fathered two litters of puppies, survived road accidents, a chip-pan fire and serious mushroom poisoning, and recovered from being lost.

Bouncer was supplied and trained by Luke Hura, who runs a canine actors' agency. Rather amazingly, Bouncer was paid more than the human cast members and his fan cards became the most popularly demanded above any other cast member. At one stage Hura revealed that the dog was worth between $100,000 and $200,000. Thirteen weeks after filming his final scenes on *Neighbours*, Bouncer died of cancer, aged only seven. Following his death, he was sent thousands of tributes from fans around the world.

Bouncer's most famous storyline was bizarre in the extreme, even by the standards of a long-running sitcom. It had Bouncer dreaming that he was getting married to Rosie, the sheepdog that belonged to Clarrie McLachlan next door. During an interview, Anne Charleston (who played Madge Bishop) revealed,

'The whole cast was mortified about that! It reduced it to a three-year-old's programme. It was very strange.' Bouncer's dream was later named the second 'weirdest' storyline in the show's history, though his contribution – as a loyal and loved Labrador friend – was celebrated by critics. Josephine Monroe commented positively of Bouncer in her book *Neighbours: The first 10 years*, stating: 'Bouncer was a hero – he even answered the phone and barked to Joe when baby Sky was in trouble – and often had major storylines of his own like the time he was run over and nearly died. But most importantly, he was a loyal and loved friend.' She also declared him one of the most-loved characters in the serial's history. Celebrating the serial's 25th anniversary, British magazine *NOW* included Bouncer among their profiles of their favourite characters, while Daniel Bettridge of *The Guardian* said the faithful Bouncer was one of the best actors to 'tread the Ramsay Street tarmac'.

In children's television the Labrador again often serves as the most easily recognisable friendly dog. In *Big Barn Farm*, a television series produced for the BBC children's channel CBeebies with a mixture of live action and animation, Digger is one of the four young animals on a farm – the Farmyard Bunch – who share adventures. Interacting with Petal the piglet, Gobo the goat and Dash the donkey, Digger is a Labrador Retriever puppy. He is the youngest of the four chums, cute, naïve and willing to please. Brimming with boundless energy, he is always eager to prove himself and put himself forward for any new jape. He is a tiny bit dim and sometimes slow to catch on, but Digger is never happier than when playing with his friends. His catch-phrase is, 'I can do that! I can do that!'

It is good for the status of the Labrador that one was written into *Lost*, an American drama which followers the survivors of a passenger jet crash on a mysterious tropical island in the South Pacific, and which has been dubbed one of the greatest television series of all time. Vincent the yellow Labrador is the only non-human survivor of Oceanic Flight 815, and his name – from the Latin *vincere*, to conquer – means 'the one who prevails'. The series was broadcast on ABC over six seasons from September 2004 to May 2010 and comprised a total of 121 episodes. In an interview, executive producers Damon Lindelof and Carlon Cuse admitted that at the show's end the only character they could promise would be alive was Vincent. The final shot of the series showed Vincent, alive, lying next to a dying character called Jack. He and Walt were the main characters and the only ones of the original characters not shown to have died by the end of the series. Thus Vincent duly prevailed. Actor Naveen Andrews, who portrayed Sayid Jarrah, joked about his theory that the series finale would feature rescue boats coming for Vincent while the graves of all the survivors were seen behind him.

Each of the episodes featured a storyline on the island with a secondary storyline from another point in a character's life. One of those characters was Vincent, who was travelling aboard Oceanic Flight 815 from Sydney to Los Angeles in the luggage department after moving to the United States with two characters called Walt and Michael. Like all the human characters, Vincent was given a pre-island back story and plenty of on-island storylines which included having as many as four owners, being attacked by a polar bear, revealing dead bodies, and so on. Critics often observed that Vincent was frequently present just before something bad happened on the island.

Vincent was played by two dogs: one a female called Madison (trained and overseen during filming by Kim Stahl) who previously worked in tracking and obedience competitions and made her TV debut in *Lost*, the other a male known as Pono, who was discovered by crew members eating at Marcos' Diamond Head Cove Health Bar. His first scenes came towards the end of the second season, but soon *Lost* fans knew all the Pono trivia. Like every well-bred Labrador, he is especially fond of children and loves water (Pono is an excellent surfer). True to the roles mostly played by Labradors in film and TV, his name means 'righteousness' or 'moral correctness' in the Hawaiian language.

Of course, in the off-screen world of celebrities the Labrador's dependability and loyalty have long attracted a following. Paul McCartney had a 'wild' Labrador that would escape the grounds of the McCartneys' house in St John's Wood, London, and trot out for nights on the town. She gave birth to a litter of black Labradors, one of which the McCartneys named Jet, presumably because of the colour of his coat, and Jet is believed to have been the inspiration for the track of the same name that appears on the iconic *Band on the Run* album that McCartney wrote for Wings in 1973. 'Jet' peaked at number 7 in both the US and British charts in March 1974, although the lyrics bear no relation to canine influence.

It seems Labradors were rock 'n' roll; Keith Richards also had a Labrador that he kept in his house in West Wittering, in Sussex. Richards succeeded in irritating his neighbours not only by often playing loud music throughout the night but also by his inability to keep control of his Labrador, which would regularly stray on to his neighbours' properties.

In the cultural sport known as celeb-watching, fed by the paparazzi, Labradors have often provided photo opportunities for their owners or added to their celebrity aura. Arnold Schwarzenegger, for example, had two Labradors: Gustav (named after his father) and Spunky (I'll let you deduce that one). They formed part of an exotic menagerie which ran to a miniature pony, a pot-bellied pig, a cockapoo and various ducks and rabbits. In 2008, Arnie signed a Bill in the State of California that provides for enforcement of 'pet trusts' that animal owners set up to pay for the continuing care of their pets after they (the owners) have died – thus giving peace of mind to many senior fellow Labrador owners.

Arnie is not the only actor in Hollywood who appears to have fallen for the charm of the Labrador. Kevin Costner is another Hollywood figure well known for his love of dogs. He keeps a dynasty of golden Labradors, the matriarch of which, Rosalita, starred alongside him in the 1989 romantic thriller *Revenge*, directed by Tony Scott. One of her puppies was named Wyatt after the lawman Wyatt Earp whom Costner played in the eponymous movie. Daisy, the third yellow Labrador, arrived in 2000, and later had to be treated for her addiction to chewing furniture and shoes. Sylvester Stallone also keeps dogs at his home in Hollywood, among them a Labrador named Flipper, while Kevin Spacey has a black Labrador cross called Legacy. Frank Sinatra had a Labrador named Leroy Brown, presumably after the 1973 song 'Bad, Bad Leroy Brown' that was the last number-one hit for American folk rock singer Jim Croce before his death – which Sinatra released as a cover version in 1974.

In the circles of literary giants, too, what could be more fitting than to learn that Ernest Hemingway had a black Labrador gundog, or that Roald Dahl, who owned an assortment of dogs, had a black Labrador called Jelly? Of course they both had Labs. Labs inspire.

In the world of still advertisements or film commercials, a Labrador is often used for several reasons. First, the breed is famously easy to train. Second, they are universally recognised as 'a perfect family dog' so by their very presence they signal domestic bliss (and their puppies are indescribably cute). Third, everyone knows the size of a Labrador so if you have one in the back of a new car that is being launched with a pervasive advertising campaign, viewers can instinctively register 'family car with generous-sized boot'. Put a Schnauzer in the back and only a minority would be able to interpret the proportions it represents within a cameo family shot. The other advantage of the Labrador is that, as the number one dog owned in the United Kingdom, the United States, Australia and so on, its appeal reaches a massively diverse ownership. In terms of a 'hearts and minds' strategy, there is nothing so winning as a puppy.

The most famous advertisement featuring the Labrador is, of course, the one that features the Andrex puppy. The appealing playfulness of a young puppy is cleverly engaged on behalf of a brand of toilet roll. The Andrex puppy first appeared in 1972 and since then there have been 130 different adverts featuring the adorable golden-coated individual. In 2004, the company replaced its advertising slogan 'Soft, strong and very very long' with 'Tuggable, huggable softness', and recently changed it to

'Be kind to your behind'. The brand is sold in the United States and Australia as Kleenex Cottonelle, and in Australia the puppy is known simply as the 'Kleenex puppy'. The puppy thus represents softness, strength and a good thing to have as an integral part of your life.

When the first advert was scripted in 1972, the original creative concept was blocked by television regulators as it was thought that the image of a cute little girl running through her house trailing a roll of loo paper would encourage wastefulness. So, in a stroke of genius, the little girl was replaced by a playful Labrador puppy who took the end of the roll in his teeth and ran through the house with it. This was accompanied by a slogan which said, 'New Andrex goes a long, long way'.

The campaign went on to become one of the best-known commercials in the country. The most memorable of these, for most people, was the 'Little Boy' variation of this advert, which showed a young boy sitting on the loo and left without any paper after the puppy has run off with the end in his mouth and is pictured entangled in the roll. In 1991, it was voted the nation's favourite advert. Having featured in more than 100 commercials and as it celebrated 40 years on TV, the Andrex puppy soft toy was released to raise money to support charities including National Canine Defence League and Guide Dogs for the Blind. The Andrex puppy even has a kennel on the internet so that younger visitors can meet the puppy, collect tokens and email comments about their own puppies in the Bark Back section of the site.

As the lifestyle marketing folk have long realised, dogs are a winner – dogs looking cute, dogs doing crazy things, dogs getting up to amusing antics. Their appeal is universal, and to harness that wittily can translate into commercial success. Tap into man's love for his canine friend with an enterprising idea and you don't have to do research on a potential market.

Beyond advertising, it's amazing how much Labrador stuff there is out there. As a Labrador owner there is an assumption that I will love anything with a Labrador on it. Over the years I've been given everything from Labrador tea towels to Labrador notebooks and even a Labrador clock. I suppose their unmistakable silhouette is easy to replicate.

It seems I'm not the only one, though. As the Labrador is the number one choice of dog in so many countries across the world, it follows that there is a huge market for Labrador novelty items. In fact, go to a point-to-point, a three-day event, an agricultural show, a Christmas Fair or a crafts market, and you are sure to find stalls selling everything from mugs and tea towels to upholstered three-seat sofas decorated with Labrador motifs or portraits or silhouettes. Vicky Elliot – who runs The Labrador Company, which sells silhouette clocks with wagging tails, cashmere scarves, bespoke Eaton bags, dog beds, cushions, fabric by the metre, key rings, notelets, throws, foot stools, mirrors, armchairs and ottomans – described one lightbulb moment. 'I bumped into an old friend who told me he now had a chocolate shop in Stow-on-the-Wold. 'You should do Labrador-shaped chocolates,' I said. 'No, wait a minute. *I* should do Labrador-shaped chocolates.' Acting on her idea, she created her distinctive range of boxed confectionery: six handmade chocolate Labradors – two dark, two milk and two white chocolate. 'The perfect little present to make people smile! Belgian chocolate.

Made in England. Fairtrade. For human consumption only.'
Within weeks, she had sold 15,000 . . . 'People can't get enough.'

The Labrador Company also extends to ranges for Spaniels
and Dachshunds, but Elliot, a former Labrador owner, says she
sells more than twice as many Labrador products as those of
the other breeds. She puts this down to the fact that people are
'wet about their dog' and also the fact that, as a Labrador is a
big dog, a Lab owner has to buy into its presence in the family
home and car, and invest in some kit. Her ranges appeal to an
upmarket audience, which extends all the way up to the man
with his customised Range Rover complete with cabinet
marquetry for guns and cartridges in burr walnut and bespoke
travelling space for the beloved Labrador gundogs. But the secret
of success behind all the notable Labrador-themed novelty businesses is the genuine affection for the breed. Look at one of The
Labrador Company's clocks with wagging tails and you see the
stance is right, the tilt of the head so familiar . . .

CHAPTER SEVEN

THE NOSE KNOWS

Inca helped find me a job, a career and a best friend. However, I'd argue her greatest achievement was finding me a wife.

The Fogles have always walked their dogs in Hyde Park. I love it there; a little bit of the country in the middle of the city. Inca and I would have our hour-long set loop through the park, seeing the same people, but one day I spotted a tall, hot blonde running with an athletic, agile brown dog. She was soon christened 'Park Girl' and I became rather infatuated.

I would look out for her in her familiar red tracksuit. I learnt to recognise the gait of her run from a distance, and Inca and I would redirect our walk accordingly. The problem was that Marina had what I call 'pretty girl radar' and would alter her course to avoid a potential stalker like me.

For more than a year we would watch in awe as this beautiful blonde and her dog dashed across the horizon in a blur. Occasionally our paths would cross and I would get butterflies, but I was always too shy to speak to her. If Inca would only 'talk' to her dog and start playing, then it would be the excuse I needed. The problem was that Inca had never really liked other dogs. I put it down to her lack of socialisation during our year on Taransay.

So one day I set a trap. Inca and I lay in a bush and waited until she appeared. I booted Inca from the bush into the path of her sleek brown dog. Inca growled, the brown dog ran faster, and the pretty blonde carried on oblivious.

In the end it took a chance meeting at a party to finally say hello. Out of her running kit, though, I barely recognised her.

'You're the man with the dog,' she smiled. That smile was so sexy.

I discovered her real name was Marina and that her dog was called Maggi. Maggi had been bought from a rescue centre in Henley and was in fact half-Lab, half-Collie. She was a beautiful dog – fast, agile, sleek and very, very funny.

I like to think it was love at first sight, but it could never be true love until we knew the dogs liked one another. Love me, love my dog. I was terrified that Inca would try to attack Maggi when we first got together, so we organised to meet on neutral ground, the Ladbroke Arms pub in Notting Hill. Apart from a little grumble, they loved each other straight away.

We spent a year going out. The four of us. We would go for dirty weekends to Holkham with the dogs. To Woolacombe in Devon – with the dogs. Our lives and our courtship revolved and evolved around the dogs. All we would talk about was our dogs. When I look back at all our early photographs, they are dominated by pictures of our dogs.

A St. John's Water Dog from the late nineteenth century.

Cora. *A Labrador Dog* (1823). Print after a painting by Sir Edwin Henry Landseer.

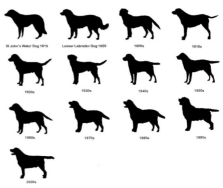

How the Labrador Retriever has developed from the St. John's Water Dog.

The earliest known portrait of a yellow Labrador. Josephine Bowes (1825–74) with her dog by Tony Dury. © The Bowes Museum, Barnard Castle, County Durham, UK/Bridgeman Images

DUKE OF BUCCLEUCH'S LABRADORS.

NAMES.	SIRES	DAMS	REMARKS
1882.			
Ned	Lord Malmesbury's Sweep, 1877	Lord Malmesbury's Juno, 1878	
1885.			
Avon	Lord Malmesbury's Tramp	Lord Malmesbury's Juno, 1878	
1886.			
Nell	Lord Wimborne's ——, 1882	Lord Malmesbury's Juno, 1882	
1887.			
Jet	Duke of Richmond's Tar, 1881	Lord Home's Dinah, 1886	
1888.			
Bess			From Lord Ruthven.
Dinah	Duke of Hamilton's Sam, 1884	Lord Home's Dinah, 1885	Sam.—See Appendix.
Trick			Dinah, by Lord Malmesbury's Nelson ex His Nell.
1889.			
Gip Nell	Duke of Hamilton's Sam, 1884	Nell, 1886	

Stud Book of the Duke of Buccleuch's Labrador.

The first registered yellow Labrador, Ben of Hyde, was born in 1899 at the kennel of Major Radclyffe.

Early depiction of Labradors: *After the Shoot* (1895) by William Woodhouse. © Bonhams, London, UK/Bridgeman Images

Betty, a Black Labrador (1911) by Evelyn Blacklock. © National Trust Photographic Library/ Bridgeman Images

Lady Howe's kennels were famous all over the world in the early twentieth century. Her Labrador Retrievers were successful both in the show ring and at field trials. (Photo by Thomas Fall)

Lady Howe with three noted dogs from her kennel. (Photo by Thomas Fall)

Ch Ilderton Ben, owned by Mrs Quintin Dick (later Lady Howe), in about 1914. He was described as an exceptionally good-looking dog, with a good head, typical of the Labrador breed. (Photo by R. Anderton)

The Duchess of York (later Queen Elizabeth The Queen Mother) and Princess Elizabeth (now The Queen), photographed at Glamis Castle in Scotland with their Labrador Glen by The Duke of York (later King George VI) in 1930. © Royal Collection Trust/ All Rights Reserved

A family surrounded by their Labradors in the garden of their Cambridgeshire home in the early twentieth century. (Photo by Compton Collier)

Two of King George VI's Sandringham dogs, shown at Crufts in 1938.

The Crufts Reserve Best in Show title 2013 was won by Labrador Retriever Romeo, owned by Franco Barberi from Cesara, Italy. © OnEdition/The Kennel Club

Before my Labrador years: with my Golden Retriever Lexington.

A Labrador Retriever living up to half of its name. © Eddie Keogh/Reuters/Corbis

Downton Abbey Labrador Pharaoh with Hugh Bonneville. © AF archive/Alamy

Bouncer from *Neighbours*.

Writer Ernest Hemingway in Sun Valley, Idaho with his Labrador Retriever in 1939. © Bridgeman Images

Black Labradors trained as search dogs for the Fire Brigade. © John Daniels / ardea.com

Allen Parton, who was seriously injured while serving in the Gulf War, with his devoted Labradors Endal and Endal Junior ('EJ').

David Blunkett, at the time British Home Secretary in the early 2000s, introduces his then new guide dog Sadie (right) to his previous guide dog Lucy (left), who was retiring. © Stephen Hird/Reuters/Corbis

Russian President Vladimir Putin with Koni. © ITAR-TASS Photo Agency/Alamy

Harold Wilson, then Prime Minister, on holiday in the Scilly Islands with his Labrador Paddy in 1975. © Trinity Mirror / Mirrorpix / Alamy

US President Clinton and his family with Buddy in 1998. © White House/ National Archive/Corbis

Labradors at war. The Normandy Landings, 1944: (Above left) A sapper of No. 1 Dog Platoon, 277th Field Park Company, Royal Engineers, with his dog Nigger, Bayeux, 5 July 1944. The dogs were used to hunt for mines, especially the all-wooden 'Shoe Mine' which was otherwise undetectable. (Above right) A sergeant of the Royal Army Veterinary Corps bandages the wounded ear of Jasper, a mine-detecting dog, Bayeux, France.

Bobs, serving with No. 1 Dog Platoon of the Royal Engineers, locates a buried mine at Bayeux, France. (Photos © Imperial War Museums)

Police training dogs with their handlers at 23rd Battalion Madhya Pradesh Police Dog Training Institute in Bhopal, India. © Sanjeev Gupta/epa/Corbis

Labradors at war. Tracker dogs in Vietnam in 1967. © WS Collection/Alamy

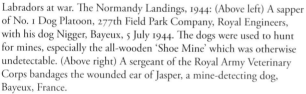

Police officers in Hyde Park, London, on patrol looking for people in possession of cannabis with a sniffer dog. © Mim Friday / Alamy

Two women police dog handlers with drug sniffer dogs, Met Police, London. © Metropolitan Police Authority / Mary Evans

RAF Wing Commander Guy Gibson with his black Labrador dog Nigger and the rest of the crew in 1942. © Daily Mail/Rex/Alamy

Ben and Inca (as a puppy).

Ben with Inca on Taransay (during *Castaway*, 2000).

There is one day that stands out, though. It was a watershed. A game changer. To be honest, it was probably the moment when I actually decided that Marina really was *the one*. Apart from my sister and my parents, no one had ever been trusted to look after Inca.

It was a Monday morning and I bumped into Marina running in the park with Maggi. I was ambling back to the car with Inca at my side, 'Why don't I take her with me?' smiled Marina. 'She could come on our run.'

If I'm honest, I panicked briefly. Marina was certainly no stranger but I had never just left Inca with someone apart from family.

'Okay,' I stuttered, and before I knew what had happened, Inca was disappearing into the distance with the blonde park girl and Maggi.

Shortly after I first met Marina, she and her family flew to Mozambique for Christmas, so naturally I volunteered to look after her dog while I was away. I can remember driving down to my parents' house just outside Arundel, in Sussex.

'Who's this?' asked my parents as Maggi marched into the house.

'Oh, just someone's dog,' I replied nonchalantly.

My parents still hadn't met Marina, or even heard about her until now. The first they knew of her was her dog Maggi. At the end of Christmas both my parents confided in me that if Maggi's owner was anything like the dog, she must be pretty special.

Marina returned in time for the New Year and the four of us saw it in at my parents' house, where we spent several days walking along the windswept beaches. It was blissful. I have such happy memories of those carefree days of young love. And that's when Maggi tried to commit suicide . . .

As always, Maggi had one of her beloved tennis balls in her mouth. She rarely left the house without one. We were splashing around in the surf on Climping Beach, a long pebbly section of the coast that runs west from Littlehampton. I picked up the ball and threw it a couple of times, then on the fifth throw I decided to give it a little more welly. The ball went careering through the air and over a wooden groyne. Without a second thought, Maggi bounded after the ball and followed it over the groyne into the abyss beyond.

My heart leapt. What was beyond the groyne? We had reached the end of the beach, so I raced to the edge and peered over. It was a sheer six-metre drop to the river estuary below.

I couldn't believe it. Had I just killed my girlfriend's dog?

'Maggi!' I shouted. 'Maggi! It was a huge drop. The water was coming in fast and with the rising tide the river was running wild. Even if she had landed safely she would easily be swept up into the current.

'Maggi!' I shouted again.

My eyes scanned the water but there was no sign of her. By now a small crowd had gathered. Alerted by my frenetic, wild calling, they had gathered by the railing. There was still no sign of Maggi. Inca pottered around, unconcerned for her new friend.

And then I spotted her, circling in the muddy waters close to the wall . . . proudly clutching the tennis ball. How on earth were we going to get her out? It looked impossible. Then I spotted a small piece of foreshore that had been uncovered by the tide and, using stones, encouraged her to swim towards it.

Now she was standing on a tiny patch of mud, surrounded on one side by a sheer wall and the other by a fast-flowing river more than 60 metres wide. The tide was coming in fast and soon the little island would be submerged. I thought about calling the Coastguard or the RNLI; they would have to rescue her by boat, I thought, but then a young boy pointed out that there was a form of ladder recessed within the wall. Without thinking, I leapt over the railings and began to descend to the little castaway dog.

The assembled crowd grew a little larger as I reached Maggi. Now how on earth was I going to get her back up? There was only one thing for it. I scooped up the soaking wet, muddy dog and began to climb the ladder.

I'm not sure if you've ever tried to climb a ladder with a heavy weight under one arm and only one hand to grip it, but it's pretty precarious. Maggi weighed 25 kilos, not an easy shape or weight to hold under one arm. I was just grateful it wasn't Inca – there's no way I could have carried her under one arm.

Slowly I worked my way back up the ladder, holding the rusting bar with one hand before taking a step and then letting go briefly to catch the next bar a little higher up. Several were broken or missing, which required a little acrobatics along the way.

I'm not quite sure how I defied gravity, but somehow man and dog made it to the top. There was a round of applause as I placed Maggi, still clutching her ball, onto the ground. If this didn't impress Marina, nothing would. I had just saved her dog. Admittedly, it was my throw that had got her into this situation, but that is a minor technicality.

Fortunately, all was well, and we didn't look back. Our fate was sealed. In years to come we would often joke about the time

I saved Maggi and how it was probably a ploy by the dogs to bring us together.

But while my actions may have looked brave to Marina, it was nothing compared to the actions of working Labradors over the years which have been nothing short of heroic.

Labradors excel as search-and-rescue dogs. A mixture of good scent detection and a desire to work has brought these dogs to the frontline of terrorist activity and natural disasters. Earthquakes, floods, tsunamis, hurricanes . . . the list is long and impressive. Where humans are prone to emotional anguish at the sights they have to deal with, dogs just go to work. They search relentlessly, day and night, for survivors of natural disasters. Then, when all hope is lost, they become cadaver dogs, hunting for the remains of victims.

Rescue dogs not only work diligently and risk injury by going into areas deemed unsafe for humans, but they also offer comfort to their human handlers. It is beyond the scope of this book to celebrate every amazing Labrador tale, but a few serve to highlight the depths of loyalty and ingenuity shown by this breed when faced with a situation in which their master is vulnerable. As one professional disaster-relief dog trainer says, 'You don't have to explain things to a Lab. They just do it.'

The recent conflicts in Afghanistan and Iraq have seen Labradors deployed across the region, creating their own inseparable bonds between soldier and dog. When Marine Pfc Colton Rusk was stationed in Afghanistan he shared a cot with his beloved dog Eli. On 6 December 2010, the day that Rusk was shot and killed by Taliban sniper fire in Afghanistan, the dog had just located IEDs (Improvised Explosive Devices) but couldn't protect his master from three Taliban bullets. When Pfc Rusk fell to the ground his dog crawled on top of him to shield him.

Rusk's family decided to adopted Eli after the tragic events in Afghanistan – he had loved that dog and his family wanted their son's legacy to live on. Eli was the second dog to be adopted by a fallen service member's family, and emotions ran high at the official repatriation. 'We're going to share the love that we have for our son with something he loved dearly,' said Kathy Rusk. 'It had given me some comfort knowing Colton wasn't alone over there. Colton would have loved knowing that [we were adopting Eli]. Like he used to say, "what's mine is his". We're Colton's family, so now we're Eli's family. [The adoption process] did get our minds off the sadness.'

The story makes my heart skip. Poignant and moving, but to anyone who has loved and been loved by a Labrador, completely relatable.

Military statisticians claim that as many as 2,700 dog teams have been in action as sniffer dogs in Iraq and Afghanistan at one time, many of them Labradors. As General Petraeus, the US Commander in Iraq in 2008, said, 'The capability the Military War Dogs bring to the fight cannot be replicated by men or machines. By all measures of performance their yield outperforms any asset we have here in our inventory.' The high regard with which the US military regards Labradors was again made clear in February 2010 when the *Wall Street Journal* reported that the US Marines shot a farmer's dog which was acting aggressively towards an explosives-sniffing Labrador. This was because they could not afford to have the valuable asset maimed or injured. 'We consider the dog another marine,' was the official line.

Dogs are used by the military for vigilance, protection, pursuit, and search and rescue, but mainly for detecting the scent of homemade bombs. Improvised Explosive Devices are responsible for the deaths of more than half of the coalition troops killed in Iraq and Afghanistan. When war dogs are in operation, the IED detection rate rockets to as high as 80 per cent. No form of technology is more efficient than an eager-to-please, non-aggressive, strong-nosed dog.

The Labrador's independent nature enables it to work off the lead, which keeps the handler a safe distance from hidden bombs. The handler keeps control with voice and directional commands and reads the dog's body language in order to raise an alert, and the trackers can pick up a scent and follow it back to the bomb's delivery boy. Dog and handler live side by side; the dogs endure the same conditions as their handlers and receive treatment for Post Traumatic Stress Disorder (PTSD) as and when it is required. They even wear tactical body armour and flak jackets to protect their vital organs. In sensitive situations that are deemed unsafe for humans to operate in, a dog can go in wearing a flak jacket fixed with a wireless camera and speakers so a handler can see what the dog sees and instruct it by audio command.

The fate of dogs in war is largely unreported; many survive to work on repeated deployments, but some are killed in action or suffer Post Traumatic Stress Disorder. The story of Corporal Kory Wiens from Oregon and his MWD Cooper, a four-year-old golden Labrador, stands out as a poignant reminder of the risks that dog and handler run in the course of duty. The close pair were killed together by an IED while patrolling in Iraq in 2007. Wiens had planned to adopt Cooper when the dog retired at the age of eight or nine, and when Wien's family received his personal effects, they were moved to unpack a large number of Cooper's dog toys. Their ashes are buried together in Wiens's home town and their story caught the imagination of animal lovers. A dog park at Fort Carson, outside Colorado Springs, is also dedicated to commemorate the duo.

The story of Gunner, a golden Labrador diagnosed with the canine version of PTSD, is an example of the incredible bond that can develop between man and dog. In 2004, an American couple, Deb and Dan Dunham, lost their son Jason to an insurgent's grenade in Iraq. Their process of grieving and healing came after they adopted an injured bomb-sniffing dog that was haunted by war, and also called Gunner. The process of healing on both sides is slow but steady. As Dan Dunham says, 'Everybody's resilient – human and dog', whilst acknowledging that he and his wife can't heal all of Gunner's scars any more than they can forget their own grief. Dan's sentiment sums it up. 'To us it's like Jason died yesterday. To Gunner, whatever happened to him – it's probably like that happened yesterday. We get up each day and find a new way to get through the day, realising that Jason's not here. We have to pass that on to Gunner.'

From the tough, dangerous life of hardship and treacherous insecurity, incredibly heart-warming stories emerge. In 2008, Sarbi, a Labrador/Newfoundland cross who worked as an Australian Special Forces explosives detection dog, went missing in action. She was caught up in a battle with the Taliban when a rocket-propelled grenade exploded close to her, injuring her handler (among a group of eight other soldiers). The force of the blast broke the lead that attached her to her handler's body armour and, in the confusion that ensued, she was nowhere to be found. She remained 'missing in action' for 14 months. The Australians kept reminding other soldiers of their loss and asked them to look out for her. Eventually Sarbi was spotted by an American soldier with a local Afghan man who was aware that the Australians were missing a dog. Sarbi was then liberated and flown by plane to be reunited with her Australian handler.

There are more . . .

Tangye, a black Labrador bought as a puppy by a British soldier from a dam worker in Afghanistan, became a camp mascot, patrolling alongside the soldiers for five years. Named after a village on the Helmand River lying opposite the forward-operating base at Kajaki, Tangye was 'fearless under fire' and would be the first to jump through a hole if soldiers blasted one into a compound wall while they cleared a village of insurgents. L/Cpl Meheux, a 44-year-old Territorial Army soldier, said Tangye had done more patrols than most soldiers and he should be honourably retired to keep him safe. 'When the lads are under contact (fire) he will run up and down the line barking and wagging his tail. It's as if he is shouting encouragement – he loves it. But we had to stop him coming out on patrol about a week ago. The IED threat is just too high. It's gone through the roof. The Taliban probably know about him and think he is a sniffer dog. I'm sure they would want to make him a target,' L/Cpl Meheux said. 'He has been such a morale-booster for the lads. It would mean an awful lot to the lads to know he was safe.'

The campaign started by the men of C Company, 3rd Battalion, The Rifles, to raise money for Tangye to be found a home in the United Kingdom was successful. With the help of

Labrador Retriever Rescue Southern England and British war dog charity NOWZAD, the costs were raised and Tangye was flown to Britain, where a home was found for him.

Perhaps unsurprisingly for a country of dog lovers, Great Britain has an official means of recognising hero dogs of war: the animal equivalent of the Victoria Cross. The Dickin Medal, a bronze medallion which bears the words 'For Gallantry' and 'We Also Serve' within a laurel wreath, was named after Maria Dickin, founder of the People's Dispensary for Sick Animals (the PDSA). It was introduced to acknowledge 'outstanding acts of bravery displayed by animals serving with the armed forces or civil defence units in any theatre of war, worldwide'. It has been presented to 66 animals since its introduction in 1943.

Several Labradors have received the award for their contributions to the War on Terror, among them Sadie and Treo. Sadie, a Royal Army Veterinary Corps arms and explosive search dog and a veteran of Iraq and Bosnia, received her Dickin Medal on 6 February 2007 for an incident in 2005 when she located a remote-controlled bomb made from a pressure cooker, filled with TNT and covered with sandbags. The device, which Sadie detected through nearly a metre of concrete, was designed to kill rescue workers responding to the suicide attack. Sadie's handler, Lance Cpl Karen Yardley, shouted warnings that quickly cleared the area as a bomb disposal team moved in.

The report on the incident read:

'For outstanding gallantry and devotion to duty while assigned to the Royal Gloucestershire, Berkshire and Wiltshire Light Infantry during conflict in Afghanistan

in 2005. On 14 November 2005 military personnel serving
with NATO's International Security Assistance Force in
Kabul were involved in two separate attacks. Sadie and
Lance Corporal Yardley were deployed to search for
secondary explosive devices. Sadie gave a positive indication near a concrete blast wall and multinational
personnel were moved to a safe distance. Despite the
obvious danger Sadie and Lance Corporal Yardley
completed their search. At the site of Sadie's indication,
bomb disposal operators later made safe an explosive
device. The bomb was designed to inflict maximum
injury. Sadie's actions undoubtedly saved the lives of
many civilians and soldiers.'

Treo, also a Royal Army Veterinary Corps Arms and Explosives
Search dog, received his Dickin Medal from Princess Alexandra
at the Imperial War Museum on 24 February 2010. Treo, an
eight-year-old black Labrador, and his handler, Sergeant Dave
Heyhoe, were deployed in 2008 as part of 104 Military Working
Dogs Support Unit attached to 8 Platoon from the 1st Battalion
Royal Irish Regiment near Sangin in Afghanistan. On 15 August
2008, while acting as forward protection for 8 Platoon, Treo
located a 'daisy chain' Improvised Explosive Device which was
designed to trigger a series of bombs on a roadside where soldiers
were about to pass. It was subsequently confirmed that the device
uncovered was new to the area and would have inflicted significant casualties. Further, on 3 and 4 September 2008, Treo's actions
on patrol were reported as saving the platoon from guaranteed
casualties, again as the result of an IED. Without doubt, Treo's

actions and devotion to his duties, while in the throes of conflict, saved many lives.

Major Graham Shannon, commander of the 1st Battalion Royal Irish Regiment, said, 'Treo's nose kept my soldiers safe from the roadside bombs planted by the Taliban to maximise injuries and deaths among troops. The Military Working Dogs play a vital role in our patrols in detecting these devices and the dogs themselves show enormous amounts of courage doing this work every day, and on many occasions while under attack. It is fitting that Treo has been recognised for the protection he afforded the troops through the presentation of his award.'

In a twist to the story, it transpired that Treo had been a very naughty two-year-old who snapped and growled at people until his owners donated him to the army to 'straighten him out'. He was retired in August 2009 and adopted by his handler, Dave Heyhoe, and his family.

For those of us with a snoring dog asleep at our feet or on our bed, it may be hard to reconcile that with the image of the real 'dogs of war'. When I think of my domesticated, non-working Labrador, it's hard to imagine her serving in battle, but it is a reminder that all the virtues and attributes for which the Labrador is famed and loved worldwide, when harnessed and channelled can and have created some of the most heroic dogs of our time.

11 September 2001 was a date few of us will ever forget. Like most people, I remember the day vividly, and I remember where I was when the Twin Towers were attacked. I was filming on a wherry on the Norfolk Broads with Inca for *Countryfile*. We were sailing the calm waters of the broads, our heavy brown canvas sails propelling us along. Inca was sitting at the front of

the wherry. It was blissfully quiet, and a world away from the events that were just beginning on the other side of the Atlantic.

Alongside the 2,606 people who lost their lives when the Twin Towers collapsed was Sirius, a golden Labrador explosive detection dog who was put in his basement kennel in the South Tower when his handler, Port Authority Police Office David Lim, went to join the emergency evacuation following the initial explosion in the North Tower. When Lim set off in response to the alarm, he did not know that a plane had crashed into the top of the tower, which was then likely to collapse. Trapped in the rubble, Lim did not get out in time to go back and save Sirius. The dog died when the South Tower collapsed.

When Sirius's body was recovered, he was accorded the same respect as all the victims. All machines were silenced and everyone lined up and saluted as Officer Lim carried out his flag-draped companion while a prayer was read. Eight months later, more than a hundred dogs and their police handlers gathered in tribute to Sirius at Liberty State Park across the Hudson River. In a moving ceremony to honour the 'thousands of police dogs who play vital roles in battling terrorists, smugglers and other dangerous criminals,' officers filed by a wooden urn and a medal dedicated to Sirius. Bagpipes played and a 21-gun salute echoed. Sirius' metal bowl, recovered from the wreckage, was presented to Lim.

Two other working Labradors caught up in the blasts were awarded the Dickin Medal for their calm and dutiful heroism. Salty (also known as Dorado) and Roselle were golden Labrador guide dogs who, remarkably, led their blind owners to safety. Salty, a four-year-old, was the trusty eyes for his master, blind computer technician Omar Eduardo Rivera, who was at work on the 71st floor of the WTC North Tower. Thinking he had no chance of escape, Rivera let Salty off his lead, urging him to go, but the dog came back to him within a few minutes and nudged him towards an emergency staircase. With the help of Rivera's supervisor, Donna Enright, Salty led his master down what must have seemed an interminable spiral of 71 flights of stairs. About halfway down, a co-worker, trying to help, tried to take Salty's lead but the dog refused to leave Omar. They reached safety just before the tower collapsed.

Roselle went on to be posthumously named American Hero Dog of the Year 2011 by the American Humane Society. Roselle was her owner Michael Hingson's fifth guide dog and they had been a team for almost two years on 9/11. Roselle was asleep under the 78th-floor desk of her owner, who worked as a computer salesman, when the attack commenced. She was awoken by the plane crashing into the building 15 floors above them. Despite the smoke, panic and confusion around her, Roselle calmly led Hingson and 30 other people to stairwell B and down 1,463 steps out of the tower. The descent took just over an hour. Just after they exited the tower, the giant construction collapsed, sending up clouds of flying debris. Once clear, Roselle calmly led her owner to the safety of a subway station, where they helped a woman who had been blinded by falling debris. When they arrived home, Roselle immediately began playing with her retired guide dog predecessor, Linnie, as if nothing important had happened. When she died in 2011, Hingson wrote a book of their 9/11 experience entitled *Thunder Dog: The True Story of a Blind Man, His Guide Dog, and the Triumph of Trust at Ground Zero.*

Many Labradors were among the 300 search-and-rescue dogs that worked at Ground Zero. They worked tirelessly, often in places that were inaccessible to humans. Where even the most professional emergency service workers struggled with emotion at the scenes before them, the dogs worked diligently. Handler John Gilkey's Labrador, Bear, found remains in more than 40 sites, but he also became a focus of comfort for fellow workers. 'I remember Bear falling asleep in a firefighter's lap . . . People would stop and pet him on the pile every day. They would discuss their dogs or ones they had owned, and for a brief minute or two they had left the terror of that massacre scene,' he said. 'He helped them as much as he kept me grounded during our tour.'

Kinsey was a black Labrador whose first job after qualifying as a Canine Commando was an 11-night stint at Ground Zero. 'She wanted to find someone alive and she would bark and nip at me in frustration,' recalled Bob Deeds, her handler from Texas Task Force One. These Labradors offered the consistency of love and loyalty in a time of worldwide turmoil.

As well as the annual Dickin Medal, which has been awarded for animals showing military gallantry for over 70 years, the PDSA also awards a civilian equivalent for animal heroism, the PDSA Gold Medal. This award was instituted in 2001.

'No human or, for that matter, animal is aware of their heroic capability until placed in an extraordinary situation requiring extraordinary action. The PDSA Gold Medal recognises this.'

To date all 23 recipients awarded the PDSA Gold Medal have been dogs, two of them Labradors and both police explosives search dogs who worked bravely, obediently and tirelessly in the terror attacks in London on 7 July 2005.

Vinnie the Lab and his handler, PC Dave Coleman, were already on duty in the City when they were urgently deployed to the terrorist explosion at Russell Square tube station, during Britain's 7/7 attacks.

Vinnie began a search for secondary explosive devices to find a clear and safe route for medical assistance to reach the many casualties. Overcoming choking smoke and poor visibility, Vinnie searched the 1.6km-long route from Russell Square to the bomb-damaged train at King's Cross and completed a search of King's Cross station. Through the devastation and human trauma, Vinnie didn't hesitate in carrying out his duties. Vinnie really was one of the unsung heroes of 7/7.

Another Labrador, Billy, and his handler, PC Rob Brydon-Brown, were deployed to what they thought was a train crash at Aldgate tube station. They were met by a sea of casualties and soon realised there had been an explosion. Billy was tasked with securing the scene by searching the length of the underground tunnel. Despite immense heat and poor visibility, Billy didn't falter from his duties and he remained on call throughout the day, attending 21 locations in response to alerts from the public.

Another Labrador honoured as a hero in the aftermath of terrorist bombings was Zanjeer, a golden boy who worked with the bomb squad in Mumbai in March 1993 and saved thousands of lives by detecting more than 3,329 kilos of the explosive compound RDX, 600 detonators, 249 hand grenades and 6,406 rounds of live ammunition. He also helped to avert three further bomb explosions in the period after the initial blasts. Following his death at the young age of eight, from bone cancer, Zanjeer was buried with full police honours, including a wreath of flowers being laid on his body by a senior police officer.

Bosnich, a Labrador cross, was awarded a PDSA Gold Medal for bravery and gallantry in leading rescuers to 73-year-old Mark Corrie, who had gone missing on the wild Cumbrian fells in August 2006. What was remarkable was that the dog, who belonged to Corrie's daughter, Lorna Farish, was not a trained assistance dog; he was simply a family pet. His story illustrates some of the inherent instinct whereby a dog will do anything to keep the person whom he is accompanying alive and safe. Corrie and Bos had set off on their regular walk in Gelt Woods near Brampton, but the sudden onset of bad weather disorientated them. Corrie wandered around for hours, confused. In exhaustion, the elderly man took shelter in a gully on Cumrew Fell, a bleak, exposed elevation. When he failed to return home at the expected time, his daughter called the police. For two days, police search dogs and volunteers from mountain rescue teams scoured the district for man and dog, but without success. A helicopter from RAF Boulmer employing heat-seeking thermal imaging cameras also joined the search, but still there was no sign of the pair. The fortuitous rescue came when four local walkers decided to investigate a dog howling on the south side of the fell, 11 kilometres away from Brampton. At the top of the first ridge they spotted Bos, whose howl changed to a persistent bark as he engaged their attention. The dog immediately guided them to where Mark Corrie was sheltering – cold, confused, dehydrated but miraculously unhurt. It was clear the dog had used his body heat to keep the pensioner warm in between his stints of determined howling and barking. Bos stayed at the pensioner's side as they waited for the emergency services, and Mark Corrie was rescued on his 74th birthday.

The Labrador that claims the accolade of 'the most decorated dog in the world', though, is Endal, a golden-coated service dog who in his lifetime was named Dog of the Millennium, earned a PDSA Gold Medal and was the subject of a book celebrating his role in 'saving' one man and his family. Saving, in this case, was about psychological stability.

I was fortunate to meet Endal a number of times over the years. Inca, too, had the privilege to meet him. Passive and kind, Endal was the typical Lab who would sit obediently at his owner, Allan Parton's, feet.

Parton was a Royal Navy engineer who suffered a severe brain injury in a car crash in 1991 during the Gulf War. After spending five years in hospital, he returned to his wife and children a changed man. His memory had been wiped. Unable to walk, talk, read, write, or remember anyone or anything prior to the accident, Parton was confined to a wheelchair, angry, frustrated and unwilling to participate in life. During the summer of 1997, Parton's wife Sandra took her husband to a charity called Canine Partners. The charity trains dogs to help people with various impairments, enabling them to have more independence.

A young dog wandered over to his wheelchair, Parton slowly gave him a pat on the head and the dog promptly jumped on to his lap. The dog was Endal, a big bouncy Labrador who was to give Parton and his family a new lease of life. The partnership with Endal brought Parton back to emotional health. They developed an incredible bond, inventing their own sign language so that they were in cahoots together. With Endal's help, Parton could pick up anything he wanted, from a hat to a hamburger.

This incredible partnership also rekindled Parton's social skills and built his confidence and ability to talk again, because Parton had to learn to do so, if only to communicate with all the people who stopped to pat his dog. Endal notched up plenty of canine 'firsts': he was trained to withdraw cards at an ATM, empty the washing machine, bark for attention at the bar in pubs, post letters, bring over the phone and collect the knife, fork and plate for Parton's lunch.

Allan was so proud of that dog. Each time I met him, he talked of nothing but Endal. Their relationship was extraordinary. The pride Allan had for Endal was only matched by the loyalty shown by his beloved Labrador. And he wasn't just good at the soft stuff. In 2002, Endal saved Parton's life when Allan was knocked out of his wheelchair in a car park and left unconscious on the ground. Without delay, Endal put Parton in the recovery position, covered him with a blanket from the wheelchair and moved the mobile phone close to his mouth. When Parton came around, the dog trotted off to alert staff at a nearby hotel. Endal's quick actions saved him that night, just as he had saved him in so many other ways before and since.

Parton once said, 'My greatest fear, because of my head injury, is that one day when Endal is no longer faithfully by my side, because of my memory problems, I will forget him.'

It is the faithful Labrador owner's greatest fear, to forget our best friends.

CHAPTER EIGHT

YELLOW COATS

While I can't say she ever saved my life, Inca certainly helped change it in ways I could never have expected.

When I rowed the Atlantic Ocean in 2006, Marina, still then my girlfriend, packed me off with a series of envelopes. One for each day I was away. In each one was a photograph, almost all of which were of Inca, Maggi, or both. They invariably made me cry.

More importantly, they emphasised just what a perfect girl Marina was. Kind, fun, clever, thoughtful, funny, beautiful, but most importantly of all, a fellow dog lover.

Marina and I talked of little else. Our Labradors, Maggi and Inca, were like our children. I think they call them fur babies. I could never have married anyone who didn't love dogs as much as I did; my family used to joke that it would be Inca that decided the fate of various girlfriends, not me. To give them all credit, they all loved Inca, but Marina was different. Inca didn't love her, she *loved* her. What's more, Marina even had her own Lab.

We spent endless weekends exploring beaches and forests with the dogs. We travelled from Devon to Norfolk with Inca and Maggi, and at weekends we would walk the parks of London together. We were a perfect match. The four of us.

Rowing across the Atlantic gave me a chance to reflect on my life, and more importantly to plan my future. I couldn't think of anyone I'd rather spend the rest of my life with. So I made Marina a little ring made from some rope we had on our rowing boat and I proposed.

A year later, Marina and I married. We tied the knot in Portugal, too far to take our matchmakers, so instead the dogs were immortalised as figurines on top of our wedding cake, and also in a letter I read out to our guests purporting to be from the dogs, and how our marriage had in fact been entirely engineered by the dogs. It probably wasn't far from the truth.

The dogs were never far from our thoughts.

To make up for them missing the wedding, we devised our honeymoon around them. I had organised for us to spend a week on Taransay, because it was important for me to show Marina the island that had changed my life, but subconsciously I wanted to take Inca back, too, and allow her to share the experience with Maggi. By now the two dogs had become thick as thieves and were inseparable.

We loaded up the Land Rover and together, once again, we began the long overland journey up to Scotland. I'll never forget Inca's excitement when we leapt from the boat onto the shore. She was home! She raced around the island to all her favourite spots – she still knew where the fence was high enough to crawl underneath and where the gates were.

Of course, it wasn't a typical honeymoon. Goodbye tropical island, azure seas and bikinis, hello rain, mud and Gore-Tex jackets. It was cold and wet and we had to cook basic food on a woodburning stove, but it suited us. We walked and walked and walked. I introduced Marina to the island while Inca did the same with Maggi. They both had to understand how important this place was to the two of us.

When I first suggested the idea of having a dog as my luxury item for my year as a BBC castaway, I promised the filmmakers that Inca would be more than just a pet. She would be a working dog, I insisted. She would earn her keep. She would play with the children, but more importantly she would help us with the farming, rounding up pigs and sheep.

Of course, this never happened. Inca resolutely remained a pet. She was scared of the pigs and felt slightly bullied by the sheep, who would knock her sideways whenever she wandered into their field. She used to try to forage in the pigs' pen until they decided her paws looked slightly tasty. I have a hilarious photo in which it looks like Inca is being devoured by four piglets, while in fact she is just being gummed by them.

Inca was never going to work, which is surprising given how many Labradors have been used by charities and organisations to help others.

I have experienced these working dogs first hand. My father helped launch Hearing Dogs for Deaf People more than thirty years ago. The idea was simple: dogs, mainly Labradors, of course, would be trained to help those who were visually impaired. The dogs were taught to alert owners to a doorbell or a crying baby and to wake them up when the alarm bell rang and warn them if a fire or smoke alarm sounded. Above all, the dogs acted as messengers of an invisible disability. Without the bright yellow bib saying 'Hearing Dog', their owners' deafness remained invisible, often leading to conflict if someone asked them something and they didn't answer.

When Inca was seven I decided to enrol her as a Pets As Therapy dog. PAT dogs are trained to go into retirement homes and even education centres for those with learning difficulties. The idea is that a well-behaved dog goes into the home to meet all the residents because dogs bring love and calmness. To become a PAT dog, the animals need to go on a course to ensure they have the right temperament to deal with everyone from the young to the old and those with learning difficulties.

Inca had been there for so many big changes in my life. She was there through the highs and the lows. She was there for births, deaths and marriages. By my side as I lived, loved and lost, from first dates to the break-ups, through the highs of my career and the lows – the paparazzi, the tabloid tales. Inca had seen it all.

I had became dependent on Inca. She was my confidant; I told her all my fears and my troubles and she soothed and calmed me when I was anxious or stressed. A head squeeze with Inca always worked.

There are so many different ways in which people show affection to their dogs. There is, of course, the clichéd head pat. 'Pat' is a terrible description – who 'pats' their dog? To pat insinuates you bounce your hand up and down on its head. A pat is what someone unsure of a dog will do.

I prefer to stroke the head. Always moving my hand with the

fur – the hand moves from the crown of the head down onto the silky ears. I like to feel the soft velvet of the skin on the inside of the ear, feel the heat of the skin. The fur of the ear is like cashmere, fine and soft. If I'm really honest, I would often rub the ear on my cheek. Again, you stroke the nose. A Labrador loves this; not only does it help exfoliate any loose hairs on their face but they like the sensation of the touch. All Labrador owners will also be familiar with the 'Labrador nudge', where the dogs nudge their faces under your hand, compelling you to stroke them.

It has been proven by research that to stroke a dog lowers the pulse. Blood pressure can even drop. Science has proven what we dog owners have long known.

Then there is the body rub; full strokes across the back and flank of the dog. And let's not forget the belly rub – Labradors love belly rubs. Inca used to groan in ecstasy when I rubbed her belly; the sensation would often trigger a nerve that would send her leg into an uncontrollable swing.

When I was sad, I used to hold her head in my hands and hold it close to my face. Those eyes. They would heal anything. A Labrador's dark eyes have a kind of knowingness within them. Wise and worldly, they can heal a broken heart and mend a damaged ego.

Can you imagine the power of a stroke, a caress or a tummy tickle for residents in homes or people institutionalised by disabilities? Often these are people with few social interactions. In many cases they have inadvertently been starved of affection. The dog is the enabler. The dog is able to act as channel for affection and a lightning rod for stress, conducting the stress down through their paws.

Dogs often work to break down social barriers – they can often act as a trigger for conversation. Any dog owner will relate to this; you would be frowned upon if you didn't engage fellow dog walkers in idle chitchat, or in the least greet them with a cheery 'hello' or 'good morning'. It's amazing how dogs enable us to rewrite our own social rules. The dog acts as a catalyst of conversation. There is no need to talk about the weather; you can ask how old he or she is instead, or perhaps comment on their glossy coat, or ask the owner if you can say hello to them.

Inca passed all the PAT tasks with flying colours . . . until it came to the paws. The final test was the paw squeeze. You could roll Inca around on the floor and blow in her face. You could pull her tail and tweak her ears. You could scrunch her scruff and lift her gums. You could pretty much do whatever you wanted . . . except touch the paws.

Of course, all dogs have their little nuances, the little quirks that make them unique. Inca's was her paws. They were gigantic, like those of a bear, but she hated to have them squeezed. I can only attribute this to an early paw-cleaning experience from which she never fully recovered. The result of touching her paws with any pressure was that she would emit a low, deep grumble. She never snapped or bit, but she grumbled like a lion. To the uninitiated it probably sounded a little scary.

The jolly trainer had been thrilled with Inca. She had kept telling me that she was a perfect candidate for the role . . . until she squeezed her paws.

Inca emitted her low grumble. She squeezed again. Another grumble.

'Oh dear.'

It took all the persuasive distraction I could muster to take Inca's attention away from the paw squeeze for her to pass the test. It wasn't quite the calibre of her yellow-coated assistant dog cousins, but it was a start.

Inca loved her PAT visits. It was mutually beneficial, of course. Inca, like most dogs, loved physical contact. She was happiest with a hand placed upon her head or body. She would nudge you until you made contact. Even when she lay down, she would lie on top of your feet, her back wedged close to your legs.

It is the reason why Labradors have worked so well as assistance dogs, perhaps one of the oldest and most iconic being the Guide Dogs for the Blind.

There are nearly 5,000 guide dog owners in the United Kingdom, with approximately 900 new partnerships created each year, and each treasured guardian-cum-companion has an average working life of five to six years. The guide dog service is an amazing charity which receives no government funding and depends solely on public support in order to enable blind and partially sighted people to enjoy the same freedom of movement as everyone else. It costs £5 per day to support each working guide dog partnership; the lifetime cost of a dog is around £50,000.

Dogs trained to provide assistance to people with disabilities need to be confident, friendly, intelligent, willing and of a stature that makes them robust enough for a harness but small enough to curl up under the seat of a bus or train. All working dogs have to fulfil clear-cut tasks, but not even guide dogs are in total control when fulfilling their assistance role; they are in partnership with a human. Today the Labrador dominates the global guide dog population, with national breeding centres dedicated to producing dogs of suitable temperament. The Guide Dogs for the Blind Association in the United Kingdom breeds up to 1,500 puppies a year, mainly using Labradors and Golden Retrievers, as well as crosses of the two breeds.

The puppies go out to family homes for their first year then return to undertake a training programme taught by specialist instructors which typically will teach them how to lead a person in a straight line from point A to point B, unless told otherwise; to stop for all changes in elevation, such as steps and kerbs; to find doors, crossings and places which are visited regularly; to stop for overhead obstacles such as tree branches; to avoid obstacles in their path; and to resist chasing cats and squirrels. Although a trained dog will guide their owner across the road, it is up to the human to decide where and when to cross safely. The constant companionship, at home and at work, keeps up a strong and rewarding level of respect and trust between the dog and owner.

Though the Labrador was late to become the guide dog of choice (the classic working dog, the German Shepherd, was initially the most desirable canine helpmate), the history of the international guide dog movement is worth recapping as a testament to the intrinsic human drive and belief in the potential of man's relationship with the dog. The first record of a dog assisting a visually impaired person is depicted in a wall painting that was excavated at Herculaneum, preserved under 20 metres of ash following the eruption of Vesuvius in AD 79. A Chinese scroll dating from 1200, now preserved in the Metropolitan Museum in New York, also depicts a blind figure being led capably by a dog.

Similar likenesses appear in woodcuts, paintings and engravings around the world up until the eighteenth century, a time which is notable for a landmark painting by Gainsborough, *Blind Man on the Bridge*, featuring a dog showing its master the way. The question is, did these figures build on a relationship with a trusty dog they already owned and loved, or were these partnerships deliberately built up to serve a practical purpose?

The first organised attempt to use dogs as eyes came in 1780 at Les Quinze-Vingts hospital for the blind in Paris. Shortly afterwards, in 1788, Josef Reisinger, a blind sieve-maker from Vienna, trained a thick-furred Spitz so impressively that people witnessing the spectacle of dog leading man didn't believe he was blind at all. The Germans and Swiss developed their own method of training dogs, but it wasn't until the First World War, when thousands of soldiers returned from the front line having had their sight damaged by poison gas, that demand prompted a guide-dog training scheme. The catalyst was an incident seen by German physician Dr Gerhard Stalling.

Strolling through the hospital grounds with a visually impaired patient one day, he had to leave the man with his dog while he treated another urgent case. When he returned, he saw from the way the dog was behaving that it was 'looking after' the blind patient. In 1916, Dr Stalling opened the world's first guide dog school for the blind in Oldenburg. The school grew and many new branches opened across Germany – preparing up to 600 dogs a year to aid ex-servicemen and blind people in Britain, France, Spain, Italy, the United States, Canada and the Soviet Union – until a lack of suitable dogs forced closure of the venture in 1926.

Waiting in the wings – or on her Swiss farm named 'Fortunate Fields' – was an American lady, Dorothy Harrison Eustis, who took up the mantle. Having studied the successful methods for training guide dogs at a large centre in Potsdam, near Berlin – which produced 12 fully trained guide dogs a month – Dorothy and her husband George were already training German Shepherds for the army, police and customs service in Switzerland. Impressed with what the Potsdam School was achieving, she submitted an account of her visit to an American newspaper, which was published in November 1927. This resulted in a flurry of letters, including one from Morris Frank, a blind man who wanted to help introduce guide dogs to the United States, and which prompted her to try to train a dog for him to take back to the States. In April the following year, Morris Frank arrived in Switzerland and trained with guide dog 'Buddy'. When Morris and Buddy returned to New York they won over sceptical journalists by crossing a wide, busy street without injury. Lo and behold, here was America's first guide dog.

Eustis went on to launch the Seeing Eye School in America and Italy. Realising that the major problem would be training suitable instructors, she returned to Switzerland and trained four instructors; two went to the Seeing Eye School in New York, one to Italy, and one, Captain Laikhoff, came to Britain at the request of two British women, Muriel Crooke and Rosamund Bond, who had heard about the Seeing Eye. In 1931, the first four British guide dogs completed their training and the four members of that first class wrote to express gratitude for the increased mobility, dignity and independence they had thanks to their dogs:

*Not only has my dog given me glorious freedom and inde-
pendence, never known since pre-war days, but also delightful
companionship* – Allen Caldwell

*A guide dog is almost equal in many ways to giving a blind
man sight itself. Judith has been worth her weight in gold
. . . I would not be without her for a day.*

Three years later, the Guide Dogs for the Blind Association was
founded in the United Kingdom.

One of the most famous guide dogs in Britain belonged to
the blind politician, David Blunkett. Her name was Lucy the
Labrador.

Blunkett and Lucy were inseparable. Beyond his own personal
reminiscences, David Blunkett's guide dogs are immortalised in
British political history. In March 1999, as Education Secretary,
he records that he was sitting listening to a speech about education measures in the Budget given by his Conservative shadow,
David Willetts, when Lucy was sick on the carpet near the
government front bench. What to do? Deputy Speaker Michael
Lord faced the possibility of suspending the debate to allow the
vomit to be cleaned up, but Government Whip David Jamieson
stepped in, calling discreetly for cleaning materials to be brought
into the chamber and dealing with the mess himself. Meanwhile,
Lucy was led out for a bowl of water. Later in the debate, Liberal
Democrat education spokesman Dan Foster made political
mileage from the incident saying he often felt a 'sense of nausea'
when Willetts spoke. Jamieson, meanwhile, passed David
Willetts a note saying his speech had given his opposite number's

dog a turn for the worse. 'He was looking quizzical because he didn't realise what had happened, and then he roared with laughter.'

In 1994, Tony Blair, then leader of the opposition, sprang up to face John Major in Prime Minister's Questions and accidentally stood on Lucy's ear. She yowled in pain, whereupon Blair uttered an apology, words which were faithfully recorded in Hansard – marking out Lucy as surely the first dog to receive an official apology from a future prime minister.

Inca never met a prime minister, but she did once meet Michael Portillo . . .

As the years rolled on, Inca and Maggi grew older and greyer, but I was away filming in Svalbard when her world, and mine, changed forever.

We had finished filming and had returned to the main city Longbearyen, and, as with so many of my overseas shoots, I had been out of contact for nearly two weeks. In that time, Marina had left several text messages asking me to call her.

'Inca's had a funny turn,' she told me calmly when I finally got through. She explained that Inca had been asleep on her bed when she had suddenly had some sort of fit in the middle of the night. It was nearly silent, and it was only because Marina had felt her convulsing body that she knew something was wrong. She had called my father and Inca was now with him while he ran a series of tests to understand what it was and why it had happened.

If I'm honest, I wasn't really worried. I assumed it was just a one-off episode and, what's more, Marina had done a good job at playing the whole thing down. How wrong I was. I flew

home and went straight to my parents' house. I rang the doorbell and, as always, Inca came flying towards me . . . and then
she collapsed.

One of her legs was aloft and she was on her side. Her face
was contorted and she was showing her teeth in a type of grimace,
and then the shaking began. First slowly and then more violently.
Her legs kicked and white foam began to appear around her
mouth as she frothed.

I was shocked. I wanted to hold her tightly, to protect her,
but my father warned me that she might bite in her disorien-
tation. All we could do was watch helplessly.

She was having an epileptic seizure. This would be the first
of thousands as her epilepsy dominated our lives. My father
spent the next week doing every test and study he could think
of to try to discover the cause. When all that failed, he sent her
to Cambridge University where she had MRI scans of her brain
and then the rest of her body. Half her thick coat was shaved
off to allow easier access for the various tests.

In the meantime, Inca became a shell of herself. She was
permanently in some kind of drug-induced stupor. With no
proven cause, Dad had been forced to experiment with various
cocktails of drugs to try to control the increasingly common
seizures, which by this time were happening up to eight times
a day.

We had discovered that one of the best ways to pull her from
the post-trance-like stupor was with a bowl of smelly food, so
we had started stockpiling cans of wet dog food and positioned
them around the house within easy reach. For up to an hour
after each seizure, Inca would sway and stumble around the

house like a drunk. She would walk into walls and fall down stairs, and then if you held a smelly bowl of food in front of her face, she would begin sniffing at the air like she was blind. The sniffing would become more and more furious as she struggled to work out where the smell was coming from until she finally noticed the bowl in front of her face. We would then let her eat small amounts before repeating the action. I'm sure it was more to do with her deep love of food than it was scientific, but it really seemed to work.

While we were able to pull her from her post-epileptic stupor, we simply couldn't get to the root of the cause and Inca's health continued to deteriorate.

'If she gets any worse,' warned my father, 'you're going to have to make a tough decision.'

It was a thinly veiled warning that her time might be up.

I was devastated. She was only seven, and it seemed so cruel. Surely I was owed more than seven years? A dog's life already seemed too short, but this was just so unfair.

Gradually we altered the concoction of medication and with time Inca began to return to her normal self. The seizures continued, but we learned to live with them. Eventually we discovered that Inca's seizures were triggered by a sudden burst of mental and physical activity: the doorbell, pursuing a squirrel, running for her dinner, chasing a ball, or just the excitement of me coming through the door.

This meant that life became a little complicated. Both my parents and I got rid of our doorbells and placed notices warning that an 'epileptic dog' lived there and not to knock or ring the doorbell but to phone our mobiles to let us know they had arrived.

The park was much more complicated, though. A simple missed scenario of someone throwing bread to the ducks could instigate a seizure as Inca's Labrador appetite kicked in and she bolted for the bread. We always knew a seizure was about to happen because one of her hind legs would pull up uncontrollably, then her whole body would freeze and she would topple onto the ground.

While we became pretty accustomed to these daily turns, it often caught other dog walkers unawares. I lost count of the number of times I knelt at Inca's side, shouting at her to try to bring her back, when other dog walkers would run over, phone in hand ready to call the vet and offer assistance. Inevitably they thought she was dead or dying, and I always felt guilty for their concern. Not that I didn't worry myself; it was just that we dealt with the seizures so frequently that they became the norm.

It's a strange thing to say, but the epilepsy became a part of her character. Her personality. Her daily life. So much so that Marina bought her a little glittery green pencil case in which we kept her medicine. The biggest impact of her illness was that it increasingly became easier and safer to leave Inca at home when I went out or away. While I trusted Marina and my family to cope with the seizures, I was worried about leaving her with strangers, even for the shortest of times, because it was in these drunken, trance-like stupors after the seizure that Inca could spend up to an hour in an other-worldly haze. To those who didn't know her she might appear normal, but those were the times when she would get herself into trouble. Sometimes she would just bolt and run, often towards water or a road, and nothing would stop her. I would need to rugby tackle her and hold her tightly to stop her drowning or being hit by a car.

In some respects I think her epilepsy brought us even closer together. I became her full-time carer, and as such I was much more acutely aware of her behaviour. I had to second guess her instinct and read every situation.

With each seizure, Inca starved her brain of a little more oxygen, and the cumulative effect of this began to affect her behaviour. While it certainly wasn't funny, there was one incident that was as hilarious as it was heartbreaking.

We had driven out to Austria for the summer. Each year we would pack up the car and load the dogs for the long winding journey to the Austrian Alps. Once there we would spend several weeks with Marina's family high on a mountainside overlooking Salzburg. One morning I came down to breakfast.

'Have you noticed anything strange about Inca?' asked my father-in-law, Jonathan. 'She seems to be behaving a little oddly,' he continued.

I looked at Inca, who had taken her usual position in the kitchen. She was standing and wagging her tail. She looked herself.

'Inca,' I called. Her head turned and she began to move . . . backwards.

She stopped, tail wagging.

'Inca,' I called, and once again she ran backwards, away from me. Somehow, Inca had lost the ability to walk forwards. Fortunately, this quirk didn't last long, and soon enough normality returned and Inca could walk again as before.

Inca's epilepsy dominated the second half of her life. I was always on edge. I hated her seizures; they made me sad. Each one damaged her brain a little more and Dad had always warned me that one day she might not come out of one.

I'll never really know what caused the epilepsy, but it was more than likely her pedigree. The small circle of breeding in the pedigree Labrador world has led to various health issues from hips to epilepsy; you just need to look at the slightly incestuous history of the Labrador and the progenitors to realise that there has been plenty of interbreeding. I have no doubt in my mind that this was ultimately the root cause of Inca's ills. Of course, I will never really know that for a fact, but it opens the debate about where the breed has come from and, more importantly, where it is going.

The recent trend towards designer dogs, whereby two breeds are mixed together, is testament to the fact I'm not the only person worried about the health risks in pedigree dogs. By mixing two breeds, the gene pools are being further diluted, mitigating some of the health risks found in traditional breeds like the Labrador. Even when it comes to new variations of dog, the Labrador never drifts far from fashion, and while it's tempting to be swayed by one of these crossbreeds, there is still something enduring about the Labrador as we know it. It is like a classic car; however much other cars progress in terms of technology, the classics are still the most covetable. They may be temperamental and break down a great deal, they may cost a small fortune in veterinary bills, but they have stood the test of time.

I suppose in some ways, by continuing to be seduced by the pure-breed Labrador, I am part of the ongoing cause.

CHAPTER NINE

ALL THE PRESIDENTS' DOGS

There can be few things in life that are as levelling as a Labrador.

In this glorious country of ours where everything, from the clothes we wear to the accent we have, is dissected in a socio-analysis of our status, the Labrador remains relatively neutral.

It has often frustrated me how the smallest nuances of our behaviour and our choices can be used to define us by hierarchy: the place in which we live, the type of home, kitchen, car, brand of clothes we have, or the school we attended. All of these elements can be examined and used to make assumptions about our social status.

Politicians are terrified of it. Look at our current incumbent, Cameron, so worried about being classed as posh that he tries every opportunity to be the people's Prime Minister. Take his obligatory annual photo in the fish market, or at the fishmongers. He is trying to say 'look at me, supporting hard-working fisherfolk'. The fish and the market are both unclassifiable.

Even the former leader of the opposition, Ed Miliband, was at it during the General Election in May 2015. He allowed himself and his wife to be photographed posing in their annexe kitchen rather than in their large family kitchen in an effort to play down his social and financial status.

Of course, dogs have been at the forefront of political campaigns for years. The dog has given politicians the world over the chance to say something big about themselves. Indeed, the very fact that they have a four-legged furry friend speaks volumes in itself. It says, 'I am a caring, considerate person', it speaks of a selfless attitude in which you think about others more than yourself. Exactly the attributes we want from a leader.

If only Labradors could speak.

The Labrador has been the pet of choice for a number of world leaders of the modern era. Safe, loyal and biddable – there's that word again.

The Labrador is safe. It's not just their character that is safe, but also what they represent. They are apolitical. Let's take some examples. If a presidential candidate chooses a Rottweiler, a German Shepherd or a Doberman, it immediately speaks volumes about the owner. Don't get me wrong; all three have their own unique character traits, and I have met many examples of each over the years, but what do they *say* about you? They say aggressive, powerful, controlling . . .

Another example is the Bichon Frisse, the miniature Poodle or Chihuahua: again, all lovely dogs, but they say high maintenance, vain, preened. Now these might be some of the traits you are looking for in a politician, but it is also likely to divide the voters.

A politican needs a dog that defies our culture of stereotyping. Of course, the Labrador isn't without its own stereotyping. Indeed, it would be a predictable choice for our Eton-educated, Bullingdon Club fighting Prime Minister. True, they have a reputation as the country tweed choice of dog, but it is so much more complex than that. Where the stereotyped owner makes up just 2 per cent of our population, the Labrador remains our most popular dog. It doesn't add up.

The Labrador is far, far more popular than that. The Lab looks as at ease in a small terraced house as it does in a stately home. You are as likely to see one in the back of a Skoda as you are the back of a Volvo. Their popularity has not gone unnoticed by those in power, of course. Over the years Labradors have been given high status within the courts of such leaders, being accorded quasi-regal treatment, special handlers, food fit for the gods and privileged access and proximity to their masters beyond the dreams of the CIA. Not only have they been present at some of the defining moments of recent history, but they have had their own role in shaping that history. What dog owner does not talk to their dog, ask him or her rhetorical questions on a daily basis? Should I do this? Should I go ahead with that? Shall I call in the secret police? Shall I invade Ukraine?

The dogs in my life have been privy to the greatest secrets I've never told. They were there during my teenage angst. They were my loyal ears in all times of trouble or confusion.

After an official visit to Romania in the 1970s that included a hunting expedition, David Steel, the Liberal politician, found to his horror that Romanians used children instead of hunting dogs to retrieve game. Disturbed by this revelation and feeling compelled to do something about it, Steel hit upon the idea of sending his host, the Romanian leader Nicolae Ceauşescu, a Labrador puppy from a litter that Gilly, Steel's black Labrador, had given birth to. He named the puppy Gladstone 'after the Balkan connection' (referring to the then leader of the British opposition's role in denouncing the Bulgarian horrors at the time of the April Uprising of 1876, when he called up Britain to withdraw its support from the aggressor Turkey). Steel shipped Gladstone to his new Romanian master, who renamed him Corbu, meaning 'Raven'. It was an inspired gift. Dog and dictator became inseparable, and Bucharest courtiers even affixed the honorific 'Comrade' to the dog.

Wrapped in dictatorial pomp, Comrade Corbu even had his own motorcade to whisk him, nose in the air, in the back of a Dacia across Bucharest. He was later paired with Shenona, a black Labrador bitch. The two dogs ate the finest cuts of meat, spaghetti Bolognese and sausages – all of which would be first tasted and tested by a special doctor before being given to the dogs. Their coats were shampooed daily with Fa, a German brand, and sprayed with deodorant. Their paws were wiped clean with a special cloth and brush. At night, the Comrades slept on a chaise longue at the foot of the Ceauşescus' bed; by day, they lolled in their 'kennel', a villa furnished with all the bourgeois trappings of a bed, television and telephone. At 2pm, the dogs would pull a blanket over themselves with their teeth and doze until 4pm. Meanwhile, says Steel, the Romanian ambassador in London would roam Sainsbury's for dog biscuits and Winalot and would send them on a weekly basis to Bucharest by diplomatic bag.

The next occasion on which the two politicians met was at

President Tito of Yugoslavia's funeral in 1980. Ceaușescu had
no recollection of Steel, and he stared blankly when the Liberal
leader greeted him. A man of fine mettle and iron will, Steel
pushed on with, '*Ça va, le chien?*' The penny dropped and the
Romanian despot burst colourfully into congeniality and hugs.

Of course, no matter how high you elevate a dog, to 'Comrade'
and even beyond, it will always remain a dog, with a dog's
instincts and urges. This was shown one Sunday in 1985 when
Ceaușescu paid a visit to Brâncovenesc Hospital, in Bucharest,
then in danger of demolition to make way for the Boulevard of
Socialist Victory. During a discussion about the future of the
hospital, Corbu's attention understandably drifted off, whereupon he espied a cat. Now, the hospital had been rat-infested
partly due to unaffordability of rat poison, so the doctors had
resorted to using cats to cull the rodents. Corbu, by then precip-
itously promoted from 'Comrade' to 'Colonel', considered it his
job to cull cats, and promptly ran after the feline, heedless of
his master's cries to stop. When Corbu caught the cat by the
throat, a bloody duel ensued. Ceaușescu screamed at his bodyguards to act. Three men leapt into the fray to prise the beasts
apart. Peace was restored at the cost of three scratched bodyguards, a wounded cat and a nose-bloodied Colonel Corbu.
Feeling that this was an insufficient price to pay, Ceaușescu
himself then struck Corbu with his fist, more in despair than
anger: his closest companion had abandoned him. For a cat.

The story didn't end there. Ceaușescu was famously paranoid
about disease and infection, and, fearing poison, he never wore
the same clothes twice. So he ordered for the Securitate to have
the cat checked for disease. The hospital was turned upside down

as doctors and nurses sought out cats and produced them for inspection by the Securitate to find the one that had earlier caused the ruckus. It wasn't until 10.30 that night that the culprit, one of many cats caught that evening, was identified by a bloody gash to his side. It was immediately hustled into a secure guarded room while the hospital's carpenter fashioned a special cage for the feline. The following morning the cat was taken to the Institute of Veterinary Medicine to be checked for disease. After a fortnight, the cat got the all clear. During those two harrowing weeks, Colonel Corbu was banned from Ceaușescu's presence. Nevertheless, the doctors knew that the incident had sealed the hospital's fate. It is ironic that a man as paranoid about health as Ceaușescus should preside over the closure of a hospital, more so because of a fight between a cat and a 'Colonel'. But at least Corbu had proven his credentials as a hunting dog.

Vladimir Putin is quickly becoming the bogeyman of our age. His muscle-flexing rhetoric is bringing Europe to the brink of war, but apart from his warmongering, little is known about the man who many describe as the most powerful in the world.

While few Russians know much about Vladimir Putin's family, almost all Russians and many others beyond Russia's borders know about Koni. As H. Goscilo writes, Koni 'serves as Putin's attribute not only in children's pictures of him, where Koni is depicted as Putin's sidekick, but also elsewhere, and with more obvious importance than the human members of Putin's family. Koni definitely holds an important place in the public's imagination as a metonym of Putin's power.'

Born in a government cynology centre in Noginsk, a few kilometres east of Moscow, which specialises in breeding crack dogs for search and rescue, Koni is a female black Labrador Retriever which was given to Putin in 2000 by Sergey Shoygu, General of the Army and Minister of Emergency Situations. Putin uses his beloved Labrador Koni for his own political power in the games of diplomatic one-upmanship that are part of the cut and thrust of life in Russia. Indeed, a cold war of sorts is being waged between Russia and the West in which presidential pets are the weapons. As George W. Bush recalls in his memoir, *Decision Points*, while he and Putin strolled the birch-lined grounds of Putin's dacha one summer, a large black Labrador bounded up to them. Putin turned to Dubya and said, 'You see? Bigger, stronger and faster than Barney [Dubya's Scottish terrier].'

In a society like Russia, which favours strong leaders and where expressions of certain emotions can be interpreted as a weakness, Koni offers an emotional crutch. As Putin once said at a press conference in response to a question about his moodiness, 'As far as bad moods go, of course I have them like any other person, but in those cases I try to consult with my dog Koni – she gives me good advice.'

Koni has become elevated to something of a national icon. She accompanies the Russian president to meetings and to greet world leaders. When Putin first met Angela Merkel, he brought Koni, knowing that the Germany Chancellor is afraid of dogs, having been bitten by one as a child. In December 2003, when Koni gave birth to eight puppies, which were given away to Russian citizens, politicians and foreign ambassadors, Koni was hailed as 'a Mother Hero', the official title that the Soviet State, keen to raise the national birth rate, bestowed on unusually fertile women. In February 2005, there was even a youth campaign to promote Koni to President.

For Putin personally, Koni seems to be the wife figure that perhaps he otherwise lacks. At a press conference in Sochi in 2003, the officially sponsored newspaper *Rossiyskaya Gazeta* reported that when it was time to begin the meeting, Putin's security detail tried to prevent Koni from entering the meeting room. Koni was having none of it. Pushing her way past the guards, she rushed down a staircase to confront Putin as he and a group of journalists made their way to the room. Turning to face Putin, Koni barked loudly at the President, as if to say, 'Where the hell do you think you're going without me?' Among journalists present was Irena Lesnevsky, founder and owner of REN TV, one of the largest private television channels in Russia. 'So who else here can bark at the President?' she demanded.

Koni repeated the trick one year later when, at a children's New Year party at the State Kremlin Palace, she gave security guards the slip and managed to join Putin on stage while he was in mid-speech to media, politicians and the public.

Food is, of course, the Achilles heel of powerful leaders, no more so than in Russia, which has a tradition of Czaricide by poison. It is known that Vladimir Putin has all his food tested for toxins, and so, not surprisingly, Koni's eating habits are food for debate and speculation. Does the same presidential protection extend to her? Putin once issued a press statement saying, 'Please don't feed my dog.' Koni, however, has her own ideas on the matter. At a meeting of members of the United Russia Party at Putin's residence at Novo-Ogaryovo, convened to discuss the local food industry, a special tea was prepared to bring the meeting to a close. While the meeting was still in session, Koni rocked up and wolfed all the food, pastries, biscuits and jellied puddings. As an astonished bodyguard said, 'Koni ate everything!'

These incidents raise questions about the effectiveness of Putin's close protection bodyguards. After all, if a dog can elude them . . . ? Putin's first question upon attending a 2008 demonstration of the Global Navigation Satellite System (GLONASS) that the Russian army had developed in answer to the American GPS system, was, 'Can I use it on my dog?' Later that year, Koni was fitted with the first GLONASS-enabled collar. Should any of Putin's rivals or enemies wish to bug or otherwise harm Koni, they must somehow distract the attention of 21 geostationary satellites that track Koni's exact whereabouts 24/7.

Doubtless, Koni is indeed bigger, tougher, stronger, faster and meaner than Barney, Dubya's terrier. It also appears that she is tougher, smarter, faster and meaner than Putin's bodyguards, too. Koni for President!

The United States also has a rich tradition of presidential dogs. Indeed, the announcement of the First Dog is arguably as important as the President himself.

'You want a friend in Washington?' Harry S. Truman, US president (1945–53), famously said. 'Get a dog.' Truman himself shunned canine company (in 1947, he passed on a gifted blond Cocker Spaniel by the name of Feller) and indeed he preferred to hustle pet-free. However, other US presidents from George Washington onwards have kept a colourful menagerie of pets – from horses, goats and parrots to lions, hyenas and even alligators. (John Quincy Adams' donated alligator terrorised White House guests from its bathroom nest; President Hoover's son Henry kept a pair that sometimes roamed the White House grounds.)

Having served his first term of office dog-free, Clinton decided one year into his second term to get a dog. Bill, Hillary and Chelsea Clinton studied various breeds. 'Chelsea wanted a teeny-weeny dog she could carry around with her, and Bill wanted a big dog he could run with,' wrote Hillary in *Living History*. 'We worked through that and finally decided that a Labrador would be just the right size and temperament for our family and the White House.'

So, in December 1997, a three-month-old chocolate Labrador puppy was acquired from Tony Harrington, a lawyer from Washington DC, who bred dogs. When puppy met president and the canine scampered into Clinton's arms, both parties were smitten. 'All we had to do was figure out a name,' continues Hillary. 'Buddy' evoked Bill Clinton's great-uncle Henry 'Buddy' Grisham, who had recently died and whom Clinton often described as a major influence.

Before naming their puppy, though, the Clintons consulted one of the White House butlers, name of Buddy Carter, to see if he objected to their puppy sharing his name. Carter loved the idea, and began to identify with the dog. Months later, when Buddy the dog was sent for neutering, Buddy the butler was seen shaking his head and muttering, 'Not a good day for Buddy today. Not a good day at all.'

Bill and Buddy the Labrador quickly became firm friends. Evoking Truman, Clinton's spokesman Mike McCurry said, 'It is the President's desire to have one loyal friend in Washington.' Buddy appears to be the first and so far only example of a Labrador as First Canine.

'We brought our family traditions, favourite pictures, and

personal mementos to make the White House feel more comfortable,' wrote Hillary Clinton when the Clintons moved into the White House. 'But it wasn't until . . . Buddy walked in with his rawhide bone that this house became a home. Pets have a way of doing that.'

Buddy the dog fell in with Bill Clinton's routine. He slept at his feet in the Oval Office and stayed up late. He strolled the White House grounds with Bill, and accompanied him to Camp David. He was present at the historic Israeli–Palestine peace talks in 1998 that took place between Netanyahu and Arafat, and he even adopted some of his master's characteristics. 'He loved people, possessed a sunny optimistic disposition, and had the ability to focus and concentrate with singular intensity,' wrote Hillary. When the Lewinsky scandal broke and Bill was in the doghouse, Buddy alone kept him company. Buddy's two obsessions were tennis balls and food; he would chase and retrieve balls until he dropped, 'then he'd get up and look for his dinner.'

While family life centred on Buddy, Socks, the feisty adopted stray cat, felt usurped. Buddy and Socks' long-standing feud became infamous, so much so that it was eventually decided that one of them must go: Socks was given away to Clinton's former personal secretary, Betty Currie.

Like Socks, Buddy littered a family of fan clubs and websites in his honour. In her book, *Dear Socks, Dear Buddy: Kids' Letters to the First Pets*, Hillary Clinton explained how letters to Buddy and Socks were sorted, read and answered at the US Soldiers' and Airmen's Home.

After President Clinton's second term expired and the family moved to their home near Chappaqua, NY, Buddy became a familiar sight tugging on his leash or chasing tennis balls. Tragically, Buddy's sunny exuberance eclipsed him. On 2 January 2002, while playfully hounding a contractor's van into the street outside the Clintons' home, to the despair of chasing Secret Service agents, he died when a car struck him. Buddy was rushed to Chappaqua Animal Hospital where he was pronounced dead. The Clintons were away on holiday.

'We are deeply saddened by Buddy's death,' said the Clintons in a statement. 'He was a loyal companion and brought us much joy. He will truly be missed.'

In 2005, the Clintons adopted Seamus, their second chocolate Labrador.

Another American statesman, Henry Kissinger, was a Labrador lover. In 1988, Kissinger lost his yellow Labrador Tyler to cancer. He was heartbroken and the situation brought out the softest side of the formidably tough National Security Advisor who had served under Presidents Richard Nixon and Gerald Ford. Gregory MacEwen, who treated the dog, was impressed that Kissinger got right down on his knees in his three-piece silk suit while Tyler lay prone and whispered into his dog's ear how much he loved him. When Kissinger was Secretary of State, he sometimes brought his Labrador to the office. Mighty are some of the names today of important US diplomats who, as assistants to Mr Kissinger, were awarded the dubious honour of taking his Lab for a walk around the block. One neighbour of Kissinger in New York recalls watching Kissinger take his ailing black Labrador out for walks in an 'open red children's wagon'. The Kissingers later had a black Labrador named Abigail. In 1994,

Kissinger successfully lobbied to have a Labrador Retriever reprieved from death by lethal injection for chasing postmen: Smokey, a five-year-old Labrador Retriever from Danville, Virginia, was found guilty of chasing (but not biting) three mail carriers in his Danville neighbourhood, thus becoming the first dog to face sentencing under Danville's tough 'three mail carriers and you're out' ordinance. Smokey was sentenced to die by lethal injection, but the case turned political when 40 members of the Italian Senate signed a petition on Smokey's behalf, and that world-class humanitarian and retriever owner Henry Kissinger urged the judge to 'Restore the dog to the owner and tell the mailman to take a different route.'

Dick Cheney, Vice President of the United States from 2001 to 2009 under George W. Bush, owned two Labradors; Jackson (black) and Dave (golden). In 2011, Dave hit the headlines for all the wrong reasons. After launching an attack on Barney, Dubya's feisty Scottish terrier (the one whom Vladimir Putin liked to mock), in full view of other guests, he was banned from the main lodge at Camp David. Dave would regularly accompany Cheney to the US presidential retreat in Maryland, and on this occasion, he joined his master in the Laurel Lodge, scene of official meals and meetings. 'No sooner had we walked inside did Dave catch sight of the president's dog, Barney,' relates Cheney in his memoir, *In My Time.* 'Hot pursuit' ensued. Clearly, Dave subscribed to his master's zero tolerance to terrorism and launched a pre-emptive strike to neutralise the terrier. The dogs ended up duelling in the dining room, where wives of several Cabinet members were enjoying breakfast.

'What's going on here?' demanded Dubya on seeing the

mayhem. It was not an unreasonable question. Cheney sedated Dave with a pastry from the breakfast buffet and then hauled the mutt back to the cabin where he and his wife Lynne were staying.

'I hadn't been there long when there was a knock at the door,' Mr Cheney writes. 'It was the camp commander. 'Mr Vice President,' he said. 'Your dog has been banned from Laurel.'

In Dave's defence, there is ample video evidence of Barney's aggressive tendencies (possibly an insecure reaction to jibes from Vladimir Putin). In 2008, Barney bit a Reuters' reporter on camera, causing a wound that had to be patched up by the White House physician.

Ever since Napoleon Bonaparte's life was saved by a Newfoundland, when the non-swimming French leader slipped and fell from a ship into the sea, dogs and French Heads of State have had a close bond, possibly closer than between French Heads of State and other human beings. 'Here, Gentlemen,' said Bonaparte, upon safely reaching shore on the back of the Newfoundland, 'a dog teaches us a lesson in humanity.' In the same vein, De Gaulle once said, apparently paraphrasing Harry S. Truman, 'The better I get to know men, the more I find myself loving dogs.'

Just as dogs have historically accompanied the French nobility, so in recent years they have become power accessories to the country's democratically elected politicians. Labradors in particular seem to be the preferred breed. This might seem a strange choice; Labradors are an unlikely pet for a French president. Few of the characteristics commonly associated with Labradors seem particularly, well, French: loyal, obedient, playful, happy, gregarious, charmingly naïve, bourgeois, reassuring and trustworthy. Yet every French president since the early 1970s has owned at least one Labrador.

While in power, Valéry Giscard d'Estaing had two black Labradors: Jugurtha, a chocolate male, and Sandringham Samba, a black male that HM the Queen gave d'Estaing in 1976 (Samba was trained in the Queen's English, suggesting a cunning ruse to introduce the language of Shakespeare and Churchill into the highest political circles of France). In retirement d'Estaing acquired two more Labradors: Beauly and Typhon. '*Il poursuit: 'Ce sont des chiens très accueillants. Quand je reviens, ils sautent en l'air de joie. Je n'ai jamais rencontré d'être humain qui, lorsque je reviens, saute avec une telle allégresse'*. 'They are very friendly dogs,' he said. 'When I come back, they jump in the air with joy. I've never met a human being who, when I get back, jumps with such joy . . .' Today, ex-President d'Estaing owns Spinee, an 'adored' golden Labrador Retriever who, in 2014, underwent surgery, much to the consternation of both the former president and Spinee's army of fans.

Labradors were the preferred power pooch for François Mitterrand, Jacques Chirac and Nicolas Sarkozy, who named them Baltique (black female), Maskou (black male) and Clara (sand-coloured female) respectively. Mitterrand, a serial Labradiste, also had Nile, a black male. Attitudes towards dogs became a political hot *pomme de terre* when, during the 1988 presidential election campaign, Jacques Chirac tore snarling into François Mitterrand, accusing him of raising the tax on dog food.

Baltique, Mitterrand's Labrador, had the run of the Élysée Palace. According to Daniel Gamba, author of *Interlocuteur privilégié, j'ai protégé Mitterrand*, when he went missing, life at the Palace stopped dead. At Mitterrand's funeral in January 1996, he had made arrangements for Baltique to travel alongside his coffin in the State cortège as it wound from Paris to Mitterrand's final resting place at Jarnac.

When Jacques Chirac finally won power in 1995, his Labrador Maskou was wrongly accused of devouring the Élysée Palace ducks. However, rumours persist of canine misdemeanour during Sarkozy's rule. The Élysée's famous Salon d'Argent is almost unchanged from the sumptuous room that Napoleon's sister Caroline Murat created in 1807, where Napoleon signed his abdication in 1815 and where President Félix Faure died in the arms of his mistress, Marguerite Steinheil, in 1899. But those fang marks in the chair legs, and those stains on the soft furnishings – whose are those? Sarko's incontinent alpha pooches, Toumi the Chihuahua, Clara the Labrador and Dumbledore the Terrier, were allegedly partial to gilded silk-swathed nineteenth-century furniture: as an hors d'oeuvres they snacked on antique sofa legs, as an entrée they gnawed at braided chaises longues, and for dessert they sunk their teeth into silk cushions. The repair bill ran to thousands of euros, excluding the cost of the new braids, silk covers and the time of the Mobilier National staff. If Sarko couldn't control his dogs, how, one might ask, could he control France? More importantly, this canine affront was a logical but dramatic response to the threat of a tax on dog food: a tax on dog food is a tax on France's patrimony!

In Britain, Labradors have proved useful both as PR tools and as voter bait to politicians on either side of the political divide.

On the left, the Jarrow March of 1936 got a PR boost when Paddy, a black Labrador, joined in and was adopted as the march's official mascot and even appeared on the cover of the newspapers. Harold Wilson, two times Prime Minister, used his golden Labrador, also called Paddy, not only to burnish his image while being photographed on holiday in the Isles of Scilly, but also to cover up his own stupidity: in August 1973, Wilson, yet to serve his second term at Number 10, fell from a dinghy into the sea and nearly drowned. Jo Haines, the Labour leader's spin doctor, blamed Paddy for the accident, despite Isabel Wolff, whose family rescued the weasel Wilson, insisting that she saw Paddy chained to a hut on the beach, looking 'affable and unperturbed'. Clearly, Paddy voted Conservative. Ken Livingstone, ex-MP and ex-Mayor of London, campaigned for the mayoralty in 2012 alongside Coco, his golden Labrador. Livingstone lost in the poll to Boris Johnson.

On the right, David Burrowes, MP (Conservative) for Enfield, Southgate, uses Cholmeley his golden Labrador to help raise awareness of responsible dog ownership. Neil Parish, MP (Conservative) for Tiverton and Honiton, owns Wilberforce, a golden Labrador and winner of Westminster Dog of the Year 2012. Edwina Currie, ex-MP for South Derbyshire, says that George, her chocolate Labrador, is 'Here for me when people are horrid,' adding superfluously that George is as 'daft as a brush'.

While dogs have obvious photogenic appeal, Andrew Murrison, MP (Conservative) for South West Wiltshire, put his finger on another reason why democratically elected politicians prefer pooches. Buster, his black Labrador, is an 'asset' on the doorsteps, he told the *Daily Mail*, because, 'Constituents' dogs can normally smell Buster on my clothes, and this makes them very friendly to me.' Result: Murrison's 'animal magnetism' wins votes.

I love the idea that this simple, humble, honest dog has been on the front line of the political elite for decades, if not centuries. It always surprises me that David Cameron doesn't have a Labrador; it would be the perfect dog for a country-living, family-loving prime minister. Come to think of it, he doesn't have a dog. Maybe that's the reason why no one really likes him. As I say, never trust a man who doesn't like dogs.

From dictators to presidents, meglomaniacs to prime ministers, all have shared their lives with the humble Labrador. Throughout history these dogs have been privy to conversations and decision making that have affected us all. If only Labradors could speak.

CHAPTER TEN

LAB OF ALL TRADES

I never cease to be amazed at the ingenuity and enterprise shown by Labradors when they are trained and willing to take on human tasks that increase the quality of life of others, particularly individuals with physical disabilities. They are often best friend, nurse, personal assistant and au pair (or should that be au paw), complete with wagging tail.

The list of roles we have found for Labradors keeps on growing. One of the new areas for these dogs has been to help children with autism. Eleven-year-old Charlie McGowan was three when he was diagnosed with autism. An apparently healthy little toddler, he lost all linguistic ability at the age of two. He wouldn't allow anyone to touch him and he stopped making eye contact with people, including his mother, Kirsty. He would only sleep for one hour each night, meaning that he was awake for the remaining 23 hours of the day. Charlie would become extremely stressed and repeatedly banged his head until he bled. His autism was so

severe that his mother was warned that by the time he turned 10
she wouldn't be able to look after him herself. Kirsty didn't give
up, though. Determined to ensure she had tried everything to
help her son, she realised she would have to do something radical.
Although Charlie could cope in his own home with a support
system around him, leaving the house was almost impossible for
him. 'We couldn't attend doctors' appointments or even go into
the shops,' said Kirsty. 'In a supermarket Charlie would become
so distressed that he would drop to the floor, scream, and bang
his head repeatedly. The only way I could get Charlie out of the
house was in a wheelchair. However, if a plane went overhead or
if a bus stopped close by, Charlie would become stressed and
inconsolable. We were unable to get out more than once a week,
it was just too much of a challenge.'

Support Dogs was set up to increase the independence and
quality of life for people with medical conditions. The charity
provides, trains and supports specialist assistance dogs to provide
help with everyday tasks for people with physical disabilities,
give advance warning of seizures for people with epilepsy, and
provide safety and support for children with autism and their
families. Kirsty put her son's name on the waiting list. 'It was
the best thing I could have ever done. I spent five years hoping
and praying every day that we would get the call. Then finally
it came and it changed our lives. There was a dog for Charlie,
a black Labrador named Bailey. Charlie's autism is so severe I
was unsure how much difference Bailey could make, but I
couldn't have been more blown away.' Charlie had never walked
on his own two feet since he was two and a half years old. When
he was first attached to Bailey, he walked straight down the

street for the first time. 'After seven and a half years my son was walking on his own,' his mother recalls. 'It makes me want to cry every time I think about it. Now we have Bailey, we finally have a life. When we leave our front door Bailey is a godsend and Charlie's best friend. Once he's attached to Bailey the world makes sense. Just having him attached to him means he can process sensory information better. And if something worries Charlie, he bends down and hugs Bailey. It's not just Charlie's life that Bailey has changed. He knows when I'm becoming stressed or anxious and calms me down. I love him and I'm so grateful for everything he does for us both.'

Support Dogs is also responsible for training the remarkable Hetty, a Labrador cross who won a Guardian Angel Award in the augural Britain's Animals Honours Award Show, broadcast on ITV in April 2013. Hetty is thought to be the world's first guide dog who is also a trained medical assistance dog. Officially she is classified as a Dual Assistance guide dog. Specifically, she can detect the signs of a seizure before her owner, Tony Brown-Griffin, who is registered blind and has intractable epilepsy, suffers one by recognising the physiological changes which are invisible to the human eye. In the past, Tony's epileptic fits had caused her to smash headfirst through a glass shower screen, fracture her wrists and break ribs falling in the street. 'The unpredictability of seizures is frightening – not knowing if it's going to happen in the middle of a busy road,' says Tony. 'Even going up the stairs would be terrifying because if I had a seizure I could fall. So much of what I do revolves around Hetty. She is fundamental to what I do. Everything I can do is because of her. Without her, I'd be stuck.'

The clever thing is that Hetty gives different signals to

distinguish the severity of the oncoming attack. Sensing a minor seizure, Hetty nudges Tony and rests her head on her lap, giving her 15 minutes to prepare herself to sit somewhere soft until it passes. If it's a major or life-threatening seizure, she paws Tony's leg and Tony knows she has precisely 42 minutes to prepare. Hetty will also lie with Tony as a comfort until she recovers. A fit can last between five and ten minutes and Tony suffers approximately two major and four minor attacks a week. Hetty is also vigilant to ensure that Tony's two young children don't witness their mother in the hold of these scary fits. Tony lost her sight six years ago, so Hetty also does the jobs that a traditional guide dog undertakes – helping Tony dress by removing her socks and trousers and helping with sleeves, taking the laundry out of the washing machine, even stripping the household beds.

As well as acting as a guide and seizure dog, Hetty has also picked up new skills. Tony also has severe food allergies, and when she was new to her, Hetty would try to alert her to a reaction but Tony would ignore her and tell her to lie down as she wasn't acting as if it were a seizure alert. 'Then one day my brother-in-law said, "Should Hetty be standing on the table?" and I turned around and she was there. Again I told her off, but about 10 minutes later I started feeling really bad with an anaphylatic shock reaction. We realised that was what she was trying to warn me of. Now she jumps up at my belt to let me know. People assume that she's misbehaving – they misinterpret her. Or when we're out, people assume she's got a sore paw because she holds it up slightly. When I explain what she does, they're always impressed.'

What other good uses can a dog's extraordinary instinct and vigorous sense of smell be put to? Dr Claire Guest, a psychologist, was convinced that dogs could sniff out cancer. While she was working to prove her hunch, she received the most emotive affirmation that she was right about the potential of dogs to operate as medical detection agents.

In the middle of experiments to train her own Labrador, Daisy, to pick up the smell of chemicals given off by tumour cells, Daisy began to act strangely around her. Instead of being her normal, placid self, Daisy seemed uptight and uncharacteristically attentive – exactly the kind of behaviour that she had been taught to display if she detected the odour of cancer. Had the dog's work/life balance gone awry? No. Dr Guest could never have anticipated that the first person Daisy would diagnose would be herself.

'She kept jumping up on me,' she told the *Telegraph*. 'One day she bumped into my chest with her nose. It was unusually sore, and there seemed to be a lump there. I had a fine needle biopsy, but it came back clear.'

After more unsettling behaviour from Daisy, Dr Guest had a core needle biopsy and was diagnosed with early stage breast cancer. She underwent treatment and has since been given the all clear.

'Had I not had Daisy's early warning, I would have had a very poor prognosis,' she said. 'It would have gone undetected for much longer and could have been more serious. I have my dog to thank for the fact that I'm standing here today.'

That was in 2009, when Daisy was just a puppy, and the charity working on this controversial technique was only one year old.

Dr Guest's dog is now the Medical Detection Dogs organisation's most distinguished 'advanced cancer dog', able to detect different cancers through smelling a patient's breath, urine or skin. She heads up a growing number of dogs now being trained as 'pattern recognition biosensors' to detect cancer in this way and, as the pioneer, was awarded the Blue Cross Medal for her work. The medal is awarded by the Blue Cross charity to an animal that has changed or saved someone's life – and Daisy had (to date then) sniffed more than 6,500 samples and detected more than 550 cases of cancer.

Daisy now helps to train a team of 12 dogs at the Medical Detection Dogs' head office and is a senior consultant for the United Kingdom's first ever trial using canines to detect breast cancer.

The science behind it is simple in theory: to harness a dog's acute sense of smell to pick out chemicals given off in cancer cells in samples of a patient's breath, skin or urine. The dogs do not meet the patients who have provided samples: they work in a laboratory setting, sniffing along a row of samples attached to a small conveyor belt. On the command of 'Seek-seek', they sniff all the samples and return to sit and bark by any which emit a cancerous smell.

The idea of your pet dog having a sixth sense and trying to warn you about something is not uncommon, but it was two doctors, Hywel Williams and Andres Pembroke, who first put forward the idea of dogs as potential medical detective agents in a 1989 article in *The Lancet*. Their claims were re-aired on BBC Radio 4 in 2001 by the orthopaedic surgeon Dr John Church (who had equally controversially introduced wound-cleaning maggots to the NHS). Dr Guest heard the programme, contacted Dr Church and together they formed a research team at the Buckingham NHS Trust, with funding from an anonymous philanthropist. They conducted ever-larger clinically robust, proof-of-principle studies – largely detecting for cancer of the bladder, breast and prostate – and published the encouraging results in the *British Medical Journal*. The voice of the sceptics has now reduced to a whisper and several cancer specialists have come out in support of the scheme. For example, Dr Alan Makepeace, a senior oncologist at the Mount Vernon Cancer Centre in Middlesex, who was initially dismissive of the involvement of dogs, told the *Telegraph*: 'The data is robust. Dr Guest's passion is driven by good science, not anecdotal evidence. There is so much we don't know about the natural world. A more effective early test could be worth its weight in gold.'

The results are not 100 per cent accurate, but the charity's recent study into the detection of prostate cancer shows the dogs achieved 93 per cent reliability compared with the 75 per cent detection of patients who don't actually have cancer when examined after traditional PSA tests, a blood test which can detect early stage prostate cancer. This work is being developed to examine the potential of offering second-line screening for men.

It would be impractical to use dogs pervasively, but their value could lie in determining whether further invasive and uncomfortable tests are needed when a patient is presenting inconclusive symptoms. Already, a prototype 'electronic dog nose' has been developed by an Israeli-Arab chemical engineer at the Laboratories of Nanomaterial-based Devices in Haifa.

Hossam Haick has created the 'NANOSE', which it is hoped could be used to analyse a patient's breath for traces of cancer.

As the pioneering charity in this area, Medical Detection Dogs has two aims in its cancer work. First, to assist scientists like Hossam Haick through their research into the development of electronic systems (E noses) in order to facilitate the early detection of cancer through cheap non-invasive tests. Second, in the short term, the charity's team of cancer dogs can provide second-line screening for cancers that are very difficult to diagnose reliably, such as prostate cancer. Dr Guest acknowledges the limitations of introducing dogs to the NHS. 'It would be impossible to have a trainer and specialist dog in every surgery,' she said. 'But dogs can be used behind the scenes to screen samples. Dogs enjoy it. There's no reason why they can't screen large numbers of samples if they get a biscuit at the end.'

The Medical Detection Dogs Centre also trains canines for purposes other than cancer detection. People with nut allergies can apply for a dog trained to detect nut traces in their immediate environment. Those with severe type one diabetes can receive a dog that will alert them when their blood sugar is reaching dangerous levels. A similar service can be provided to sufferers of Addison's disease, a hormonal disease that causes the adrenal glands to malfunction and not produce enough of the steroid hormone known as cortisol.

Karen – one of many to consider themselves blessed in being supported by Medical Detection Dogs – refers to her chocolate Labrador Coco as her 'knight in shining armour with a waggy tail'. Karen suffers from Addison's disease and her condition was exacerbated due to the removal of tumours found on her adrenal glands, which left her with no cortisol reserve in her body at all. If cortisol levels become dangerously low, the patient's condition becomes critical and can lead to death if they are not treated quickly. An Addisonian crisis causes severe pain, convulsions and unconsciousness; pain seizures which lead to collapse and hospitalisation; severe allergic responses, and narcolepsy – a malfunction of the sleep/wake regulating system which causes sleep attacks and paralysis.

Coco is the first dog in the world that has been trained to assist an Addison's disease sufferer. Karen has very little time from the moment of starting to feel unwell to a full-blown crisis, but Coco, who carries her injection kit with him in his vest, will warn her when the cortisol levels are dropping and will persist until he gets the message through. 'People have already noticed that I am much more confident since having Coco,' says Karen. 'I sleep better knowing he will alert me if my levels drop while I'm asleep. I can also relax when out and about knowing that Coco is there to look after me. As long as I have my knight in shining armour with a waggy tail with me by my side, I'm not scared of anything anymore.'

Diabetes is on the rise in Britain and thus the avoidance of dangerously low blood sugar levels (hypoglycaemia) is an acute daily issue for many people. When the condition is accompanied by loss of warnings it has a dramatic effect on the lives of both the person with diabetes and their family because low blood sugar levels are very dangerous if left untreated. Symptoms vary from confusion to seizures to comas, and can become life-threatening. An inability to detect a 'hypo' is particularly common in young children and adolescents as a result of their stage of growth and development. With their amazing sense of smell the dogs are trained to detect minute changes in blood sugar levels. When these levels fall or rise outside the normal range they will warn their owner, get help and fetch any vital medical supplies.

In the case of Cherry and Zeta, a characterful black Labrador who was Britain's first Diabetic Hypo-alert dog, it has been a joint learning curve. Zeta was deemed the family pet after being declared not fit enough to train as a guide dog, but when Cherry, who had been an insulin-dependent diabetic since he was 29, began to lose his hypoglycaemic warning symptoms, his wife enquired about re-training Zeta as one of the Diabetic Alert Dogs she knew existed in Australia and North America. She contacted Claire Guest, who came to stay for a few days and taught her how to train Zeta to alert when Cherry's blood sugar was low. Zeta was a quick learner and gave Cherry and his wife a new sense of security. Like all Labradors, though, she has her own personality quirks. In Zeta's case, she doesn't do night duty! She sleeps and snores through everything.

The Labrador's finely honed skill to detect scents also comes in very useful for the police force. Just as they are an integral part of bomb detection teams in the army, Labradors are an important element in the detection of drugs as well as missing persons and police suspects.

A law enforcer also enjoys extra personal security with a dog. In the fifteenth century, parish constables often took their dogs to work for company and what would now be termed 'back-up'. According to the Metropolitan Police Service (MPS), the first use of dogs by the police was believed to be in 1888 when two bloodhounds were used during the Jack the Ripper murders to try to track the killer through the streets of Whitechapel and Spitalfields. The Home Office had suggested Sir Charles Warrens, Head of the MPS during the Ripper investigation, use bloodhounds to sniff out the murderer. Warren himself was sceptical about a dog's ability to pick up one scent from pavements where people had been walking all night, but, after trials in two London parks, he was won over and gave instructions that, in the event of another murder, the victim's body must not be touched until bloodhounds could be brought to it and put on the scent. The policy was short-lived, though, because the owner of the bloodhounds couldn't agree on a suitable fee for the services of their dogs with the police. On the sole occasion they were called upon in the immediate aftermath of the murder of Mary Kelly, the owner had taken back their dogs so that they were no longer available to the police.

In 1914, following experiments in Germany and elsewhere in Europe, the Met introduced 172 dogs of various breeds to accompany officers on patrol. In that inaugural year of police dog use, an officer and dog were commended for saving a person from drowning in a lake. The dog was rewarded with a new collar.

1938 was the Year of the Police Labrador. Two Labradors became the first genuine police dogs and their beat to patrol was in Peckham, South London. Following the Second World War, six Labradors were reintroduced to combat crime, supplemented in 1948 by the first German Shepherd to be employed by the police. The dogs were very successful and their numbers grew to 90 by 1950 within the dog section, which was then based at Imber Court, in Surrey. In 1954 the current MPS Dog Training establishment at Keston, in Kent, was opened, where all dog-training courses now take place. Since then the Dog Support Unit has been at the forefront of police dog training, constantly exploring new ways to use the special abilities of these animals to improve officer and public safety, and to detect and prevent crime. Today, around 250 dogs of various types work across the MPS.

The role of the Dog Support Unit (DSU) is to provide police dog and handler teams to support their colleagues across London, and to respond to emergency calls where their unique skills can be used to help make London safer. Specific dogs have specific skills. For example, German and Belgian Shepherd dogs most often act as general-purpose dogs to undertake roles such as – and here is the official job description – searching for suspects and missing people, locating objects dropped or concealed during a criminal incident, following a track left by a person on the ground, chasing and detaining a person who runs away when challenged to stop, disarming violent armed suspects and controlling hostile crowds.

Some of the more specialist skills include support of firearms teams and something called – with tremendous understatement – 'line access' work, whereby officers often have to get themselves and their dogs up and down the outside of buildings, or even boats, using abseiling skills. The dogs are trained to cope with being tied to their handlers, via a harness, in order to achieve this kind of operation.

Labradors, alongside Spaniels, are trained to find specific scents. These include drugs, both hidden and being carried on a person in public; cash (banknotes); explosives; firearms; human remains and blood. Explosives search dogs work exclusively in bomb detection. All dogs can be called to operate calmly and happily in crime scenes, buildings, open spaces, vehicles, vessels, aircraft and transport infrastructure centres such as stations and bus terminals, and often accompany officers who are executing search warrants.

The police dog team of Sergeant Martin Proctor and his handsome black Labrador Dylan was awarded the Queen's Gallantry Medal in 1988 for exemplary bravery following an incident on the London Underground. In the summer of 2014, Sergeant Proctor retired after 36 years as a police dog handler, and Dylan, after eight years of sniffing duties, also bowed out for some well-earned rest and playtime. Part of their annual beat had always been ensuring the grounds of the All England Lawn Tennis Club were safe during Wimbledon fortnight. Working in the England Garden Party atmosphere for two weeks each year was such a contrast to normal explosive detection work that Sergeant Proctor deliberately chose to retire after the Championships. For a self-respecting retriever, Wimbledon is absolute heaven, with its secret cache of lost balls and rabbit-shaped furry camera microphones. 'He's extremely playful. That's what makes him such a strong dog. It's all fun to him,' said Sergeant Proctor. 'There's a giant tennis ball under a glass floor panel in the museum and let's just say he gets VERY interested in trying to get at that! We both love it.' Fellow behind-the-scenes staff at the tournament responded in kind: Dylan was one very popular dog. His last day on the beat saw him more fêted than your average champion. As he carried out his final search of the grounds ahead of the day's play, Dylan was mobbed with presents, photo requests and affectionate pats. Camera crews ran backwards to catch him in his handsome

Day-Glo harness and he duly lay down, rolled over and offered his tummy for a tickle.

'I couldn't ask for a nicer dog. Each police dog is independently licensed and I was told he wouldn't make it when he was young, but I've had dogs since 1988 and he's the best I've ever owned,' said Sergeant Proctor. 'We took a shine to each other straightaway. He's got a lovely temperament, but when he works, he clicks on and just searches. He's the ultimate pro. We're a team and we're going to miss all this.'

Police dogs work under several occupational hazards. First, they are the 'shield' for their handler, being at the epicentre of an explosion should they detect and set off a bomb, or on the frontline of gangsters involved in illegal goods trafficking. Second, if they become renowned for their success in thwarting criminals, such as drug smugglers, they themselves become 'Wanted' by the bad guys and have a price slapped on their head. For example, in an article in the *Telegraph* in 2013, Boss, a Labrador who helps lead police to stashes of drugs within the vast slum cities or favelas in Brazil, was named as the most wanted sniffer dog in Brazil. A powerful drug kingpin was said to have issued a 'death order' against the eager young Labrador, who had led police officers to a haul of more than 1.5 tonnes of drugs within twelve months. In October 2012, Boss was assigned nine protection officers after the police intercepted a message on the radio from a gang leader in the Manguinhos favela with an order to 'target Brownie' – a reference to Boss. Nine months later, in July 2013, he was still at work, uncovering 6,919 packets of cocaine worth more than £300,000 during an operation in the Favela do Rola on the west side of Rio. He also sniffed out 236 packets of cannabis, 14 blocks of cannabis and a stash of automatic weapons.

The scenario is not exclusive to Brazil, though. In Colombia, police guards were monitoring food for Agata, a champion drug-truffler, for poison. In 2007, a report in the *New Straits Times* in Malaysia told of death threats issued against sniffer dogs Lucky and Flo, whose personal expertise lay in detecting pirate CDs and DVDs.

If you've travelled around the United States by Amtrak train, the chances are you've seen a K-9 at work. Strategically deployed at stations throughout the system and involved in up to 1,000 train trips a month, the Amtrak Police Department K-9 teams provide a psychological and physical deterrent to potential threats from explosives. Up to 50 bomb detection teams – which translates into one handler and his Labrador per team – play a proactive role in the prevention of terrorism. At least a dozen of the teams are certified 'vapour-wake' dogs, which are trained to detect the smell of a suicide bomber, i.e. to determine the smell of explosives left in the wake of a person as they pass by. As Captain Deborah Myers of the unit says, 'The dogs are very dependable. They're more dependable than any piece of equip-ment . . . I have a dog there, it's a safe area.'

For explosives detection, the dogs begin training from 13 weeks of age, and it includes a year-long stint in prison. During an 11-week training programme at either the Auburn University Canine Detection Training Centre in Alabama or the Transportation Security Administration facility at Lackland Air Force Base, in Texas, the dogs have a lot of fun playing hide and seek with their favourite toys and tennis balls – exercises which are canny sessions in teaching odour recognition. During that time, they are partnered with a handler. The dog is the nose; the handler is the eyes and brain, taught to recognise changes in their dog's behaviour as a response to 'alerting' on a potential threat. This could be a tail signal, a head held high or 'acting stealthy', like they're sneaking up on some prey.

There has to be a lot of trust between dog and handler. Those that don't excel over 11 weeks of training don't make the cut. A lot of factors make a good explosives detection dog, says John Pearce from the Canine Detection Research Institute: 'a lot of play, a lot of desire and motivation to hunt. It's like a big game of hide and seek, looking for their toy or their tennis ball.'

All this is a far cry from my own dogs. To all intents and purposes, despite being a crossbreed, Maggi looks exactly like a Labrador. The only characteristic that gives away her mixed genes is her ears. She has the unmistakable 'r'-shaped ears of a Collie; she also has the sheepdog head tilt. At first glance most people assume she is a pure-bred Labrador, but get to know her and you recognise the obsessive compulsive attributes of the Collie.

Maggi has the most incredible coat of any dog I know. A rich brown that borders on red during the winter and bleaches to strawberry blonde in the summer. Where Inca's life was largely dominated by her love of food, Maggi is obsessed with tennis balls. I don't mean in an occasional play kind of way, but an OCD crazy kind of love. She could chase a ball all day and stare at one for even longer. I often used to wonder if she had merely confused it for a sheep. A friend of Marina's once bought her a tub of 200 multi-coloured tennis balls, after which our house resembled one of those children's ball parks.

Wherever Maggi went, there was sure to be a tennis ball.

Apart from my parents' dog, Maggi was the only other dog that Inca ever really liked. Inca never really liked other dogs; I could probably say that Inca disliked most other dogs – she was more into people. I'm not sure if it was because she was bullied by the Collies on the island, or because she wasn't properly socialised, but Inca just really wasn't into other dogs. She would crouch down, holding her head close to the ground in a form of submission while baring her teeth in a snarl. She would usually give the other dog a couple of seconds to read her behaviour before letting rip with her snapping jaws.

At first it was quite funny. It seemed such unlikely Labrador behaviour, particularly from a female, but her aggression towards other dogs became more and more pronounced. She seemed to focus all her doggy angst, rage and hatred towards particular breeds. At the top of her death list were, somewhat unexpectedly, Boxers.

Personally, I've always liked Boxers, but Inca HATED them. If she spotted one, and she could identify one from several hundred metres, she would chase it down and attack it, or try to, until one of her seizures felled her to the ground. Poor Inca.

Maggi took all of this in her stride. Maggi wasn't really into other dogs either. If she could choose anything as a best friend it would be a tennis ball. Though loyal and kind, Maggi isn't really into people either. Maybe it is the Collie in her, but she rarely tolerates more than a fleeting stroke on her head. She certainly never likes a cuddle.

Maggi and Inca had a strange dynamic of affable acceptance. Although I like to think they were inseparable, I'm not sure either of them was really that concerned when they were separated. We would sometimes divide them between my parents and Marina's parents to share the burden.

Children was as much of a shock for Inca and Maggi as it was for us. Ludo was our first born. He arrived on 9 December and he turned our world upside down, for the better of course, but it meant we were pretty dizzy for a while.

Both Marina and I had read plenty of books on the effect children can have on family pets, particularly if they are used to being fussed over. Maggi and Inca had had several years of playing the role of our surrogate children and now they were about to be usurped by a screaming child. I prepared myself for jealousy and angst, but the dogs took Ludo's arrival in their stride. In fact, Ludo's arrival had an unexpected effect on her.

The only time I saw anything verging on jealousy from either of the dogs was the first day we took Ludo to the park. He was barely a week old and we bundled him into his pram and took him to Hyde Park. The dogs sniffed around his pram in curiosity; neither of them could really understand what this screaming, pooing little thing was. Eventually Inca stood in front of the pram and began to scrape mud and leaves into the air, and straight into the pram. This was no accident. I had never seen her do it before and it was so well directed that I'm sure it was a sign of her frustration.

Yet Inca loved both of our children, Ludo and Iona, and having them around seemed to spur her ailing body on. Ludo would squeal with delight whenever he saw her, placing his face close to hers and staring into her eyes. Nothing gave me greater pleasure than seeing the children and the dogs together.

Having children gave me the final insight into the Labrador as a family pet. Some would argue that this is their greatest role. Think of a family pet and, more often than not, you'll imagine a Labrador.

The Labrador has all of the perfect traits. It is true there are many breeds well suited to children, but the Labrador has the added bonus of being both tolerant and wanting to please. It is this double whammy that makes them a trustworthy choice.

Of course, no one can ever trust any animal 100 per cent, but I'd argue that when it comes to trust and Labradors, that percentage is in the high 90s.

Inca would sit there as the children squeezed and poked her. To be honest, I think she enjoyed the physical contact. I have a wonderful photograph of Ludo sitting on her back while Inca lies care-free on the lawn.

I suppose we need to ask ourselves what we want from a family pet. I'd argue you need calmness, happiness, a willingness to please, a team player, tolerance and, above all, loyalty. A family dog is a projection of your core values. For me, a family dog says I am not the most important person or thing in this family. It is about shared responsibility.

In many ways Inca became a third pair of eyes on the children. I'm not sure she would have done anything if something serious ever actually happened, but I found her a reassuring presence. Maggi tolerated the children, but she was never that into them. I imagine that might be the Collie blood in her. Given half a chance, she would happily round them up, but from the beginning we'd notice Maggi slinking off upstairs whenever the children were about.

Inca, on the other hand, gained a spring in her step – though I still suspect it had something to do with the shower of food that descended from the children's highchairs.

Inca didn't just gain two children when Ludo and Iona came along – she also gained a couple of kilos.

CHAPTER ELEVEN

LABS OF WAR

When I was a boy I remember reading the stories about the 'dogs of war'; these were the tales of the maverick mercenaries who acted as guns for hire, working in war zones from West Africa to Central America.

As a boy, the 'dogs of war' were the real-life heroes of Boys' Own adventures. It never occurred to me to question why they were called dogs let alone challenge the morals of their escapades.

'Cry "Havoc!", and let slip the dogs of war' comes from Shakespeare's *Julius Caesar* (Act 3, Scene 1, line 273, to be precise). It was uttered by Mark Antony shortly after the assassination of Caesar. There is an ongoing debate about whether the Bard's use of the phrase 'dogs of war' was a metaphor for soldiers rather than four-legged warriors straining at the leash to snatch at the spoils of battle, but scholars agree that there is precedent for the literal translation, and dogs have been used in warfare since ancient times.

So where do Labradors come into this?

As early as 4000 BC, the Egyptians prized dogs for their role as sentries, hunting companions and guard dogs – and as snarling offensive weapons to let loose on their enemies. The ancient Egyptian word for dog was *iwiw*, which is an onomatopoeic reference to its bark. Hyper-alert and vigilant, the dog was well suited to act as a mobile alarm system, boosted by its acute sense of hearing and smell.

If you think about it, it's a great bit of kit. There are numerous depictions in paintings and murals of ancient Egyptian breeds that resemble modern Salukis, Greyhounds and Mastiffs. Preserved remains of leather collars and carved *stelae* stones reveal the names given to these dogs: Brave One, Reliable and Good Herdsman – the names give a tiny insight into the dogs' reliability and fortitude. Whatever warlike purpose dogs have served – from sentry duty through to sophisticated detection – they have a long history of being employed in some, often noble, capacity.

In *The Odyssey*, Homer's dogs appear as hunters capable of squaring up to savage animals like lions and bears. They are depicted as guards for public buildings and for valuable herds of sheep. Canine fighting skills encouraged the resourceful Greeks, Babylonians and Assyrians to dress their dogs in armour, complete with spikes, to ensure the dogs could participate in hand-to-hand, or paw-to-paw, combat. That was, of course, before the invention of gunpowder.

As the nature of warfare evolved, so did the role dogs that could play. In the eighteenth and nineteenth centuries, Native Americans used dogs as sentries and pack animals to carry their belongings. In the Russo-Japanese War of 1904 to 1905, the Russian Army trained ambulance dogs. In the Spanish-Moroccan War of 1919 to 1926, dogs were schooled to run along the front lines to draw enemy fire and give away the enemy's gun positions. The potential of a dog's trainability seemed limitless.

Faithful, loyal and agile, the dog seemed a natural choice.

The role of ambulance dog showed how man and canine can work well together even in high-stress jobs. Often the dogs would be used to search for wounded personnel under the cover of night, within a marked territory on the battlefield – injured soldiers often hide themselves from further danger, making themselves invisible to both friend and foe.

A dog's acute sense of hearing enables them to detect the sound of a wounded man's breath or groans even when they are inaudible to the human ear; their super-sensitive nose can ferret out the scent of a man lying in a concealed place, perhaps unconscious. The ambulance dog works in several ways; the dog can be trained to return to his handler and lead him to the wounded man, he can be taught to bark to communicate his location, or to work on a long lead to lead a human medic to the right spot. We've all seen images of Red Cross dogs proudly wearing saddles with pockets to store bandages, first-aid dressings and very often a flask of stimulant (or brandy). In the early twentieth century English ambulance dogs wore a light saddle marked with the Geneva Cross with a loud bell hanging from a leather collar. The Russians equipped their ambulance dogs with small lanterns as well as bells. There are many depictions of Labradors working as ambulance dogs, too.

It is strange but true that the qualities that make a good

soldier are as readily found in a dog (of particular breeds) as in a human. Candidates preparing for interviews for roles in the military services are advised to stress personality traits such as courage, dependability in the line of duty, enthusiasm, decisiveness, unselfishness, integrity, loyalty, a good spirit and a willingness to follow orders and strategies. Many a breed of dog boasts that package of qualities. In 1808, Lord Byron wrote in an epitaph for his beloved Newfoundland dog, Boatswain,

> *In life the firmest friend,*
> *The first to welcome, foremost to defend,*
> *Whose honest heart is still his master's own*
> *Who labours, fights, lives, breathes for him alone.*

Lord Byron was summing up what we dog owners have always known, but his observations also confirm why dogs working in war zones have become canine war heroes themselves.

Many a poet and statesman has been moved to pay tribute to the dog as ultimate wingman, a living creature you want next to you in the trenches or the foxhole. Most famously, Napoleon recalled this cameo scene in his memoirs: 'I walked over the battlefield and among the slain, a poodle killed bestowing a last lick upon his dead friend's face. Never had anything on any battlefield caused me a like emotion.'

In the theatre of war, soldiers say a dog is much more than a best friend; the dog is both an extension of yourself and your guardian angel. So when does the Labrador Retriever fit into the war dog tradition? As the breed was only officially recognised with Kennel Club status in 1903, it is to the Great War and twentieth-century wars that the Labrador's qualities first came to notice. The very same traits that attracted the Newfoundland cod fisherman and later the British aristocracy would lead the Labrador firmly into the fold of battle.

Field-Marshal Haig acknowledged the essential role of dogs in the British Army in his final despatch from the First World War. The introduction of trained dogs to the war effort was solely due to one Lieutenant Colonel Edwin Hauteville Richardson, who fervently believed in the vital role that a well-trained dog could play in combat alongside troops in the trenches. Were it not for him, dogs may never have been used by the British Army.

Edwin Richardson's story is pretty moving. The youngest son of a farmer, he grew up an animal lover. At school, he learnt about dogs being trained on the continent for military purposes and decided to find out more. He studied canine history and the use of dogs in warfare by the ancient Greeks and by the French during Napoleon's era, and later went to Sandhurst military academy. On passing out, he and his wife bought farm-land on the east coast of Scotland and began to experiment with training dogs for military purposes. He had been inspired after observing a curious incident in 1895 when, shooting on a friend's moor in Scotland, he noticed a German man buying a sheepdog from a shepherd. It transpired the man had been sent by the German government to buy a large number of Collies for the German Army, because they were so useful in searching and returning to a given spot. From 1900 onwards, Richardson began training dogs as 'ambulance dogs' with the help of officers at nearby army camps. He travelled to Russia and Germany to pick up tips on how dogs were used by police and army forces on the continent. His dogs – initially mostly Airedale Terriers – proved useful comrades in these experimental scenarios, by day and by night, prompting officers to request an official recognition of war dogs. Several attempts were made to persuade the Army of the potential usefulness of dogs in protecting ammunition dumps and factories against enemy saboteurs, but Richardson and his supporters made no headway in getting a commission. However, in the early years of the Great War, and with no official military dogs attached to the British Army, the War Office suddenly contacted Richardson to request that he form an official training school for war dogs.

In 1916, in response to a request from the Royal Artillery, Colonel Richardson began to train dogs as messengers. He trained two dogs, Wolf and Prince, and sent them to the front line. The dogs' ability to take vital messages about reinforcements, artillery and positioning during heavy bombardments was perfect. The idea was for a soldier to attach a message to the dog's collar, send the dog 'over the top' of the trench, and expect the dog to convey the message a few kilometres away within minutes. It worked.

I used to do the same with Inca. Marina and I used to spend holidays and long weekends in an idyllic little cottage high on the cliffs overlooking Putsborough Sands on the North Devon coast. I used to use it as a writer's den. I would sit at the window overlooking the ocean and Lundy Island beyond while Marina would lie on the beach below and read.

We used the dogs to send messages between one another. I

would place a note in a plastic bag tied to their collars and send them down the steep cliff. It worked a treat. The dogs became so good at it that I ended up sending ice cream down to her, or at least I did it once . . . until Inca worked out how to get the ice cream out of the bag and into her mouth. Like I say, Labradors love food.

Fortunately for the army, their dogs were used to transport messages rather than food.

A source material on these highly trained messenger dogs, which is in the archive at the University of Edinburgh, reads: 'One of their first tasks was to carry a message four miles to brigade headquarters from the front line through a smoke barrage, a task completed within an hour. It soon became clear that dogs were faster, steadier, more nimble across shell holes and muddy terrain, and more difficult to spot than human messengers. The two dogs were trailblazers. With Wolf and Prince having proved the usefulness of dogs at the front, demand for more messenger dogs grew and Lt-Col Richardson was asked by the War Office to establish his British War Dog School in 1917.'

Individual officers began to request dogs for sentry and patrol duties, as well as in messenger roles. The Richardsons sold up and moved to Shoeburyness, in Essex, where the Colonel established the first training centre for British military working dogs.

Richardson trained hundreds of dogs, mostly gathered from rescue centres. Not all dogs made the grade, though; some were too flaky to adopt a disciplined, task-specific mindset. Just like the soldiers, the army required focused, dedicated candidates. Each dog underwent intensive training for weeks to 'go over the top', cross tricky terrain, swim canals and leap over barbed wire entanglements, all the while ignoring the whistling bullets and explosions around them. Demand grew. All over Britain, police were instructed to send strays of any breed to the school. The War Office even appealed to the public to donate their own pets.

Now I am a patriotic soul. I have even spent a small amount of time in the military myself, as an officer cadet in the University Royal Naval Unit, but there is no way I would ever donate my dog to the war effort, however dire the situation. Some of the letters accompanying the donated family pets are heartbreaking. One lady wrote: 'I have given my husband and my sons, and now that he too is required, I give my dog.'

Can you imagine this kind of selflessness today?

Richardson's training regime at the British War Dog School encouraged kindness, gentleness and reward. It also acclimatised the dogs to loud battlefront conditions by feeding them amid similar noise, working them through mock trenches and encouraging them to run towards the crackle of rifle fire. It was also designed to build up the bond between dog and handler.

The nature of warfare was quick to change, and soon war became a far dirtier proposition.

'Keeper Davis talked of his dogs, Joe and Lizzard, who could cover three miles at night in twenty minutes, and they are just the same on any front that we go to.' Keeper Brooks, reporting on one of his dogs, Tom, spoke of how the dog was gassed and hit by shrapnel but was quite well again after a fortnight's rest. Keeper Swankie's dog, Ginger, suffered from shell shock but eventually recovered and was back on duty, and 'able to cover a mile in just three and a half minutes.'

By the end of the First World War more than 20,000 dogs had served on the front line, 7,000 of which had been family pets before war had broken out.

Lt Col Richardson is quoted: 'The trained dog considers himself highly honoured by his position as a servant of His Majesty, and renders no reluctant service. From my observation along this line I have, in fact, come to the conclusion that a dog trained to some definite work is happier than the average loafing dog, no matter how kindly the latter may be treated. I certainly found it to be the case with the army dogs.'

Although many owners of family pets may find this hard to read, these observations do in fact concur with those of many animal behaviourists, who conclude that a busy dog is a happy dog.

During the same period, Red Cross institutions in many countries employed Mercy Dogs to identify and comfort the wounded men on the front lines, but it is Richardson's Tactical Dog programme that formed the lasting legacy. Dogs used in war are now officially titled Military Working Dogs (MWDs) in the United Kingdom. The Defence Animal Centre in Melton Mowbray, Leicestershire, which opened in 1946, is home to the Joint Service Dog School which trains approximately 300 dogs a year and offers 22 handler courses, ranging from explosive detection to search and protection. It offers the most sophisticated dog training in the world. The high demand for these dogs prompted the army to consolidate five MWD squadrons into the first Military Working Dog regiment in March 2010. The regiment has nearly 300 soldiers and 200 dogs, supporting world-wide operations.

Labrador

Richardson's book, *British War Dogs*, was used as a training manual by the United States' Quartermaster Corps in 1942, when it started its first official K-9 Army. Today, the American services have 2,800 working dogs, divided into four categories – including one category of specialised search dogs (SSDs) starring our friend, the Labrador Retriever. The Lab has proven invaluable in locating improvised explosive devices, the number-one killer of coalition forces in Iraq and Afghanistan.

What makes a Labrador suited to work in a warzone? In a world of technologically sophisticated weapons detection systems, the Lab's best assets are its nose and ears. They reign supreme on the ground. An average dog smells 50 to 100 times more sensitively than an average person and they remember smells better than things they have seen.

I have seen this first hand on the course of hundreds, if not thousands, of dog walks over the years – the daily sniffathon, as I call it. Can you imagine if humans greeted one another by sniffing one another's bottoms?

The physiological reason for this is that dogs' olfactory centres consist of approximately two billion olfactory receptors compared to 40 million in humans. Labradors are particularly brilliant at tracking ground scent (as opposed to airborne), thanks to an extraordinary ability to distinguish one individual scent and follow it despite thousands of competing smells.

As far as the ears go, dogs have a broad hearing spectrum which allows them to hear frequencies as high as 35,000 cycles per second (Hz) compared to humans' upper limit of 20,000 Hz. Their ability to hear high-pitched sounds means, they are able to detect incoming shells before a soldier can. They can close their inner ear to filter out background noise and focus on a task at hand. Erect ears are better than floppy or fold-over ears, which is why German Shepherds are particularly good for scout work rather than sniffer duties.

In general terms, dogs are near-sighted, but their sense of smell and hearing compensate during bright daylight hours. It is a fact that dogs don't see as well as humans during the day, but from dusk through the night to dawn they have superior vision because in the retina of their eyes there are more rods (responsible for light sensibility) than cones (responsible for colour), which respond better to dim light.

Temperament, as well as physiology, influences whether a dog makes a good war worker, and this factor became more important as gradually the employment of dogs became increasingly specialised. During World War Two, Doberman Pinschers were initially the preferred dog for the Marines. When the military changed tack and began preparing dogs more as scout dogs than sentry and messenger dogs, they had to look beyond Dobermans, who were excellent sentries but were too excitable and skittish on the battlefield. Bloodhounds have excellent scenting ability but they are too noisy to be used as tracker dogs. So German Shepherds, with their famously stable temperament, emerged as first-choice combat dog. By the Vietnam War, Labrador Retrievers were the number-one choice as trackers because they could be trained to be quiet. A dog's ability to withstand climatic extremes also has to be taken into consideration. In Vietnam, the dog handlers were warned to expect losses due to heatstroke.

Today dogs are celebrated as war heroes. The Animals in War

Memorial at Brook Gate, Park Lane, in London, is a powerful monument to all the animals that served, suffered and died alongside the British, Commonwealth and Allied forces in the wars and conflicts of the twentieth century. The monument comprises two different levels separated by a dominating wall. On the lower level, two laden mules struggle on towards a flight of steps that leads through the wall that symbolises the war experience. On the other side, a bronze horse and dog stand facing into the gardens, bearing witness to the loss of their comrades and symbolising hope for the future.

There would be no accolade for these dogs of war were it not for the steadfast companionship they enjoy with their handlers who have proudly told of their exploits down through generations. And so it is that in war there are countless heart-warming stories of dogs' loyalty, devotion, bravery and courage as their role evolved. Among these, it is fascinating to look at where and how the Labrador features throughout twentieth- and twenty-first-century warfare.

The Labrador is first notable as a mascot dog. There is a wonderful photograph of the then Wing Commander Johnnie Johnson (he later became Air Vice Marshal CB, CBE, DSO & Two Bars, DFC & Bar) standing in front of the propeller of his Spitfire, cigarette between his lips, greeting his beloved black Labrador, Sally, the squadron mascot. Johnson was one of the most celebrated RAF flying aces of the Second World War. He flew alongside Sir Douglas Bader and, with a tally of 34 victories over Messerschmitt Bf 109s and 20 Focke-Wulf Fw 190s, emerged as the highest-scoring Western Allied fighter ace against the German Luftwaffe.

Clearly, a black Labrador was the fashionable squadron accessory. The iconic example of this is the Dambuster dog, a male
black Labrador Retriever belonging to the legendary Wing
Commander Guy Gibson, whose presence is still felt today at
RAF Scampton, Lincolnshire, where he is buried.

Guy Gibson was the first Commanding Officer of the Royal
Air Force's 617 Squadron who led the 1943 Dam Busters raid
– immortalised in the film starring Michael Redgrave and
Richard Todd – which resulted in the destruction of two large
dams in the Ruhr area. He was awarded the Victoria Cross,
but lost his life later in the war at the age of 24, having undertaken more than 170 operations. In a biography of his life,
Dambuster: a Life of Guy Gibson VC, Susan Ottaway describes
the memorable role of Gibson's black Labrador called Nigger.
(The name was commonly given to dogs before it became
taboo in the late twentieth century. To avoid offence, I shall
refer to Gibson's beloved dog as N.) In 1941, Guy and his wife
Eve acquired a puppy who was 'full of character'. N went
everywhere with Guy, having beers bought for him in the
officers' mess (no one's drink was safe with N around), and
even accompanying his master into the cockpit on flights. N
would curl up on the floor and sleep, quite unconcerned about
the chugging noise and action that surrounded him. Life as a
commander of 106 and later 617 Squadron was stressful and
lonely. Gibson was the boss; he couldn't spend the evenings
with the other lads, and while living away from Eve during
the war years, he came to rely on N for companionship. They
would go for long walks in the grounds of a nearby country
estate and sometimes go out on a boat together on the estate

lake. They would attend social occasions together, as commander and squadron mascot. N became quite a hardened drinker. He was adored by the rest of the squadron and even wore on his collar an Iron Cross that had been crafted for him. Man and dog were devoted to each other.

During preparations for the 'bouncing bomb' Dambuster raid, which took place on the night of 16–17 May 1943, it was decided Guy would coordinate the operation by radio. He would use certain code words to simplify the procedure. Words such as 'Dinghy' and 'Nigger' would signify that the targets had been destroyed. 'Nigger' (Morse code: -. .. --. --. . .-.) was the code word Gibson would use to confirm the breach of the Möhne Dam. As Susan Ottaway relates, 'It was, perhaps, a horrible irony that the word 'Nigger' should have been chosen to mean the destruction of a target, for, on the night of 15 May, as Guy was writing out his operation orders, his beloved dog, N, was killed by a car outside the main gates at Scampton. Group Captain Whitworth brought Guy the awful news and told him that N's body had been taken to the guard room. It is not hard to imagine how Guy must have felt at that moment. N had been his faithful companion since he first came to live with him as a puppy down in Kent. They had shared so much and, when times were hard for Guy, N had always been there with a friendly greeting for his master. The dog's death was a devastating blow for Guy, and, coming as it did, the day before the most important mission he had ever flown, was a disaster. Guy was, however, a true professional in his work and was determined not to let this personal tragedy affect the raid. His time for grieving would have to wait until the raid had been satisfactorily carried out. Knowing that some of the crews might regard N's death as a bad omen, Guy asked that they should not be told until after their return.

The next morning Guy discreetly arranged the burial of his dog. He did not want to do it himself but asked that it be carried out at midnight that night, the precise time he was due to be over the target. Ottaway reports that he spoke to a Flight Sergeant in the station workshop and asked him to build a coffin for N, but the man refused to do that for a dog and a row ensued, with Guy losing his temper. The burial was carried out by Flight Sergeant Powell, 617's disciplinary NCO, to the letter of Gibson's instructions, and at midnight his little four-legged friend was laid to rest. Marked much later by a proper stone, the carefully tended little grave remains to this day on the grass outside the original 617 Squadron offices at RAF Scampton. As history relates, the mission was successful but the squadron suffered loss of crew. On 18 May the men of 617 Squadron were given special leave but Gibson stayed in his office, which overlooked N's freshly dug grave, and, full of emotion himself, wrote letters to the families of those who had not returned.

The Labrador picked to play the part of N in the 1954 film *The Dam Busters* was an army dog, trained in mine detection. He had never been involved in film work before but was hailed a natural actor in the role, obediently following the director's instruction. However, in one scene, he had to trot past the place where the real N was buried. He dug in his heels and could not be persuaded to go near the grave. He couldn't even be dragged past it. Since his death in 1943 there have been many sightings of the ghost of N, so could the actor dog detect something? In

November 2011, it was reported that paranormal investigators, given special permission to stake out the RAF base which is now home to the Red Arrows, claimed that the spectre of the dog's spirit tried to communicate to them as they have picked up activity on their electronic detection equipment. And so the legend lives on . . .

The Red Arrows' first mascot was also a Labrador – a golden-coated dog called Dusty. He belonged to Squadron Leader Henry Prince, an aerobatic display pilot who flew at Red 7 in the original line-up in 1965. Dusty was often observed at his master's feet during briefings and occasionally ventured into the cockpit. He was photographed wearing flying helmet and goggles with his paws over the side of the Folland Gnat jet trainer. Sadly, like N, Dusty met a tragic end on the eve of a milestone event in his master's life. He died on the day before the Red Arrows' first ever display in May 1965, hit by the propeller of an aircraft as he followed at the heels of an airman who had rushed out to speak to the Chief Flying Instructor. Dusty was buried at RAF Fairford in a small grave on the north side of the airfield, marked by a gravestone and a white picket fence. On 24 June 2014, a group of children from Kempsford Primary School, whose parents are all serving members of the RAF, cleaned up Dusty's resting place as part of the celebrations to mark the 50th display season of the Red Arrows.

Labradors came into their own as serving war dogs towards the end of World War Two leading into the Vietnam War, which waged from 1955 to the fall of Saigon in 1975.

The British government rejected US requests to send troops to Vietnam, but even so there was significant indirect practical support from Britain, much of which went under the radar. The contribution that involved Labradors was in offering the US Special Forces training in jungle warfare using tracker dogs. During World War Two, Britain had initiated successful 'recce' patrols as a tactic for finding pockets of Japanese soldiers hidden on the Pacific Islands. They trained their tracker dogs at the Jungle Warfare School in Malaysia. In 1966 – eleven years into the Vietnam War – Britain allowed the United States to begin training 14 tracker teams there as well. Thirty dogs supplied by the British made up these first 14 teams. The 63rd Infantry Platoon Combat Tracker team, for example, received Bruce, Lucky and Sambo – valued comrades who lived in well-constructed kennels with concrete runs, wash points, drainage, chain-wire enclosures and secure covered accommodation. The dogs were well looked after. During World War Two, US soldiers had elevated the status of dogs, listing their canine comrades as wounded or killed in the compilation of casualties with accompanying remarks stressing their courage or devotion. This practice was forbidden by army regulations, but the bold defiance demonstrates the immediate respect held by the men responsible for handling the dogs. They agreed that a dog's action was often the difference between life and death for a platoon.

A distinguishing feature of Vietcong strategy was to ambush and then disappear quickly into the night. The US and Army of the Republic of Viet Nam (ARVN) soldiers needed a means of tracking the Vietcong back to their enclave where the larger force could be eliminated. The purpose of the tracker team is to find retreating or evading enemy troops, but not to engage with them. 'Locate and wait' was the name of the game. Black or yellow Labrador Retrievers were preferred because of their super-sensitive noses and their strong ability to scent on the ground. A tracker dog is trained specifically to follow only one scent, which it learns by sniffing a footprint or blood spot, giving the dog a unique signature smell to follow. Ideally they would be deployed within a three-hour window of known enemy presence, but in certain conditions a scent trail could be followed up to 24 hours later. The tracker dogs were able to detect enemy soldiers with ease because the Asian diet was based on rice while the American diet was based on wheat. The resulting body odours are quite different to the dog's keen nose. Tracker dogs are not taught to attack or to alert to booby traps or tripwires, though many did through natural instinct.

Private Peter Haran of the Royal Australian Infantry wrote a memoir about his time as a War Dog Operative in South Vietnam teamed with his Labrador Kelpie cross, Caesar. Life in the J – as the Aussies referred to the jungle – was stressful, and in *Trackers* Haran brings it to life complete with Aussie slang and gallows humour. A tracker team of dog and handler had to be on standby for rapid deployment. Haran's description of a memorable sortie is pretty vivid:

> *A dog team was called for. It was my turn, so I grabbed my combat gear, collected Caesar and went to the 2 RAR helicopter landing pad – codenamed 'Eagle Farm'. There were three of us. My cover man, a machine gunner, myself and of course, Caesar. We boarded a Huey (UH-1 Iroquois helicopter), took off, and within ten minutes we arrived at the D Coy position. We quickly deplaned and were taken to the*

contact site. There was a great deal of blood scattered on the sandy ground as well as streaked along some bushes. My cover man said 'I'm ready when you are'. The Pl Commander (who had been commanding 12 Pl for only one week) gave the order to commence the track. Caesar began his track at a fast pace and the tracking team followed at the end of his leash. 12 Pl did not patrol on the track, they were aware of the land mines and preferred to move off the sides of the track. My cover man and I had no choice but to honour where Caesar wanted to go, and he wanted to go on the track where the strongest enemy sign was. We patrolled for a couple of hundred metres, when we came upon a T junction in the track.

This was a dangerous situation and I willed Caesar to point. He did not. Instead, Caesar came straight back to me and sat on my foot. He had never done this before. We were now stopped and exposed in the middle of an open track. The next thing, there was a terrible explosion and we discovered that the Pl Commander had stepped on a mine. It exploded and blew off both his legs. An engineer splinter team arrived and began clearing the mine blast area with their counter-mine equipment. Once cleared, the casualties were treated and evacuated by DUSTOFF medical helicopter. The two sappers then went in front of Peter and continued their sweep for mines along the track which lead to the T junction. At the T junction the sappers removed a large anti-tank mine and four M16 anti-personnel 'jumping jacks'. Caesar had never received any training in mine and explosive detection, but he was suspicious of what he found at the T junction and for good measure, came back and sat on my foot so that I would not continue toward the danger. Soon after, we were all airlifted by helicopter back to our base at Nui Dat. That was the worst day I was to experience during my tour of duty. That day haunted me then, and continues to do so to this day.

At the end of his tour of duty, Haran had to hand Caesar over to another dog handler. The farewell was heartbreaking:

In the last day, I went up and I actually spoke to him through the cage. I said, 'This is the way they run the war – I'm going, you're staying. I don't want you to forget me 'cause I won't ever forget you'. And I turned and I walked away. He had his bowl in his mouth, expecting food – and I heard the bowl hit the concrete. And as that happened, I felt this ton of lead just fall straight through me from the top to the bottom.

Later, in 1970, Caesar was retired to the Australian Embassy in Saigon. Haran thought he'd long said his goodbye to his faithful dog, but on 3 October 1987, he had tucked into the beer with some mates after the march in the Welcome Home Parade when someone pressed something into his hand, saying 'This is for you'. Haran took the item to a private spot and had a 'cathartic experience'. The item was a silver identity disc engraved D6NO3 CAESAR that had hung from his collar during his lifetime. Dog and handler were reunited.

It won't surprise you to hear that Caesar was a Labrador.

It is hard to imagine the Labrador, from its ice-wrapped origins in Newfoundland, working diligently in the steaming, triple-canopy jungle environment of Southeast Asia, but their genetic docility remained strong and they could tolerate the heat reasonably well. They would be trained for eight months, starting at the age of two, and would be expected to work in the combat zone for six years or so. The relationship between dog and handler had to be strong as the detection alerts were silent and subtle – a tail wagging, a raising of the head or twitching of an ear. The handler would be vigilant in spotting any change in behaviour that might not be recognisable to others. The Labrador's gentleness and friendliness also allowed for short transition periods between different handlers, practical in the high-stress arena of war.

In 1968, the US Army started training their own tracker dogs at Fort Gordon, Georgia. In 1968, they sent 10 tracker teams to Vietnam; in 1969, another 10, scattered throughout South Vietnam. On paper, the tracker strategy looked good, but the flaw was that the tracker teams themselves were sometimes ambushed, because dogs trained to follow a ground scent weren't trained to alert when the enemy was near. Nevertheless, the Labrador was as immersed in war experience as was its human comrades. Photographs show Labradors poised to jump from helicopters, standing guard while their handler sleeps, stalking through the jungle, sleeping with their noses on their handlers' legs, wearing an M1 combat helmet for a photograph or – sadly – resting in dog cemeteries.

When the war was over, the tracker dogs were left behind. There was no precedent for this: dogs had been demilitarised and brought home after World War Two. Like tanks and other specific items of war, the dogs were classed as 'equipment' and would be left behind. The news that most of the 4,000 dogs were to be handed over to the Army of the Republic of Viet Nam – who did not want them – prompted high emotion. The Vietnamese considered the black Labrador trackers bad luck. The dogs were large compared to their new handlers and many were scared of them. One platoon, aware that the Vietnamese had no affection for the dogs, was reported to have put their dogs down rather than leave them to an unknown fate. The prevailing belief was that the dogs became another source of 'walking protein' for the ARVN troops.

In 1970, when the American public learnt of the decision to leave the hero war dogs in Vietnam, there was outrage. Animal lovers and politicians tried to file bills in Congress, but despite the newspaper headlines the decision was not reversed. A concil-iatory gesture was announced that allowed all 'healthy' dogs to return. Out of 4,000 dogs, only 120 were transported out; 500 were listed killed in action.

Thirty years later, it was President Bill Clinton – himself a Labrador owner – who signed into law HR 5314, that the Department of Defense release old and infirm war dogs to their handlers, civilian law enforcement agencies, or other responsible civilians.

The dogs of war were reunited.

CHAPTER TWELVE

THE END OF THE INCAS

I always dreaded the end. Even from the beginning, I worried about the end. I am certainly no pessimist; on the contrary, I consider myself an optimist. A fatalist. But I have experienced the pain before. You never forget losing a dog. It haunts you.

Time waits for neither man nor dog, and one of the brutal truths of the natural order is that man outlives most other species. I always knew it would happen, but nothing really prepared me for the sudden shock.

I was on the Isle of Wight on a family holiday with our dogs, Inca and Maggi. Inca's deterioration had been rapid. At 12, she had lost full control of her back legs and even walking had become difficult. She would often collapse while eating or, worse, while relieving herself; frequently I found myself holding her while she did her business. I had to carry her in and out of the car, and soon she couldn't even get up from her bed.

To make the decision to let my best friend go was one of the hardest decisions I have ever had to make. 'Are you prolonging her life for you or for Inca?' asked my dad. It was a question he has posed countless times over the years in his capacity as a vet.

Suddenly I was not just his son but a client with his beloved dog. Dad never made the decision for me; he wanted me to decide when the time was right.

'You'll know,' he had once told me.

I was about 8 when I first experienced the pain of losing a dog: Honey, a beautiful Golden Retriever. She had belonged to my mother, Julia Foster, then a famous actress. It was the perfect love story; my mother took her beloved dog to the vet, where she met a swarthy vet who would soon become her husband and, more importantly, my father.

You see, my father is key to this whole story. The canine blood that flows through my body was inherited from him. If the Fogle family had a crest it would most certainly be of dogs. They are to our family what chocolate is to the Cadburys. Breed is irrelevant. Dogs are in the Fogle DNA. Nature AND nurture.

Honey was the first dog I knew and the first dog I lost. I can remember snapshots. I can remember her becoming old, lying in her rectangular wicker basket that sat beneath the window of my parents' bedroom. I can remember the lumps on her belly. I recall coming home from school and my parents leading me into their room. I remember lying on her lifeless body, already stiff. I sobbed. I think it was the first time I ever sobbed like that. Uncontrollable emotion that I didn't really understand. She was gone but death was still abstract. She had gone, but where to?

I remember Dad carrying her lifeless body down the stairs and it was the last time I ever saw that red-blonde coat of hers. We weren't sure where to bury her. We didn't have a garden in our London house so some friends volunteered to let us bury her in their garden in Sussex. She's still there, of course, beneath an apple tree.

Bereavement for a pet is a strange thing. I was overwhelmed with a feeling of betrayal; I had cared for and protected this dog, who in turn had showered me with loyalty and love: the unspoken bond of trust between man (and woman) and dog.

The week following her death was awful. I was a wreck. I suffered panic attacks. I couldn't stop crying. It was like losing a limb. My shadow had gone. It was like a small flame had been extinguished within. There was a yawning gap in my life.

Time is a great healer. You never forget, but the ache begins to wane.

Then there was my beloved Liberty, also a Golden Retriever. She died while I was away doing a ski season in France. And Lexington, she died while I was marooned on the island of Taransay. My mother sent me a letter to tell me the sad news. On the envelope she had written very clearly, 'OPEN IN PRIVATE'. I of course ignored her advice and opened it on camera. I promptly burst into tears. Each of those losses had been preceded by an extraordinary life. Each of those dogs had their own unique impact on me, but Inca was the most powerful. Perhaps it was because of the intensity of our relationship. Maybe it was because she was MY first dog, as opposed to our family's.

Inca was cremated. For a long time her ashes remained in a little urn at my parents' house. I couldn't bring myself to scatter them. I had always been certain that her ashes belonged on Taransay. It was her island; it was where she was at both her healthiest and happiest.

But a lot had happened in the 10 years since we had been marooned together. The island had changed hands and Inca had become a London dog. The park was more familiar to her than the wild machair of the Western Isles. So there was really only one place that she belonged: Hyde Park, where she had so many walks and where she had helped me find the love of my life.

I bought a small beech tree sapling. It is hidden in a corner of the park, close to where Marina and I had first seen one another. A tree seemed so symbolic. I could think of Inca each time I saw it.

A year after Inca had died, my parents, my sister, Marina and Ludo all walked through the park accompanied by more than a dozen dogs, including Inca's daughter, Lola, and all of her canine friends. I carried her ashes in a little bag while my mother had packed a hamper full of champagne and Bonios. We gathered around the little tree, Inca's tree, and I took her old dog tag from my pocket. I placed it low on the tree and, using a little wire, attached it to the base of the trunk. I then scattered her ashes. I placed a hanging Bonio in the tree in homage to that insatiable appetite and we raised our champagne glasses to Inca.

It was sad, but it was also uplifting. I have a photograph – perhaps one of my most precious photographs – of a lush green meadow; trees are in full leaf; it looks rich and luxurious. It is of me, Ludo and all the dogs gathered around the little tree.

It was simple but symbolic. For anyone who has never loved

and lost a dog it would be meaningless, but for anyone who has loved, lived and lost a friend like Inca, I think it is a rather touching legacy. A growing object of beauty.

For me, that simple ceremony was a way of saying thank you. Thank you to a little black dog who helped shape my life. She changed it in ways I never thought possible. Inca brought me so much happiness and pleasure over the years. We shared so many adventures together. It seemed fitting that one chapter would end here in the park where it all began.

My most prized possession is a painting – a painting of Inca. Marina commissioned the artists Oli and Suzy to paint her. Oli and Suzy are two of the most talented artists of their generation; they have focused on wildlife, painting everything from African wild dogs and elephants to Amazonian anacondas and polar bears. Apart from the fact that the duo paint together, their individuality comes in the interaction of the animal with the work of art – elephant footprints, claws, even shark bites.

Marina somehow persuaded them to paint Inca and had planned to give me the painting for my 40th birthday. It was a sign of just how much Inca meant to me . . . and that Marina knew it. This wasn't any old painting. This was something special.

Marina gave me the painting early. Inca had died a few weeks after its completion and Marina thought it would bring me some comfort.

I cried when I saw it. It is perfect. It IS Inca, made all the more poignant by her muddy paw prints all over it. The slouch. Her paws. Her head tilt.

I love that painting. It makes me smile. As Dr Seuss wrote,

'Don't cry because it is over, Smile because it happened'.

It is the sad inevitability that we will almost always outlast our dogs.

After she died, I wrote her story for the *Sunday Telegraph*. I received hundreds if not thousands of letters and emails. Strangers would stop me on the street. My story was just one of millions and millions of Labrador tales – all slightly different, all with the same hero, the loyal, kind, thoughtful, generous, hungry friend.

Why is it that dogs have such a powerful pull over us all? What is it about our four-legged friends that can reduce a grown man who has rowed the Atlantic and been swimming with wild Nile crocodiles to a weeping wreck?

My father has experienced the power of bereavement for over forty years. Mine was far from unique. Many people are more devastated at the loss of their beloved dog than they are at the loss of a family member. Perhaps it is because the bond is so unique. It is one of utter physical dependence from the dog, like that of a carer and their charge.

In many ways it is more intense than many other relationships, both physically and psychologically. The bond between person and dog is very physical – hugging, stroking and in many cases kissing. For many people it might be their only form of physical contact. Even for those who are married, there is arguably more physical touch between the human and the dog.

Humans can show their emotions between one another using words or even gestures, but for a dog it is often physical. I wonder whether it is this intimacy that tightens the bond.

The physiological connection is also unique. We are more

likely to be honest to our dogs than to another person. When I say honest, I don't mean that we lie to other people, but we are less likely to 'edit' what we do or say. Mainly this is because the conversation is one way – there is no way the dog will ever repeat what it has heard or even seen.

How many of us have whispered our worries and our woes to our dog? I have unburdened myself of countless worries over the years. Inca was privy to more secrets than any member of my family. I've no doubt this is the reason the dog becomes and extension of you. You can really be yourself with your dog. I mean, 'singing, dancing, and funny voices' yourself.

In a constantly shifting world, a dog can be a stabilising force. For me in particular, Inca provided me with a stabilising consistency in an ever-changing world. She was there to witness the key moments in my life. My loss of anonymity. My struggle to reintegrate into society after my year in isolation. My various relationships. Travel. Work. Fame.

My world is one of nomadic travel. For more than 15 years I have travelled the globe. I spend more than seven months away from home. There is no consistency in my life. Family, of course, has since changed all of that, but through my bachelor years, Inca was the one consistency in an unstructured world.

I would travel off to remote corners of the globe to return to my little Notting Hill flat and Inca was always there to greet me. Of course, it meant she had two families, as it was my parents who always looked after her while I was away. But Inca never held it against me. She never complained. She was always there, wagging her tail and leaning against my leg.

It is a combination of that consistency with unfailing loyalty that leads to this inseparable bond. A dog, you see, will always forgive. A stroke and a handful of food and all is forgotten.

Humans are so much more complex. You can't really argue with a dog.

There is nothing quite like waking to a dog licking your face. A house feels empty without the greeting of a wagging tail. A five-minute trip to the corner shop for some milk is rewarded with a welcome like we've been gone for a year. It makes us feel special.

Dogs simply don't have the emotional complexity, the layers that we have. And at the top of that list, I'd argue, is the Labrador. I would say that, wouldn't I? But as this book has proved, I am far from the first and certainly won't be the last lover of Labradors.

A Labrador offers much more than just loyalty and love; they combine those qualities with a subdued intelligence and an eagerness to please.

Inca was the best thing that ever happened to me, but I'm far from unique in that situation – as these pages have demonstrated, Labradors have achieved a global dominance that is quite extraordinary.

There are, of course, plenty of other popular breeds, many of which share numerous similar personality traits – the Golden Retriever, for example – but the Labrador is still king.

'Will you get another dog?' was the mantra for the couple of years after Inca died. I needed time. I couldn't bear the thought of another dog so soon after. We still had Maggi and it was simply too soon.

But as all Labrador owners will know, their coarse long hairs – be they black, yellow or chocolate – get into your soul.

Labradors get under your skin. And before long you begin to crack as you are haunted by the Labrador spirit, willing you to begin again.

The Labrador has morphed from fisherman's friend into man's best friend over the course of a hundred years. Dependable and biddable, they have evolved into one of the planet's most popular breeds.

Celebrated in popular culture, loved by dictators and presidents, valued by the military and prized by charities, the Labrador has become a jack of all trades. Multitalented and multifaceted, all of these credentials are wrapped up in a dog that also looks perfect.

Their size, shape, head, ears, eyes, nose and tail are all perfectly proportioned. Look at a seal and you will see a Lab. I'd argue that not only have they evolved in their tasks, but also in their appearance. They have become irresistible. I defy the hardest of souls to walk past a Labrador and not feel compelled to stroke it.

I've never really trusted someone who doesn't like a Lab. What isn't there to like?

I still miss Inca. I think of her often. The thought of getting another dog felt so disloyal. Inviting another dog into her home and her car just felt wrong.

But eventually we all relent . . .

CHAPTER THIRTEEN

A PERFECT STORM

All good things come to an end.

It's incredible how something or someone can come into your life and turn it inside out. The arrival of my first child changed my life; the arrival of my second child, my daughter, changed it forever.

But sometimes life throws you a curve ball. It catches you off guard. My third child was stillborn. I don't want to dwell. It was the worst time of my life, from which my wife and I will never really recover. You learn to deal with it, but it's always there. During that long week in an Austrian hospital we tried to focus on what we had rather than what we'd lost. We buried Willem and tried to console ourselves with dreams about our future.

'We're getting a puppy,' smiled Marina. A tear trickled down my cheek.

Neither of us was under any illusion that a puppy would ever make up for such a traumatic, life-changing loss, but it would be something to look forward to, a break from the bleak storm in which we found ourselves trapped.

A puppy would give us something positive to focus on as a family.

There was never any question in my mind as to what it would be. We'd get a Labrador puppy.

The children were delirious with excitement; since the day he could talk, Ludo had resolved to follow my father, his grandpa, into veterinary medicine. He cares and worries about animals more than any other child I've ever met. His teachers invariably comment on this compassionate streak.

I suppose it shouldn't be that surprising given that it was dogs that brought both his parents and his grandparents together.

I called up Sussie Wiles, the breeder from whom Henry Holland Hibbert had got his Labradors, the closest I had come to the original progenitors.

'A litter has just been born,' she said.

'There are four black bitches and you can have first choice.'

It was surely destiny.

On the day that we were to meet our puppy, I woke up at 5am. My heart was racing. I hadn't had this kind of feeling since I was a child on Christmas Eve. The anticipation and excitement of the stocking. I sipped a coffee alone downstairs. It is a rare moment of silence in our house before the children stir.

I felt a mixture of excited nervousness. In just a few hours' time everything would change forever.

The careful dynamic of our household would change. It had taken several years of nappies and sleepless nights to reach this place and now we were going to shift it again.

My pensive reflections were soon interrupted by a cacophony of children. Breakfast, dressing, teeth, old dog walking and soon we were in the car heading west.

It's funny how sometimes you spend your life searching for something, only to find it right underneath your nose. And it seemed to be in the most unlikely of places: Uxbridge.

My life has taken me to the furthest corners of the world and to each and every corner of the United Kingdom, and now we were on our way to Uxbridge in west London, barely twenty minutes from where we lived. I had passed the sign many times. I must admit I had only been to Uxbridge once before in my life, nearly 12 years ago, when for some inexplicable reason I was sent there by Graham Norton to do a live insert from the town centre into his Saturday night TV show. If I remember correctly, I was standing in a temporary DJ booth in the middle of the city centre being pelted by rubbish from drunken local youth. Happy days.

Of course, this wasn't our first trip to Uxbridge. We had made several visits from the first time we had met the litter. Marina hadn't been so sure about getting a puppy from a breeder; she was wary about it, being more keen to rehome or adopt a dog from an animal shelter. She had experienced first hand the health issues that had dogged the pure-bred Inca's life and she was naturally concerned that we would merely repeat the process with another Labrador. But it's incredible the sway that a litter of pups can have on attitudes and moods. I genuinely believe that if we catapulted a litter of pups into almost any situation, they could diffuse the tension. Conflict, fights, arguments could all be settled with a cuddle from a newborn pup.

I could see Marina melt as she cuddled each and every puppy in the litter. Ludo and Iona, too, had fallen silent as they hugged, squeezed and nuzzled the black and yellow fur.

We had agreed that we would take a black bitch. (I hate those two words; they make you feel like a racist bigot. In one of the strangest email correspondences I have ever had, I found myself in the very unlikely and rather worrying position of asking Prince William if he knew of any black bitches at Sandringham.) Labrador colour is a personal and probably quite an emotive issue. In some ways, a little like the breed, I think people often choose the same colour with every dog they get.

I grew up with blonde Golden Retrievers. My childhood was dominated by their blonde hair that coated my clothes in yellow and white swathes, but long before I chose Inca, I had always known I wanted a black Labrador. I can't say why. I just wanted one.

Many of the dog owners I met during my Labrador research had insisted that black was the only true authentic colour, and that yellow and brown had come latterly. Black, after all, was arguably the best camouflage for those out hunting or shooting, their colour merging with the environment.

Of course, by choosing a black Labrador, as I had with Inca, I had merely replaced the swathes of wispy thin blonde Golden Retriever hair that had dominated my childhood, with the brittle black hairs of the Labrador. Inca's hair had plagued me for more than a decade. I used to dread her moults. They happened like clockwork. Hair would cascade from her body like a waterfall, forming tides of fur around the house. She would leave perfect impressions of her body on the bed, carpet and rug. Like the police chalks of murder victims drawn at the scene of a crime, Inca would leave silhouettes of herself. You could always tell exactly where she had been.

I would try to remove as much fur as I could by hand to minimise the fur tsunami around the house. I would stand over her and, using my fingers like a giant comb, I would drag at her fur. Armfuls of the stuff would fall to the ground; puffed with air, I would create mini mountains of the stuff. I filled whole bin bags and still the fur fell.

It's one of the downsides of having a dog that moults, particularly if they have a big thick lion's mane of a coat like Inca, but these are some of the sacrifices we make as owners.

As for sex, I have only ever known girl dogs, or bitches to give them their correct terminology. Why 'bitch' I have no idea. I always think it makes me sound like Tupac Shakur or some gang member from the Bronx.

Like the choice of breed and colour, sex is a very instinctive choice. Perhaps if you have never had a dog before, you might find yourself more easily swayed, but I have only ever had female dogs. Over the years I have built up a general stereotype of male dogs. They are brutish and arrogant. They race up with their head held high in an authoritative manner. Most fights I have ever witnessed have invariably involved male dogs. They are much more physical than bitches (there's that word again), using their bodies to assert their authority.

How many times have I had to shake a male dog from my leg after it has mistaken it for a female dog? I reckon we have all experienced a humping dog on our leg, but I reckon I've had it more than most. Maybe it is the symptom of being a vet's son, or perhaps I just have a really fit leg, but I have lost count of the times I've had to shake a humping dog from my leg. I'm not sure who it's more embarrassing for either. The dog, the owner or the humpee?

And if it's not humping, it's leg cocking. Where female dogs always seem rather elegant with their urination, squatting unobtrusively, their male counterparts seem to relish the opportunity to cock their legs little and often . . . on anything and everything.

Just a few months ago I was walking in the park when a large Weimaraner ran up to me and confidently lifted its leg against me, releasing a cascade of pee down my leg before I even had time to react, before racing off. Leg cocking is used to mark territory and it is this territorial character that I have always found a little overbearing in the male.

That is not to say, incidentally, that bitches are perfect. On the contrary, there are plenty of aspects that are just as difficult, if not worse, the hardest being the season. Why it's called a season rather than a period like in women I have no idea. I have always assumed it is something to do with their breeding season. Unfortunately there is no such thing as a dog tampon. If you have never had a female dog then I'll leave the mess to your imagination.

When I first met Marina, she used to dress her dog Maggi in special doggy 'pants' complete with a hole for the tail. Poor Maggi would skulk around looking humiliated. They were, of course, only meant to be worn around the house and in the car, but she would often end of walking from one to the other in her pants. If dogs could blush she would have been puce.

So here we were, making a decision about a new dog. We

handled each and every pup, examining their legs, tails, heads. To be honest, they were barely two weeks old. Their eyes were yet to open and the only distinguishing factor was their colour. We had a selection of six black pups, four of which were bitches. Of these four, apart from a tiny variable in size, there was nothing in it.

Pat White had told me of the 'puppy aptitude' test, a way of scientifically choosing the correct puppy for you. 'Biddability and compatibility,' she had explained, 'are the key traits in the correct dog.'

'Whatever you do, don't let the children choose the puppy,' she had warned.

'So which one do you want?' Marina had asked Ludo and Iona as we cuddled the litter.

Despite the best advice, I think both Marina and I are driven by instinct. We both knew deep down that it would be nearly impossible to choose a puppy using any sort of scientific reason at two weeks.

As it happened, Sheila instructed us to return a month later, at six weeks, once the puppies had developed more of their characters and personalities.

Since that first visit we had returned several times to watch the growing pups. On the penultimate visit we had been asked to make our decision.

Even at six weeks, there was very little to differentiate them. Some were a little more sleepy and docile, but that was probably because they were a little sleepy. As I have already explained, I am often guided by instinct. To be honest. I am a firm believer in destiny. What will be will be.

It came down to two pups, only distinguishable from one

another by their slight size, variation. I had chosen a slightly larger one than Marina and the children. Instinctively I think I had wanted a Labrador on the larger size, while Marina wanted a more 'portable' version that could be easily squeezed into the car between bags and children.

'Paper, Rock, Scissors,' smiled Marina. 'Best of three wins.'

Marina and the children won. Of course they won. They chose the small pup with a pretty face. A thin piece of pink wool was tied around her neck. She would be ours and we hers. That little pink necklace marked out our future together.

It had felt strange leaving her for another two weeks, knowing that she was our pup. But now we were returning to bring her home. To envelop her into the Fogle Family fold.

We pulled up at the farmhouse.

I can remember collecting Inca like it was yesterday. By coincidence it was less than thirty minutes from here. So much had happened in the fifteen years since I had picked up Inca. My life had changed beyond recognition. I had been a young, single, naive 25-year-old still living with Mum and Dad when I had collected Inca. Now I was here with my own family.

I can even remember picking up my childhood dogs, Liberty and Lexington. There is something so monumental about the day you collect a dog. It's not on the scale of the birth of a child, but there is nonetheless something monumental and life-changing about it. It is a moment when two, or in this case five, lives collide.

We knocked on the door. Sussie answered and we went through to the front room where all the pups were still in the whelping box. The pups were now eight weeks old and a riot of dogs raced towards us.

There at the front was the little pink-collared pup. We scooped her up and cradled her.

There is something a little sad about taking a pup from the warmth, safety and comfort of its brothers and sisters. For eight weeks they had eaten, slept and played together. She had long been weened from her mother but this was still a moment when she would be taken from her nest.

I suppose it's all about perspective. The little pup may be leaving its siblings but it is also heading for a loving home.

I love this idea that throughout the world these litters of Labradors have been primed and prepared by their mothers to bring love and companionship. I am a sucker for anthropomorphism. I can't help but imagine the pups being tutored in how to be as cute and kind as possible.

David Attenborough once hypothesised that dogs are arguably the most conniving parasite on Earth, who through evolution have become as sweet and loving as possible in order to ingratiate themselves into our homes.

Is there anyone in the world who doesn't like a puppy? Kittens, calves, lambs . . . they all have a cuteness, but none of them really comes close to a puppy, with their perfect little faces. A puppy has the ability to melt the facade of the toughest gangster or the hardest politician.

The 'parasite' hypothesis goes on to speculate that through cuteness, puppies have evolved to get closer and closer to man. First by living within communities, then into gardens, next houses, and now, for many of us, even our beds.

Our beds? If you aren't a dog lover, look away now, though I doubt you would have chosen this book in the first place unless you had already been hypnotised by the allure of the dog. What is it that encourages us to allow these animals onto, and in many cases into, our beds? They are the descendants of wild animals, after all.

But that is the whole point. The puppy has evolved to look as sweet and cute as possible in order to secure its place with mankind. Now the same could be said for any puppy, but I disagree. I think the Labrador puppy has a particular, indefinable allure. Just look at the popularity of the Labrador puppy in marketing. They are everywhere. Hollywood films choose them as the ultimate family pet and everything from loo roll to beer has used them in advertising.

Sussie handed me a little bag that contained the puppy's worldly possessions – a worn toy pheasant and a small blanket from the box. Both would bring the smell of familiarity to help her adapt to her new life.

Clutching her tightly, we walked to the car. Marina held her on her lap as we waved goodbye.

It was a journey to a new life for us all.

For Marina and me, it was a new chapter in our marriage together. Dogs had brought us together, but the dogs had always had personal familiarity. The puppy years of both Maggi and my late dog Inca remained a mystery to one another. I had never known Maggi as a pup. I had seen the photographs and heard the tales, but for me she was Maggi, the older dog.

Now we were embarking on a new adventure with a puppy together, *en famille*.

We weren't really sure how Maggi would react. There is no kind way to introduce a puppy to a geriatric dog. I worried about how Maggi would interpret the situation. 'Here we go', she says, 'they think I'm about to kick the bucket, so here's a little pup to replace me.'

It is impossible to explain a situation to a dog. Excuses or explanations don't cut it.

Still clutching the puppy under my arm, we walked into the house. Maggi was fast asleep on the sofa. Since she had turned 14, she had taken to sleeping for most of the day in a happy, contented slumber. The commotion and noise of squealing children woke her and I could see her sniffing the air.

We placed the little pup on the floor and Maggi sniffed her briefly before wandering off. I wish I knew what she was thinking. The puppy was deliriously happy to meet another dog.

We still hadn't named her. Naming a dog is not like naming a child. There is no need to discuss and speculate how the child is going to feel in years to come. No need to second-guess the teasing opportunities that come with a name. A dog's name is much more flexible.

It was a choice between Tatty and Storm. Why? You may well ask. I wish I could come up with a fantastic anecdote or yarn, but the simple truth is that I liked both names. I had very nearly called Inca Tatty, and I had always liked Storm or Stormy.

We got the children to call out the name at the top of their lungs to see which one tripped off the tongue more easily, and Storm won.

Storm she was.

From the minute she arrived into our home, this little pup became a firm part of the family. It's amazing the power of a pup to bond a family. Even Maggi lowered her guard and began to enjoy this little bundle of fur's company.

Ever since my little boy, Ludo, was born, he has wanted to work with animals. Ludo loves animals. I mean really loves them. Last summer, in Austria, we were cooking ribs on the barbecue. They were delicious but we simply couldn't get Ludo to try them. Normally an adventurous eater, he kept refusing. Eventually, after a huge amount of bribery, I managed to persuade him to try a little. He nibbled a sparrow's peck from one of the ribs and told me triumphantly he didn't like them. Now I'd believe him if this was liver or pâté or sushi, but these were the tastiest ribs I'd ever tried. It was as if he didn't want to like them.

A few days later we were in the car, when, apropos of nothing, Ludo suddenly piped up, 'Daddy,' he said, while peering through the window, 'do you know why I didn't like the ribs?' He continued, 'It was because I didn't like the thought,' he explained. 'I didn't like the thought of eating from the little animal's ribs.'

I was blown away. This was coming from a five-year-old boy. My own son. He decided on his own valuation to question eating various forms of meat. He had already told us that he didn't like beef, but now he was explaining that it was the thought, not the taste, that he didn't like.

'Why do we have to kill animals?' he asked.

For the first time I was genuinely lost for a satisfactory answer. I could have said it's because we are omnivores and that we need to eat meat, but he had a valid question. My own son was challenging my own decisions and sentiments. Suddenly I didn't really have an answer. Why would we welcome dogs into our homes while at the same time happily allow people to kill animals on our behalf to sate our appetite? It seems so contradictory. How can you love one animal enough to allow it into your house while you happily eat another?

I have often worried that society has lost any sense of connection between the meat we buy in a supermarket, or even from a butcher, and the living animal from which it comes. We live in a sanitised society where the horrors of the abattoir are hidden behind doors. Meat is packaged to look less like meat. It's as if we don't want to admit to ourselves the provenance of the bacon or the burger. It has become an abstract food, not much different to a chocolate bar or an apple.

Allowing a dog into your home provokes more thoughtful debate. Ludo's deep love of animals, and in particular Maggi and now Storm, has led him to question our animal morals.

Storm is our dog, but deep down she is really Ludo's. Ludo loves that little dog more than anything else. It takes me back to my own childhood and the deep love I had for my two dogs when I was growing up. Ludo would scoop little Storm up under her belly and march her around the house. He would place her into her bed, and from the beginning he would help to feed her and come with me to the park to walk her. A puppy brings responsibility, which is an important and joyful lesson for children.

This little pup has re-energised our home. With her youthful enthusiasm she has created a new dynamic. In the morning she sits next to the bed and stares. Even with my eyes closed I can feel those Labrador eyes like laser beams, willing me to wake from my slumber. At the first sign of movement, she comes closer and lifts her front legs onto the bed and licks my face.

The excitement with which she greets each morning is infectious. She wakes long before the children. I scoop her up and take her down to the garden. Just me and her. It reminds me of the time when Inca was my sole companion, all those years ago. We'd wander down to the barn together, light the wood-burning stove and sit there alone. Just the two of us.

Fifteen years later and I was doing the same with Storm. The slouch, the head tilt, the protruding back leg. The echoes of Inca are uncanny.

The Labrador must be one of the most versatile breeds in the world. Guide dogs, hearing dogs, police dogs, bomb detection dogs, drug sniffer dogs, war dogs, search-and-rescue dogs, truffle-sniffing dogs, cancer-sniffing dogs, epilepsy dogs, autism dogs, assistance dogs, fishermen's dogs, politicans' dogs, rock 'n' roll dogs, family dogs . . . the list goes on.

I know it sounds saccharine, but these loyal black dogs have been my guardian angels over the years, silently guiding and directing me. They are always there. Loyal, kind, happy and optimistic. As we have discovered, they have extraordinary versatility as well as an untarnished and unwavering loyalty. They offer a tonic to many of the ills of the world. We can learn a great deal from the Labrador.

The humble Labrador has changed my life. It is little surprise then that the Labrador has become the world's most popular breed. Man's Best Best Friend . . . Forever.

INDEX

ACKNOWLEDGEMENTS

Thanks . . .

To Sarah Edworthy who helped me gather the history and unpick the story of the Labrador.

To my father for introducing me to my lifelong passion for dogs.

To Sussie Wiles and family for our beautiful little Storm and to Richard Edwards for his useful comments on the manuscript.

To Sam McColl for loving our dogs even more than we do.

To Myles Archibald for hanging on so long and to the team at HarperCollins.

To Julian Alexander and the team at LAW.

To everyone who helped me while writing this book.